Sir Wilfrid Laurier and the Romance of Canada

~

ALSO BY LAURIER L. LAPIERRE

1759: The Battle for Canada

Canada, My Canada

SIR WILFRID LAURIER AND THE ROMANCE OF CANADA

~

LAURIER L. LAPIERRE

à Louise Bréleu

Laurier is Canada

Canada's we are

own to be free

Published in 1996 by
Stoddart Publishing Co. Limited

Distributed in Canada by
General Distribution Services Inc.
30 Lesmill Road
Toronto, Canada M3B 2T6
Tel. (416) 445-3333
Fax (416) 445-5967
e-mail Customer.Service@ccmailgw.genpub.com

Distributed in the United States by
General Distribution Services Inc.
85 River Rock Drive, Suite 202
Buffalo, New York 14207
Toll free 1-800-805-1083
Fax (416) 445-5967
e-mail Customer.Service@ccmailgw.genpub.com

Cataloguing in Publication Data
LaPierre, Laurier L., 1929–
Sir Wilfrid Laurier and the romance of Canada

ISBN 0-7737-2979-8

1. Laurier, Wilfrid, Sir, 1841–1919.   2. Canada –
Politics and government – 1896–1911.•   3. Prime
ministers – Canada – Biography.   I. Title.

FC551.L3L36   1996   971.05′6′092   96-931247-4
Fl033.L3L36   1996

Designed by James Ireland Design Inc.
Printed and bound in Canada

~

To Dominic, Thomas, Cary, and Laura

~

L'union entre les peuples, le secret de l'avenir.

[The unity of the people is
the secret of the future.]

Bien de puissantes nations pourraient ici venir
chercher une leçon de justice et d'humanité.

[Mighty nations, indeed, may well come to us
to seek a lesson in justice and humanity.]

Wilfrid Laurier, 1864

CONTENTS

~

ACKNOWLEDGMENTS

I have incurred many debts in my rediscovery of Laurier's life. I wish to acknowledge them now.

Bruce Westwood of Westwood Creative Artists is my agent. He is a warm and kind man, a thoughtful and persistent agent, and a friend. Thank you.

Jack Stoddart, president of Stoddart Publishing, understood instantly what it was that I proposed to do and made it possible. Thank you.

Donald G. Bastian, managing editor of Stoddart Publishing, has been more than encouraging, patient, and understanding. Thank you.

Nicole Keefler is a researcher of extraordinary skills, a conscientious observer of life, both past and present, and a woman with a flair for what is important. She has not led me astray. Thank you.

Rosemary Shipton, my editor, has edited this book with courage, respect, and generosity. Its readability is due to her astonishing skill, if not genius. Thank you.

In the preparation of this biography, both Nicole Keefler and I have encountered much kindness and cooperation from the officials and staff of museums, archives, historical sites, and libraries. We would like to thank them for their generosity in placing their advice, help, and time at our disposal. Among those many, we would particularly like to thank Annette McConnell at the McCord Museum in Montréal, Jennifer Fong at Laurier House in Saint-Lin, Stéphanne Boily and Richard Pedneault at Laurier House in Arthabaska, Father Laiberté and Anne Leblanc at the Collège de L'Assomption, Sharon Shipley and Jack D'Aoust at the National Library of Canada, Stephen Davis at Parks

Canada, Harvey Slack at the Canadian Fund, and Georges Lagacé at Laurier House in Ottawa.

My gratitude as well to Jean Pigott, Susan Scotti, Guy Côté, Martin Hunter, the Reverend Paul Lapierre, and my Ottawa family.

I have a need to tell you the story of Wilfrid Laurier. You see, he has been a part of me since the day my paternal grandmother, who was an indefatigable Liberal and had seen him once from afar, commanded that I be named after the *grand homme* she so admired.

In my rambling youth, I, of course, paid no attention to him at all. My elders mentioned him from time to time, but he had no relevance for me. It was only when I enrolled in the history department of the University of Toronto, where in time I would obtain a doctorate, that I began to notice this tall, handsome, poetic, and dramatic man who inhabited our history, as a prime minister and statesman, in the first two decades of the twentieth century. However, it was not until my discovery of Canada through the television program *This Hour Has Seven Days* in the early 1960s that he wove himself into my psyche. He became the inspiration of the love I came to have for this, my Canada. He nurtured that love in me and fired the words and images I have used in countless speeches and encounters as I criss-cross this country from sea to sea to sea.

Yet at no time before 1993 was I compelled to write the story of his life. This need came only with the collapse of the Charlottetown accord in the referendum of the previous year. I took great pride in supporting the new constitutional arrangements brought forward, because, in my heart and mind, they went a long way to resolve our multifaceted national crisis. More important, they appeared to be the *projet de pays* — the national undertaking — of the twenty-first century which would confirm, once and for all, my understanding of Canada as the prototype of the political ensembles of the next millennium.

One day, in the midst of my depression that followed this national failure of heart, I was reading about the federal government's creation of Alberta and Saskatchewan in 1905. A phrase that Laurier used then struck me. The time had come, he said, to put the stamp of Canadian nationality on the lands that stretched endlessly between Manitoba and the Canadian Rockies. No sooner had I read that remark than my depression went the way of all previous ones — into the pool of resolution.

For it's quite a concept, this stamp of Canadian nationality. Laurier had certainly spent a considerable part of his life drawing it and affixing it wherever he went, in whatever he said, and in the actions he took as leader of the Liberal Party (1887–1919) and prime minister of Canada (1896–1911).

But where is that stamp in the 1990s? We are approaching a new century: we need an inspiration if we are to put our mark on it. We live in tormenting times: we need the confirmation that Canada is worth having. We tremble on the brink of disunity: we need to affirm our future through reconciliation. We share an insecure and divided planet: we need a vision of justice and humanity. At this juncture in our history, a biography of Wilfrid Laurier as the passionate expression of the kind of person he was, the times in which he lived, and the vision he kept before him as "a pillar of fire by night and a pillar of cloud by day" would do us all good.

The time had finally come for me to tell his story.

~

Laurier has been studied in learned treatises, scholarly books, and brilliant essays. Comprehensive as these may be, they have spoken much of Laurier's *political* times and little of his *personal* times, with the exception of his "romance" with Émilie Lavergne. Even though I must talk of the politics, I believe it to be secondary, because it has no significance without the private Laurier. For his life to have any value in our day, I must, as much as possible, rediscover him in the intimacy of his soul. I must also find what he concealed from those about him. And, above all, I must measure the cost of his official acts in relation to his well-being. To do so, I must read between the lines to reconstruct the main relationships, events, circumstances, and moments that marked his life.

Many of his important speeches are quoted extensively in the book.

Laurier's words were consequential: they meant something of value in his time; they added to a moment or a decision; they influenced action and moved an entire nation. Today, they perform the same tasks. We, Canadians and *Canadiens*, must let these words and their spirit move into our souls and there kindle a genuine fervour for our land, our people, and our country.

Laurier L. LaPierre, OC
Ottawa, July 1996

PART I

"COME AT ONCE!"
1841–1896

1

FOR THE LOVE OF ZOË

On Tuesday, 12 May 1868, when the telegram came in the late afternoon, Wilfrid Laurier was practising law in a small town in the area of Québec known as Les Bois-Francs. He was twenty-seven years old and had grown into a tall and fine-looking man, but was frightfully thin. His chestnut brown hair, which he combed back on his head in one great swoop, was thick, naturally curled, and high on his forehead, revealing finely shaped ears. A narrow and long nose led to a mouth that could only be described as sensual, an impression reinforced by the slight projection of his chin. If seduction was in his lips, romance was in his eyes. They were of roughly the same colour as his hair, deeply set, and, with their dark bushy eyebrows and long eyelashes, enhanced the pallor of his skin. He was often ill with chest complaints, a weakness that had already killed his mother and his sister. But in two days, he had an important court case, a case that might well establish him permanently in his career. He opened the envelope, stared at the signature, read quickly what was imprinted on the page, and scowled: "Viens à Montréal tout de suite, j'ai quelque chose de très grave à te dire. Séraphin Gauthier." [Come at once! A matter of urgent importance. Séraphin Gauthier.]

What was that urgent matter? Zoë, obviously. At first he decided he would not go. But later that evening came a rushed telegram: "Forget your murderer. Your destiny is being determined here."

It was by then 11:30 p.m. Quickly, he changed his mind. He could always work on the train, and it would do him good to see the Gauthiers again and ascertain what was happening with Zoë. There was a train in forty minutes. He would be on it for the six-hour journey to Montréal.

~

Wilfrid Laurier met Zoë Lafontaine when he first came to Montréal to study at the Faculty of Law of McGill University in the fall of 1861. He was then twenty years old and she was five months older.

The Lauriers had no relatives in Montréal, but Wilfrid's mother had once made a close friend in Saint-Lin who had moved there. In the last stages of her illness, Marcelle Laurier became close to the wife of the doctor who was treating her, Phoebé Gauthier. Before she died, Marcelle asked Phoebé to keep an eye on Wilfrid and to help him in any way she could with his studies. Phoebé agreed. However, in 1849, a year after Marcelle's death, her own husband died, forcing her to leave Saint-Lin and settle in Montréal. There she married one of her late husband's cousins, Séraphin Gauthier, who was younger than she. From 1849 until she opened the door of her house at 25 Saint-Louis Street, around the corner from the Champ de Mars, to Wilfrid and his father, Carolus, she had not laid eyes on any of the Lauriers. She had, however, kept some contact with the parish priest, who had given Carolus her address. Wilfrid didn't remember her at all, and she was surprised that he had developed into such a handsome young man. Seeing them on her doorstep, she remembered her promise. Over tea, she and Carolus agreed to a price for Wilfrid's board. It was to be paid in both cash and kind.

The house he was to live in was in a noisy neighbourhood between Saint-Hubert and Berry Lane, where practically every spring the St. Lawrence invaded the basements of the houses and created smelly living conditions. The house was a dark, cold, and damp place, with a basement and three storeys and no central heating. In the basement Wilfrid found the kitchen, various storerooms, and the bathroom. On the ground floor were the living room and the dining room. Above it lived the Gauthiers and the Lafontaines, who occupied a small room and a sitting room. His own bedroom, which served him as a study as well, was to be in the front on the top floor. It was narrow and tended to be gloomy, especially in winter. But it had a small window. From Saint-Lin, Phoebé asked him to bring his bed, his bedding, a chair, a dresser, and a desk. From time to time, she told him, other *pensionnaires* occupied the other rooms on his floor. It didn't take much for Wilfrid to realize that the Gauthiers needed the money.

When their business was over, the Lauriers drove back to Saint-Lin, to return in the first week of September. No sooner had he arrived on Saint-Louis Street than he found that living with the Gauthiers was like living on a merry-go-round. Séraphin, who was about ten years older than Wilfrid, was a clerk in a pharmacy and was studying to be a doctor. They had three children: Emma, Annette, and Louis. Also living with them was Séraphin's brother Stanislas and a woman by the name of Lafontaine and her daughter, Zoë. On his first visit in the summer of 1861, Wilfrid met only Madame Gauthier. The others, though, were all there to greet him when he arrived for the opening of term at McGill.

Wilfrid lived at that address during the university sessions of 1861–62 and 1862–63. The Gauthiers, who moved practically every year, then moved east to 70 St. Mary, a not much better location, and Wilfrid went with them. At that new address, his living arrangements hardly changed. By that time, Madame Lafontaine, the estranged wife of Godfrey-Napoléon Lafontaine, had died, but Zoë continued to live with the Gauthiers in return for a little housework and for teaching the piano to the children, a task her mother had done before her. Zoë's piano was the only valuable possession she had.

Zoë Lafontaine was a good musician. She played remarkably well and was an even better teacher. She was patient and consistent. The family adored her, especially Emma. Even though the Gauthiers were far from being rich, they were hospitable. Their children often brought friends to visit — mostly on Sunday afternoons. Séraphin invited colleagues of his who, like him, were studying for the professions, and Phoebé always had a couple of interesting people she had met on the street while shopping. There would be a little to eat and drink, but the guests didn't come for that. They were there to relax, laugh, talk, sing, and even dance. Zoë, the pianist, was often at the centre of those activities. She played and led them in song and provided the music for their frolicking. Every now and then her father, who began to reappear in her life, arrived with his new wife.

From time to time, Wilfrid attended. Sometimes he would bring a couple of friends, mostly of the *Rouge* persuasion. Séraphin, who sympathized with these radical opinions but lacked the time to participate in political activities, would be enchanted, and serious conversation would ensue. Eventually, the talk faded away as the young people gathered at the piano, surrounding Zoë and singing to their hearts' content. Thus he came to know her, to admire her, to be joyful in her company, and to love her. And she reciprocated.

From the beginning they were quite compatible. She was as shy as he was. She sympathized with his recurring cough and tried to make him comfortable in his bouts of illness. When he was around and she played for the whole family, she liked his brooding eyes plunging into her. For his part, her company gave him comfort. He found her unpretentious, but certainly not without humour; courageous, with a quiet affirmation of who she was; affable and reserved at the same time; and beautiful enough to stir emotions within him that he had not experienced often, if ever, before. He liked her mouth, small and fragile, and the roundness of her face; and, above all, he marvelled at her circular, large, and light-golden eyes. He could peer into them forever, he was convinced! Still, he wished that she would dress more fashionably, adorn herself with ribbons and colour, and comb her black hair differently from the straight parting in the middle that she fancied. She looked so severe! She did not read very much, but she was fascinated by the authors he talked to her about, even though many of them were on the church's forbidden list. Often, they talked of religion. There was no satisfaction in that area for either of them. In his eyes, she was overly zealous in her practice of doctrine and uncritical of what was being asked of her. In return, she deplored his refusal to attend Mass, his ardent and impatient censure of practically all clerics and their practices, and his unwillingness to return to the cradle of his faith. He was often impatient with her over these matters and she retreated, sad and morose, leaving him convinced that he was without "aucune volonté, aucun sentiment," as he once wrote to her.

Her modesty and the religious differences between them, though, did not impede the attraction. Slowly and gradually — encouraged by the romantic Gauthiers — they found more and more time alone and their love flowered into a relationship. At some point or other, they took it for granted that one day they would be married and live happily ever after. All the Gauthiers agreed, except Phoebé, who feared that Wilfrid's illness could not be contained. Laurier, more than he was willing to admit, shared that view — even as he sang with Zoë at the piano, or danced a quadrille with her, or walked in the summer air with her on his arm, or sat quietly beside her reading one of his favourite books, or whispered the sweet nothings of love.

Wilfrid was never without the thought that what ailed him had brought pain to his family, had killed his mother and his sister, and was now devouring him. He was always afraid of this godforsaken demon inside him which he came to know too well. He acknowledged its symptoms more than its name: he had been coughing a dry cough for years; he was always pale, and the pallor became more pronounced as he grew older; and he was often sad beyond reason and indifferent to what was going on about him. As a friend once said, in those days Laurier "walked among us, a shadow of himself." He was convinced that he had tuberculosis. Both Phoebé and Zoë did not doubt it as well.

He moved with the Gauthiers from Saint-Louis Street to St. Mary Street to Craig Street. He had to pay his board out of his meagre revenues, forcing him to work from dawn until late in the night, often going without food, and unable to tame his listlessness and physical weakness. In such circumstances, there was little time for Zoë. They talked, but never for long and certainly not satisfactorily. Most of their discussions ended with her dissolving into tears and him being even more impatient and disoriented.

By the time he graduated from McGill, Zoë wanted to get married. He didn't. Over and over again he explained to her that he couldn't support her, he was probably dying, and their life together would be miserable. Better wait and see what the future brought. Over and over again she explained to him that his circumstances didn't matter, she could give piano lessons to earn some money, together they could live as cheaply as one, and their love would conquer all. He didn't buy any of it and he never formally proposed. He resented being pressured, and she took his refusal as a sign that he didn't love her.

On 9 May 1865 Séraphin, who was then thirty-two years old, received a licence to practise medicine in Canada East. He was a doctor. With his new professional and social rank, Séraphin and Phoebé felt it necessary to move to another location, in a better house and neighbourhood, where he could practise his Hippocratic art from his home. The address chosen was on Dorchester Street, number 385. By June 1866 Séraphin's house and practice were located at 132 Saint-Laurent, between La Gauchetière and Dorchester. He was successful and he no longer had any need to take in boarders. He asked Wilfrid to move out. It was an agreeable departure and it was long overdue. Zoë was becoming more persistent and he more reluctant. Phoebé had not changed her opinion about the nature of Wilfrid's illness, and her disapproval led to arguments and animosity between her and her husband. She was becoming impatient with Wilfrid's inability to make up his mind about anything. He no longer fitted in. He realized that and he welcomed the decision he should leave. He took rooms at 23 Saint-André.

Zoë knew that Wilfrid was getting away from her. She could hardly bear the pain. Nor could she stay at the Gauthiers indefinitely. Without Wilfrid asking her father for her hand, only a bleak future faced her — unless she looked elsewhere. There was ample opportunity. The Gauthiers, with their new-found wealth and status, entertained even more. All sorts of people — artists, politicians, professional and business men — filled their salon practically every week. Zoë played as she had always done and many men flirted with her. One evening, in the summer of 1866, she met Pierre Valois. He was about twenty-two years old, a student in medicine at the École de Médecine et de Chirurgie de Montréal, where he had met Séraphin. Zoë and Pierre became friends and he fell in love with her. Unsure of what was to become of her and craving affection, she did not turn him away.

As Valois entered Zoë's life, Wilfrid retreated from it. The fall of 1866 came and his body couldn't any longer bear the endless hours of work, worry, and deep depression that echoed in every part of him. In November he went to live in the country in the Eastern Townships — first in L'Avenir, next in Victoriaville, and then in Arthabaska.

The period between the fall of 1866 and the summer of 1867 was the worst of times for him. He was constantly ill, his business went bankrupt, his depression deepened, and he had no contact with Zoë, except for a few letters written in haste which left them both only more frustrated of their future together. However, after a lengthy bout with hemorrhages, endless coughing, and dilapidating weakness that kept him in bed for six weeks in the spring of 1867, he had the need to reach out to her. But the doubts and the conflicts and the vacillations came back in full force. A part of him told him that marriage to her was impossible for all the reasons they had discussed together; another insisted that he, too, was entitled to happiness and marital bliss, that he could overcome his "malady of the lungs," as the newspapers called it, and that he could build a loving and fulfilling relationship with Zoë.

In a moment of frankness, or desperation perhaps, he wrote her a poem that was meant to convince her of the impossibility of what he called "notre grand projet" — their marriage in the not-too-distant future. In this poem, he was the butterfly who, irrationally and senselessly, allowed itself to be singed by the "pale light" of a solitary lamp. Having suffered in the process, what perverted pleasure, he asked, compelled it to seek new "tortures"? He knew the answer, of course. It was this never-ending compulsion he had to climb the inaccessible summit of the mountain of ambition. He paid dearly for the pursuit of this folly — the best of his blood — only to fall the victim of his unrelenting passion.

À un papillon

Doux petit papillon, à peine dans la nuit
Commence de briller ma lampe solitaire,
Comme le plomb fatal, qui vers le but s'enfuit,
Tu tombes palpitant sur la pâle lumière.

Et chaque fois pourtant tes pures ailes d'or
A la flamme brûlante ont laissé des parcelles:
Quel atroce plaisir peut t'amener encore
Y chercher aujourd'hui des tortures nouvelles?

Comme toi, papillon, jadis naïf enfant,
A gravir du succès l'inacessible cîme,
J'ai versé sans profit le meilleur de mon sang,
Et de ma folle ardeur suis retombé victime.

To a Butterfly

Sweet little butterfly, hardly has my solitary lamp
Begun to burn in the darkness of the night,
Than you fall shivering upon its pale light.

And yet, to the inexorable flame
You sacrifice every time

A little of your golden wings.
What self-serving pleasure this night
Brings you to seek new tortures?

I am like you, little butterfly,
For I too return to the unyielding light
And spend, without any gain, the best of my blood,
Falling victim to my foolish ambition.

With the unfolding of the summer of 1867, his health took a turn for the better and his desire for her dominated his emotions. He therefore went to Montréal shortly before the inauguration of the Confederation of Canada on Monday, 1 July 1867. They spent a few days together. They were nice days. "My dearest Zoë," he wrote, "I have done nothing else but think of you since I left Montréal." Never would he forget those days in which they again came to the decision they would marry. "I am delighted to think," he affirmed, "that I will have the best wife in the world."

In the month of August he went to Montréal to see her practically every week. In his correspondence with her, in which he passes abruptly from the formal *vous* to the familiar *tu*, he told her much about his life, his preparation for the first elections of the Confederation era, his meetings with influential people.

Yet throughout the fall of 1867 there was confusion in his relationship with her. In his letters, he became more formal. On 6 September, for instance, he rambled on about a *grande soirée* that he was to attend, before telling her that he would not be coming to Montréal every week as he had done. Oh! He still loved her as much, he wanted her to know, and profoundly at that. But the demands of his law practice, the new life he was forming, and the uncertain behaviour of his malady made the six-hour train ride too time-consuming and onerous. Moreover, Wilfrid was not capable of solemn declarations, of passionate entreaties, and of sudden and direct resolutions. He preferred to agonize as he thought out every possible eventuality to whatever decision circumstances compelled him to make.

She fought back. She did not receive his decision calmly, and whenever he missed the weekly letter they had agreed on she reproached him with neglecting her. He defended himself, assuring her, sometimes with the *vous*, sometimes with the *tu*, that he was devoted to her.

She was, by then, under considerable pressure to marry Valois. Over and over again her friends, even her spiritual confessor, told her that she had to abandon Laurier and forget the plans the two of them had made together. He was a lost cause incapable of supporting her, an agnostic damning his soul, a butterfly going from one pleasure to the next, and a philanderer incapable of doing the right thing by her. They tried to convince her that he was unreliable and indecisive, and that he would not amount to much even if he lived a long life. More and more Phoebé, who was the leader of the anti-Wilfrid forces, pressed her to make a decision about Valois. He had been patient, kind, attentive, determined — everything Wilfrid wasn't.

By the time Wilfrid saw Zoë in the first week of January, the die was cast. She was shy in his presence and he sensed that a decision was imminent. In spite of that, he did not formally ask for her hand and he made no arrangements to see her father.

Shortly after Wilfrid returned to Arthabaska, she told him that she intended to marry Valois sometime in May. It would be a double ceremony with Emma and her fiancé, François-Xavier Coutu. She nevertheless hoped that they would remain friends. He assured her that he wanted only her happiness, yet he was desperate. "Why has heaven refused me wealth and health?" he cried to her. "Adieu, ma bonne Zoë." He was certain he would never love again.

~

By 7:15 on the morning of 13 May 1868, he was at the Gare Bonaventure in Montréal. Séraphin's *cocher* was waiting for him and in silence he was taken to the house on Saint-Laurent and dropped at the door leading to the medical office. The door was unlocked. Séraphin greeted him warmly as they walked into the surgery.

"J'ai bien des choses à te dire. However, what I have to say can wait. What I want you to do now is get undressed so that I can examine you."

Wilfrid did what he was told. While in the background came the noises of the family getting up, Séraphin left hardly any part of his body unprobed.

"You are not tubercular, but you suffer from chronic bronchitis. When it flares up — generally when you are tired, the weather soaks you to the bone, and things aren't going as well as you would like — it becomes severe and painful, constricting your lungs, making it difficult for you to breathe. You spit blood. You become exhausted, depressed, and God knows what else. But none of it is life-threatening. If you take care of yourself and have someone decent and kind to look after you — and I don't mean a doctor — you can live to a ripe old age. Now, let's go for a walk. It's a nice morning. When we return, we'll have break-fast. Viens."

Séraphin picked up his walking-stick and led the way. They walked for close to an hour and Séraphin talked. His life, he said, had been miserable for months. His household was in a state of war. There was no peace to be found and for reasons he could not understand he was made the culprit. "Phoebé est absolument impossible; Emma hardly speaks to me; the others give me looks that could kill a bull, and the servants may be putting arsenic in my tea! Et tout ça, because of Zoë and you." He stopped and looked Wilfrid straight in the eyes and asked: "Do you love Zoë?"

"You know I love her. I have told her often enough. Why do you ask me such a question?"

"Then marry her!"

"Impossible! You know the reasons as well as I do. And so does Zoë."

Séraphin would have none of Wilfrid's excuses. Somewhat grandly and a little irritably he said: "Do you think that Phoebé and I were rich? I was a simple clerk and a student with many years to go. But it did not stop us. There were even children. So don't tell me you can't afford a wife! Your career is just beginning. You fear that your illness may have left you sterile or impotent or both, but how do you know? Let time determine that. As for not passing on your *maladie* to your children, there is no evidence that there is anything malignant to pass on."

"Je ne sais pas quoi faire! Zoë told me several months ago that she would marry your friend Pierre Valois. Is the date fixed?"

"Oui. Pierre became a doctor yesterday. It was no longer possible to avoid fixing the date of his wedding to Zoë. That's why I wired you. The date is set for the end of May. A double ceremony with Emma and Coutu."

Back at the house, Séraphin took him to the living room and went to look for Zoë. He found her in her room surrounded by the women of the house. He sent them all away and took Zoë downstairs to Wilfrid, without giving her any time to let Emma beautify her.

Her eyes were all puffed up, her forehead deeply creased and red, and her hair, generally imprisoned tightly around her head, dishevelled. In her black dress, without a hint of colour, she appeared more severe than usual. Séraphin knew that she didn't look her best, but "ce n'est pas ça qui compte," he kept repeating. Besides, Wilfrid was also the worse for wear. He had slept only a little on the train, his clothes were all wrinkled, his hair scattered, he had not shaved since the previous morning — and he coughed.

Wilfrid is terrified. She comes in and he bows stiffly as she sits down on the edge of a chair. He remains standing by the fireplace. She does not look at him. She waits. Séraphin's voice comes through the door. "Allez-vous en!" he yells. There is the noise of several pairs of feet running away. They both burst out laughing. She stands up and comes beside him. She takes his hand and her beautiful eyes sweep up at him. It has to be now or never! Formally, he asks her to marry him. Formally, she accepts.

What is important to Zoë is when the marriage will take place.

"Aujourd'hui," she says, smiling up at him.

"Today? But . . ."

"Aujourd'hui," she repeats more firmly this time.

He smiles, takes her in his arms, and repeats: "Aujourd'hui."

After that, it was mayhem. Emma, who, in spite of her father, had been listening at the door, burst into the room, followed by the rest of the Gauthiers, servants and all. Séraphin, who had spent the intervening time with Phoebé, entered majestically with her on his arm. Phoebé embraced the two young people, who were hanging on to each other for dear life. Zoë whispered to her, "Aujourd'hui!" Phoebé didn't flinch. "Certainly!"

When Zoë told the others, Emma shrieked: "Moi, aussi!"

"If the four of you are to be married today," said Séraphin after a brief moment of consideration, "there is much to be done. Wilfrid has to be on the train tonight."

He made a quick list and barked out orders. Phoebé and the girls were to find suitable clothes while the cook and the other servants prepared for the small wedding feast that would follow the ceremony. The driver was sent out to find a couple of carriages for hire. Once they arrived, Wilfrid, after borrowing twenty-five dollars from Séraphin to cover various expenses, went off in one of them to find Zoë's father at the address she gave him along with a note. Not finding him at home, Wilfrid rushed to the bailiff's office where he worked and it was there that he formally asked Godfrey-Napoléon Lafontaine for the hand of his daughter in marriage. Monsieur Lafontaine gave his blessing and agreed to give the bride away. Then Wilfrid went on to see the vicar general of the diocese to secure the necessary dispensation for the reading of the banns and, after him, to the parish priest, Chanoine Édouard-Charles Fabre, the future archbishop of Montréal, to fix a time for the double wedding.

By 2:45, Séraphin and Phoebé, Emma and François-Xavier, Zoë and Wilfrid were with the notary. It took about one hour to draft the contract, which contained eight articles. Wilfrid and Zoë each retained full ownership of their personal effects and property. Zoë brought sixteen shares in the Capital Fund of the Société permanente de construction of Montréal worth about eight hundred dollars, a 1799 piano with the signature of manufacturer John P. Craig on it, clothes, some jewels, and a few pieces of furniture, all of which were diligently enumerated. For his part, Wilfrid provided Zoë with a three-hundred-dollar annuity. He further agreed to contribute whatever furnishings he had to their joint enterprise and to pay his share of the expenses incurred for Zoë and him to live together.

The wedding took place at 8:00 in the evening in a chapel attached to the Roman Catholic Cathedral of Montréal in the parish of Saint-Jacques. There were about twelve guests, in addition to the four young people about to be married. Emma, who had been planning her wedding for months, was all in white. Zoë, who to Wilfrid was radiant, was in a pale grey corded silk dress with a blue sash around her waist. She had her mother's gold chain and locket around her neck. The white veil on her head didn't conceal the fine features of her face.

When they had repeated their full names to him in a clear voice, the curé asked Wilfrid if he consented to have Zoë as his lawful wedded wife before God and before their parents, friends, and relatives assembled. He answered "oui," and the procedure was repeated for Zoë. On receiving their mutual consent, the priest took them by the hand and joined them in marriage, while making the Sign of the Cross over them: "Ego jungo vos in matrimonium — in nomine Patris, et Filii, et Spiritus Sancti. Amen."

Before the last blessing, they and their witnesses signed the register. It was by then close to 9:30. In less than an hour, at 10:10, Wilfrid's train to Arthabaska would be leaving from the Gare Bonaventure.

There was no time for him to go back to Séraphin's for supper and a celebration. They filled the carriages as best they could, leaving Wilfrid and Zoë alone in the Gauthiers'. All the way to the station he held her hand and stayed very close to her. They made plans. In a day or so, she would send her piano and her belongings by train and he would forward fifty-five dollars to Séraphin to cover these expenses and repay the good doctor. He hoped to come on the following Sunday to take her to his lodgings in Arthabaska, where they would live until they could build a home of their own.

Arriving at the station, he remained with her until the last possible minute, then kissed her goodbye.

2

SAINT-LIN AND L'ASSOMPTION

Wilfrid Laurier belonged to a family that was poor in belongings but rich in pedigree. His heritage was deeply rooted in the life of Canada. In 1676 François Cottineau *dit* Champlaurier, who had arrived from St. Cloud in France as one of the soldiers in the Carignan-Salières Regiment in 1665, was living in Lachenaye, where he married Madeleine Milot of Montréal, the granddaughter of Augustin Hébert, one of the twelve companions of Paul de Chomedey de Maisonneuve at the founding of Montréal in 1642. Wilfrid's grandfather, who changed the family name simply to Laurier, and his father were direct descendants of that union. His mother was also from the region, her father being a large farmer in the village of L'Assomption, a few miles away from Saint-Lin. On her father's side, her ancestors in Canada dated back to 1687, while through her mother she came from the soil of l'Acadie —Acadia—her forebears having been exiled by the British in the eighteenth century.

Wilfrid's grandpapa Charles Laurier was born in Lachenaye in 1777. He was a most ingenious man. He taught himself mathematics and land surveying and was a recognized surveyor appointed under royal patent. His duties brought him all over the seigneurie and he was, therefore, well known in Saint-Lin. As a surveyor, he had an honourable profession that made him a natural leader of the people, settling their disputes, speaking on their behalf, reading and writing their important documents, and making sure, in a most litigious nation, that good fences made for good neighbours.

He was also an amateur astronomer, a scientist of sorts, and an inventor of some reputation. He was the first to seek a patent for an invention from the legislature of Lower Canada. In 1822 he invented what he called the *loch terrestre*, or land log. This device was made up of dials and could be attached to a carriage wheel. As the wheel turned, the dials recorded the number of revolutions, thus providing the distance traversed at any given time. The legislature granted him a patent in 1826.

In January 1805 he had married Thérèse Cusson in the parish church of Lachenaye. They had only one child, Charles, who took the name of Carolus. He too became a surveyor, first as an assistant to his father and then in his own right. On 8 April 1834, when he was barely nineteen years old, he married Marie-Marcelle Martineau, who was the same age. On the morning of their wedding, as was the custom, Carolus asked his father for his benediction. Charles blessed them with the admonition that they were to be for each other in all circumstances: "Fear and pray God, my children, so that He may grant you *l'Esprit de la sagesse* [wisdom]. And, in all cases, treat others as you would want them to treat you." As a wedding gift, he gave the newlyweds a lot in the village of Saint-Lin on Saint-Antoine, one of the four streets of the village, and near the Achigan River. It was in this house, after many miscarriages, that Marcelle gave birth to her only son, Wilfrid, on 20 November 1841.

It is a good thing that the small bedroom in which the woman lies is next to the kitchen. It has been such a cold week. She shivers and there comes a great movement inside her. The sage femme of the village, who arrived a few hours before, hearing her moans, rushes into the room and issues orders all around. Lukewarm water is brought; hot towels, sheets, and other paraphernalia are assembled on the unpainted pine chest of drawers; and over and over again the woman about to give birth hears the inevitable "Mais poussez! Poussez donc!" She does as she's told, but only pain rewards her efforts. In her anxiety, she glances at the baby's cradle lying next to her double bed and a faint smile appears on her lips, as if in anticipation of the beautiful moments that will follow her ordeal. Again the movement and the pain, more compelling this time, and, with a final heaving push and sigh, the child appears. He is declared to be a fine boy. Two days later, on a warm day, he is taken to the parish church of Saint-Lin de Lachenaye, where, with his father in attendance, his four grandparents, his godfather and godmother, the parish priest baptizes him: Henry-Charles-Wilfrid, "in nomine Patris, et Filii, et Spiritus Sancti. Amen."

When Wilfrid was born, his parents were well established in Saint-Lin. His father was a respected member of the élite of the village. No sooner had they taken up residence than Carolus was asked to be one of four landowners to sign his name to an official document confirming the selection of the churchwardens for the newly created parish. His prestige increased with the years, but in Wilfrid's infancy he lived in the shadow of his father. After the elder's death in 1844, however, Carolus came into his own, with the villagers referring to him as Monsieur Carolus and looking to him for guidance. In 1845 he was appointed justice of the peace, or commissaire pour la décision sommaire de petites causes dans la paroisse de Saint-Lin. As such, he was in charge of keeping the peace, issued summonses, heard and passed judgment on cases of little importance, and took and certified depositions on oath. Two years later, in 1847, the governor general, Lord Elgin, named him a lieutenant in the Third Battalion of the Leinster Militia. In 1850 he became a school commissioner and later, when his son was in his early teens, Carolus served for seven years as mayor (1855–62). By all accounts he was a good official, honest and upright, who could rally dissenters in the process of organizing the much-needed municipal services. At the same time, he didn't allow himself to be trampled by ecclesiastical authority. He was a firm proponent of a clear demarcation between ecclesiastical authority and civil authority. Wilfrid often heard him preach on that principle.

Unfortunately for the family fortune, Carolus was not as frugal as his father had been and he tended to be more easygoing. There was not much money at any time. He worked hard as a surveyor, farmer, and lumber merchant, and his family did not live in penury — but it was not easy.

Wilfrid was seven years old when his mother died of tubercular consumption. Her dry hacking cough, general emaciation, fatigue, and hemorrhage of the lungs taught him about pain. She was thirty-three when she died, pregnant. His sister, Malvina, was eleven when she, too, died from the same disease. He remembered that his mother, when she was up to it, took him to the *lisière des bois* and there in the woods she would sketch a flower, a blade of grass, an arrangement of rocks, or anything else that took her fancy. She described it all to him. Later, at home, she read to him and hung her paintings on the walls.

His Maman Adeline became his new mother in the same year that his own mother died. She had come to live with the Lauriers when Malvina was born.

Maman Adeline was not like his mother, or at least what he remembered of her, but she became a second mother and he loved her. The best memory he had of Maman Adeline was the way she welcomed him with open arms when he returned home from playing or from school. He needed to be loved in those days. Often, he would climb on her knees to eat his bread and jam, all the while smothering her with kisses.

He remembered watching the logs float down the Achigan River to market. Invariably, he wanted to be on one of those logs going far away. He also recalled what fine cooks both his mother and his Maman Adeline were. The Lauriers ate well, but not more than anyone else in the village. He was fond of buckwheat pancakes with maple syrup and the boeuf à l'ancienne. At Christmas they always had a mountain of tourtières and sugar pies, and dozens and dozens of cro-quignoles, those mouth-watering cookies only *Canadien* women can make.

Oddly enough for him, the good times of his youth also included going to church. He was fond of the ceremonies, particularly when he made his First Communion and was confirmed. He also listened carefully to the parish priest, who after Sunday High Mass would instruct the children of the village on the tenets of the Faith, which was so much part of their national character and which Wilfrid later seemed to misplace somewhere along the way. In those days, the practice of religion was not as oppressive for him as it was on his wedding day, but it certainly was omnipresent.

On 24 June it was Saint-Jean-Baptiste Day — their national holiday. No one would miss it for the world. In the morning they had High Mass in a splen-didly decorated church, after which there were picnics, games, and, to end it all, fireworks at night. The men consumed much beer and often became intoxicated. Everybody, including the children, went to bed late.

As for his father, Carolus, Wilfrid liked his laugh, his sense of life, and his combative spirit. Carolus was a handsome man, and Wilfrid saw much of himself in him. From time to time, Wilfrid would go with Carolus on a sur-veying expedition, and he became aware of how people looked up to his father and valued his opinions. He was a leader in Saint-Lin. Carolus was a great talker, like Wilfrid's grandpapa. He argued with priests and bishops, and he thundered against the *autorités*. Listening to him about politics, the state of national affairs, and the future of *les Canadiens*, Wilfrid came to believe that it was Carolus who encouraged him to be a rebel of sorts. It certainly accounted for his distrust of all things clerical.

Gradually, Carolus came to the conclusion that he could not keep his two establishments. In addition to the house in town, he had a farm in the upper concessions. After his wife's death and his marriage to Adeline Ethier in 1848, he vacated the house on Saint-Antoine and moved to his *terre d'en haut*, which he had acquired earlier. He lived there until he sold it in 1857, then returned to his former residence.

Even though Carolus was far from being a wealthy man, he never skimped on education. Unlike many of his neighbours, he was an ardent believer in educating his children. However, he was not helped by the attitudes that existed about him. It was the time of the *guerre des éteignoirs*, when ratepayers considered educational reform as just another insidious way of taxing people. It was also the time when the church insisted on affirming its pre-eminence in educational matters and when most fathers believed that all boys needed was an elementary ability to read and write and know their catechism. Carolus opposed that trend and was determined that his son would have the best education he could provide. He would go to great lengths to see that Wilfrid entered the ranks of the liberal professions.

Until Wilfrid's twelfth or thirteenth year, there was no school for boys in Saint-Lin. The responsibility to educate Wilfrid in his early years fell largely to his mother, his father, and to some itinerant lay teachers who appeared from time to time. In that way, Wilfrid learned to read and write, developed some notions of mathematics and French grammar, and picked up smatterings of English.

Carolus deplored the nonchalance of his neighbours, the dismal state of education in Saint-Lin, and the constant battles between ratepayers and the parish priest over schools. In the summer of 1851, when Wilfrid was ten, Carolus decided to do something revolutionary about his son's training. He would send him to the English school in New Glasgow for the next academic year, which was scheduled to begin on 5 September.

New Glasgow was seven miles west of Saint-Lin and also on the Achigan River. It was an idyllic spot. The river wove its way through the village, and the falls, where there was a seigneurial mill, were quite impressive. The forest was not far from the settlement and was perfect for walks and games. Wilfrid was told that around eighty settlers from Glasgow, in Scotland, had come to that part of the world in 1820. By the time he went to school there, many of their descendants had left for the farms of southern Ontario; but many remained to till the soil, conduct business, and join with the Protestant and Catholic Irish and a few French families to build a village of about eight hundred souls.

The school Wilfrid went to was at the top of the hill and was called Fort Rose School. It was a wooden schoolhouse, small, with one window on each side, a door in front, and another in the back that gave access to the outhouses. Technically, it was a Protestant school, but no one was turned away because of religion. It was open to both boys and girls. The teaching was totally in English. Wilfrid did, though, learn French on his own by reading books that his parents borrowed for him from the library in Saint-Lin. It boasted some four hundred volumes. There were also the newspapers that came from Montréal: *La Minerve*, *La Patrie*, and *Le Pays*. As well, his father would often help him keep up in his mother tongue, for he was determined that Wilfrid would speak and write both languages fluently.

The school year began in early September and ended in the first week of July. There were, of course, many holidays. Not as many, though, as in Catholic schools. They learned grammar, English literature, arithmetic, as well as religion. Those who were not of the Protestant faith could be excused, but Wilfrid chose not to. He liked to compare their faith with his — in so far as he could. And he didn't wish to miss religious history. His fascination with history began in New Glasgow. The teacher, Sandy Maclean, always had a glass of Scotch on his desk and he read beautifully from the classics of his country of origin and from those of England. Often Wilfrid did not understand a word, but it did not matter.

To a boy of ten or eleven, New Glasgow was full of marvels. He never felt isolated there, nor could he ever remember being lonely. Everything he needed was at hand and he was quite busy, going to school and helping behind the counter in John Murray's shop. Murray was the village tailor and a great friend of Wilfrid's father, but he had a large family and was not able to take Wilfrid in. Besides, he was a Protestant, and Maman Adeline didn't want the dear son she had inherited to live with Protestants. It was bad enough, she used to say, that he was attending a Protestant school. When he wasn't too busy, Murray would read to him from his Bible: the King James version, it was. Ah! It was quite beautiful. Through their religious obligations, the Murrays instilled in him a feeling for literature that Sandy Maclean transformed into love.

Wilfrid spent two years in the home of a New Glasgow Catholic Irish family by the name of Kirke. Life at the Kirkes' was not as gay as at the Murrays'. They had no children his own age and there was not much reading from the Bible and singing of psalms. Kirke, who was in his early sixties, was, however, a mine of information on the Rebellion of 1837–38. He had been a member of the local committee that was formed to support the cause of the *Patriotes*. He was all in favour of liberty from the English. He and his family had suffered in Ireland at the hands of the Anglo-Protestant oligarchy there. Like their French counterparts, the Catholic Irish of New Glasgow objected to the control of the economy and their political life by the *Château clique*, as the oppressors were called, and their allies. However, he and the others were not very keen on an armed rebellion. A few went by foot to the battle of Saint-Eustache, but the majority remained in their village, contenting themselves with acts of intimidation.

Once a month or so, Wilfird went back to his family. Even though there was a sort of primitive road to Saint-Lin, it was not very useful except by foot. When he returned to Saint-Lin, Carolus would come and fetch him and they would walk the miles to Maman Adeline, only to return the same way a few days later. If the weather was good and the road passable, which was not very often, Carolus would drive his *carriole*. In winter, they could use the *traîneau*. There were lanterns or beacons marking the road, so they would not get lost. A few times, they went up by canoe. There was much pleasure in that.

Then, when he was almost thirteen years old, it was time to go to the classical Collège de L'Assomption.

~

In the early afternoon of 5 September 1854 Carolus and Wilfrid arrived at Madame Guilbault's house at the corner of Saint-Pierre and Saint-Hubert streets in L'Assomption, about twenty miles east of Saint-Lin. The house was long, with several windows giving onto the street. On the first floor, there was a formal parlour, a dining room large enough to accommodate a dozen students, a kitchen, and Madame Guilbault's private quarters. On the second floor were several bedrooms capable of lodging three or four boys each. All hygiene facilities were outside.

Madame Guilbault, a large woman with a warm smile, was affable and a strict disciplinarian. She was in charge — in loco parentis — and she tolerated no nonsense. She would house and feed Wilfrid, and he would have to obey the schedule and regulations established by the Collège de L'Assomption, where his father had enrolled him the previous summer. If he didn't do what he was told, he would be sent back home. The *pension* was about ten cents a day and was included in the fees payable to the college, in advance, every three months. Looking at Wilfrid's paleness, she concluded that he was a sickly child. She informed his father that should any student fall ill, the directeur of the college would determine whether the patient could stay home — in which case she would look after him with tenderness.

Both father and son agreed, and Wilfrid's belongings were stowed in one of the bedrooms upstairs. Wilfrid had brought from home a *baudet*, or small sawhorse, on which he placed a straw mattress and some woollen blankets. He had his chamber pot, a basin in which to wash, and some towels fashioned from rough material.

Carolus and Adeline had agonized over sending Wilfrid to L'Assomption. They wanted him educated well enough to enter the professions. But it cost money — approximately twenty or thirty dollars a year for tuition, *pension*, and incidental expenses — an enormous sum for a father of few means. After much deliberation, it was decided to cut here and there and make do with less. The cost of Wilfrid's food could be paid in kind. Adeline sewed his uniform of blue cloth with white ribs and a blue sash. It was to be worn on Sundays and holidays. She made the rest of his clothing of woollen cloth, flannel, and linen, and from the wool she spun herself. She sent him to Madame Guilbault's with a couple of grey linen blouses or *sarraux*, as she called them, a coloured belt to cheer him up, a wool jacket and two pairs of pants, a few pairs of socks she had knitted from leftover wool, some underwear made from flour or sugar sacks, and a single pair of boots that had belonged to Carolus. No item in this wardrobe could be described as fancy, let alone elegant. The belt, though, was a great success. To save the cost of washing his clothes, Carolus was mandated to come once every three weeks to fetch the dirty ones and replace them with clean ones.

They both admonished Wilfrid to be frugal with whatever purchases of school materials he might need. Armed with this litany of do's and don'ts, Laurier arrived at L'Assomption.

Having finished with Madame Guilbault, Carolus and Wilfrid went to the college. It had been founded twenty-two years earlier and had acquired a reputation in the region. The exterior was formidable. It was a two-storey cut-stone building divided into three wings: two on the sides and one in the rear. There were many windows, each with several square panes of glass. When the Lauriers walked in, Abbé Médard Caisse, a severe-looking man, greeted them in the parlour to the right of the entrance. While Carolus went to the office to pay the tuition and the *pension*, a senior student showed Wilfrid around.

The vastness and emptiness of the interior, viewed in a dark light, were intimidating to the young lad. Across the hall from the parlour was the library, with some two hundred volumes and two flights of stairs leading to the storage area above. In the left wing was a small and not elaborate chapel, the office, the refectory for the priests, and the kitchen. In the right wing were three small, dark classrooms and a long recreation room, which also served as a study hall.

The furnishings were primitive. Wood benches and a few long doors placed on workhorses served as tables. In Wilfrid's time, students did not have individual desks, and it was only in 1859, after he had been at the college five years, that the doors were replaced with wooden tables. There were several wood-burning stoves. The student showing him around mentioned that it was quite cold in winter and to have his mother sew him warm clothes. Oil lamps were scattered around — the bare minimum — which Wilfrid would have to trim and monitor when his name came up. He was shown where the outhouses were, and when he asked shyly about drinking water, the student pointed through a window to a small pond. In winter, he added, the ice was thick.

Wilfrid met a few students in the recreation room, along with a couple of professors. After an awkward interlude, Carolus, his business done, fetched him to return to Madame Guilbault for his supper and a good night's rest. School started in earnest the next day.

At 5:25 the following morning Madame Guilbault woke him up, along with the other students in her house. He had twenty minutes to get dressed, wash his face, and run to the college. By 5:45 he was in the chapel, looking around and wondering what prayers he should be saying and what on earth one did while meditating. In the study hall, he listened to various briefings from the director of the college, the prefect of studies, and the prefect of discipline.

The director, the Reverend Alfred Dupuis, welcomed the old and the new students, especially those of the 22e Cours (1854–61), the one Wilfrid was enrolled in. There were twenty-three of them and they all sat together under the supervision of their English teacher, George Mount, a taciturn ecclesiastic who hardly spoke a word of French and who was reputed not to make any effort to understand those he was in charge of. After his welcome, the director became more precise and less friendly. Everyone was to study hard or he would be thrown out. Insubordination of any kind would not be tolerated. In the winter of 1852–53, he reminded them, eighty students, members of a secret society called Les Flambards, were expelled because they had the temerity to rebel against the authority of the priests. Their fees were not refunded.

Moreover, the students had to be polite at all times, keep healthy, and, above all, pray to the Virgin to avoid sins of impurity. He ended his remarks by reawakening in them the terrifying reality that the school year would last until the middle of July. There would be a half-day's holiday each week until Easter, and after that a whole day. He gave the list of regular holidays, and indicated the special ones. He was quite firm: the presence of the students was required every day while the school year lasted. No going home for any holidays. Wilfrid felt a jolt in the bottom of his stomach, and a fit of coughing followed. It always happened like that! The director waited patiently for him to recuperate.

It was the préfet de discipline, Abbé Caisse, who made Wilfrid note the daily routine. At 5:25 it was wake-up time, followed by ablutions and the walk to the college. By 5:45 he had to be in his seat at chapel for morning prayer and meditation. Fifteen minutes later there would be a one-hour period in the study hall. Mass was at 7:00, after which the students went to their boarding houses to eat breakfast, which generally consisted of bread, some rancid butter, and barley coffee with lots of milk. On Sundays, Madame Guilbault added some salted pork drippings. At 8:00 Wilfrid went to class until 10:00, followed by a fifteen-minute break till 10:15 and an hour and a half study period. By 11:45 he was hungry and tired, but he had to go to chapel for the Angelus. Then he ran home to lunch, where he ate a thin soup, a small quantity of roasted or boiled meat, potatoes, and an apple or some maple syrup that had seen better days. He devoured the food because he had to be back to play with his friends and be in the study hall by 1:00. Another two hours of classes followed, and at 3:50 there was a twenty-five-minute recess; then from 4:15 to 6:00 there was more study. Between 6:00 and 6:30 the director supervised a period of spiritual readings. After that exercise, Wilfrid rushed to Madame Guilbault's one more time for a supper of *ragoût* — a brown sauce in which swam some meat and potatoes. He was entitled to a glass of milk, which Maman Adeline had insisted upon and which Carolus paid for with some other product. Returning to the college, he could walk around and talk until 8:00, when he went into the chapel for prayers. Mercifully they didn't last too long, and by 9:00 the students were generally in bed.

Recess was taken either inside in the *salle de récréation* or outside in *la cour*, an area that increased in size throughout Wilfrid's stay at L'Assomption. There he would sometimes join in a game of *paume* or *pelote*, in which players bounced a hard ball off the wall of the college with their bare hands. To play it well, one needed agility, quick reflexes, and endurance. Wilfrid had these qualities, but not the physical energy to go with them. He tired quickly. If truth be told, physical exercise was never his forte and he seldom indulged in it. He never mentioned playing baseball or any other game of exertion, but contented himself with walking, talking, and walking some more.

Halfway between L'Assomption and the small town of L'Épiphanie, the college owned a vast property filled with elms and maples, with a creek running through it. It was called the *bois des écoliers*. This was Wilfrid's favourite place and he would visit there as often as time allowed, especially on the weekly holiday that fell most often on a Thursday. This was the day he most looked forward to. All week the students worried about the weather. All week Wilfrid and his friends Louis-Joseph Riopel and Joseph Marion studied the heavens, searching for the right stars, and asking endless questions of the *maître des salles*, generally a benign ecclesiastic who was as keen as his charges were. Wilfrid, who seldom prayed, did so fervently on Wednesday nights. They sang the Salve Regina, the canticle to the patroness of scholars, the Virgin Mary, ever so clearly and loudly. They were desperate to be heard! Generally their prayers were granted. Riopel became weary of Wilfrid taking the credit for the fine weather. He claimed it was all due to him because he prayed fervently all the time.

Marion, for his part, insisted that the Virgin was making up to him for his missing arm.

Wilfrid arrived at the college coughing. His father had informed the priests of this affliction. Almost every year, in the rainy seasons of the fall and spring and in the depths of winter, he tended to cough more and occasionally had to take to his bed under the care of Madame Guilbault and the watchful eye of the director. It was at L'Assomption in his fourth year that Wilfrid had a *hémorragie* — that he spat blood for the first time. It was a wintery Thursday afternoon and he was seventeen years old. He and the other students had gone to the *bois des écoliers*. He had been sick for a couple of days before and had not totally recovered. He was late in his *composition* and was somewhat discouraged. Nothing seemed to be going right. He and his friend Oscar Archambault were walking along a path near the frozen creek when, all of a sudden, he stopped with a severe pain inside and a general feeling of weakness. His throat was on fire and his lungs were about to explode. In panic, he ran as best he could a little ways into the wood. There he coughed and coughed, and the more he tried to suppress it so as not to alarm Archambault or the others, the more he coughed loudly and desperately. Removing his hands from his mouth, he saw to his horror that his mittens were covered with blood and that more blood was pouring onto the snow with every breath he took. He thought he was going to die. He did not pray, nor did he make any promises to God to end his torment. How long it went on, he didn't know, but it finally stopped. By then he was sprawled on snow stained with red, and with patches of blood on his jacket. He rested there for a while and when he heard Archambault calling him, he got up quickly, washed himself as best he could with snow, and erased the evidence of his ordeal. When he came back to the path, he was so pale that Archambault took him to the *abri*, or shelter, which was on the property. Archambault spoke to the préfet de discipline about Wilfrid not being well, and he was sent back in the horse-driven sleigh that had brought the food.

Religion permeated the whole fabric of the college. In fact, the college existed to form men who would accept the teachings of the church, defend its rights and prerogatives, and be an example to those less educated. The best way of serving God and the church was to become a priest. Many came, but few were chosen. Out of the twenty-three boys who joined the 22e Cours with Wilfrid, only four appear to have taken Holy Orders. The teachers were either priests or ecclesiastics — students sent to the college to learn theology in preparation for their ordination. There were no lay teachers in Wilfrid's time. The guiding hand of God could be experienced in every classroom and dominated every subject taught. Recreation began with prayers, as any other activity did. On Friday evenings, the first quarter of the recreation was devoted to the *Chemin de croix*, the journey that symbolized Christ's march to Calvary. Assignments were headed with "J.M.J. aidez-moi" [Jesus, Mary, Joseph, help me], or "Omnia per Mariam" [All through Mary], or even "Laus Deo Semper" [Praise be to God always]. There were yearly retreats; months dedicated to Mary, the dead, St. Joseph, and the Sacred Heart; novenas, particularly before Pentecost, the Immaculate Conception, and the feast of St. Thomas Aquinas, who was seen as the special guide of students of philosophy and theology; and *octaves* after the celebration of certain feast days, notably that of the Blessed Sacrament in May. Students were encouraged to stop by the chapel on their way to all activities, either to say a short prayer or to make a simple genuflection and the Sign of the Cross. All these practices were in addition to the daily prayers, the Mass, the Rosary, and various other religious exercises, all of which were obligatory. The spiritual merged seamlessly with the secular.

In his first year, Wilfrid selected a spiritual director among the priests to whom he went at first frequently, then less so after his sixteenth birthday. As for a confessor, he didn't have a regular one, even though the students were encouraged to do so. He seldom went to confession, and to Communion hardly at all. Eventually he was thrown out of the Congrégation de la Sainte-Vierge for his general indifference to religion. Every year while he was at L'Assomption, though, he did his Easter duties. Wilfrid observed all the externals of religion, as he did for a great part of his life, but the kind of faith Riopel and some of the others had eluded him. The notion of an all-encompassing Being, or a God, was no problem to him, but he couldn't join fully in the exuberance of it all. He liked the ceremonies, though, the ritual and the music, and he seldom missed attending Sunday Mass.

Religion to Wilfrid was a process to save his soul. The spiritual, in contrast, was nourishment to feed his soul, and that sustenance it received from the books he read, the nature around him, and the friends he had. Over the years he developed a socio-religious attitude that he didn't deviate from: he went to church and did what was required; he caused no scandal, nor did he question or discuss the religious practices of others; and he lived his life with the suspicion that his salvation would take care of itself.

Sometimes in the spring and early fall, Carolus, Maman Adeline, and his half-brother Charlemagne would make the journey from Saint-Lin to attend a particular Sunday or Feast Day. More often than not he would get special permission to accompany them to the Martineaus', his mother's relatives who lived in L'Assomption. Other times they would be invited to the Archambaults' house.

Such visiting, though, had to wait until they had heard the speakers on the church steps. Generally, the *cérémonie*, as Wilfrid called it, would begin with announcements of various kinds; the notary, or someone who could read, would scan some excerpts from the newspapers and, after that, came the speeches. Joseph Papin was the most eloquent. Wilfrid would do almost anything to hear him. Papin had been a student at the college before Wilfrid was born and in 1854 was elected as a *Rouge* to the United Legislature of Canada as the member for L'Assomption. He was a founder of the Institut canadien and of the newspaper *L'Avenir*, which the priests of the college condemned almost daily. The students were asked to pray for the electoral demise of the *Rouges* so as to ensure the salvation of the faithful. When Papin became a defender of nondenominational schools, Wilfrid found himself supporting him — quietly, of course, and only among his friends, for he was certain he would be expelled if the priests knew of it.

Joseph Papin inspired Wilfrid. In his youthful enthusiasm, Wilfrid thought Papin one of the most brilliant men to grace Canada's political life. Wilfrid gladly suffered the punishments he received for sneaking out of classes and other activities to hear him. Papin gave Wilfrid a political vision with liberal ideas, words to express them, a voice to articulate them, and the courage to suffer the price.

In his third year, Wilfrid became enthusiastic about law. Papin and the other fiery *Rouges* he met at L'Assomption were all lawyers and he often skipped study and classes to go to the court-house to hear their briefs. "That's me!" he told Marion, who wanted to be a notary. Throughout the rest of his years at the college, he went back to the court-house as often as he could. His knees were hard put by all the kneeling he was forced to do as punishment for breaking the rules.

The seven-year course Wilfrid followed at the Collège de L'Assomption was divided into seven categories: Éléments, Syntaxe, Méthode-Versification, Belles-Lettres, Rhétorique, Philosophie 1, and Philosophie 2. In his first year, he was introduced to the subjects that would remain constant throughout the 22e Cours: French and Latin grammar, history, geography, and English. He came in contact with the glories of French literature — before the French Revolution, of course — in his second year. In the third, his intellectual life began in earnest with Virgil, Cicero, Catullus, Sallust, Horace, Bossuet, Racine, Corneille, along with much history and even more poetry. The same authors found their way into the program in Belles-Lettres and Rhétorique. In his last two years, he devoted his time to philosophy à la St. Thomas Aquinas, along with some Greek, astronomy, physics, and mathematics, all taught by the same ecclesiastic. In addition, Wilfrid studied the rudiments of liturgical chant, agricultural science, and drawing. He excelled at none of these, but he had a good singing voice. He played no musical instrument, but he liked to listen to the piano and the organ.

In his sixteen-hour day, Wilfrid spent approximately two hours in various spiritual exercises, two hours in recreation, four hours in classes, and a little more than four hours in study periods. Three hours were allocated to washing, eating, and going back and forth from the college to Madame Guilbault's. He was a busy lad.

Each study period was assigned to a subject, so that every course would be prepared before class. Daily homework had to be done faithfully and handed in on time; there were tests and competitions of various kinds almost daily; regular formal debates in French, English, Latin, and Greek, with the winning side receiving a flag with the Latin inscription *Victoria* embossed across it; lengthy compositions that took five hours to write; and oral examinations each semester. These examinations, held in February and July, lasted several days and were open to parents and the general public, who came in large numbers to the torment of the student body. Teachers and other members of the staff first asked questions of each student to test his general knowledge and his specific understanding of the various subjects he had taken. As an interlude, students gave orations on particular issues and topics. Then it was the turn of the audience to seek answers to what interested them, most of which had little to do with what the students had learned. When the director decided that the tormentees had had enough, he presented the prizes to the most erudite students and terminated the misery with a short talk and a prayer. At the end of the year, a graduating student made an eloquent speech thanking the authorities on behalf of the boys, and the director congratulated them all and sent them home.

Wilfrid had much to learn at the Collège de L'Assomption. Unfortunately, the quantity was accompanied by a severe lack of quality. Since all formal contacts with France were more or less broken off after the British Conquest of Canada in 1759–60 and the French Revolution of 1789, there were few adequate textbooks. Professors at the college dictated their notes to the students, a tedious and monotonous process. Moreover, these notes came largely from teachers who were not much older than twenty and who had no formal training in education. The majority of them were ecclesiastics on their way to ordination. In fact, they were there to study theology and sacred scriptures from one of the resident priests at the college. Their knowledge on any given subject was extremely limited. However, what they lacked in erudition they more than amply made up in enthusiasm.

In Wilfrid's years at L'Assomption, Norbet Barret, a remarkably cultured and intellectual priest, held the position of préfet des études. His task was not simple. He was responsible for the effective application of the program, the proper teaching methodologies, the adequacy of the note-textbooks, the rigorous standards to be applied, and the harmonious development of the intellectual life of the college. It was his decision to keep a register of each student's progress. He insisted that all members of the teaching staff provide him with weekly marks and comments on each of the students. He kept his register faithfully, issuing lists each week in which the students' names were read out loud in order of their overall standing in class. Every month there was a special ceremony in the study hall at which he announced the monthly results of each student. Twice a year he dispatched a bulletin of their son's progress, or lack of it, to the parents. He summoned students constantly to discuss their marks and their intellectual and general comportment. He introduced the practice of either refusing readmission to students who did poorly or making them repeat the year.

He initiated *la classe des faibles* for those who needed extra help. Forty percent was the passing mark, and he fought relentlessly to maintain the high standards he desired so ardently. He was not well liked, but he persevered and Wilfrid benefited from his courage and dedication.

Barret was a vigorous and exacting man, a purist, a harsh disciplinarian, and he pursued Wilfrid relentlessly to combat his student's natural tendency to indolence. He knew that he had a remarkable pupil in his care and a rebellious one on his hands. How to tame the latter without endangering the former? There is no doubt that he overlooked many of Wilfrid's infractions to the regulations. Like his young charge, Barret appeared to desire more liberty, but he could not allow discipline to deteriorate. This is why Wilfrid often found himself *à genoux*, kneeling in front of the whole student body for an hour or so as a punishment for having run away to pursue some political escapade. Once as he was about to kneel as ordered, he sensed that his classmates would rebel and he made clear his disapproval. With a single gesture of his hand he commanded them to be quiet and to return to their studies.

In relentless pursuit of the highest standards possible, Barret encouraged students to follow their particular intellectual interests in small groups outside official study time. A year before Wilfrid arrived at L'Assomption, Barret founded a literary circle called L'Académie française for a more detailed study of French literature and writing. Wilfrid became a member in his second year and was president at least four times. When Barret established an English Academy, Wilfrid joined it as well. Wilfrid was not at all satisfied with the teaching of English at the college. It was too theoretical and was taught by ecclesiastics who had little interest in English literature and history. The students took advantage of the teachers' incompetence to fool around and cause havoc. Wilfrid remedied the situation by reading on his own, translating a variety of texts, and speaking and writing English whenever he had a chance. Barret's academy gave him a splendid opportunity, and he made ample use of it.

On special occasions, Barret would organize a *discours de circonstance*. Often he chose Wilfrid, particularly for the celebrations around Saint-Jean-Baptiste Day. Wilfrid's patriotic speeches aroused the enthusiasm of his colleagues and of all those who listened to him. He was clear in his thought, natural in his gestures, and his voice, beautiful and sonorous, echoed far. Wilfrid was also involved in another of Barret's innovations: the *récréations latines*. Held about once a week, the students attempted to spend an entire recess period speaking only Latin.

Barret also continued an old practice he had been part of when he was a student at the college in its first years: the *débat oratoire*. In these debates and presentations, students discussed topics that arose from class work or from some event of national or international importance. These subjects would be discussed mostly in French, but sometimes in Latin, Greek, or English. Barret was always there scrupulously examining the content for its orthodoxy, correcting errors in grammar and pronunciation, and encouraging greater efforts.

From his first year, Wilfrid became an enthusiast of these debates and he always participated in them. He read many of the newspapers that found their way into the college library, as well as whatever contraband his *Rouge* friends in L'Assomption could procure for him. Consequently, he became knowledgeable about the public affairs and great issues of his time both within the province and elsewhere. Often he chose to debate a particular question one way, only to exercise himself the next time around by arguing the opposite.

At the end of his first year in Philosophie, for instance, he delivered an oration at the final convocation in favour of the temporal power of the papacy, a topic that was much discussed at the time. He argued well that to deprive the pope of his *pouvoir temporel* was to rob him of his liberty to act in accordance with the lofty interests of the church. Catholicism was in peril, he made bold to say, situated as it was in the midst of the *atmosphère empoisonnée* that prevailed in this century of error and impiety. The oration was extremely well received. At the oral examinations at the end of his stay at the college, however, some visitors implored him to repeat it. With dignity, some foolhardiness, and much courage, he refused. "I never accepted the notion of the temporal power of the pope." And that was that.

Besides orations, compositions, and debates, Wilfrid practised his art of Rhétorique by acting in the *séances* or plays that the college mounted a few times each year and to which the general public was invited. Barret made certain that these plays were classical works, in keeping with the teachings of the church, and worthy of student participation. One such play was Racine's *Athalie*, which was presented during Wilfrid's first year and repeated three times thereafter.

The Collège de L'Assomption, though, did not live by the spiritual or the profane alone. It conquered through *la Règle et la Discipline*. Regulations and discipline: these were the mortar with which the various blocks used to build the edifice of a good and learned *Canadien* devoted to the church were cemented. Almost every act and every minute were preordained. The bell rang five minutes before the beginning of an exercise and five minutes before the end of it. All written assignments had to be presented on regulation paper. In oral presentations the student had to stand up and answer the questions posed to him with courtesy and respect. He had to accept with humility whatever punishment was inflicted should he fail to answer correctly. And the *règlement* never changed, though it was adapted from time to time. Between 1833, the year the college was founded, and 1933, the daily schedule was hardly modified.

In January 1857, when Wilfrid was fifteen years old, he encountered an individual who became one of the few persons he would remember with annoyance and, at times, anger all through his life: Ignace Bourget, bishop of Montréal. For over thirty years, Bourget dominated the affairs of the church in Québec and was directly responsible for the religious crisis that permeated that period. A man of astonishing cruelty, a pharisaical bureaucrat and a dictator at heart, his energy consisted largely in meddling. Since the college was situated in his diocese, he spent a week there interfering. He met with the priests and the ecclesiastics discussing the affairs of the college and their role within it, and he spoke with the students in groups or individually. Wilfrid met him along with the members of his Cours. Bourget's ultra-conservative character and agenda didn't appeal to him and, if Bourget was warned of Wilfrid's unorthodox views, the prelate avoided any confrontation with him.

Wilfrid did well — in fact very well — at the college. He was much admired, often the centre of attention, and always polite and courteous. "You must always think of others," Barret used to tell him, and he remembered that all his life. He studied regularly and worked hard. He also learned fast. If he didn't always come first, it was because his lethargy prevented it or he was not interested. He was always frank, diplomatic, assertive, loyal, and a good companion, even though he had a certain hauteur, or loftiness, which Barret and the disciplinary prefects attempted to eradicate without much success. A leader by temperament, he learned to curb his intransigence, and his colleagues respected him for his sang-froid in holding the controversial views he did and for his ability to express and defend them. His weakness, which Barret recorded often in his *régistre,* was indolence. It almost amounted to laziness, according to the good father. All were convinced that he was capable of greatness if he could only harness his energy.

Indolence or not, he succeeded rather well. In 1856 in his third year, he was first over all, second in Latin grammar and oration, and first in English, history, and geography. Three years later he won prizes in seven out of his eleven subjects. Carolus was proud, and Maman Adeline knew that the sacrifices she and the others had made were worthwhile.

Then it was 8 July 1861. He took leave of his friends, Louis-Joseph Riopel, Joseph Marion, Oscar Archambault, Arthur Dansereau, and Joseph-Israël Tarte. In one way or another, these friends would always be part of his life, even if they didn't share his religious or his political views. Together they had dreamed of the great deeds they were going to do. Together they had worked and prayed and played and suffered punishment. Together they had exchanged ideas, even intimate thoughts and deeds. Together they had grown up. He bid Madame Guilbault farewell, thanked the priests and the ecclesiastics who had taught him, and, late in the afternoon, boarded Carolus's *calèche* with all his belongings and went home to Saint-Lin to the house in which he had been born nineteen years before. The most important and difficult part of his journey to adulthood was over.

3

MONTRÉAL

Wilfrid had been to Montréal a couple of times before entering McGill University. The first time was with a delegation of students that Father Barret took to participate in the celebrations of Saint-Jean-Baptiste Day. With Barret watching them like a hawk, he had no opportunity to roam around the streets of the city. However, what he did see pleased him, especially the crowds parading up and down or sitting under the trees. From afar, he noticed the contour of McGill. He made up his mind to be a lawyer. Even though there was one other law faculty beside McGill's, that of the Collège Sainte-Marie with thirty-one students, he never had any doubt where he would go after L'Assomption. It would be McGill.

During the summer of 1861 he journeyed to Montréal to register, find a legal firm in which to article, and secure lodgings. His father made the thirty-mile journey with him. Montréal was by then a city of some 90,000 souls — just under half of them French-speaking — who occupied more and more space up the mountain and along the St. Lawrence. The city was so vast that the previous May the Montréal City Passenger Railway had been incorporated; it had become too difficult to get around on foot, and most people couldn't afford to hire a carriage. The entire rolling stock of the new public transport system consisted of four cars, each drawn by two horses. In winter the cars were replaced by sleighs. Its daily operation was from 7 a.m. to 10 p.m. and the fare was five cents. Wilfrid would use it often.

The 1860s also marked the beginning of an industrial boom for Montréal as the city continued to be the financial centre of British North America. Well served by rail, waterways, and roads, it was an undisputed metropolis.

Automated flour mills and elevators propelled by water power dotted the landscape. The wealthy and the élite built large houses on quiet streets. Some of these residences on Sherbrooke Street were single-dwelling homes, while on Sainte-Catherine and Dorchester continuous rows of houses with terraces abounded. As Wilfrid made his way to the building that housed the Law Faculty, he liked what he saw. But he never became enamoured of the city, largely because he preferred rural to urban living.

He had no difficulty being accepted at McGill. He had an impressive academic record from L'Assomption, he spoke English, and he was charming and polite. The dean and the registrar had no doubt that he would do well. No one asked about his health. He paid the yearly tuition fee of about three pounds ten shillings.

He was then directed to the offices of a lawyer by the name of Rodolphe Laflamme, whose office was at 6 Place d'Armes, to see if he could article there. In his pocket he carried a letter of introduction given him by one of his *Rouge* connections in L'Assomption. Wilfrid was well aware of Laflamme's credentials as a Liberal, a democrat, and a *Rouge.*

Toussaint-Antoine-Rodolphe Laflamme, a graduate of and professor at McGill, was thirty-four years old when he encountered Laurier at the door of his office. Admitted to the bar in 1849, he was, by the summer of 1861 one of the most prominent members of the Montréal legal fraternity, a Queen's counsel, and the *Bâtonnier,* or highest official of the bar. He was also one of the busiest lawyers in British North America. According to an eminent judge of the time, Laflamme in some years had as many as four hundred cases in the Superior Court alone. He was frequently charged with important cases before the Court of Appeal and the British Privy Council. Between 1857 and his death in 1893, a number of the most important legal cases in Canada found their way to his desk. At McGill, Laflamme taught real estate law and customary law, which included such matters as fiefs and servitudes, successions, donations and wills, contracts and marriages, community of property, and mortgages.

Laflamme, who belonged to a wealthy Montréal merchant family, was born ten years before the Rebellions of 1837 and 1838. The word "rebellions" is a misnomer. What happened in Lower and Upper Canada with Louis-Joseph Papineau and William Lyon Mackenzie were attempts — sometimes serious, often badly planned and executed, and from time to time ludicrous — to change the political process and social organizations of both societies, living as they were under a regime of patronage, perks, and the dictatorship of a monopolistic and arrogant clique of profiteers. In many ways, "revolutions" would be a better term. However, the leaders' natural tendency to conservatism and the fact that many of them ran away to the United States, leaving their supporters to be executed, deported, reviled, and abused by the British authorities and their cohorts or to fend for themselves rather diminishes the word "revolutions." During the uprisings, Laflamme was at the Petit Séminaire de Montréal studying Latin, Greek, and church doctrine. By the time he graduated in 1845, at the age of eighteen, both Union Government and Wilfrid Laurier were four years old.

Laflamme became a lawyer in 1849 at a time when the moderate Liberals Louis-Hippolyte LaFontaine and Robert Baldwin, with a good assist from Governor General James Bruce, eighth Earl of Elgin, were bringing about Responsible Government, a system that makes the executive responsible to the legislature elected by the people. This way of governance endures to this day.

To Laflamme, there were two basic impediments to the freedom and development of the *Canadiens*. First, their inability to control their institutions democratically endangered not only their liberty of action but also their survival. Second, the ecclesiastical/clerical structure was oppressive and tended to focus the energies of the people into an agenda that originated in the ancien régime before the reforms brought about in Europe by the French Revolution.

With the collapse of the Rebellions, John George Lambton, first Earl of Durham, was sent to Canada to examine the causes of dissatisfaction that had led to the insurrection in two of Great Britain's colonies in North America. He arrived in Québec at the end of May 1838 and returned to London four months later. His *Report on the Affairs of British North America* was published the following year.

Durham's *Report* had many recommendations, at the core of which were two basic principles. The first was Responsible Government, or the system whereby the crown in all internal matters takes the advice of ministers who enjoy the support of the people, regardless of the views of the governor general or the British colonial authorities. Only this system, he insisted, would establish the foundation of an efficient and popular government, ensure harmony among the various powers of the state, and bring the influence of a vigorous public opinion to bear on every detail of administration. Without this grant of power, he affirmed, Canada and the other North American colonies would be lost to Great Britain, for they would find shelter in the United States of America.

The second basic principle was that Responsible Government could be recognized only if a British majority was available. That is why he rejected a federal union in favour of a legislative one. The 400,000 English-speaking inhabitants of Upper Canada should be joined in holy matrimony with the 150,000 English inhabitants of Lower Canada to create the majority he needed. There would be 550,000 *Anglais* to 450,000 *Canadiens*.

Durham's need to entrust the functioning of Responsible Government to an English-speaking majority arose from his observations about the causes of the Rebellions in Lower Canada. He wrote: "I expected to find a contest between a government and a people: I found two nations warring in the bosom of a single state: I found a struggle, not of principles, but of races; and I perceived that it would be idle to attempt any amelioration of laws or institutions until we could first succeed in terminating the deadly animosity that now separates the inhabitants of Lower Canada into the hostile divisions of French and English." His plan, accordingly, would achieve this goal on a political level since it would simultaneously settle the question of race.

But there was more. The result of the recommendation would mean the utter and complete assimilation of the *Canadiens*. This Durham viewed as good. As a people "with no history and no literature," as persons with a "peculiar language and manners," and as a nationality "destitute of all that can invigorate and elevate" its members, the entry of the *Canadiens* into British civilization would be welcomed as the gift of a generous and compassionate conqueror.

The British authorities firmly rejected the notion of Responsible Government on the grounds that the governor general, being an employee of the Colonial Office, could not at the same time be answerable to colonial ministers whose advice might contradict his instructions. They agreed, however, to unite both Canadas, Lower and Upper, and in 1840 passed an imperial act to that effect. As for the desired English-speaking majority, they hoped to achieve it by creating a legislature of forty-two members from each of the Canadas and where the English language would dominate, especially since French was proscribed.

Both of these stipulations inflicted a grave injustice on the peoples of Lower Canada. It meant that Representation by Population, a fundamental tenet of British parliamentary democracy, was denied them, and it burdened them with a share of Upper Canada's debt, which was much greater than that of Lower Canada. It also condemned the *Canadiens* to the status of a perpetual minority, without even the recognition of their language. This Union came into effect nine months before Wilfrid was born.

While Laflamme was in his teens and Laurier in his infancy, the *Canadiens* united in one common purpose — to defeat Union at best, or, if that was not possible, to minimize its impact as far as their survival was concerned. They were successful with the latter. With LaFontaine as their leader, they allied themselves with the moderate Reformers of Canada West under the leadership of Baldwin. LaFontaine gave his maiden speech in French in the legislature in 1842. Two years later a unanimous resolution made French an official language, to which the British Parliament assented in 1848. And Responsible Government fell into place in 1849. The *Canadiens* had defeated Durham. They were now full-fledged members of the administration, without having had to assume an English character. They had also weakened considerably the reality of legislative union. Union Government was more or less dead. All that remained was to bury it.

In the meantime, though, Papineau had returned from exile in 1845 and, after the victory of 1849, the political unity of the *Canadiens* began to disintegrate over two questions of some importance. The first was what to do about the Union. LaFontaine was of the opinion that with the developments of 1844 and 1849, the break-up of the Union was not so important. The *Canadiens* had demonstrated that they could accommodate themselves very well within it. Consequently, Union no longer needed to be repealed. Many accepted his position, but a few did not. Among this minority were the Laflammes and, eventually in the 1860s, the Lauriers. In these circumstances, two political formations emerged: the Liberal-Conservative one or the *Bleus*, and the Liberal one or the *Rouges*. After Confederation, the former would break up into the *Ultramontains-Castors* and the school of George-Étienne Cartier; and the latter, which had already split in two factions during the Union, would eventually find its unity within the Liberal Party. Both were dedicated to the promotion of the best possible means to assure the survival of *la nation canadienne*.

The second matter of importance had to do with the principles that should inspire the *Canadiens* in their political life. LaFontaine and his group, once the dispute over the French language and Responsible Government had been decided positively, became more inclined to the maintenance of the status quo and, therefore, more conservative. The *Rouges*, on the other hand, grew more radical. Since progress was inevitable, they argued, "he who keeps the middle path is shattered; he who does not go forward is crushed." Papineau became their mentor. He brought them liberal ideas; he infused in them notions of republicanism; but, unlike his pupils, he was utterly opposed to the separation of church and state and maintained, as the seigneur of Montebello, his devotion to feudal tenure. Inspired by him, they preached the gospel of republicanism and democratic liberties. In their political creed or program, published in January 1850, they listed their objectives: widespread education, free trade, decentralization of the judiciary, codification of laws and the liberty for every man to defend his own cause, free circulation of newspapers, decentralization of power through the establishment of municipal organization, elective institutions in all areas, representation in the legislature based on population, universal suffrage, parliamentary sessions fixed by law, abolition of seigniorial tenure and the tithing system, equal rights and justice for all citizens, repeal of the Union, the independence of Canada, and annexation to the United States. On their own, they challenged the nascent Ultramontanism or clerical domination of politics, joined in freethinking organizations, read books forbidden by Rome, and fought the priests and bishops and any other form of tyranny.

∿

When Wilfrid arrived at Laflamme's study in the fall of 1861, he had some knowledge of the struggle that had been waged and he associated his political ideals with those of the *Rouges*. He was ready to do his part.

Wilfrid found in Laflamme a kindred spirit and a kind and generous friend. Laflamme was a tallish man, aristocratic-looking, and not bound by any vows of marriage or allegiance. He was his own person, proud, disdainful, and a little of a misanthrope. A *grand seigneur* with expensive tastes, he lived in a succession of large houses either with his brother or alone and with a menagerie of horses and dogs. He was often seen parading them in the streets of Montréal. He belonged to the best of clubs — all English — and he was a high liver. However, he remained constant in his Catholic faith despite his opposition to the clerical pretensions of his bishop. In court, he was generally boring and he hardly opened his mouth to present his arguments. He came alive only when his adversaries interrupted him or argued with him. Then he was a sight to behold, full of verve, eloquence, and precision, and most articulate. He would always have the better of them. What surprised Wilfrid was that Laflamme spoke French with a slight English accent. The young man soon picked that up for himself.

As they sat and talked about Wilfrid's life, Laflamme realized that his pupil-to-be had potential. He decided to facilitate it. He offered Wilfrid a job along with a small stipend, roughly equivalent to the yearly fee Wilfrid paid the university in his overall tuition for Laflamme's courses, as was the custom. When the interview was over, both had decided that they would make *bon ménage* together: Laflamme would provide the opportunities, and Wilfrid would do the work with all his energy and enthusiasm.

In early September 1861 the term began. McGill's Law Faculty was also a child of the Union period. Established when Wilfrid was barely three years old, it was still in its growing phase when he entered its portals. It had no permanent staff, hardly any books in its library, and it expected its students to obtain for themselves the practical knowledge they needed from the law offices in which they were articling. However, the professors were all reputed lawyers, the standards high, and the curriculum was broad, with an emphasis on the fundamentals.

Wilfrid arrived at the Gauthiers' the day before courses were to begin, settled into his small room, read as was his custom, and went to sleep early. The next morning he was out of the house with the rising sun and walked to Laflamme's office. A more advanced student who was also articling there introduced him to the routine of the office and took him around the neighbourhood, showing him the good places to eat and drink and how to get to the two important places he needed to be: the Law Courts and Burnside Hall on Dorchester Street where he was to attend classes. Both were close to Laflamme's offices. After lunch, he received his first assignment — putting legal documents in chronological order. At 3:45, Laflamme rushed out of his office. It was time to go to class.

On the third floor of Burnside Hall, Laflamme introduced him to the dean, John Joseph Caldwell Abbott, later to be prime minister of Canada, who was responsible for Commercial Law. There were three other professors there as well: Frederick Torrance, who taught Civil and Roman Law and who spoke Latin with a British accent Wilfrid could hardly understand; Professor Lafrenaye, whose specialty was the French Civil Code and the history of the laws of France, Great Britain, and Lower Canada; and a lawyer by the name of Carter, who brought the complexities of Criminal Law to the classroom.

He was at his lectures from four to six, as he would be five days a week for the rest of his life at McGill. There were eleven students in the first year, five of whom were *Canadiens*. The courses were given in either French or English, depending on the professor's preference. If he studied regularly, completed all the courses, passed the examinations, wrote a good thesis, and was recommended to the university by the dean and the faculty, he would graduate in three years with a Bachelor of Civil Law degree upon paying a fee of one pound five shillings.

In his first year, it was all introductory, with the general principles of law and contracts and with the origin and history of law. In the second, studies became more focused and he was introduced to criminal law and the whole expanse of commercial contracts. He also continued with varied aspects of legal history. The third year covered the same courses but in greater depth, except for the introduction of international law.

At L'Assomption, he had accumulated an impressive record. At McGill, it was more moderate. There was more to do. In his first year, in 1861–62, he was second in his class. The following year his ill health seriously interfered with his studies, and his marks were the worse for it. However, in his final year, he did extremely well and graduated second in his class of eleven. It was his thesis, though, that marked him. It was a prerequisite for all graduating students and he ranked first.

His days at McGill were full and he didn't have much time for leisure. He was up at dawn and he worked at Laflamme's office from 8:00 in the morning until 3:30 in the afternoon preparing documents, attending at Court, interviewing clients, and carrying out whatever tasks were given him. After that came two hours of lectures. Often in the evenings he would return to the office to finish what needed to be done and to study because it was too noisy at the

Gauthiers' to permit much concentration. Walking was his only form of exercise. He had few social contacts with the other students in the faculty, nor did he have anything to do with university life outside his lectures.

He often forced himself to think in English and to write it, experimenting with the various styles of famous writers, particularly that of that great constitutional lawyer Goldwin Smith. In his relentless pursuit to master the English language, he translated from French to English and vice versa; he read the English poets, particularly Milton, Burns, Tennyson, Shakespeare, and the essayists; and he studied parliamentary rhetoric and oratory, conquering John Bright and crying over Lincoln's Gettysburg address. No one could move him more than Abraham Lincoln, both in his heart and in his imagination.

That quest of English remained with him all his life, and he added more and more authors as he went along, particularly the splendid Thomas Babington Macaulay. Later in his life many *nationalistes* would reproach him for his love of English, which they thought detrimental to his *devoir* — his duty to French language and literature. They accused him of contributing to the death of French in North America, to which he replied in 1886: "So long as there are French mothers, the language will not die." The nationalists also decried his slight English accent when he spoke French. He had one, no doubt about that. He had developed it not at the Murrays' or the Kirkes' of New Glasgow, but by reading out loud the speeches and the poetry of the English authors and poets he revered and by associating with Laflamme. He also had a little French accent speaking in English.

His political and constitutional ideas were forged and given focus through his reading. He discovered the horror of slavery through *Uncle Tom's Cabin*. After devouring it in one night, he was a determined abolitionist. Free trade entered into the realm of possibilities; individual freedom was more anchored into his psyche; constitutional liberty developed into a beacon of light that could never be extinguished; and the conviction that the people had the power to search and find and choose that which was best for them was affirmed, reaffirmed, and confirmed.

His life was also taken up by other activities, largely engineered and encouraged by Laflamme. Laflamme's office was often the centre where the best of *Rougeisme* gathered. There he met Antoine-Aimé Dorion, who taught Wilfrid the difference between being a Whig in the British tradition and a Radical in the French; his brother Eric Dorion, the enfant terrible of them all; the Doutre brothers — Gonzalve, whose religious persecution was a high drama in his time, and Joseph, who fought a duel with George-Étienne Cartier; Louis-Labrèche Viger, in turn a seminarian, a journalist, a lawyer, a merchant, a politician, a scientist, and a company promoter; and Louis-Antoine Dessaulles, the editor of *Le Pays*, another *Rouge* newspaper but less controversial than *L'Avenir*; and many others. Through Laflamme, he had his entrées into the world of ideas, opinions, and sentiments.

Others, more conservative than he was, also found their way into the enclave, men such as Laurent-Olivier David, Hector Fabre, Joseph-Adolphe Chapleau, and Louis-Amable Jetté, all of whom were to occupy a large place in his life. Friends from L'Assomption like Oscar Archambault and confrères from McGill such as Henri-Lesieur Desaulniers and Arthur Taschereau also came on occasion. The *Rouge* group was not of uniform opinion. In that cauldron of ideas, much was fermented, and the debates and the discussions went on and on. It was an intense intellectual life.

At the beginning of October 1862 Laflamme had Wilfrid admitted to the Institut canadien. Perhaps it was Laflamme's birthday gift to him, for a month later, on 20 November 1862, Laurier was twenty-one, the age signifying independence, adulthood, and manhood. Carolus and Maman Adeline sent wishes and cakes and money for a new suit; the Gauthiers had a party; Zoë played the piano more divinely than ever before; his friends took him for a drink; and Laflamme smiled.

The Institut canadien had been founded in Montréal to meet the needs of educated *Canadiens* who had no way to pursue their intellectual endeavours effectively. It was to be a rallying point, a centre to improve the mind through free inquiry, an institution inspired with pure patriotism. It had a library and a reading room, and it organized debates and lectures on subjects such as the role of the clergy in civil affairs that were important to the elites of the city.

The members of the Institut of Laflamme's generation were quite knowledgeable about the opinions of American thinkers. In fact, American views on democracy, on a secular society with many religions living in social harmony, and on state rights and non-denominational schools, not to mention the great economic success of the Americans, greatly influenced the young men who belonged.

It was no wonder that they preached the virtues of the annexation of Lower Canada or Canada East or Québec and of Upper Canada or Canada West or Ontario to the American Manifest Destiny. Laflamme defended the notion in the main newspaper of his group, the left-wing *L'Avenir*, which he helped to found in 1847. In these articles and in his speeches, he didn't hesitate to claim that the annexation of Canada to the United States was the only avenue to prosperity, secular progress, and educational reform. So enthusiastic was he that a month after he had been called to the bar he became a member of the board of the Montréal Annexation Association. He was barely nineteen years old.

In those early years, the members of the Institut didn't attach much importance to the political and secular thought of Great Britain in so far as freedom, liberty, and liberalism were concerned. That attitude was not without reason. The Laflammes of the middle 1840s and 1850s didn't see much liberal thought in the application of a political constitution that was more or less an instrument to destroy their people as a distinct society in North America. The "Britishization" of Québec's liberalism was to be Laurier's essential contribution to the political thought of Québec. That contribution would not come, though, until 1877.

The Institut thrived — it had seven hundred members in 1857 — until the bishop of Montréal, Monseigneur Bourget, condemned it in 1858. Bourget, who had become the second bishop of Montréal in 1840, was an advocate of the submission of the lay order to the episcopal and clerical one, or the supremacy of the church over the state. For the entire second half of the nineteenth century, the political battles in Québec centred on this question. Bourget became the arch enemy of the Institut. He condemned its eight-thousand-volume library and ordered all good Catholics to comply.

No sooner had Wilfrid become a member of the Institut than he immersed himself in its library, consuming what had been forbidden or not available at L'Assomption. During his five-year stay in Montréal, he was deeply involved in the activities and the administration of the organization. Twice he served as vice-president, and in the fall of 1863 he was named to a committee to meet with the bishop of Montréal to try to effect a reconciliation. The bishop received the members, but no accommodation could be reached. The Institut, its library, and its membership remained condemned.

Even though the principle of free inquiry was strongly implanted in him, Wilfrid's interest in the Institut was in its library and its discussions. This craving for books and intellectual discourse brought him to another group of young *Canadiens* in the spring of 1862. When Bourget put the Institut canadien under interdict, many of its members left to establish the clerically inspired Institut canadien-français. The library there was meagre, freedom of inquiry did not exist, and debates and discussions tended to be dull. He stayed only a few months.

However, there was an association of law students in which he participated. The Institut des lois had no connection to McGill, but its membership was made up of those who were preparing themselves for the bar. Some of them did not frequent any university, preferring to learn all they needed to know through apprenticeship. Meeting on the last Friday of each month, the members discussed whatever they felt to be of importance: the relationship of religious practice to civic life, the inequality of the tithe, the impact of denominational education, and much more. In their view, the participants tended to be more liberal than conservative. Wilfrid became a member almost as soon as he arrived at McGill. He participated in most of its activities and was president in his final year.

In both of the organizations he favoured, the Institut des lois and the Institut canadien, he came into his own and honed his skills as a debater. Early on, he was considered a star. His arguments were well presented; his delivery was clear and capable of being heard in a large hall; and he continued, as he had done at L'Assomption, to toy with both sides of a question. Yet he perceived a change in his intellectual approach and attitude. It was not the first time that conflicts arose about his thoughts, opinions, and values. He had gone through all that at the college. There the demarcation had been very clear: it was either the right way, which was the church's; or the wrong way, which was his nascent *Rougeisme*. He had chosen the latter and had stuck to it. At McGill between 1861 and 1864, however, and during his subsequent stay in Montréal until late 1866, the contest between sets of ideas was not so easily resolved. The free-for-all discussions he engaged in and the greater variety in his reading acquainted him with a wealth of opinions and values that were presented in a non-authoritarian environment. Furthermore, McGill introduced him to British thinkers who provided him with an alternative intellectual and political dimension. Before McGill, he doubted if the liberal tenets he held could be realized outside radicalism. Now, he was presented with a possibility that suited his natural tendency to seek harmony through reconciliation or compromise.

~

The afternoon of 4 May 1864 was beautiful. It was Convocation Day at McGill. Molson Hall, above Sherbrooke Street and at the end of the long driveway bordered by trees, was filled to capacity with the parents, relatives, and friends of the students who were about to graduate. Carolus was there, as were Séraphin, Phoebé, and Zoë. Maman Adeline had stayed with the children at Saint-Lin. The professors in the Faculty of Law walked in solemn procession with their colleagues from other faculties behind the members of the Convocation: governors, the principal, the vice-principal, the deans. Eventually, the students walked in. There were 177 medical students, 11 in law, and 1 in civil engineering.

After the usual prayer and speeches of welcome, graduates from the Faculty of Medicine were honoured. Rodolphe Laflamme then read the standings and awarded the prizes to the students of the Faculty of Law. Wilfrid received first prize in customary law and the law of real estate and second prize in both criminal and constitutional law. Then he knelt in front of the acting chancellor of the university and received his Bachelor of Civil Law.

When his classmates had all collected their degrees, Wilfrid walked to the podium to give the valedictory address — in French. He stood for a moment and looked over the assembled crowd. He found Carolus and Zoë. A small smile appeared on his lips. He coughed a couple of times, but when he began to speak in his clear and well-modulated voice, his tall, thin, melancholic figure dominated the hall. Members of the audience advanced to the edges of their seats; Carolus sat up proudly; Zoë, nervous, sank back at the first cough.

Wilfrid spoke of the lawyer's sense of justice, of his mission to render to each according to his due, of his willingness to embrace liberty as the basic condition of all, and of his responsibility to participate in the affairs of society. "Nothing on earth is more precious than justice," he proclaimed, "yet nothing is more difficult to obtain." He ended with a plea for unity between the two language groups of the country, for reconciliation and harmony among them.

It is to our glory that race hatreds have ended on Canadian soil. There is no longer any family here but the human family. It matters not what language the people speak, or at which altars they kneel. . . .

You have heard French and English names here, graven on the tables of honour. You have heard some address you in English, and I . . . am speaking to you in my mother tongue; I am speaking to you in French.

There is glory in this fraternity of which Canada can never be proud enough. Mighty nations, indeed, may well come to us to seek a lesson in justice and humanity.

At that early moment in his life, Wilfrid Laurier grasped that "the unity between the people" was "the secret of the future."

Many in the audience didn't understand a word he said, but few were left indifferent. There was a nobility in his movements and in the cadence of his words that appealed to them. Many of the phrases and the sentiments were predictable and served the occasion well, but there was something else: an intellect about to be reckoned with; a personality that would emerge in time; an emotion being untethered; and a journey beginning. They applauded politely, heard more speeches, thanked God, and went home. The next morning, the reporter in the *Gazette* related that a "valedictory address had been read in French by one of the members of the graduating class." He didn't mention a single word Wilfrid had uttered. And the graduates forgot to sign the Register of Convocation.

Thus ended Wilfrid Laurier's passage through McGill University. He left without any sorrow and never returned, not even to receive the honorary degree of Doctor of Laws that the Senate of the university conferred upon him in 1898. On the other hand, he visited the Collège de L'Assomption five times — in 1873, 1883, 1893, 1901, and 1918.

A new life was about to begin.

~

By the end of October 1864, Laurier and his friend from college days, Oscar Archambault, were in partnership together. They opened an office on Sainte-

Thérèse Street, kitty-corner to Saint-Vincent Street. There they hoped to make their fortune, at a time when all thinking people were awash in the collapse of the Union and the possible creation of the Confederation of the colonies of British North America.

Confederation had become a necessity because British North America was on the verge of disintegration. In United Canada, no government could be maintained for any length of time and no attempt to deal with this failure proved successful; in the colonies by the Atlantic, none could afford the vast costs of the transportation system that needed to be built if they were to prosper at all; in Great Britain, the government had lost interest in its North American territory; and in the United States, the Northern armies, victorious against the South in the Civil War of 1860–65, wanted to invade Canada and the other colonies in retaliation for the support Great Britain had foolishly accorded to the rebels. For good measure, the Americans also abrogated the Reciprocity Treaty that had made all of British North America somewhat prosperous during the preceding decade. Obviously, a new constitutional arrangement was necessary. Otherwise, British North America would cease to be.

The formula proposed to save it all was the federation of the provinces: Newfoundland, Prince Edward Island, Nova Scotia, New Brunswick, Canada East (Québec), and Canada West (Ontario). The principle was accepted at the Charlottetown Conference in September 1864 and, a month later, delegates to the Québec Conference adopted seventy-two resolutions on which to base a new country.

That new country, to be called the Dominion of Canada, was to consist of as many British colonies in North America as could be welcomed or cajoled into it. They would be united together in a federal union in which the national interests would be the responsibility of the central government sitting in Ottawa, and the purely local matters would be left in the hands of the provinces. However, the decisions of the provincial legislatures could be reserved for the scrutiny of the federal government, and could also be vetoed if the Government of Canada considered them inimical to the overall interests of the country. English and French were to become official languages to be used at the federal level and in the legislature and courts of Québec. The Dominion of Canada would be governed by an executive branch composed of a governor general representing the sovereign and appointed by the imperial authorities without the necessary consent of the people or their representatives, and a council chosen by the governor in accordance with the principles of Responsible Government; a Parliament, or legislative branch, composed of a Senate appointed by the executive to represent the regions and a House of Commons elected through universal manhood suffrage and in accordance with the gospel of Representation by Population; and a judiciary named again by the federal executive. In the seventy-two resolutions, no definite provision was made for the creation of a Canadian Supreme Court as the court of last resort, nor of an amending formula.

It was this constitutional arrangement that Laurier's friends and associates were to battle for almost three years — with him contributing his piece from time to time.

Meanwhile, the legal partnership Laurier had formed with Archambault could not be made profitable even after the brilliant Henri-Lesieur Desaulniers, a classmate at McGill, had joined the firm in December 1864. By March 1865 it was obvious that clients were staying away in droves, and Laurier bowed out, having received an offer from the mercurial Médéric Lanctôt. His friendship with both Archambault and Desaulniers was not impaired by this possibly cavalier decision.

Laurier's health had been deteriorating dramatically since his graduation. While studying law, he had often been severely ill, especially in his second year. He had always rallied, but these grave bouts of illness drained him of energy and left him pale and lethargic, depressed and frightened. It took him longer and longer to recover, and any extra exertion or anxiety could trigger other attacks. With his admission to the bar, he had to earn his own living. Carolus's financial assistance ended with his graduation. He chose to practise in Montréal, not because he liked the city, not because of Zoë, but because the large city offered more opportunity, was close to his family, and his friends and contacts lived there. Totally on his own, he tried to make ends meet. However, his legal business was unprofitable and his debts mounted. His financial problems activated his sense of desperation, precipitating fits of coughing, difficulties in breathing, and some loss of blood. Unable to rest for long periods, to the chagrin and worry of Maman Adeline, he became weaker and weaker and, thus, less resistant to his demon. Going into partnership with Lanctôt could assure him a steady income as Lanctôt was popular and drew clients.

Laurier had met Lanctôt shortly after his arrival in Montréal. He liked him immediately. He appreciated Lanctôt's passion, his brilliance, his fiery nature, his energy, and his great gift of oratory. On the other hand, Lanctôt often frightened Laurier. The man was so erratic, extreme in his opinions, often consumed by rage, and obsessed with vengeance. They met often in Laflamme's offices, or at court, where they tried to resolve all the ills of mankind and, particularly, those of their country. They both described themselves as patriots and as liberals in philosophy, and they asserted that they would devote their lives and careers to the betterment of their people. Like Laurier, Lanctôt endured poor health — and he drank too much. For his part, Lanctôt saw in Wilfrid "un homme de l'avenir," a man of the future. In his partner, Lanctôt felt the poet, perceived the lawmaker, experienced the orator, contacted the thinker, and was moved by the inner torment he beheld. "Il fera son chemin!" Laurier would make it, Lanctôt was certain.

Lanctôt was short, blond with a high forehead and a long beard. He was about three years older than Laurier. His father had participated in the Rebellions, for which he was arrested and exiled. That event marked Lanctôt's life. After becoming a lawyer, he began to publish *La Presse* and to oppose the Confederation scheme. He was the soul of the opposition to it, spending his time not only writing articles and making speeches, but also rallying to his cause all the young people he could find. He had no doubt that Confederation had been proposed solely to anglicize the *Canadiens*. Should the scheme go through, he thundered, a majority hostile to the interests of his people would be created to destroy them. He would have none of it.

Publishing *La Presse* and making speeches against Confederation, however, meant that he could not devote much time to his law practice. This is where Wilfrid came in. From March 1865 until November 1866 he ran the firm as a junior associate. The offices were at 24 Saint-Gabriel in the legal district. The work was plentiful, the interruptions unending. He worked from dawn to dusk. He had little time to participate in the debates about Confederation swirling around him.

Still, he did find some time to become involved in the discussion. He could hardly avoid it. Lanctôt, consumed by his rage at the Anglais, the curés, and

George-Étienne Cartier, who led public opinion in favour of Confederation, made his office the rallying point of the campaign against it. Laurier attended a few planning sessions, spoke at a couple of meetings in 1865 and 1866, and wrote some articles in the anti-Confederation newspaper *L'Union Nationale*. He even joined a secret society Lanctôt founded, Le Club Saint-Jean-Baptiste, which met on the street of the same name right across from a convent of teaching nuns. There were oaths to take with a dagger pointed to the heart, secret passwords to observe, and other fancy footwork. Many anti-Confederates belonged to it; but it didn't last long.

Laurier had no difficulty accepting that Union Government was dead and that, in spite of achievements such as the use of the French language and Responsible Government, it had been a failure. What then could replace it? He was not an *indépendentiste* and he had only toyed with annexation. The real solution belonged to the *Rouges*: a federation of Canada East and Canada West that could lead in time to the larger union of all the British North American colonies. This solution would allow for growth and adjustments, and would leave the *Canadiens*, practically all of whom lived in Canada East, in full command of their development. What was being proposed in 1864–65 was a larger union which, in his view, would result in the *Canadiens* being vastly outnumbered and made vulnerable to the sizeable majority that could be arrayed against them. In other words, it was another way of achieving what Durham and the Union had been unable to do. Confederation had to be opposed.

Yet Laurier's heart didn't seem to be in it. His main obligation, he felt, was to make a success of his law practice. Only that would establish his reputation, pay the bills, and ensure his future. Moreover, Lanctôt was drinking more and more, and so busy was he with the Confederation proposals that he did hardly any work in the office at all. In the circumstances, Laurier worked relentlessly.

He found a place, a little above Dorchester Street and about twelve blocks east of the Gauthiers, at 23 Saint-André. To go to his office, he walked along Dorchester Street to Saint-Denis, where he boarded a horse-drawn tramway. After a short journey, he got off at Gosford Street and proceeded on foot to his office on Saint-Gabriel, passing the Champ de Mars, the Court-House, and Notre Dame Church. He would return the same way at night, but often after 10 p.m., when there was no public transport, he walked all the way home. He generally arrived there exhausted and soaked to the bone.

To set up house takes money; Laurier had none. Carolus came to the rescue, driven by Maman Adeline, who had become almost frantic about his deteriorating health. Hemorrhages came and went with greater regularity and his exhaustion was more extreme. He ate less and became thinner. He had no money for drugs and medication. In view of his son's poor pecuniary condition and worsening health, Carolus rented the house in Saint-Lin and came to live with his family and furniture at the Saint-André address at the end of May 1865. Immediately, Laurier improved and saw his future more brightly. He continued to work endless hours, but he found time to help the anti-Confederation cause. He also found greater enjoyment in his work at the Institut and immersed himself in its activities and library. Life took on a new meaning.

But not for long. By the fall of 1866 his family had returned to live in the country, his relationship with Zoë was strained, and once again he was over-worked, anxious, and depressed. One day, in October, he collapsed, with blood leaking out of his mouth and spattering the papers on his desk. A doctor was summoned, who repaired some of the damage, handed out some drugs, prescribed rest and good air, and admonished his friends to see that he took good care of himself; otherwise, he wouldn't live ten years, if indeed he could recover from that particular bout. A message was sent to the Lauriers in Saint-Lin and, within days, Maman Adeline arrived with Carolus, who had to return to Saint-Lin to look after the children. He spent a month convalescing with her on Saint-André.

At this low point in Laurier's life, Antoine-Aimé Dorion, the leader of the *Rouge* — or of the Liberal Party of Canada East as he preferred to call his polit-ical group — suggested a solution to ease Laurier's predicament. At the begin-ning of November 1866 Dorion's brother Jean-Baptiste-Eric died. He had been an ardent *Rouge* and had founded a newspaper called *Le Défricheur* in the little town of L'Avenir. Dorion proposed that Laurier should take Eric's place, publish and edit the newspaper, and practise law. "We need to continue Eric's work in the Townships," Dorion said, "and the air of the country will be more suited to Wilfrid's condition than that of the city." He arranged for a *Rouge* fundraiser, Louis-Adélard Sénécal, to assist financially, and he found a willing partner who would also print *Le Défricheur*.

The little village of L'Avenir, which had first been called Durham, had been the home of Eric Dorion since the 1850s. It was roughly half French- and half English-speaking, half Protestant and half Catholic. Through *Le Défricheur*, which he founded while Laurier was in his second year at McGill, Dorion had filled the minds of his readers with the best that *Rougeisme* had to offer during the last four years of his life. In the process, he often encountered the wrath of the clerical authorities. The paper was only moderately successful and *Rouge* ideology was hardly making headway. Dorion himself, though, was quite popular. There were possibilities. But Laurier hesitated. His departure meant leaving Lanctôt in the lurch. Even though the thought of losing his partner depressed him, Lanctôt was insistent: *la campagne!* So were Laurier's parents, though they hardly knew where L'Avenir was. Laurier and Zoë had no arguments about his leaving. It was the best solution there as well.

By 17 November, three days before Laurier's twenty-fifth birthday, it was all arranged. Dorion's friends had found him lodgings, and the offices of *Le Défricheur* were to be used both to publish the paper and as a law office for Laurier. He said good-bye to Zoë, and that evening his friends gathered to honour him at the Hôtel Saint-Louis. They were all there to drink his health and toast their friendship. Most of the participants were *Rouge*, but many were not. Oscar Archambault remembered L'Assomption; Laurent-Olivier David and Joseph-Adolphe Chapleau teased the radical in Wilfrid; Louis-Amable Jetté, whom he had known at L'Assomption and who was a moderate *Rouge*, preached moderation; and Laflamme spoke eloquently about his former pupil. It was left to Médéric Lanctôt to sum it up: Wilfrid was worthy to continue the *oeuvre national* that Eric Dorion had inaugurated in that part of the world. The next day, after many admonitions from Maman Adeline, who had filled his luggage with food she had been cooking for a week, Wilfrid, all bundled up, left by horse-drawn carriage for L'Avenir. Ten days later his first edition of *Le Défricheur* appeared.

In it he swore allegiance to the principles and programs of the *Rouges*, of Papineau, and of Dorion. He opposed, he wrote, all those tendencies that were inimical to the well-being of society and that were antireligious. Regarding Confederation, he wanted his readers to know that he opposed it, because the project was false in its conception, iniquitous, immoral, and "cruel dans ses détails."

L'Avenir, however, was not for him. Well-intentioned as he was, he was still not Eric Dorion. His readers sensed that, as did everyone else. He lost subscribers and few, if any, sought his legal talents. He wasn't recovering as fast as he had hoped; in fact, his health was actually deteriorating, aggravated as it was by the mountain of bills he was accumulating. He had no choice — he had to find another venue. About one month after arriving in L'Avenir he announced that as of 1 January 1867, *Le Défricheur* would move from L'Avenir to the village of Victoriaville, some thirty miles farther north. Before he left for his new destination, he wrote a scathing article against Confederation in which he repeated all the arguments that Lanctôt and the others had used around Montréal.

Victoriaville was more appealing because it offered more opportunities. The population was mostly French speaking; the Grand Trunk Railway serviced the town; the principal court of the district was close by; and, to Laurier's thinking, Victoriaville could, in time, develop into an important commercial centre. Both his newspaper and his law practice could flourish better there. He spent the Christmas season installing himself, found a building in which to house his paper and his legal practice, and, by the first of the New Year, he was ready. But he was not welcome.

Wilfrid was a *Rouge*. He was the editor and, apparently, the sole writer of a newspaper founded by another *Rouge*. As such, he was an enemy of the church. He had to be stopped before his nefarious ideology took hold in the Bois-Francs, a region in the diocese of Trois-Rivières. Over the spiritual welfare of the people and the powers and prerogatives of the church reigned the co-adjutor, Monseigneur Louis-François-Richer Laflèche. Laflèche, who would appear frequently in Laurier's life to do him wrong, was a petty tyrant who was ordained a priest three years after Wilfrid's birth. He served as a missionary in the North-West, and returned to Québec in 1856 to be a professor at the Collège de Nicolet, vicar general of the diocese, and then co-adjutor, or associate bishop, of Trois-Rivières, with the right to succeed the bishop already installed. He was an impossible man, critical to a fault, severe, and a megalomaniac, though these characteristics were camouflaged under his apparent devotion to the church and its mission. Laflèche declared war on Laurier as soon he arrived in Victoriaville, a war that was to last until the bishop's death in 1898. In this conflict, the curé of Arthabaska, Philippe-Hippolyte Suzor, who was also the most powerful clerical figure in the region of Drummond-Arthabaska, served as Laflèche's commander in the field.

It was a violent war. Laurier could never fathom the virulence of it. From the pulpits of churches, priests denounced him and his views. They called him every name under the sun. One day he was a *révolutionnaire* and a monster; the next, a blasphemer and a hypocrite. They more or less invited the people to arm themselves to defend their religion and their rights. They forbade their parishioners to buy *Le Défricheur* under pain of mortal sin, a condition that would damn their souls to the flames of hell. To stop Laurier, they founded a newspaper of their own, *L'Union des Cantons de l'Est*, in which they attacked him mercilessly — and wounded him in the very depths of his being.

But Laurier learned to give as much as he got. "Any authority that is arbitrary, unjust or iniquitous, tyrannical," he screamed in *Le Défricheur*, "need not be obeyed. You want war; you shall have it!" He had a pen and a paper, and he knew how to use both. "Rira bien, qui rira le dernier."

Unfortunately for him, the clerics won. Under interdict, few people bought his newspaper, driving him into bankruptcy. Sénécal and the publisher and printer accepted the inevitable, and funds were no longer made available. His law practice suffered and more debts piled up. He became discouraged and fell ill. Three months after he had relaunched *Le Défricheur* in Victoriaville, he had to close it and cease publication. He gave his *maladie*, which was taking alarming proportions, as an excuse. He remained, though, in Victoriaville.

He never forgot what the priests had done to him in the name of God. At the mention of Bourget or Laflèche, anger would mount in him; his upper lip would crease in a tight line, and his eyes, generally soft, would light up with outrage. When, a few years later, he became somewhat friendly with his parish priest, Suzor, he asked him why they had been so bent on destroying him. "Oh, we felt you were growing too powerful," the priest answered. To which Wilfrid replied: "Did you not consider that you were depriving an honest man of his livelihood, destroying the investment in which I had put everything I could find or borrow?" For an answer, all he got from the reverend man was a shrug.

With the arrival of Confederation, elections to the first Parliament of Canada and the first legislature of the newly formed Province of Québec were to be held at the beginning of September. He plunged into the fray with all his enthusiasm. On 1 August 1867 there was a meeting of the Liberals of the constituency at the Hôtel Boisclair. According to a newspaper of the time, the purpose of the meeting was to force a well-known Liberal of the region to abandon his candidacy for the provincial legislature in favour of Laurier. Everybody except Laurier, who didn't drink, was drunk; the meeting was turbulent and the matter was dropped. In one of his letters to Zoë, he mentioned how pleased he was to be considered. He attended more sober meetings to discuss it further, but it came to naught. This didn't prevent him, however, from travelling extensively in his part of the province to attend rallies and to speak at them. He described these activities as "mon amusement à moi." By the end of August he was exhausted. Nevertheless, he was at it again four days before the elections. He even neglected his practice to be part of it all. And he moved.

Earlier that year, in February, while he was on an errand, the *côcher* driving the horse-drawn sleigh took him beyond the railway station and headed off on Saint-Christophe road. They travelled some five miles through a dismal plain covered with snow and came to a river. They crossed a rickety wooden bridge and arrived in Arthabaska, also known as Saint-Christophe or Arthabaskaville. This easy little town of about two thousand souls was nestled in a valley bordered by the Alleghenies, dominated by Mont Saint-Christophe and Mont Saint-Michel and bathed by two rivers: La Rivière Nicolet and La Gosselin. Laurier liked it. He returned in the spring and in the summer. By then the maples and the poplars were full of life, the roads were covered in mud, and carts had to make two trips up the steep hill with their cargoes. The people he talked to were friendly, and he decided to look for a place to stay. In September he moved into the rambling red-brick house of Docteur et Madame Médéric Poisson, where he rented a sitting room, which also served him as a library, and a bedroom. His *pension* and lodgings were expensive for the country, but it was the best he could do.

He liked the Poissons. The doctor was the coroner for the district and Madame Poisson was as devout as Zoë. She went to church every morning. At first, she didn't want him in her house. The parish priest had often told his flock that Laurier was a monster and she feared losing her soul. He set out to prove to her that the *Rouges* were "des êtres avec qui on peut vivre sans danger." He convinced her that she was safe. She found him charming and polite, and not dangerous at all. The house was clean and he shared it not only with the Poissons but with forty birds living in a tall and beautiful aviary. He found it pleasant to wake up every morning to their joyous music, and it generally put him in a good humour for the rest of the day. From time to time, he wished Zoë was with him. But she wasn't — yet.

4

POLITICS: THE BEGINNING
1871–1877

After the High Mass on Sunday, 28 May 1871, Laurier came forward on the steps of the church and agreed to be the Liberal candidate for the county of Drummond-Arthabaska in the provincial election that was to be held in July. The previous summer, the Liberal organizers had approached him, but he had been reluctant to accept until he had evaluated the support he could count on. His political friends in Arthabaska and elsewhere in the county were most supportive. But again he had delayed the decision. He was ill most of the fall and winter of 1870–71, and even the new spring didn't help his health much. He was depressed, he was coughing and bleeding, and he acted in a most indecisive and dissatisfied way. He neglected Zoë, who had by then settled quite nicely at the Poissons', and made her generally miserable.

She was opposed to his being a candidate. They were happy in Arthabaska together, she reminded him constantly. All that peace and quiet would end when he entered politics. Every time they discussed his possible candidacy, she told him frankly that the role of wife of an active politician was difficult for her to accept. Every time the priests or some editor attacked him, it hurt her. "Tu vas en mourir, tu sais." He would die of it, she feared.

He delayed his decision until he received a letter from Dorion in the middle of the month of May. The party counted on him, Dorion wrote, to bring this electoral district into the ranks of the Liberal Party. He was told that he was the only one able to do it. "J'espère que vous ne nous ferez pas défaut," Dorion mentioned casually. To Laurier, it was an order. He couldn't fail the party or Dorion.

~

In Europe in the early nineteenth century, Catholics were divided into two groups. On the right were the Ultramontanes, who saw the pope as the Vicar of Christ, the head of the church, supreme in all temporal authority. Emperors, kings, rulers, politicians — all had to submit to his will or face condemnation. On the left were the Catholic Liberals, who accepted the spiritual authority of the pope and the church while framing it around the doctrines of the liberty of conscience, the separation of church and state, and the reconciliation of church doctrine with modernity, especially liberalism. Laurier considered himself in this camp.

The church did not want any of this Catholic Liberalism. It was an error, the pope declared in 1864, to accept that the Roman pontiff can and should reconcile himself to progress, liberalism, and civilization. Five years later, at the First Vatican Council in 1869, the six hundred patriarchs, archbishops, bishops, abbots, generals of religious orders, and theologians in attendance conferred on him the gift of infallibility. After that, Ultramontanism became the order of the day.

In Canada, the ecclesiastical conquest of the political soul of the *Canadiens* began slowly. At mid-century, some Catholic politicians followed the lead of radical liberals in Europe, founded the Institut canadien, and opposed Confederation in 1867. The bishops, divided at first, rallied when their influence, their power, and their *Magisterium*, their collective rights and prerogatives, were questioned, endangered, or minimized. Since they were all omnipotent in their dioceses, they could impose their interpretations of the declarations they signed together with impunity.

Five Quebec bishops were particularly involved in the Liberal-Ultramontane battle that raged in Québec during the first ten years of Confederation — a battle in which Laurier was often the most visible target. In the Ultramontane corner, where the supremacy of the church was unquestionable and the authority of the bishops and the priests as agents of that supremacy was untouchable, was Ignace Bourget, bishop of Montréal from 1840 to 1876. In 1844, four years after its foundation, His Excellency declared war against the Institut canadien. Technically, there were several reasons for the conflict: the books in the library of the Institut which Catholics were forbidden to read; the membership of both Catholic and Protestants, an association that might, in his view, encourage heresy; the political discussions on church-state relations; and the anticlerical language that often prevailed. The real basis for the bishop's opposition, however, was that the members dared to think for themselves and generally acted without regard to their first duty as Catholics: to defend the interests of the church and to do what they were told. Condemning them and their Institut in 1858, while Laurier was still at L'Assomption, Bourget wrote in a pastoral letter that because they considered themselves competent to judge the morality of their library, no Catholic could belong to the Institut under pain of excommunication. Many of the Catholic members obeyed, but others stayed. The Institut was still under interdict when Laurier joined it in 1862. In Bourget's view, he, like the others, was a rebel against the church.

Appeals to Rome were launched, but were not successful. During the First Vatican Council, the Institut was rudely condemned, the authorities finding just cause in Bourget's actions. By this time Laurier was no longer a member, residing as he did in Arthabaska. He never regretted having been a member of the Institut. What he did regret, however, was the sorry comedy of the Guibord affair, which weakened the Liberal Party by making it appear more radical and revolutionary than it was.

Joseph Guibord was a member of the Institut when the condemnation came from Rome in July 1869. He didn't obey the bishop and was excommunicated. In November of that year he died, without making peace with the church. He was not able, therefore, to be buried with a religious ceremony, nor could he be interred in the Catholic cemetery where he had already bought a plot. The parish priest offered to bury him in the section reserved for those who die outside the church, but his widow refused. When she sued the church, Laflamme and one of the Doutre brothers represented her. The matter went all the way to the Privy Council in London, where, in 1874, their Lordships found in favour of the widow. When Guibord's body, which had been kept in the Protestant cemetery, was taken to the Catholic cemetery in September 1875, a mob attacked the *cortège* and barred the way. It was only two months later, on 16 November, with the mayor of Montréal, a judge, and 1235 soldiers in attendance, that Guibord was finally buried in the plot next to his wife, who had died in the meantime and within the fold. Reinforced cement was poured in the grave and soldiers stood guard over it. That same day, Bourget deconsecrated the ground in which Guibord was laid to rest. With great relish, the bishop wrote to his faithful: "There reposes a rebel who has been buried by force of arms." Bourget's ally in the battle against *Rougeisme* was Laflèche, the coadjutor and, after 1870, bishop of Trois-Rivières. It was Laflèche who had more or less ordered Laurier's bankruptcy when he was the editor of *Le Défricheur* and he had pursued him relentlessly ever since. To him, Laurier was the embodiment of a great evil that lurked around his diocesans. If they voted for him, Laflèche was certain that revolution would ensue and that the church would suffer or be destroyed. When he accused Laurier of treason against the church, of being a fomentor of evil and a seducer through hypocrisy and bad faith, Laflèche meant every word. When he or his priests threatened the Catholics of his diocese, should they dare to vote for Laurier, the bishop knew what he was doing.

But not all bishops agreed with Bourget and Laflèche. The primate and archbishop of Québec, Elzéar-Alexandre Taschereau, opposed the intervention of clerics in politics. He had been instrumental in obtaining the unanimous consent of his colleagues to a statement in a pastoral letter that was issued on 14 May 1868. Priests were strictly forbidden to involve themselves in the political life of Québec. He meant to see that policy adhered to, especially since he feared a negative reaction from the Protestants who were, after all, in the majority in the country. In letters and conversations with the archbishop of Toronto, Taschereau had come to realize that clerical intervention in Québec politics endangered the church in the rest of Canada. Unless the crisis was resolved in favour of the British political way of life, Rome would intervene. Of that, Taschereau was quite certain. His views were more or less acceptable to Charles Larocque, the bishop of Saint-Hyacinthe, and, to a lesser degree, to Jean-Pierre François-LaForce Langevin in Rimouski.

In 1871 an event occurred that accentuated the rivalry between bishops and politicians in Québec. On 21 April 1871 *Le Journal des Trois-Rivières* published a document that had been prepared by a group of eminent Conservatives closely linked to the interests of the church and subsequently vetted and approved by Bourget and Laflèche. The document was a political manifesto called the *Programme catholique*. Its ideas were to be part of Québec politics long after

Laurier's death. Its purpose was primarily to boost the fortunes of the fumbling Conservative Party by supporting a group of politicians who would subordinate their party's interests to those that were religious and racial — the language, traditions, and religion of what was then called *la nation canadienne-française*. This group believed, probably sincerely, that Confederation had created unique conditions to permit the church ample liberty of action in the pursuit of its mission. The role of the lay person was to assist that mission. In other words, Québec formed a state within a state, with an established church, and it was only right that political decisions be subjected to ecclesiastical directives and scrutiny.

To achieve that objective, it was necessary for the *Programmistes*, or Ultramontanes as they came to be called, to get power and to keep it. Their alliance with the clerics would achieve that end. The manifesto stipulated that they would generally support electorally only those Conservatives who accepted their platform. In return for ecclesiastical support, they would rid Québec of those laws on marriage, education, the creation of parishes, and many other areas that the bishops considered inimical to the church's rights and the smooth administration of its affairs. They also promised to frame any new legislation in accordance with the canons of the church. They vowed to destroy the Liberals and, in the process, the evils of liberalism.

Laurier was under no illusion: the bishops couldn't fail to see the benefits that the *Programme catholique* brought them, but would they support it? Unlike his friends, Laurier had his doubts. Bishops, he argued with David and others, generally do not like laymen interfering in their affairs. "Mark my word," he said, "they will insist that the *Programme* is nothing more and nothing less than the laymen's 'empiètement sur les droits des Evêques' — encroachment on their rights." He was correct: that is exactly what most of them said. Moreover, the archbishop of Québec was concerned that the *Programme* would irrevocably divide the Conservative Party, leaving the door open to a Liberal electoral triumph. To Taschereau and his supporters in the church, this was the calamity to avoid. Laurier found the archbishop's analysis valid. To Dorion and others he stated categorically: "The Conservative Party may well break under the strain. I cannot see Joseph Chapleau, Arthur Dansereau, Joseph Mousseau, and other so-called Liberal-Conservatives allying themselves with the Ultramontanes, this worst class of Conservatives. It is just not possible. They will never, any more than we would, accept being the agents of the church or subordinating themselves to the dictates of the bishops. Never! They will therefore resist and, failing victory, what then? Will they join us?"

Laurier was prophetic on all counts. The majority of the bishops disassociated themselves from the *Programme*. However, they were so circumspect in their opposition that it became an important Conservative instrument in provincial politics in the fight against the Liberals for almost a quarter of a century. But for the first ten years of its existence, it had relatively little electoral success. After that, it was a different story. The spirit of the *Programme* has lasted to this day. Ultramontane nationalism was founded on the conviction that the security and survival of the *Canadiens* didn't rest on federal parties or coalitions or brain trusts. Rather, it was only by building on their traditions and their institutions, and by emphasizing their religious and racial differences, that they would survive. This provincial focus explains why the Ultramontanes never had a distinct federal program and and why they were seldom at home in Ottawa. The same may also be said of those who followed them.

If the Conservative Party was having a *crise de conscience*, so too were the Liberals. They did not want to be condemned any longer, and they resented being associated with the radicalism of the past and censured from pulpits and in pastoral letters. They, too, wanted to be accepted and secure. Consequently, on 25 January 1872, some nine months after the *Programme catholique* was first published, Louis-Amable Jetté and the moderate elements of the party founded the *Parti national*. "We are a national party," its founders declared, "because ... we are attached to our nation and because we have pledged our unswerving loyalty to Canada above the whole world." They stood for the abolition of the Legislative Council, the election of senators, secret ballots and fixed elections, the abolition of dual federal and provincial representation, greater freedom for Canada in treaty making, increased provincial automony, and, as a departure from earlier *Rouge* policy, protection of Canadian industry. *Le National*, the quasi-official Liberal newspaper, even proclaimed its devotion and obedience to the church.

Laurier and practically all the *Rouges* of the pre-Confederation era participated in organizing the Parti national, but he did so with little enthusiasm.

His health prevented him from assisting at founding conventions and meet-ings. He approved of most of the policies that the Parti proposed, however, including protection of industry, even though he was more inclined to be a free trader. He was to regret that support.

~

Laurier's campaign for election to the provincial legislature in 1871 almost proved Zoë right. Through it all he was often sick, bleeding, shivering with fever, and breathing with difficulty. She and those who worked with him actually feared the consequences. It was too late, though, for her to plead with him that he stop. In spite of the exhaustion that followed the *assemblées contradictoires*, those political meetings that drew two to three thousand people and formed the chief means of political communication in those days, he waged a most ener-getic campaign. The Conservatives and the *Programmistes* were constantly after him, interrupting, calling him names, and starting fights. Since Drummond-Arthabaska was in Bishop Laflèche's diocese, His Excellency used his newspa-per, *L'Union des Cantons de l'Est*, to remind his spiritual sheep that Laurier was a *Rouge* and, as such, an enemy of religion. With the help of Laurier's parish priest, the Abbé Suzor, Laflèche organized the clergy. Every Sunday the Liberal candidate was attacked, often personally, and condemned. Zoë was torn, fre-quently angry, and in tears at the injustice of it all.

But Laurier ploughed on. A thousand times through the month of June he stressed that his Conservative opponent had done nothing for the county since his election in 1867. Armed with facts and figures, he slowly got the elec-torate to consider carefully if transportation had improved, if industry had flour-ished, if the flood of immigration to the United States had stopped, and if the educational system served the needs of their children. Whatever was valid for Drummond-Arthabaska, he reminded them over and over again, was true as well for the rest of the province. He refused to deal with his *Rouge* baggage. Yes, he had edited *Le Défricheur* — but that was then; this was now.

At first the men were curious about this new *poulin*, this new pony in their neighbourhood. The women, who didn't vote, stood behind their husbands, brothers, or fathers and listened carefully. What they saw pleased both sexes: a tall, twenty-nine-year-old man, handsome and dignified in his top hat and *redin-gote*, his exposed hair floating in the wind, his eyes piercing the crowd, and his voice deep and seductive. He made sense to them as he addressed the ups and downs of their daily lives. Using arguments they could all understand, he appealed to a better day in words that were intelligible to them and full of nobility. In the middle of the campaign, they sought him out.

Often returning home late at night, he would work until dawn on his arguments and then fall into an agitated sleep, watched over by the ever-present Zoë. Morning came bringing delegations of voters, the *calèche* to take him to yet another meeting or picnic or *assemblée*, and the insults. He realized he was driving himself, possibly beyond endurance, but he would not let Dorion down. He would deliver Drummond-Arthabaska.

By the beginning of July, when the campaign had nine or ten days to go, it became obvious to the Conservatives that he was going to win. They redoubled their efforts. Bishop Laflèche wrote to his priests ordering them to greater ardour in the defence of the cause of right. Suzor ascended the pulpit to warn his parishioners that if that infidel Laurier won, he would resign his *cure*. Zoë was aghast. That Sunday night many came to tell the good Father that they didn't want to lose him — but not enough.

In 1871 the government in power determined when voting would take place, generally on two consecutive days, and it hired the scrutineers and other officials who were needed. It also drew up the electoral list. As a result, the dead voted often. Since there was no secret ballot, the voters would declare their vote openly, leaving themselves susceptible to creative revenge. Votes were bought in full daylight, party discipline was lax, intimidation was constant, and the priests used the administration of the sacraments to get their way. In such a system, it was not easy to be a democrat.

On 9–10 July 1871 the *Programmistes* lost; they elected but one candidate. The old Conservative administration won about forty-three of the seats, but none of them were new faces. As for the Liberals, they could count on perhaps twenty supporters, depending on the issue — a slight gain over 1867. About five of these men were new to electoral office.

In Drummond-Arthabaska, Laurier won — with a majority of nearly a thousand votes. He was so exhausted that he was practically an invalid and was not able to go to Mass on Sunday, the 9th. Next day he was at home with the Poissons and Zoë when the noise in the street in front of the house interrupted their conversation. It grew louder and louder and sounded joyful. It was no guarantee of victory, however, for the Conservatives could be celebrating at his expense. Unwilling to open the door to a mob in frenzy, they waited for the knock on the door. It came loud and clear. Madame Poisson opened it and soon the living room was filled with supporters. Laurier received the news calmly but with great delight. He saw pride, and alarm, in Zoë's eyes. The majority was unbelievable! He thanked them in his usual fashion. "We have, my wife and I," he said, looking only at Zoë, "spent happy days here, in this house, in this village, living with our friends. It is possible that we shall see these days again." He smiled shyly and squeezed her arm as he went outside to greet the crowd that had come with the heralds of victory. After an hour or so, Dr. Poisson ushered them all out and ordered Laurier to bed. Dorion's trust had not been misplaced.

Through the month of July, letters poured in to congratulate him and to predict that "la carrière parlementaire sera ta vie!" If Zoë read in such a prediction that her husband's life would be spent in Parliament, she must have been frantic. On the other hand, it is quite possible that after 10 July 1871 she knew that it would be so.

Arthabaska, le dimanche, 23 juillet 1871

Mon cher Oscar [Archambault]:
How can I thank you for your good letter! Of all the congratulations that have come to me, it is yours, and yours alone, that I looked for. Yours, I knew, would come from a friendly heart. My own heart leapt when I saw your writing and read the post-mark L'Assomption. At that word, my whole life, our whole life in college, our life as students passed before my eyes like a flash. In an instant I surveyed ten years of my life. How many memories, how many happenings, how many intimate thoughts, how many anxieties, how many hopes buried by the hand of time surged up in my heart again as freshly as ten years ago. I said to myself then with what joy I would throw to the winds

my *député*'s seat if I could find myself back in that blessed time.

Yes, my friend, I am now a member of Parliament; I have scored a triumph, a real triumph; I have beaten the government; I have been carried through the portals with nothing to help but popular sympathy. Yet, once more, I would sacrifice all that to find myself back at nineteen with my poverty, but with my hopes, with my illusions, with your friendship. There is in the depths of my heart an enduring regret that the hand of time does not efface; regret that we have not been able to realize the dreams of our youth, that we have not been able to carry on beyond the threshold of life that union of our careers that we had planned so long. How many times I find these thoughts in my head, those regrets in my heart. I say to myself: What is the use of regretting what cannot be helped? What is the use of complaining of the implacable edicts of destiny? Yet the very instant afterward I find myself again dallying with the same thoughts, the same regrets.

Assuredly I ought to be perfectly happy. It rests only with myself to be happy, and I would be were it not for this regret. I do not know what you think about it, but for me it is a sorrow at every moment.

Like you, I regret that you have not been able to make your entrance into political life this year. We would have come together, we would have been able to work together, we would have tasted again something of the great days of yore. That opportunity is not lost; however, it is merely postponed. At the next election your turn will come. You will carry by assault that fine county of Assomption of Papin's which now lets itself be hypnotized by a wretched côterie. I know that will be a large struggle to fight, but the goal is worthy of your striving.

As for me, I do not have the ambition with which you credit me. I am entering political life without any preconceived ideas, without seeking any personal advantage, without desire — or, if I have any desire, it is that of making my ideas triumph. We are, it is true, in an era of transition, and there is a fair field for anyone who will take the trouble to strike out on his own path. There was a time when I felt tremendously ambitious, but age has dissipated these dreams of adolescence. I am turning into a positivist.

Adieu, my dear Oscar, or rather, *au revoir*. I suppose that I will see you at Québec this winter during the session. Accept my regards and those of my wife, and please remember me to your family whose many kindnesses to me will never vanish from my memory.

Ton ami,

W. Laurier

It came to pass that, by this time, Father Suzor had been cajoled into staying as the parish priest of Arthabaska. Zoë was relieved.

~

By Tuesday, 7 November, Laurier was in Québec City and had rented a room at the Hôtel Saint-Louis. The lieutenant governor came in great pomp to open the new session of the Québec legislature. According to most observers, he had little to say. There were balls and soirées and dinners to mark the event. Zoë stayed in Arthabaska; the former Speaker was re-elected; and the lone *Programmiste* announced he would support the Conservative government.

Laurier didn't arrive in Québec a total unknown. He had been part of provincial politics since the middle 1860s, but he wasn't in the first tier. He didn't represent an urban constituency, and he had never campaigned provincially. However, his success in Drummond-Arthabaska had been noticed. From it, he had emerged as the most promising figure of the new generation of Liberals. He had met the principal leaders of his party and, in the small political community of Québec, he knew most of the Conservatives. The only member of the legislature who could be said to be a friend, even though they were politically unfriendly, was Joseph-Adolphe Chapleau, who had been at L'Assomption in Laurier's time and had battled him and Médéric Lanctôt over Confederation. Chapleau was in his second term as member for Terrebonne.

The ceremonies didn't overly impress Laurier. He complained to Zoë that the legislature had nothing to do except partake in endless rituals that he found fastidious and almost unreal. He was bored to death. When he wrote to her he had just finished giving his maiden speech.

The Liberal caucus had chosen him to reply to the Speech from the Throne. When, on 9 November, the Speaker recognized "l'honorable député de Drummond-Arthabaska," his demeanour, as usual, inspired confidence and sympathy. He glanced at his notes, which he had well memorized. His eyes took in the mood of the audience. Everyone was there — George-Étienne Cartier, Joseph-Édouard Cauchon, Joseph-Adolphe Chapleau, his leader and members of his caucus — and the benches opposite were also filled to capacity. The press had registered in great numbers and the galleries were packed with the general public. They all seemed to expect something from him which was exciting and unscripted. Could he not but disappoint them? He became nervous, even slightly agitated.

His first words were a question: "Le tableau qu'on a mis devant vous, est-il bien l'expression de la vérité?" He thought not. The reality of everyday life in Québec was far from the rosy picture painted by the government. "We are told that we are rich," he continued, but if anyone poked around he would find a malaise, *une gêne*, a discomfort that hid great suffering. The cause? The absence of an *industrie nationale*. That was the cause of the vast exodus of *Canadiens* to the United States. Québec was bleeding to death. Many babies were born, but when they became adults they could find no work and were doomed to poverty and exile.

As a *Canadien*, he was mortified that the citizens of British origin in Québec succeeded better than his people: "We must frankly acknowledge that down to the present we have been left behind in the race." There was a buzz in the room and some murmurs of discontent. He quieted them. There was no shame there, he reminded them, for after the Conquest the *Canadiens*, "desirous of maintaining their national inheritance intact," set themselves up apart from those living with them and even from the "outside world." The result, he said firmly and with some courage, was to keep the *Canadiens* "strangers to the reforms that were constantly taking place beyond their boundaries" and, fatally, to shut them up within the narrow circle of their own old traditions and way of life. That could no longer be. The moment had come for the *Canadiens* to be part of the modern world, the world of commerce, industry, science, and the arts *de la paix*.

He finished with an appeal to solidarity and to reforms of various kinds that would establish democracy on a better footing, create a new educational agenda, improve transportation and communications, and institute a policy of industrial development to ensure Québec's future. He sat down and a deadly silence followed. Then the applause and the "Bravos" came from everywhere, even from the galleries. Chapleau nodded his pleasure. The press rushed out to file their enthusiasm for this new star. He had not disappointed. He had again met the expectations.

In this first parliamentary address, he focused on matters social, economic, and national that were peculiar to his people. He wanted major changes in outlook in *Canadien* society in Québec. Tradition was not so important to him, especially if it interfered with progress. He was a Liberal, and a Liberal was for change, not the preservation of the status quo. The retention of a small *Canadien* society tied to the land and largely uneducated was to him no guarantee for the future. He made that quite clear and, in the process, enunciated what would be a guiding principle throughout his life. Still, if a shift had to be made from a rural to an industrialized society, it was up to the only government the *Canadiens* controlled to devise policies that would realize that objective. He was at a disadvantage here, though. Economics was never a subject he was comfortable with. He therefore contented himself with listing some generalities about how to create an *industrie nationale*. He was not able to determine the practical means to bring it about.

His second speech in the Québec legislature, on 22 November 1871 — two days after his thirtieth birthday — dealt with the question of dual representation. The issue was the constitution, the rights and liberties, guarantees, and division of responsibilities and powers in the federation, and the difference between legality and legitimacy. There was not a single hesitation in his presentation. His arguments rolled out unimpeded by unfamiliarity, and his delivery of the words that clothed the thoughts was masterful.

There were two moments in that address that invoked the future. Looking around the Chamber and to the seats of the government, where many of the provincial deputies were also federal members, he almost whispered what he knew they all saw clearly: "With a single mandate," he said, "Québec is Québec; with a double mandate, it becomes merely an appendage of Ottawa." In that single sentence he heralded the Canadian constitutional principle of provincial auton-omy. In that principle lay the protection of the rights of the *Canadiens*. The second moment came when, in rhetoric seldom heard in political debate until that day, he set out the framework of Canada's constitutional social contract between his people and their fellow citizens with whom they shared the land.

> When a people accepts a constitution, they make the sacrifice of a portion of their liberty, a generous sacrifice by which each gives up something belonging to himself individually for the benefit of the security of the whole.
>
> When a people accepts a constitution, they trace out themselves the circle that they assign to their liberties. They say to themselves, in a sense: This space belongs to me; here I can speak, think, act; I owe no account of my words, my thoughts, my acts to anyone except to my own conscience and to God; but as regards society, here its domain begins and mine ends, and I shall not go further.
>
> Still, like all human works, constitutions are not perfect. New horizons, which were not before perceived, are constantly opening up, and unsuspected abuses are discovered. It is then the duty of the legislature to step in and enlarge or contract, according to needs and circumstances, the circle within which the institutions of the country move.

When the vote was taken, the double mandate remained for the present, but Laurier had the satisfaction of watching Chapleau vote for its abolition. In 1872 Ontario did away with it and when, a year later, the federal government made it impossible for a provincial member to sit in Parliament, the practice died.

During his term as a member of the provincial legislature, Laurier did not participate actively in the debates or in the affairs of the province. He spent most of his time while the House was sitting handling his legal business. Québec as a city didn't appeal to him. He hardly walked; he spent most of his days and nights reading and preparing briefs; and he wrote to Zoë frequently. Mercifully, he kept repeating, the sessions were not long and he could return to the security and comfort of Arthabaska. He did, however, make friends.

~

The politico-religious crisis that was developing all around him compelled some attention on his part, though he watched it without much active interference. After the provincial election of 1871 and the federal election of 1872, the *Programmistes*, reeling from their lack of electoral success, began their campaign against Catholic Liberalism in earnest and, as they insisted, its associate, the Liberal Party. The *Programmiste* strategy bore fruit in the provincial elections of 1875.

By this time, the clergy was directly involved in influencing the outcome of elections and the political activities of the state. All the previous episcopal *mandements*, letters, and circulars to the clergy stipulating restraint were discarded. In the elections of 1875, in which clerical interference was pervasive, the province elected 39 Conservatives, 19 Liberals, and 5 Independents. Cauchon, who was by then a Liberal, threatened to have the results annulled on the grounds of "influence indue cléricale." However, such a policy was not without risks, as Joseph-Israël Tarte, Laurier's friend from L'Assomption, who was by then a sort of *Programmiste* and editor of a fiercely Catholic newspaper *Le Canadien*, reminded the Liberals. The Catholic people of Québec would not take kindly to priests and bishops being dragged before lay tribunals as common criminals. Eventually, saner heads prevailed. A month after the elections, Archbishop Taschereau was asked to declare officially that the Liberals of Québec were not guilty of the condemned Catholic Liberalism and to affirm that the Liberal Party as it existed in Canada was simply an ordinary political party that sought reforms for the welfare of the people and in keeping with the constitution of the land. In other words, there was a distinction to be made between Catholic Liberalism and political Liberalism, and they asked him to make it.

The archbishop and his colleagues refused to do so. In their *mandement* of 22 September 1875 they stayed within the bounds of papal directives and did not condemn the Liberal Party as such. However, they asserted that the evil of Catholic Liberalism was alive and well in Québec. Since it was the greatest enemy of the church, no Catholic could in conscience be un libéral catholique. They reaffirmed the right and, indeed, the duty of priests to be directly involved in politics. They gave two reasons for that affirmation. First, a priest was an elector like every other man and, as such, he was free to exercise his right to express his opinion. Second, a priest, in concert with his bishop, had the God-given responsibility to guide the consciences of his parishioners in all matters that involved the moral law of the church and its teachings, rights, and prerogatives; he had, therefore, to intervene in politics to point out what was right and what was wrong. Anyone who argued otherwise was guilty of the sins of Catholic Liberalism.

As for the clergy, the bishops ordered that no priest should agree to appear before a civil tribunal; rather, he should request that he be judged by an ecclesiastical court. Should a priest be condemned, he should suffer that persecution patiently "par amour pour la Sainte Église." In conclusion, they stipulated that priests should never discuss temporal matters in the pulpit, but should limit themselves to the enunciation of principles, remain in communion with their bishops, and not participate directly in electoral contests.

Priests and laity were not fooled by the clever and convoluted language of the bishops. They understood perfectly well that the Liberal Party was condemned. All its adherents were to be opposed, and the priests had a duty to eradicate evil in their parishes. When a major opportunity was presented to them in the federal by-election of Charlevoix in the Saguenay district of Québec, also in Taschereau's archdiocese, in January 1876, the clergy joined in with a vengeance. Political questions receded into the background as religious matters became the only issue. The electors were reminded time and time again that Liberals had strangled priests in the French Revolution. Did they want that to happen in their beloved province? To the objection that the Liberal candidate was also a well-known Catholic and devoted to the church, it was replied that Victor-Emmanuel and Garibaldi were also Catholics and they still waged war against the church in Italy. Surely at the hour of death, electors would rather be on the side of the pope than with these traitors. Women were ordered to refuse their conjugal "duty" to husbands who were Liberal partisans, and children were made to kneel and beg God that their parents not be damned should they have the temerity to vote for the Liberal candidate. When electors asked directly whom they should vote for, the cagey priests contented themselves with informing them that "le ciel est bleu, l'enfer est rouge" — heaven is blue, hell is red — an analogy impossible to misinterpret in Québec.

By this time, the Protestants were up in arms. A month before the election in Charlevoix, Liberals who were not Catholics founded Protestant Defence Associations in Montréal and Québec to fend off clerical pretentiousness and to protect those who might be persecuted over matters of conscience. Meanwhile, in English Canada, the Roman Catholic minority sent requests to Rome for the papal authorities to put the Québec bishops in their place before the church became a target of repression all over the country. Bishops in the other provinces had made their peace with political Liberalism, and they couldn't understand why their French-speaking colleagues couldn't do likewise.

Unable to obtain any form of justice from the Québec ecclesiastical authorities, the Liberals sent their *mémoires* to the Vatican as well. They brought the matter of the Charlevoix election before the courts in accordance with Canada's Election Act of 1874, which forbade undue influence in elections. The court of first instance, presided over by a *Programmiste*, took one year to find no evidence of undue influence, since the priests had performed nothing more than their sacerdotal duties. Furthermore, the judge found them immune from the scrutiny of the temporal power in the exercise of those duties. An appeal was immediately lodged with the Supreme Court of Canada, which had been established the year before. On 19 December 1876 the Court, in a unanimous decision, declared the Charlevoix election null and void on the grounds of undue influence of the worst kind. Ironically, the brother of the archbishop of Québec wrote the verdict. Still, in the 1877 by-election, the Conservative candidate won again.

Rome, having been deluged with petitions, *mémoires*, and conflicting opinions, decided to send a papal legate to see what was going on and to try to sort it out. Bishop George Conroy, bishop of Ardagh in Ireland, arrived in Québec on 24 May 1877.

The stage was set for Wilfrid Laurier to find a way out of the morass in which Québec religion and politics had been thrust.

~

By the time the religious-political war in Québec was raging in the middle 1870s, Laurier was no longer a member of the Québec legislature. Rather, he was the member for Drummond-Arthabaska in the federal Parliament of Canada, having been elected in 1874. Such a move was inevitable. His career as a Québec provincial politician was getting nowhere, and he had ceased enjoying whatever kudos it brought him. He took part less and less in provincial politics, which he found banal, and concentrated instead on his law practice. He spent as much time as possible with Zoë in Arthabaska and took care of his health. Zoë hoped that the political bug had been ejected from his being, but it was not to be.

What brought him to consider moving from the Québec legislature to the House of Commons was a series of events that he found intriguing. With the federal elections of 1872, the vulnerability of the Conservatives became apparent. Their majority in the House was reduced, giving hope to the Liberals for the next round. Furthermore, the Pacific Scandal of 1873 brought down the government of Sir John A. Macdonald and replaced it with a Liberal one under Alexander Mackenzie. The Liberals had arrived in Ottawa, but would they ever succeed in Québec? Laurier had his doubts. Then, when Mackenzie called an election for January 1874, the federal Liberal incumbent in Drummond-Arthabaska announced his retirement.

Laurier was in bed. He had returned from his last session in Québec with a bad cold and he was guarded by the indefatigable Zoë. The cough irritated the lungs and caused hemorrhages. His fever increased and, at times, he was delirious. He fought the despondency that accompanied the illness, as well as his tendency to be morose, discouraged, and inhibited at times like that. Zoë would entertain no thought, no discussion, about politics. Christmas came and went, and still he didn't recuperate.

One fine, cold day a group of local political friends came to see him. Zoë wouldn't let them in. They insisted and Laurier, hearing the commotion, asked that they be allowed. Against her better judgment, she did as he wished. Propped up in bed, pale and dishevelled, he listened while they talked of his candidacy. They understood that the campaign would be rough, but he would have all the help he would need. The Conservatives were presenting a candidate who was not as popular as Laurier, and the Liberals could retain the seat if he ran. Moreover, they insisted, he was bored in Québec, his stature and reputation were growing in the party, federal issues were complex and required the attention of his keen mind, and a federal political career would benefit his law practice. They were sure he had the potential to be a Cabinet minister, and they dismissed his concern that Ottawa was far away from Arthabaska and that the sessions were longer than in Québec. When he mentioned his health, one of them replied that electoral excitement had always made him feel better in the past. Before they left his sick room, he had agreed. When Zoë came in to let the gentlemen of the Liberal Party out, he was already making plans. He looked more animated than she had seen him in weeks.

The election campaign was arduous and bitterly fought. He almost drowned crossing the Nicolet River near the little village of Horton in his constituency. Liquor flowed on both sides; money changed hands to buy votes; and the great issues of the day, particularly the corruption of the Conservatives as illustrated in the Pacific Scandal, were debated in countless *assemblées contradictoires*. The Conservative candidate, though, lacked Laurier's rhetoric, intelligence, and charm, and the clergy stayed relatively quiet. At the end of January 1874 Laurier was elected by a majority of 238. He was Ottawa bound.

When Laurier entered Parliament, the Liberals had won 138 seats out of 206, with 54 percent of the popular vote. In Québec, the Liberals had elected thirty-five to the Conservatives' thirty, a gain of eight over 1872. They faced three problems that could seriously affect the future of Canada: the construction of the Canadian Pacific Railway, which was caught in a scandal of giant proportions; the agitation in Manitoba, which emphasized racial antagonism and threatened to disrupt national unity; and the economic recession caused by the panic of 1873.

What to do about the railway? Laurier was damned if he knew. When British Columbia entered Confederation in 1871, the federal Conservative government led by Macdonald and Cartier committed itself to building a transcontinental railway within ten years. It would be a national work of astounding proportions filled with formidable difficulties, heavy costs, and little return for years to come. The Liberals, on the other hand, considered it foolhardy and irresponsible. Their principal newspaper in Toronto, the *Globe*, saw it as a rash and disastrous step dictated by a handful of people 2500 miles away. The Parti national, which grouped the various shades of Québec Liberalism, also thundered against it. Laurier, who was later to build a transcontinental of his own, appeared to share that opinion. By the time the Liberals left office in 1878, the cause of the transcontinental was not far advanced.

Laurier did, however, take a strong stance in the debate over Manitoba. The insurrection of 1869 — an insurrection caused by Macdonald's bungling of the integration of the Hudson's Bay Company lands, which Canada had bought in November of that year, into the constitutional framework and social fabric of Canada — was still being felt when Laurier went to Ottawa in 1874 to help govern the country. The most contentious event had been the execution of Thomas Scott, a surveyor from Ontario, an Orangeman, and a foul-mouthed racist. That a "savage," the Métis Louis Riel, had put to death a white man was, to say the least, unacceptable. An army was sent to rectify matters and to establish Canadian rule in the territories. When hostilities ceased, Cartier had created the province of Manitoba in 1870 and had allowed for language and educational rights similar to those in the Québec constitution. By the fall of 1870, all was quiet on the western front. But not in Ontario and Québec.

Ontarians were incensed at the "murder" of one of their own and, in addition, they were anxious to offset the influence of Québec by extending Ontario's role in the West. A little Ontario, or even a series of them, in the former lands of the Hudson's Bay Company would do quite nicely. Consequently, they wanted punishment for the leaders of the insurrection and the rule of law to make the West safe for them to take over. The government of Ontario offered $5000 cash for Riel's arrest. *Canadiens*, in contrast, had trekked all over the western prairies before Orangemen and Ontarians even knew such territories existed. In the process, they had opened the West and had intermarried with the First Peoples and created a new nation, the *Nation métisse*. Some, but only a few, saw the possibilities of a *Canadien* western immigration to counteract the drain of population to the textile mills of New England. Let bygones be bygones, *Canadiens* urged, and grant Riel and his cohorts an unconditional amnesty.

In typical fashion, Macdonald sought to arrest Riel and Ambroise Lepine while at the same time he gave them money to flee to the United States and negotiated an amnesty with the bishop of Saint-Boniface, Monseigneur Alexandre Taché. Unfortunately, the terms were never written down and, as such, were open to various interpretations. Had Scott's execution been covered? Macdonald said no, as did the Liberals when they took office; the bishop said yes.

By the time the elections of 1874 arrived, warrants had been issued for both Riel and Lepine, who had returned to the Red River Valley in 1872. Lepine was arrested, but Riel fled and had the gall to let his name stand as a candidate in Provencher, Manitoba, in the same elections that brought Laurier to Ottawa. When Mackenzie and the Liberal Cabinet heard the news, they were stupefied, fearful of the consequences in Ontario. They asked Taché to intervene to prevent this calamity. No fool, the bishop asked in return for a written and formal statement from the Liberal government stating that an amnesty would be granted. Mackenzie refused. Riel was elected by a majority of 127 votes over his Liberal opponent. Would he come to Ottawa to be sworn in? Would he be allowed to take his seat? What would Mackenzie do, the leader who had mentioned Riel often during the campaign in Ontario and accused his Conservative opponents of treason for promising an amnesty to a rebel and a murderer? And what position would Laurier take when the time arrived?

Tuesday, 26 March 1874, was a painfully cold day in Ottawa and the opening day of Parliament. Laurier had arrived the previous Sunday and had taken up residence at the Russell Hotel. On Monday he was sworn in, with his Québec friends attending. At the caucus meeting he was assigned the task to second, in French, the reply to the Speech from the Throne that the Mackenzie administration had prepared. The Liberal Whip showed him where his seat would be, to the right of the Speaker and far to the back. Then, on Tuesday, he walked with his colleagues to the Senate Chamber to hear the Speech read by the governor general, Lord Dufferin.

On that day, as well, as the crowd was milling around the foyer of the Parliament Buildings, three men entered the House. One of those men was Louis Riel. He was heavily bearded, elegantly dressed, and no one recognized him. With his companions, he walked about the lobby, smiling at people and acting in an ordinary manner. Shortly before 1 p.m. he and the member for Rimouski who was accompanying him entered the Chief Clerk's Office. Riel took the oath, signed the register, bowed to the clerk, and walked out. Looking down at the signature, the clerk was astounded. He rushed down the hall to inform the minister of justice, Antoine-Aimé Dorion, and within minutes the news was all over the place. But Riel had disappeared.

It was under these circumstances that Laurier spoke in Ottawa for the first time on 30 March. As he stood up to speak, he appeared to many members as a country bumpkin. His long chestnut hair, which tended to fall gracefully on both sides of his face, intensified that impression and made him look much younger than he was. Many were in attendance, having heard of his eloquence. He didn't disappoint them as he delivered an innocuous speech about the wide margin of liberty Canadian citizens enjoyed under the constitution; about the harmony which prevailed among the races and which was unparalleled anywhere in the world; about Liberalism in Québec being founded on the political principles of British Liberals; and about the useful possibilities of the government's plan for the country. He spoke with assurance and, as an observer remarked at the time, with the self-possession of the practised orator: a charm of manner, a touch of dignity, an air of candour, and a natural eloquence. The members applauded and the prime minister congratulated him, as did the leader of the opposition, the Right Honourable John A. Macdonald. Speaking in French, however, he was understood by only a minority in the House.

The business of governing the land came to a standstill until the matter of Riel, who was by then in hiding in Montréal, was settled. In the second week of April, things came to a head. The government appointed a committee of the House, chaired by Donald Smith, a former official of the Hudson's Bay Company, to inquire into all matters pertaining to the North-West Rebellion, including the matter of amnesty; the Conservatives moved a motion to expel Riel; the Liberals moved that the motion was premature and that the House should wait until Smith had handed in his report; and Laurier's Conservative friend, the affable Joseph-Alfred Mousseau, along with the Seigneur of Terrebonne, the dour Rodrigue Masson, presented a motion to order the government to grant full amnesty.

On Wednesday, 15 April, Laurier rose to speak. It was his first speech ever in English. He was fearful that in its course he would frequently "murder the Queen's English." He had done his homework, however, researching all the legal precedents he could possibly invoke to prove that, in accordance with British law, "no person on British soil can be arbitrarily deprived of what belongs to him" — as the Conservatives wished to do with Louis Riel. No one had clearly shown, he contended, that Riel had committed an act of murder and that an indictment to that effect had been laid against him. These were not legal technicalities and subtleties; they were "the guarantees of British liberty." Since the days of the Magna Carta, he went on, "never has it been possible on British soil to rob a man of his liberty, his property, or his honour except under the safeguard of what has been termed in this debate technical expressions and legal subtleties."

Turning to the matter of amnesty, he called on the Conservatives to set the record straight. In the meantime, Riel had to be given the benefit of the doubt. "I for one shall never declare that this man is a fugitive from his country's justice" until Riel was proven to be so. The House would do well to wait for Smith and his committee to finish their work. However, he was not prepared to accept Mousseau's unconditional amnesty, even though he was in favour of one. Again, it was premature. As for the rebellion in the Red River Valley in 1869–70, he was proud of it. "What were they fighting for, these brave men?" he asked his colleagues. All Riel and his friends "wanted was to be treated like British subjects and not to be bartered away like common cattle. If that be an act of rebellion, where is the one amongst us who, if he had happened to have been with them, would not have been rebels as they were?" In conclusion, he affirmed that, "taken all in all, I would regard the events at Red River in 1869–70 as constituting a glorious page in our history, if unfortunately they had not been stained with the blood of Thomas Scott. But such is the state of human nature and of all that is human: good and evil are constantly intermingled; the most glorious cause is not free from impurity and the vilest may have its noble side."

He had spoken for an hour in excellent English. He who had no formal training in the language spoke it better than most natives. Yet, even though Laurier had been calm, logical and thoughtful, and his speech had been regarded as the best in the debate, and the members had applauded him for over five minutes, he was not able to convince the House. By a vote of 124 to 68, Riel was expelled from Parliament and his seat declared vacant.

Matters, however, did not rest there. Riel dominated Canadian politics for another year or so. Five months after his expulsion, he was re-elected *in absentia*. He didn't come to Ottawa this time.

In November 1874 Lepine was found guilty of murder and was condemned to death by hanging. A powerful agitation developed in Québec to prevent his execution. The governor general heard it and, early in 1875, without the advice and consent of his ministers, he commuted Lepine's sentence to two years' imprisonment. In the session of 1875 Donald Smith reported that Macdonald and Cartier had indeed promised an amnesty. This was enough for Mackenzie to act. On 11 February he moved that all those who had participated in the rebellion be pardoned, with the exception of Riel and Lepine, who were to be granted an amnesty after a five-year banishment, and a Fenian by the name of O'Donoghue, who was to be banished for life. Riel was stripped of his seat in the House of Commons and he left for the United States. Lepine refused the amnesty and served his full jail term, being released from the penitentiary in October 1876. Meanwhile, Laurier had met with Riel while he was staying at a rectory not far from Arthabaska. He found him quite charismatic but highly disturbed, and considered him a monomaniac.

Could Laurier support Mackenzie's policy? He had, after all, participated in a campaign in favour of Riel, even though he had little sympathy for the Métis leader. He and other Québec Liberals had taken "this Riel question and kindled the enthusiasm of the people for him and his friends." No doubt it was done to chastise Macdonald's government, which had done little to alleviate the situation, but in the process he had broken the vow he had made to himself to "éliminer du domaine de notre politique les questions de race et de religion." He was aware of that and, in a letter to his Liberal friend, James Young, he admitted as much: "We have been imprudent in intensifying the feelings of the people as we have done." He was not about to repeat the same mistake. He wanted the agitation stopped and the matter closed. And so he supported his government in February 1875. He took the occasion, though, to remind the House that "our nation is composed of individuals of different creeds and races." Consequently, all had to be treated equally and, in the pursuit of public affairs, one could not forget that simple fact. With that, the matter of Riel was laid to rest — for the next ten years.

But the economic situation would provide no respite. Beginning in 1873, the demand for Canadian goods declined in the United States and in Great Britain, and Canada's vulnerability to external financial fluctuations caused real hardship. Businesses, even the most prosperous, went bankrupt; banks failed and credit became hard, if not impossible, to obtain; mills and shops and factories closed; thousands of workers became unemployed; and many had no bread to feed themselves and their children. Such were the economic conditions for the entire period of the Mackenzie administration.

Since the federal government's revenues were mostly based on import duties, it needed to find some ready cash. In 1875 the tariff on most imports was increased by about $2\frac{1}{2}$ percent. But the cry for a higher tariff to supply greater revenues to the state and to protect Canadian industries from being slaughtered in their own markets became more vociferous. Mackenzie and the minister of finance, Richard Cartwright, were free traders; Laurier had supported free trade when he was a *Rouge* in his youth, but had switched to moderate protection with the *Parti national*. In 1876 the government toyed with the idea of increasing the tariff yet once again, but at the last minute changed its mind. Laurier followed suit.

"I do not deny that I have been a protectionist, which I still am," he said during the debate on the matter, "but I am a moderate protectionist." Perhaps it was safe to say, he added, that free trade was an ultimate goal to be striven for; in the meantime, though, protection "is a matter of necessity for a young nation, in order that it may attain the full development of its full resources." He posed a question: To what extent does Canada need protection? He answered it: "I consider that the present tariff affords sufficient protection . . . The depression is not particular to this country, but is universal and affects highly protected as well as free-trade countries."

Yet the position of the Liberal Party in both Québec and the rest of the country kept deteriorating, partly due to the depression, but also because it was not able to inflame the souls of the electors. It had no sense of nation building, and it was constantly hampered by questions of leadership. Mackenzie and his people gave Canada many things that were worthwhile — the Supreme Court, secret ballot, one-day elections, the North-West Mounted Police, the Royal Military College, door-to-door delivery of mail in major Canadian cities, and honest government. But leadership remained a problem.

The leadership in question revolved around Alexander Mackenzie and Edward Blake, with Laurier often caught in the middle. Mackenzie had been born in Scotland in 1822 of poor parentage. When he came to Canada in 1842 to make his fortune — which he did laying bricks and stone — he brought with him his radical politics and his interest in reforming the world that he knew. He entered politics in 1861. Blake, in contrast, was eleven years younger, an Upper Canadian of wealth, a graduate of the University of Toronto, a Liberal, and a formidable lawyer. In 1867 he was elected to both the Ontario legislature and the House of Commons, and became premier of Ontario in 1871, with Mackenzie as his treasurer. When dual representation was abolished in 1872, both men opted for the federal scene.

Blake was recognized for his intelligence, and almost everyone in the party, including Mackenzie, had wanted him to become leader in 1873. One who didn't share that opinion was Mackenzie's minister of finance, Richard Cartwright, who doubted Blake's qualities as a leader. After refusing to accede to the leadership, though he was surprised when his refusal was taken seriously, Blake entered the Cabinet as minister without portfolio, only to resign three months later. His support couldn't be counted on during the elections of 1874, but in 1875 disenchantment with Mackenzie was such that the rank and file of the party pressured Blake to return to the Cabinet. Mackenzie again offered him the prime ministership, but Blake contented himself with becoming minister of justice, a post he gave up two years later to become president of the Privy Council. In the elections of 1878 he remained studiously quiet, went to Europe, and lost the constituency in which he stood.

Laurier was somewhat put off by Mackenzie, whom he found incapable of vision and action. In Blake, eight years his senior, however, he found a genius, a contemplative and hardworking man, shy and aloof, and a most constructive statesman. They often found themselves in the Parliamentary Library, poring over tomes and discussing with each other what they read. They became intimate friends, and remained so through the vicissitudes of their political life. They trusted each other, discussed issues frankly, and sought always to reconcile their opinions. Obviously, Laurier favoured Blake over Mackenzie as leader.

Laurier also felt let down by Mackenzie. He didn't expect to be in the Cabinet at the beginning of the Mackenzie administration. However, in 1875 the minister of justice, a French Canadian, resigned to become a justice of the Supreme Court. Who would replace him? Mackenzie favoured Cauchon, who had his entrée at the archbishop's palace, knew everybody, and had thirty years of parliamentary experience. Blake supported Laurier, who represented the future of the party. This difference of opinion created a difficulty that could only be resolved by testing Laurier. If he could organize a Liberal victory in Bellechasse, which the former minister of justice had held, he would be elevated to the Cabinet. In November 1875 the Liberals lost and Laurier was punished.

Cachon was anointed in December 1875 — to the great annoyance, and even anger, of many Québec Liberals.

Another vacancy came about in October 1876. Laurier was not even considered. His former professor and mentor, Rodolphe Laflamme, became a minister in November. A month later came another opening and there was some talk about Laurier, but Cauchon was instrumental in killing his candidacy in the bud. Another man was appointed. Mackenzie apologized for his decision, citing circumstances beyond his control and the need to consider regional representation from Québec in the Cabinet. Laurier didn't believe a word of it.

But Laurier was resilient, secure, and determined. He would prevail at some point or another. When, in June 1877, Cauchon fell out with Mackenzie and Blake and was appointed lieutenant governor of Manitoba, Laurier was slated to succeed him. First, however, he had to wait for the episcopal authorities to clear up the matter of political Liberalism versus Catholic Liberalism. He decided to give them a hand.

5

" I   A m   a   L i b e r a l "

In July 1867 a new era opened for the *Canadiens*. For the first time in their history, they had a government and a legislature they controlled and they could freely and effectively participate at the highest levels of the federal Parliament and its courts of justice. It was a splendid opportunity for men like Laurier who thrived on politics, had ideas, displayed qualities of leadership, and made themselves available. However, by 1877 it was apparent that, at neither the provincial nor the federal level, the interests of the *Canadiens* were as firmly entrenched as the constitutional order had prophesied. The government in Québec appeared little more than an adjunct to the federal agenda, and the influence that the *Canadiens* were counting on in Ottawa had become weak and uncertain. Furthermore, the confusion between political Liberalism and Catholic Liberalism more or less authorized the clergy to intervene in politics, rendering the autonomy of Quebec's politicians fragile at best.

In this period of uncertainty, the Club canadien, a Liberal political club, invited Laurier to speak on Canada's brand of political Liberalism in Québec City on 26 June 1877. Alexander Mackenzie and some influential Québec Liberals, including Rodolphe Laflamme, were uneasy, fearing that Laurier would inadvertently disrupt the careful negotiations going on at the time between the Liberal Party of Canada and the papal authorities. It would be better, Mackenzie wrote in a letter, to postpone the lecture to a later date. Even Zoë got into the act. She was afraid that he would become embroiled in an endless confrontation with her cherished men of God.

Laurier was confident, however, that something had to be done — and quickly. "We cannot wait," he pointed out to Zoë. "In a few months it may be too late and our party will be the loser for it." To Laurent-Olivier David, who trusted him not to say anything foolish, Laurier said with some emotion: "Surely, if we cannot now speak plain common-sense language, the fate of our party is in a desperate condition — a worse one than we are now in as we wait for Rome to pronounce on our political purity."

~

At 6:30 p.m. on Tuesday, 26 June 1877, the young men who had invited Laurier arrived to pick him up at his hotel for the drive to the Salle de musique, a public hall on Saint-Louis Street, which could seat about twelve hundred people. He was surprised at the large number of *calèches* and cabs either parked around the building or lined up to disgorge their occupants, and at the many who were making their way on foot. In an antechamber off the main hall, he met some of the leaders of the Liberal Party who had come from as far away as Montréal to hear him. There were even a few from Ottawa. Journalists came in great numbers, most of whom he knew. Many, like his friend Tarte, were *Programmistes* and had made much political capital out of the evil of Liberalism. David was there, as was Ernest Pacaud, his unofficial electoral agent from Arthabaska, who brought a note from Zoë. Archambault had sent a telegram, and many Liberals sitting in the Legislative Assembly of Québec, including the leader of the opposition and the leader of the provincial wing of the party, the grand seigneur Henri-Gustave Joly de Lotbinière, entered shortly before he was to speak. The Anglican arch-bishop of Québec appeared, as did a couple of Protestant clergymen, three or four Roman Catholic canons, several diocesan priests, a Jesuit or two, and many lay and clerical professors from l'Université Laval — more than two thousand people in all. At long last the chairman of the Club canadien announced: "Le temps est arrivé, Monsieur Laurier!"

He rose deadly pale — so pale, in fact, that people thought he might be ill. But Laurier advanced to the front of the stage and, lifting up his head, he searched the audience just as his listeners scrutinized him. He would state clearly where he stood, what he believed in, what he was after — and they would hear his terms. The echo of his voice would go as far as Ottawa, through Montréal, and reverberate in every village, parish, chancery, seminary, and college in

Québec, even in the house where Bishop Conroy, the papal legate, was in seclusion. No one would be spared.

He went immediately to the heart of the matter. At first his voice trembled and he feared he would cough, but it passed quickly.

> *Je sais* that in the eyes of a large number of my fellow countrymen, the Liberal Party is a party composed of men of perverse doctrines and dangerous tendencies, pressing knowingly and deliberately towards revolution.

Glancing up from his text, he saw many heads bowing in agreement. He didn't tarry, but went on immediately:

> *Je sais* that in the eyes of a portion of my fellow countrymen, the Liberal Party is a party of men with upright intentions, perhaps, but victims and dupes of principles that are leading them unconsciously but fatally towards revolution.

Again the bowing of heads in agreement, and a few in disagreement. Then:

> *Je sais* that in the eyes of another and not the least considerable portion, perhaps, of our people, Liberalism is a new form of evil, a heresy carrying with it its own condemnation.

Without giving them a chance to decide to nod one way or another — and he sensed that they were done with that exercise — he went on to repeat that he knew all these fears. That was why he had accepted the invitation to speak — to make his stand, to expose for all to hear the political principles that animated his soul. He would have it no other way.

His Liberalism was not Catholic Liberalism, and had nothing to do with it. As long as Liberals were identified with it, however, "we would be obliged to abstain completely from taking any part in the management of affairs of state, and then the constitution — that constitution that was granted to us for our own protection — would be no more than a dead letter in our hands." That was not his destiny. Nor was his political creed influenced by continental liberalism. The history of that liberalism "has been written in letters of blood." Rather it was in English Liberalism that he sought his inspiration. And the great British historian, Lord Macaulay, whom he so admired, gave him the words:

> Everywhere there is a class of men who cling with fondness to whatever is ancient and who, when convinced by overpowering reasons that innovation would be beneficial, consent to it with many misgivings and forebodings.
>
> We find also everywhere another class of men, sanguine in hope, bold in speculation, always pressing forward, quick to discern the imperfection, whatever exists, disposed to think lightly of the risks and inconveniences that attend improvements and disposed to give every change credit for being an improvement.

Laurier counted himself among the latter.

To those who pretended that his Liberalism was camouflaged republicanism, he responded:

> The form matters little; whether it be a monarchist or republican, the moment the people exercise the right to vote, the moment they have responsible government, they have the full measure of liberty.

And with those words he affirmed, solemnly and movingly, who and what he was politically:

> I am a Liberal. I am one of those who think that everywhere, in human beings, there are abuses to be reformed, new horizons to be opened up, and new forces to be developed.

The Liberals in the audience applauded; the others sat on their hands, but only for the moment. When everyone was quiet again, he resumed:

> Our souls are immortal, but our means are limited. We constantly

strive towards an ideal that we never attain. We dream of good, but we never realize the best.

We only reach the goal we have set for ourselves, to discover new horizons opening up, which we had not before even suspected. We rush on towards them and those horizons, explored in turn, reveal to us others that lead us on ever further and further.

And thus it will be, as long as man is what he is, as long as the immortal soul inhabits a mortal body: his desire will be always vaster than his means, and his actions will never rise to the height of his conceptions. He is the Sisyphus of the legend: his work, always finished, must always be begun again.

This condition of our nature is precisely the one that makes the greatness of man: for it condemns him irrevocably to movement, to progress. Our means are limited, but our nature is perfectible and we have the infinite in our arena. Thus, there is always room for the perfecting of our nature and for the attainment by a larger number of an easier way of life.

This, in my eyes, is what constitutes the superiority of Liberalism.

Now the applause was louder. He had already spoken for more than half an hour, yet there was much more he had to say. He sensed that no one was tired of hearing him and that more than one found in his words an inspiration to pursue the exigencies of his dreams. Many, because they had experienced it over and over again, agreed with him: more revolutions have been caused by Conservative obstinacy than by Liberal exaggeration. It was not possible to compress each man's pursuit of liberty and his goals. Whenever it had been attempted, history taught, there was explosion, violence, and ruin.

He found the inspiration for his political activity in two sources: the British Liberal Party and the Canadian Liberal Party. In the former, the reforms undertaken in England by statesmen such as Charles Fox, Daniel O'Connell, Charles Grey, and John Russell were the handiwork of Liberalism. Through them, the oppressed were defended, Catholics obtained the rights and privileges of British subjects, the rule of the landed oligarchy was abolished, the suffrage was extended to the working man, and the Church of England was disestablished as the state religion of Ireland. "Members of the Club canadien, Liberals of the province of Québec," he proclaimed, "there are our models! There are our principles! There is our party!"

In Canada, the Liberal Party was as old as the liberty it fought for. By 1848 all *Canadiens* belonged to it; the split occurred later, leading to exaggerations in language — in the call for a "complete revolution" in the province — on the part of "young men of great talent and still of greater impetuosity of character"; young men who had grown up with the colonial authorities' vengeful abuses towards those who had participated in the Rebellions of 1837 and 1838 and the massive repression imposed on the general population; young men the oldest of whom was hardly twenty-two years of age; and young men on whom the clergy brought down a "merciless war." The English population, "friendly to liberty, but equally friendly to the maintenance of order, also ranged themselves against the new party." Consequently, they and their party, he and his party, were not accepted, not even declared acceptable.

Yet he felt great pride belonging to it, exaggerations and all. It was his party that had, for almost thirty years, "taken the initiative in all the reforms accomplished in that period." In the meantime, "the generation of the Liberals of 1848 had almost entirely disappeared from the scene," and the young of that generation, "now grown into men, disavowed the rashness of their youth." He and his fellow Liberals, the young men of the Club canadien to whom he was speaking on that June night, were still proscribed.

He took a sip of water from the glass on the table next to him and put down the papers he was clutching beside the glass. He scrutinized the audience one more time and, inside, he felt himself smiling. The time had come to attack. Bracing himself firmly on his legs, he said softly, without anger but with *puissance,* to Bourget and Laflèche and the rest of the bishops, to Suzor and the priests who were harassing him and others, to the *Programmistes* and the Conservatives who were putting Cartier to shame:

> You wish to organize a Catholic party. You wish to organize all the
> Catholics in one party, without other bond, without other basis, than
> a common religion.

He felt the anger rising among some in the audience. He stared at them and silenced them with two questions:

> Have you not considered that if you have the misfortune to succeed, you will draw down upon your country calamities of which it is impossible to foresee the consequences?
>
> Have you not reflected that by that very fact you will organize the Protestant population as a single party, and then, instead of the peace and harmony now prevailing between the different elements of the Canadian people, you throw open the door to war, a war of religion, the most terrible of all wars?

They stopped squirming. They were not to rest, however:

> Je vous accuse.... In the face of Canada, I accuse you! You do not understand your country, nor the times in which we live!

The battle cry could not be over until he had dealt with the central issue. The Liberals, he indicated, were accused of wanting "to silence" the bishops and to prevent them "from teaching the people their duties as citizens and electors," and to "relegate the clergy to the sacristy," thus hindering them from sharing in politics. Well:

> In the name of the Liberal Party and of Liberal principles, I repel this assertion. I maintain that there is not one Canadian Liberal who wants to prevent the clergy from taking part in political affairs if they wish to do so.

Laurier was a friend of liberty. He couldn't restrict anyone's liberty of action. It would be an affront to the principles he held most dear and which determined his political career. "No!" he intoned with such force that a few were startled: "Let the priest speak and preach as he thinks best; such is his right, and no Canadian Liberal will dispute that right." He continued:

[But] I am here to speak my whole mind, and I may add that I am far from finding opportune the intervention of the clergy in the domain of politics, as it has been exercised for some years.

I believe, on the contrary, that from the standpoint of the respect due his character, the priest has everything to lose by meddling in the ordinary questions of politics.

Still, his right to do so is indisputable, and if he thinks proper to use it, our duty as Liberals is to guarantee it to him against all denial.

There was, however, a *caveat:*

This right is not unlimited. We have no absolute rights among us. The rights of each man, in our state of society, end precisely where they encroach upon the rights of others.

The right of interference in politics ends at the point where it encroaches upon the elector's independence.

In Laurier's view, in the constitution, and in the law of the country, every man was entitled to the full enjoyment of his opinion. That meant that his opinion could not be forced from him "by fraud, threats, or corruption"; otherwise, government would not be exercised through the consent of the majority. It would be "government by the minority." And that was unacceptable.

I am not one of those who parade themselves as friends and champions of the clergy. However, I say this: like the most of my young fellow countrymen, I have been educated by priests and among young men who have become priests. I flatter myself that I have among them sincere friends, and to them at least I can and do say: Consider whether there is under the sun a country where the Catholic Church is freer or more privileged than it is here!

Why, then, should you, by claiming rights incompatible with our state of society, expose this country to agitations of which the consequences are impossible to foresee?

Softly, and more to himself and to the few seminarians in the crowd, he repeated, "Why?" Then it was time to end:

> I address myself to all my fellow countrymen without distinction, and to them I say: We are a free and happy people, and we are so owing to the Liberal institutions by which we are governed, institutions that we owe to the exertions of our forefathers and the wisdom of the mother country.
>
> The policy of the Liberal Party is to protect these institutions, to defend and extend them, and, under their sway, to develop the latent resources of our country. That is the policy of the Liberal Party. It has no other.
>
> Merci.

He sat down exhausted and drenched. There was a moment of silence. Then two thousand strong, friends and adversaries, clerics and journalists and politicians, the ladies, the young Liberals and seminarians, the doyens of the political parties, the ushers — all were on their feet. The applause was deafening and it went on and on. Finally, he stood up and acknowledged it all. Had Laurier died at 10 p.m. on 26 June 1877, his place in the history of Canada would have been assured.

~

Next day, two priests from the Séminaire de Québec visited a small house in Sainte-Foy near Québec City. They delivered to the papal legate residing there Laurier's speech in its entirety. Bishop Conroy thanked them and went back to his study to ponder what he should do with it.

~

Three months later, on Monday, 8 October, Laurier was sworn in as minister of inland revenue in the Mackenzie administration. He became the Honourable Wilfrid Laurier, PC, MP. Nineteen days after that he was no longer a member of Parliament, for in those days, every member of the House of Commons called to the Cabinet had to undergo the tortures of a by-election on the grounds that his status had changed and his electors had the right to pronounce themselves. Laurier's contest was to take place between his nomination on 8 October and polling day on 27 October.

His speech on political Liberalism had cooled some of the hot heads in the Conservative Party and the press. During the summer months of 1877, political life in Québec was relatively calm. Newspapers laboured, relatively harmlessly, to analyse Laurier's address. For the Liberals, he had set the record straight; for the Conservatives, he had confused the issue. His inspiration, they insisted, didn't come from England but from the radicals and revolutionaries of Europe. And life went on merrily, except that the crops in the province were poor.

Bishop Conroy was putting the final touches to his instructions to the bishops; John A. Macdonald was royally entertained all over the province; an army of Orangemen, with their insignia and flags and bigotry, invaded Montréal in July to make threats that the conquest next time wouldn't be so beneficial to the vanquished; Laurier, like all other politicians, went to picnic after picnic to Zoë's annoyance; Médéric Lanctôt died at the age of forty; and Chapleau, speaking at Saint-Lin at the end of August, hinted that a coalition of talents from both parties was an idea he liked, especially with a man like Laurier.

On 9 October, when Laurier arrived in Arthabaska, it was a rainy day. Not a good beginning. Pacaud had organized a huge demonstration with two hundred carriages and the streets decorated with arches, flags, and bunting. It was still raining at the *assemblée contradictoire* held in L'Avenir, where only seven hundred people came; but the newspapers were well represented, as were both parties. Laurier was seconded by Honoré Mercier; the Conservative candidate by Chapleau. In Laurier, Mercier, and Chapleau, Québec found its most articulate leaders and its greatest orators. The assembly went well for both sides and they all remained friends.

Two days later, on 11 October, Bishop Conroy had his day. Since his arrival in Canada in May, he had been busy attempting to establish a uniform line of conduct among the bishops which they should all adhere to in their relations with political parties. In practice, he was to convince them not to interfere directly in politics and to remember that the pope, in condemning Catholic Liberalism, had not meant to censure political parties that called themselves

Liberal. "All those act wrongly," Rome said, "who, without other resolve, declare that the church condemns one of the political parties in Canada (that called the Reform Party), a party which has already been warmly supported by some of the Bishops themselves." On *influence indue* and the bringing of priests before the civil tribunal, the Holy See pointed out that there would be no need to question the competence of the civil courts if priests never mentioned either party by name and never placed the influence of their ministry at the service of a particular party.

Between May and October, Conroy had visited eastern and central Canada, where he discussed the politico-religious situation with bishops, priests, nuns, politicians, judges, and ordinary citizens. Every day a mass of documents, proposals, counter-proposals, accusations, and justifications appeared on his desk. He saw the prime minister, who was shocked to hear that his political party had been represented in Rome as "an extreme revolutionary party closely related to the Red Republican Communes of France and Italy." In September, having exhausted every source of information, he summoned the provincial bishops to Montréal to approve a new *mandement* he had prepared for them and which he made public on 11 October.

The *mandement* approved the distinction between Catholic Liberalism and political Liberalism which Laurier had made. The individual elector was free to determine in his heart which candidate and which party was best for a Catholic to support. As for the clergy, they were told to stay out of politics, contenting themselves, in public as well as in private, with an explanation of the principles that could guide the electors in their choice. No more claiming it was a sin to vote for the Liberals! No more refusal of the sacraments for political purposes. Laflèche had lost. Laurier had won. But little good it did him.

~

It is quite late. His political allies, his friends, are all in Arthabaska with him for this momentous day: Pacaud, David, Fréchette, and many more. They have just left. Zoë is begging him to go to bed. He cannot! He feels his demons awakening inside him. He has been defeated. His Conservative opponent has received twenty-four more votes than he.

It is hard to take. Defeat always is. This one, tough, more than all his other setbacks. He is totally torn apart. No one — not even Zoë — knows how much. It was so unexpected. Again, everything about him is in shambles, shattered, and he will have to decide whether he will pick up the pieces or not. It will not be an easy decision.

"This is much too hard!" he whispers.

Yet he smiles. His hand had not trembled as he lifted his glass, after the announcement, to propose a toast to better days; and he had remained calm and composed. Yet, inside, he cried.

An hour later, he is still there, sitting alone. Zoë finds him in tears and racked with a pain that shakes every part of his body. Caught in a fit of coughing, his breathing is irregular and short and, it seems to her, that he is almost incapable of producing it. She wants to call the doctor. He begs her not to. So she gathers him in her arms and, rocking him back and forth, like the baby she never had, she talks softly to him. Gradually, her words begin to penetrate his being and to make sense:

C'est l'histoire de ta vie! You will rise again and undo this terrible wrong. You're too fatalistic . . . So am I when it comes to you.

Remember: ten years ago I told you that if I had only two years of happiness with you, I would be satisfied. We both believed then that you had only two years to live . . . Bien! We have been married almost ten years. And I still have you . . . and I'm still happy.

Alors! Prends ton courage à deux mains! You have lived beyond your expectations. You have achieved things you only dreamed of at the Collège and at McGill, when I was less in love with you than I am now.

Viens, mon Wilfrid. Tomorrow will come soon. And your courage will carry you forward. I'll be there! *Tu as encore tes idées à défendre.* They haven't taken your ideas away! You still have them! You need to defend them! *Viens. Ça ne fait que recommencer!*

He allows her to put him to bed, in their bed. And he sleeps a fretful night, the cats and dogs, their "children," all quiet about them.

~

What did happen between 8 and 27 October 1877? Was he too confident of victory? Was he as well prepared as he should have been? Was his organization sloppy? Was he at his best?

At the beginning of the campaign, it was the common wisdom of his political friends that the Conservatives would pay him the courtesy of not opposing him. There were precedents to that effect, both in Great Britain and in Québec. Laurier thought otherwise. Bishop Laflèche would certainly not permit it. Furthermore, the Conservatives needed to get at Mackenzie through him. If they could defeat him, it would be a sign that the Liberals were on their way out. And if they could cut him down to size before he got really started, so much the better. "I will be opposed," he told Zoë sadly. To the others he added more cheerfully, "The struggle awaits me. I am ready."

Laurier was right on both counts. Again he became the target of the *Programmistes* and the curés, with an assist from the moderate Conservatives. Again he was a Liberal of the worst kind, the friend of Garibaldi, and an ally of Guibord. Again he was a rebel and a revolutionary condemned by the pope and the bishops in their episcopal letters. This time, though, something new was added. Laurier, a *ministre* of the crown, was transformed into a minister of the Protestant faith, a Presbyterian at that! It was further alleged — and taken seriously — that he had refused to have his children baptized. It was obvious to the whole country that he had no children, but it made no difference. Zoë laughed at the accusation, but she didn't when she read somewhere that her husband was of the opinion that priests ought to marry. When things got a little dull, the English population of the constituency was told he had once belonged to a secret society that was sworn to crush the English race on the American continent. Irish Catholics were informed he had become an Orangeman.

On the first day of the war — for a war it was — Israël Tarte was sent from Québec City to run the Conservative campaign. Every Conservative, young and old, feeble and sturdy, *Programmiste* or not, Tarte could dislodge from somewhere in the province arrived as well. Adolphe Chapleau came in a special train loaned to him by Louis-Adélard Sénécal, and Arthur Dansereau made a few appearances and bombarded them all with inflammatory articles and pronouncements.

Charles Thibault, a most infuriating man, sat in the bishop's *calèche*, always with a telegram of some sort from the Vatican encouraging the electors to vote against Laurier. They were busy all over the place. Tarte mounted a courier system using the young men of the Club Cartier from Montréal. Sénécal, who had switched his political allegiance because Mackenzie had refused to make him a senator, arrived the last weekend with two rich friends. They proceeded to buy everything that walked; liquor flowed endlessly; and fights broke out even in the schools, where the pupils fought the election by tearing up rivals' textbooks and giving each other bloody noses. The adults were not much better.

Laurier gave them as much as he received. Ernest Pacaud was in charge and he, too, knew what to do. Night and day, Liberals arrived from everywhere in Québec. Members of the Club canadien of Québec City and the Club national of Montréal invaded the towns, cities, and quiet countryside to carry messages, round out voters, harangue the crowds, and interrupt and boo the Conservatives. Pacaud kept them all on track. He was as good as Tarte.

Meetings were generally well attended. On nomination day, five thousand people came to hear the *gros canon*s of both sides. They stayed for the entire seven hours that it took. Unfortunately, there was a fight and a Liberal from Victoriaville was wounded. He died a few days later. There were many *assemblées contradictoires* devoted largely to the religious evils of Liberalism and little to political substance. Liberals composed songs, the most famous of which was:

> Pas d'Thibault! Pas d'Thibault!
> C'est Laurier qu'il nous faut!

Tarte, not to be outdone, wrote one of his own which was all about a crow holding in its beak a faded "laurier," or leaf, which the good people of Arthabaska would have no use for:

> Maître Corbeau, sur un arbre perché
> Tenait dedans son bec un laurier tout fané
>
> . . .
>
> Eh quoi, dit il, les gens d'Arthabaska
> Ne voudront pas du laurier que voilà!

In the early days of the campaign, Laurier was confident. Even as late as 22 October he was able to write to Mackenzie that "everything is going well. The only thing I fear is bribery. If there is no bribery the majority cannot be less than 300." It was only in the last week that it dawned on him and Pacaud that he could lose. He redoubled his efforts, but too much had already been said and too many had been bought with the $5000 Sénécal and his prosperous pals had contributed. In a constituency of 3200 registered voters, Tarte managed to have 3800 vote. That extra six hundred came from outside Drummond-Arthabaska, with all their expenses paid in addition to the Sénécal bonus. And the federal Liberals did little to help him. Thus, Laurier lost by twenty-four votes. A year later, the courts annulled the election when the Conservatives officially admitted that they had bought many votes.

~

At the beginning of November Laurier went to Montréal to meet Mackenzie. Their interview didn't go very well. Laurier thought that the prime minister blamed him, and only him, for the defeat. When Mackenzie talked of overconfidence, Laurier reminded him, somewhat angrily, that, having won in 1874 with such a comfortable majority, he felt himself entitled to assume that he could make it this time as well. He didn't mention the obvious facts that the government was not well liked and that the party had put little effort into his being reelected.

What galled Laurier was the open bribery. He showed Mackenzie, with Pacaud's figures and charts, how the three largest parishes in the county of Drummond — Saint-Guillaume, Sainte-Germaine, and Saint-Bonaventure — had been bought. Pacaud had calculated that they would have a 150-vote majority there. On the Friday night before the election, Sénécal had arrived with two other railway contractors for the provincial government. They went on buying votes as in the old days. His majority in these parishes was reduced to two votes. It was the same everywhere. It was amazing that he lost by so few votes.

Meanwhile, Pacaud had gone to Québec City to look for a seat. Laurier was offered three: Québec-Centre, Québec-Est, and Iberville. He decided on Québec-Est. If he were to run again, Laurier wrote to Mackenzie, the party had to help with its prestige and its funds: "I am the last card of the party in this province. If I am sent down the party is well nigh gone down completely . . .

I cannot undertake a new fight unless we are determined to carry it."

Mackenzie, who had doubts about appointing Laurier to the Cabinet in the first place, consulted widely before engaging the party. By the middle of the first week of November, he agreed to Laurier's terms. Pacaud was ready. It would be Québec-Est. The incumbent resigned almost immediately. A special train took Pacaud, a remarkable man by the name of François Langelier, and a group of electors from the constituency to Arthabaska to offer Laurier the Liberal nomination. With Zoë smiling at his side, he accepted, and the same train took him to Québec City and yet another campaign. He would stay with Langelier, who promised Zoë that he would look after his candidate well.

Québec-Est became the political centre of the country. The Liberals strained every nerve to get Laurier elected — as did the Conservatives to get him defeated. John A. Macdonald gave orders to his Québec lieutenant, Hector Langevin, that "no pains should be spared to beat Laurier. See all our friends. Explain to them how much depends on the victory." He even asked one of his henchmen, the contractor Thomas McGreevy, to spend much but to spend it wisely. Chapleau was dispatched to Montréal to raise funds. He wasn't very successful with the *Canadiens*. After a week of labour, he had only $500 from French-speaking merchants and partisans. But he had more than $5000 from English-speaking businessmen who wanted to make a point about protection by helping to defeat Laurier.

Laurier and the Liberals had learned their lesson. They left it to the Conservatives to be overconfident. The young men of the Liberal clubs, the old patrons of the party, the rank and file who filled Québec-Est, and the students who skipped their classes and gave up their sleep were determined to do what needed to be done — and as legally as possible. They would be even tougher than the Conservatives; they would be everywhere; and always — *toujours* — this time around they would be ahead of their enemies. They would know where every vote was and they would see that it was registered on polling day, when they would challenge everyone they had not met, talked to, and inspired. They would not let a single attack go unrefuted. Laurier would spend his time talking about protection and free trade, and how the federal government could help to solve local problems. He promised, for instance, that the government would negotiate with France the entry of Canadian ships in French ports on the same conditions that prevailed for British ships. Above all, the Conservatives, who were running a businessman, were not to be left to argue that Laurier, as a free trader, would ruin industries, force factories to close, and send the working men to ruin and perdition. Rather, Laurier explained that protection was an additional tax on bread, coal, and every other basic necessity of daily life. People listened.

In one of his charges, Thibault, for the first time in his career, became exasperated with the crowd. Every time he opened his mouth to speak, thousands of others opened to sing over and over again and in cadence:

Thibault est à l'eau
Dondon
Thibault est noyé
Dondé!

Finally, he lost it. He uttered words so horrible that even the Conservatives disowned him. He dared to state publicly that Madame Laurier disliked her husband. It wasn't true, he hastened to explain. It wasn't what he had meant to say. But it was unacceptable, nevertheless. Women didn't have the right to vote and they were not to be sullied in the political arena, especially by name. Chivalry would not permit it. Five days before the end of the campaign, Thibault left in a hurry.

Since Québec-Est was under the vigilant eye of the archbishop of Québec and not the pontiff of Trois-Rivières, the clergy kept quiet. It was a blessing and allowed for a more rational discussion of the worth not only of the candidates, but also of party policies.

All through the campaign Laurier felt confident, but not overly so. He didn't know Québec-Est well, but the Langelier brothers, François and Charles, guided him through all the pitfalls. They advised him on what to say, how to please, and when to mention the name of his predecessor, who was well liked in the county and was owed many debts. By 23 November, the newspapers reported that the Conservatives had no show, and Laurier wrote to Mackenzie that the election was assured. Everybody breathed a sigh of relief.

On Wednesday, 28 November, the men of Québec-Est went to vote. Both sides were confident of victory. The fifth Battalion of volunteers had taken its position in Jacques-Cartier Square, while the B Battery was confined to barracks in case of a serious disturbance. Three hundred special constables had been hired to help the provincial police, whose responsibility it was to guard every polling station. The members of the local police force were kept in reserve. More young Liberals arrived on the night train from Montréal and places in between, a little worse for wear. Betting was ferocious and, apparently, favoured the Conservative candidate.

Election day was a cliff-hanger. By 11:00 a.m. balloting was lively everywhere and fights had broken out. The election was hard to call, but the Conservative was said to be ahead. By 1:00 p.m. everything was quiet in Québec-Est and the Québec *Chronicle* announced a victory for Laurier by seventy votes. Then the working men were said to be going strong for the Conservatives. By 2:15 p.m. five hundred people had voted in the previous hour. The Conservatives claimed that the day was theirs: 862 for their candidate; 725 for Laurier. At nightfall, after the closing of the polls, the final count was 1864 for the Liberals and 1548 for the Conservatives. Laurier would go to bed with a majority of 316. The Liberals arranged for a special train to take him home to Arthabaska and then on to Ottawa.

Before Laurier was allowed to rest, however, there had to be a celebration. Torches were lit and a mile-long procession was formed. He proclaimed for the whole country to hear: "I have unfurled the Liberal standard above the ancient citadel of Québec, and there I will keep it waving." He kept his promise. He represented the electors of Québec-Est until his death in 1919.

The triumphal train got under way on Saturday, 1 December. Close to six thousand persons saw him off to the ferry that took him to the train station in Lévis, where one thousand more cheered him. Many of his friends were on the train with him, and they stayed on it while he rested with Zoë and received the congratulations of his friends, the addresses of the *notables* of Arthabaska, a warm letter from the parish priest, and telegrams of joy and loyalty from everywhere in the country. He also took the time to write to his family back in Saint-Lin announcing his good news. By the time the letter arrived there, Carolus had read of his victory in the newspapers and Maman Adeline had gone to church to light a lampion of thanksgiving.

He parted from Zoë again and went down to Montréal via Saint-Hyacinthe, with several stops along the way. Everywhere there were banquets or receptions, and speeches and more speeches. When the train travelled in the night, farmers lit fires in their fields to herald the victory. In Montréal there were processions and congratulations and accolades. They all took pride that he had gone to the very door of the Conservative government in Québec and had beaten it at its own game. What did that single act not hold for the future?

On the evening of Wednesday, 5 December, Laurier neared his destination. In Prescott, a delegation from Ottawa that included the mayor and both a French-speaking and an English-speaking Liberal member of Parliament boarded the train and travelled with him to the capital. Flares and fireworks lit the track all the way. Once arrived, he was cheered and complimented. He responded in kind, speaking too long, no doubt, for it was pouring rain. After his speech, a procession formed: first came a fireworks van, next a band, and then two carriages; Laurier rode in an open landau, drawn by four white horses, getting soaked to the skin; following him were four more carriages, six cabs, another band, five cabs, a band, nine cabs, yet another band, seven private carriages, and many citizens on foot. The parade took them through the main streets of the city, as the fireworks van sent out Roman candles and other coloured lights. At the prime minister's house, where Laurier was to stay for a few days, the Mackenzies came out on their porch to greet him. Laurier made yet another speech in both languages, and Mackenzie prophesied that the Liberal flag which Laurier had caused to fly over Québec would also float in triumph over every capital in the Confederation. Before he bid them all goodnight, he led them in three cheers for the queen. For Laurier, however, there was still a reception at the private home of a Liberal supporter. He was not feeling well.

In mid December, Laurier returned to Arthabaska to Zoë, to the cats and dogs and birds and fish, to the family that came for Christmas, and to his sick bed. He spent most of December there, and for the rest of the winter of 1878 he was hardly of any use to his government or his party during the session. He was almost useless as well during the provincial elections held in May, which saw a Liberal government installed in Québec. By June there was talk of a federal election, and Laurier was determined that he would not be caught unawares. Mackenzie, however, delayed calling the election until 17 September. The campaign galvanized Laurier's energy and overcame the *indolence* he had felt since the previous November. He travelled from one constituency to the next and undertook his first tour of Ontario. He came back with the strong conviction that the government was going to be defeated. When he mentioned his fear to Mackenzie, the prime minister took out his charts to prove him wrong. Laurier, as practically the entire party, wasn't convinced, but the electoral activity went on and he nurtured Québec-Est. A frantic Zoë worried about his re-election and the money to pay for it all. Three days before the elections, he wrote to her, telling her not to worry. The money was in hand. "Ne t'alarmes pas! All is going well. In three days it will be over."

And it was. The Liberals elected 69 members; the Conservatives, 137. Macdonald was in; Mackenzie was out. In Québec, the Liberals lost thirteen seats. Laurier was victorious by 778 votes. On 9 November he was no longer a minister of Her Majesty, Queen Victoria. The Liberals would not see power again until Laurier brought them there eighteen years later.

6

ZOË, WILFRID, AND ÉMILIE

unday, 26 June 1881, was going to be a nice, clear day with only a light wind. Émilie Lavergne, the wife of Laurier's legal partner, woke up early to nurse her sixteen-month-old son, Armand, and soothe her daughter, Gabrielle, before turning them over to the maid and going back to bed. An hour later her husband, Joseph, woke up. The family had to get itself organized for one of the most important social events of the week: the High Mass. Suddenly, Émilie remembered.

"Joseph, c'est l'anniversaire de Zoë," she said to her husband.

"Mais oui. I know that. She's forty today. There is a *fête* for the children this afternoon, then dinner for the adults at 8:00 tonight."

The High Mass was at 10: a.m. They walked to it arm in arm, greeting their neighbours and friends along the way. The hill to the church was hard to climb, so the ladies had time to admire one anothers' *toilette*. Shortly before the Mass was to begin, the Lauriers arrived in their *fiacre* and walked to the pew they bought every year. With them were Carolus and Maman Adeline, with two of their children and one grandchild, and the Gauthiers.

Everyone in the church seemed to be aware of Zoë's birthday. They smiled at her fondly. The Mass was uneventful — Father Suzor having left the parish in 1878 — and the sermon rather boring. But the organ music was engaging, for the organist, Roméo Poisson, didn't hesitate to mix the religious with the profane. While Zoë received Holy Communion, her husband stayed in his pew. After the service, many proffered their congratulations and good wishes. Zoë kissed Émilie on both cheeks, reminding her not to forget to bring the children around at three for the *fête*. Then she went home.

La fête was a great success. The *famille* was all here.

Carolus looks frail. He is now sixty-six. Still the same, though: interested, keen to learn what he does not already know, and aware of what goes on, but suspicious of any form of authority. "When the Liberals are back in power," he advises us, "the politicians will remember to exercise authority wisely. It will be a novelty."

Zoë tells me I am just like him. Good! Except that I do not tell jokes as comfortably as he does — and I do not have his inventiveness with children. Too bad!

Would he be the secret carrier of my disease? It has dawned on me. Always, I thought it was my mother, but no Martineaus, as far as I know, have had problems with their lungs. All of Carolus's children, on the other hand, have weak lungs. My sister, Malvina, died when she was eleven and I almost did often enough — and probably will in a not too distant future. Of Carolus's five children with Maman Adeline, Doctorée is generally weak; Romuald-Charlemagne is said to be healthy now, but was often ill in his youth; Ubald is certainly not long for this world; Carolus has always coughed; and only Henri has never complained. He is a fine-looking young man of eighteen who loves Arthabaska and wants to come and live here. I hope he will.

My friend Oscar Archambault, his wife, and their three children arrived last night on the train with David and Fréchette. They spent the whole time, I am told, talking philosophy and poetry. I will not let them talk religion.

The Lavergnes came to the fête and will come back for dinner along with all the Pacauds, the Poissons, and the other friends. So many people are coming and going all day that we have had to hire additional help. Otherwise, Zoë and I would be prostrate, along with the two servants.

At the *fête* for the children, Ubald was in great form. Regardless of gender, he organized them in platoons to storm the hill in the park, with Émilie walking with Armand all dressed up in a military uniform. She ruined her shoes! Later, with Henri as marshall, there was a parade. The boys had been ordered to bring their *charrette à deux roues*, a two-wheeled wagonette. The girls decorated them and were pushed in all their finery around Zoë and Oscar, who served as judges. There were races of all kinds and games; a talent show that Joseph produced; then ice cream and cake. We had a pleasant surprise. Aurèle

Suzor-Côté brought Zoë a painting of the valley as seen from the top of our hill. He is twelve years old and he paints with such fervour! Zoë has decided to adopt him.

By five o'clock the children went home, so the adults could rest and dress for dinner, which is at eight.

Zoë and I love Arthabaska. There is a peace in this nature that invigorates me. I tend to be more serene here than anywhere else, and I always long to come back to it. That will be so for the rest of my life. The trees, the flowers, the air — they remind me of the times I walked with my mother near the forest or in the fields in Saint-Lin. There is also time to read and to prepare what I must do. Arthabaska is the centre of my universe. I am elated that I settled here and that Zoë came to live with me, here, as my wife.

~

For the first ten years of their married life, Laurier and Zoë lived in rented rooms in the Poisson household. In 1876 they bought about eight acres of land on the rue de l'Église, where they built a house and moved into it two years later. It was two storeys high, almost directly across from the Lavergnes and their legal office, and three miles from the railway station. It was made of brick and exuded comfort. Situated some fifty feet from the street, with tall maples flanking both sides of the winding drive, it had seven steps in the front leading to a narrow *perron* adorned with white columns. On the second floor there was a balcony with a delicate rail around it, and a round Roman dormer window just below the pyramid roof. The windows were high and elegant, and a verandah ran across the back of the house. In summer it was always filled with flowers, and the Lauriers would spend hours there, reading, having a quiet lunch, resting in their rocking chairs, and entertaining. It was also the only place where Zoë would allow smoking. Entering the house through a tall double door, guests and visitors found themselves in a wide hall with a tall carpeted staircase leading to the second floor. On the left was the drawing room, which ran the entire length of the house. It had a large fireplace, silver silk curtains, and, like the rest of the house, it was filled with the Louis XVI furniture Zoë favoured, good art by local artists, and her piano. On the right of the hall was the parlor, the dining room, and the kitchen at the rear. Upstairs were the library, the bedrooms, and the bathroom.

Laurier's favourite room was his library. It was his meditation room, where he could read his beloved books undisturbed, keep the mementoes of his life, and make important decisions. Few were invited into the library: David always, Ernest Pacaud from time to time, Émilie never. In antique glassed-in bookcases, he kept a fine collection of French and English authors, many works of philosophy, a few of theology, and several volumes of poetry, speeches, and other books of rhetoric. On the walls were portraits of the famous Liberals he knew and of his family.

Behind the house, the park was covered with maples and elms. Zoë loved it as it was and she refused to have it manicured. In the middle was a little hill, or elevation, with a flight of stairs adjacent to it. From that height, there was a splendid view of the valley and of Mont Saint-Christophe and, not too far away, Mont Saint-Michel.

That house was the oasis and the refuge of his life, and he came back to it as often as he could. It sheltered him from the storms raging within and without; it calmed and soothed his demons; and, through it, he reached out to Zoë, his family, his friends, and, above all, the children. He had none of his own, but he and Zoë adopted those of others. They would come for what she called *la fête* — parties, sporting events, and picnics. Over the years, Zoë's half-sister, Mathilda-Georgina, commonly known as Maggie, lived with them for a while, as did Emma Gauthier-Coutu's daughter, Yvonne; and there was always a half-brother, a nephew, or a grandniece to brighten the Lauriers' state of mind and lighten their hearts. Every creature, big and small, human or not, was welcome in their home.

~

When Laurier arrived in Arthabaska in the fall of 1867, he found an active social life and met many of the *notables* of the place: the Beauchesnes, the Garneaus, the Béliveaus, and others who were rich country folk, independent of judgment, tenacious, and interesting. Over the years, business friends came his way along with professionals, lawyers, notaries, and doctors like the Cannons, the Pacauds, the Poissons. Later, there were the artists whom Zoë nurtured and accepted and courted. He was also involved in the political swirl, at the centre of which were the Pacauds, a large family of fourteen siblings: seven brothers and seven sisters. Five of the brothers lived in the Bois-Francs: the ultra-Conservative newspaper in the area described them as the seven plagues of Egypt, the seven capital sins, the seven Maccabees. All gave good parties, bringing together around a bottle of port the best Liberal minds and personalities of the region. Laurier was generally present at these gatherings. Three of the brothers played a significant part in Laurier's early life in Arthabaska.

Édouard-Louis Pacaud (or Louis-Édouard, as he was sometimes referred to) was the dean of the Arthabaska bar when Laurier arrived there. He was rich, powerful, controversial, and drove Father Suzor to madness. Pacaud liked Laurier immediately and was instrumental in convincing him to run for the Québec legislature in 1871 and, three years later, for the House of Commons — in both instances pacifying Zoë. The notary Philippe-Napoléon Pacaud also lived in the vicinity of Arthabaska in the 1860s. He sent cases in Laurier's direction, hosted parties, and sued his parish priest. He was the father of Laurier's long-time friend and election agent, Ernest. Lastly, there was another brother, Georges-Jérémie, who had caused great scandal when he and his family left the church on the declaration of the pope's infallibility in 1869. He was rumoured to live in a haunted house, but superstition could not deter Laurier from visiting and listening to Madame Pacaud play the piano.

Ernest Pacaud came to live in Arthabaska in 1870 to practise law and, a year later, he founded *Le Journal d'Arthabaska,* which he edited until his departure for Trois-Rivières in 1877. Laurier contributed frequently to Pacaud's paper, as he did also to *L'Electeur,* which Pacaud established in Québec City in 1880. Pacaud was younger and much smaller than Laurier, darker, not as handsome, and he grew a mighty moustache. Full of energy and enthusiasm, he was always excited and catapulted everyone into his activities, some of which were rather suspect. Pacaud admired Laurier and, where the latter agonized over decisions, the former arrived at them too quickly. He was also as superb a political organizer as Tarte — and as tireless. Laurier was convinced that Pacaud had changed his life by forcing him to take politics seriously. Pacaud never doubted that Laurier would be the greatest statesman Canada ever produced, and the best prime minister. Laurier might have a genius for making friends, a charm to draw people into his circle, an intellectual grasp of the issues, and an astounding rhetorical capacity, but Pacaud would contribute the practicality and the dogged loyalty that marked the Pacaud clan. He taught Laurier everything that was to be known about the day-to-day practice of politics: how to get votes, how to buy electors, how to use patronage, how to do things that were sometimes deplorable but necessary, and how to handle the bitter disappointments that a political career made inevitable. Often Pacaud was not prudent enough for Laurier's taste and he embroiled himself in actions that were *malhonnêtes*, but Laurier preferred not to know about them.

When Laurier first opened his law practice in Arthabaska, he had an absentee partner by the name of Eugène Crépeau, a Conservative in politics and a good conversationalist. They shared an office, but hardly worked together. By 1870 that partnership was dissolved. Laurier, however, maintained his association with the third partner, Édouard Richard. Again the partnership was more nominal than real. Richard was an invalid who was unable to read because of some terrible brain tumour. Yet he went regularly to the office, had an encyclopedic knowledge of the law, and was an avid politician. In spite of what he called his *défaut de santé* or poor health, he ran as a Liberal in the federal elections of 1872 and 1874 for Mégantic, where he was elected. In 1878 he refused to let his name stand and he left for Winnipeg, and then Battleford and Regina in the North-West Territories. He soon became rich and, when he published his two-volume history of the Acadians in 1895, he was an author of international fame.

The first effective legal partnership Laurier had was with Joseph Lavergne, from 1874 until 1897, even though Laurier, after becoming leader of the Liberal Party in 1887, spent less and less time working as a lawyer. Lavergne, aged twenty-seven when he began, was six years younger than Laurier. He was a quiet man, efficient, indefatigable, and loyal. He was a friend of the Pacauds and had his entrée in all their houses. Ernest, no doubt, introduced him to Laurier sometime in 1872. They continued to meet at various soirées — Lavergne, being a bachelor, was much in demand. Zoë found him a kindred soul, for his interest in politics at that time was marginal; he was an actor, and he preferred to think the best of people. In 1874, when it became obvious that Richard would never be an active partner, Laurier invited Lavergne to join the firm. He soon became a friend and the partnership flourished. Their office had four small rooms, and the only person with a window was the clerk, who faced the street. In the back there was a large wooden stove that kept them warm in winter. The heat circulated above them, reaching them through holes in the walls.

The Pacauds were determined to marry Lavergne off and they introduced him to a relative who came to visit, a lady Laurier had encountered before he was married. She was about nineteen then and had flirted with him and every other man at the party. He soon forgot her, except for the fact that she was quite opinionated. Émilie Barthe was born in Montréal in 1847, the daughter of the writer Joseph-Guillaume Barthe. He was a *Rouge* politician and had been imprisoned for three months in 1839. Later, the family had lived in Paris for a few years. The Pacauds were successful in their matchmaking, and Joseph and Émilie were married on 29 November 1876 in Arthabaska. Émilie met Zoë for the first time at the wedding and renewed her acquaintance with Laurier. The Pacauds helped to buy the large house in which the Lavergnes moved after their wedding. It was on the same street as the Lauriers, but closer to the parish church.

Émilie was not a beautiful or even a pretty woman. Her teeth were crooked and she was rather short, but she appeared taller because she always walked with her head held high and ever so gracefully. Her eyes were almost yellow but large, she tended to *avoir-du-poids*, and she was bitchy as hell. But she dressed magnificently. She bought clothes designed in Paris and their arrival at the house always caused a sensation. Lavergne was summoned from his office and the servants assembled, together with the children once they were old enough. The boxes, wrapped in an expensive black tissue, were solemnly opened. The dresses were removed with a cackle of Ahs! and Ohs! and, after many exhortations, Émilie would rush upstairs with the maid and return a half-hour later decked out for the conquest.

Her reputation as a seductress — a reputation concocted largely out of nothing by romance-starved Canadians and *Canadiens* — has come from certain qualities Émilie exhibited in public: her gaiety, her body language, and her *coquetterie* — that feminine virtue that makes a little go far. She was a good conversationalist, she read a great number of novels and *romans feuilletons* mostly in French, and she had the knack of remembering everything she read, or overheard, or was told — an advantageous gift in a woman such as Émilie. She knew how to please a man and to destroy an adversary, and she had a genius for picking friends and managing connections. She was also opinionated, judgmental, fond of ridiculing others, and dismissed everything that was not European or British. For her, only the English knew how to eat, how to dress, how to serve tea, how to behave in the living room, how to manage a house, and how to be a superb hostess. She was all that. She had acquired this admiration for all things British in Montréal. She didn't seem to mind that this obsession was directed at a group that had jailed her father and at least two of her uncles. If she had not been such a devout Catholic, she would have made a spectacular femme fatale.

She settled well in Arthabaska society, playing the perfect hostess, the kind matron, the considerate wife. She helped with bazaars, treated her servants well, and doted on her children. She had two, Gabrielle, born in 1878, and the "incorrigible" Armand, as he was fondly referred to, followed in 1880. For the rest of his life, Laurier, who was not Armand's father or godfather, took a parental interest in both of them — and was disappointed.

As luck would have it, Zoë liked Émilie. In so far as these things mattered to her, she saw herself as physically more attractive than Émilie. Granted, Zoë didn't walk or dress like Émilie and was never at home in high society, but she had a great capacity to learn — and she did, her natural poise ensuring her success. In Émilie she found her exact opposite, as if Émilie completed her. Émilie's gaiety, vivaciousness, and aplomb only served to enhance Zoë's qualities of devotion to the large family she had adopted and the simplicity of her lifestyle. She knew herself to be sound of judgment, to be clear in her objectives, and to accept the inevitable with faith and confidence; she certainly didn't need Émilie to teach her how to cook English food. Émilie fashioned the future; Zoë lived to fulfil it. Zoë was unpretentious; Émilie wanted to be not only a duchess in Britain but *la grande dame* of Arthabaska. Zoë had no pretension to be any of that. With the same determination she used to teach herself English when circumstances demanded it and become the first art patroness of Canada, she had more or less taught herself to play the piano, cook and garden, maintain a well-kept house, receive guests with grace, care for animals, and entertain.

All through her life with Laurier, Zoë was pleased with what she was doing and with who she was. She was constantly involved in parish bazaars, in raising funds, and in organizing *fêtes* for the children of her friends in the parish. One time when she was raising funds for a cause dear to the curé Suzor's heart,

Lavergne told Laurier that the priest, who had been ill, was recuperating in direct proportion to the funds raised. Laurier was unable to keep a straight face. "If you manage to raise $800," he wrote to her, "you will add twenty years to his life. If it is $1000, he will live until he is one hundred and twenty." She didn't consume books as Wilfrid or Émilie did, but she kept up with what was going on politically and she read everything written about her husband. From the earliest moment of their marriage, she made herself familiar with the kind of life he led, the causes he espoused, and the political world in which he lived. She was also quite shrewd about politics, and her sound judgment and almost prophetic analysis helped him considerably. To be Laurier's wife was quite enough for Zoë.

He wrote to her almost every day from wherever his legal practice, his family obligations, and his political duties took him. When she travelled to Montréal to see the Gauthiers, he gave her news of their "children," whom they cherished together and for whom they had names like Ti-Paze, Delphine, Fanny, and Aurèlie. "Mademoiselle Topsy," he explained in one letter, "is determined to take the place of her mistress in our bed. Ah! This child gives me much torment. Twenty times a day, I must let her out; then let her in; she must be fed breakfast, dinner, supper: I pity those who have large families." When one of these animals died, he grieved with her, and they would love the others even more. They were most choosy about the family or child to whom they gave their offspring.

Zoë had, therefore, no anxiety in tolerating the relationship between Émilie and Laurier that began shortly after the Lavergne wedding and which matured over the years. In more ways than one, she encouraged it. Zoë was no fool. She knew well that she couldn't be all things to Laurier: he was a many-faceted man — and a most insecure one. She would nurture his soul and take care of his body; Émilie could satisfy his mind and intellect. She had no fear that he would overstep the line. She knew him to be attractive to women and they to him, but she also realized that his normal indolence wouldn't get him into trouble. She dismissed with a smile the rumours and the innuendoes. She knew her Wilfrid! And she never misread Émilie.

What of Laurier? As he got to know Émilie better in the 1880s, they developed an intimate relationship that became vital to their well-being. Unfortunately it was then — and has been ever since — misconstrued by some of their neighbours and acquaintances, by social gossips, journalists, and historians in search of romance. From the intense platonic attachment they had for each other, their relationship mushroomed into the Canadian love affair of the century. It even came equipped with a love-child.

Laurier's relationship with Émilie was a public fact and it was well known in Arthabaska and in Ottawa. When he was away during the sessions of Parliament, he wrote to her as often as three times a month. Forty or so of these letters, dated 1890–93, have survived, plus a few thereafter. During the first decade of her marriage, Émilie and Laurier had little opportunity to spend time together without the scrutiny of others. But they enjoyed each other's company and saw each other as often as they could. Both prone to loneliness, misunderstanding, and solitary pursuits, Émilie found in Laurier someone with whom she could share her interests. They gossiped and she made formidable judgments about their friends and neighbours. They read out loud to each other and exchanged books; she introduced him to light reading, and he presented her with a more intellectual diet. She learned fast, was interested in everything, and did her homework. She was the first woman he could converse with about topics and issues that captivated him. She amused him. He liked her clothes, her joie de vivre, her irreverence, and her independence of spirit. Like her, he admired English ways, and he may even have been a greater anglophile than she was. Certainly he was intellectually.

Sex didn't enter into their relationship. He liked women, he admired them, he sought their company, and it pleased him when women were attracted to him. He was a most competent flirt. But neither Laurier nor Émilie was prepared to throw away their future by endangering the present. She couldn't contemplate a life without her children — a certain fate should she become an adulteress. As for Laurier, he was desperate to reach the *cime de la montagne* — the highest pinnacle possible.

~

By 1884 Laurier's finances were in good shape. The legal practice was prospering and, each year, was bringing in three to four thousand dollars for him. In addition, he had his parliamentary indemnity, which he considered satisfactory. He was careful with his pennies (he had inherited that from his grandfather) and invested them well — never, though, without Zoë's participation. They exchanged financial opinions and information, and they discussed their separate assets, leaving them both entirely free to do as they wanted with them. She worried constantly, however, that there would not be enough. They managed somehow to meet the financial objective they had given to themselves: to have adequate capital *sous la main*. He consulted the best stockbrokers and money traders, and they found him quite astute. It was important for him to have money, capital. He once admitted to Zoë: "Avec l'argent on est à l'abri de tout ce qu'il y a de plus fâcheux dans la vie"—With money one is secure from the misfortunes of life. What he desired most was to work hard as a lawyer and watch his profits accumulate, slowly but surely. He admitted with satisfaction that he had not much money, but enough "pour me payer des caprices" — for small and unnecessary luxuries.

As for his old age and Zoë's security after his death, there was, beside whatever capital he was gathering, the $3000 policy he was able to procure for the first time in 1884. In addition, throughout his life, he was a member of the Independent Order of Foresters. As such, he would receive old age benefits when the time came.

~

As a member of Parliament, Laurier was obliged to live in Ottawa part of the year. On average, the sessions were about three months in length, from February until some time in May. Prior to 1885, there were not many express trains and the journey from Arthabaska to Ottawa was tiring. It meant taking the train in Arthabaska in the middle of the night, arriving in Montréal at about 6:30 in the morning, and leaving again at 8:00 a.m. to get to Ottawa some five or six hours later. Often the trains were late; the Pullman Palace service, however, tended to be efficient and pleasant. The return journey was about the same. On his arrival either in Ottawa or in Arthabaska, he was always exhausted. Often he didn't reserve a berth, and when he did, the poor condition of the bed caused him much discomfort.

The capital city of Canada had nothing distinctive about it apart from the Parliament Buildings, for there was little that couldn't be found in every other Canadian city of comparable size. It was, in fact as well as in spirit, a mishmash of four distinct towns: a Lower Town, with its market and houses built in the style of those found in Montréal; a Centre Town, which served as the business core of the city; a Sandy Hill area, which was reserved for an élite who built large houses in imitation of British castles and churches in the Gothic tradition; and an Upper Town, where Parliament was located, along with the more fashionable hotels on Sparks Street.

The place was also drowning in garbage, the sewers being unable to absorb all the refuse. The stench sometimes was unbearable. The Ottawa of the 1880s didn't in the least look like the capital of a booming country: the railway cut the city in pieces; dirt was a fact of daily existence; electricity didn't arrive in the streets until 1885, and the horse-drawn tramways were only slowly replaced by electric ones; Sparks Street was struggling to become the Broadway of Ottawa; and, though the market area was alive, it was difficult to police.

Until he became prime minister in 1896, Laurier stayed at the Russell Hotel at the corner of Sparks and Elgin streets. It was at first a three-storeyed stone building with a tin roof, a porch-covered door on Elgin Street, and a ladies' entrance on Sparks Street. In 1875, a year after Laurier began to go to Ottawa, a primitive central plumbing system was installed, followed, a few years later, by steam heating. Before that, every room had a small coal stove. It had a good bar, which served as the unofficial House of Commons. More deals were made there than in the halls and offices of Parliament. If the lodger was someone important or moneyed, his room was comfortable and relatively large. Laurier's generally was. The food, however, was *détestable*.

Laurier was terribly lonely most of the time. No sooner had he arrived in Ottawa than he wanted to be back in Arthabaska. He missed Zoë's cooking; his small office, where, undisturbed, he could look after his affairs; the talks with Lavergne and the conversations with Émilie. Above all, he missed his library, in which he could read his books in peace. Political life came to interest him less and less: "The only benefit I have in being in Ottawa," he wrote, "is the indemnity."

It was not all bleak, however — even Laurier had to admit that. When spring came, Ottawa became more than tolerable. "Un temps sans pareil," he once told Zoë; "un soleil admirable." He attended readings of Shakespeare, and in May 1882 he encountered Oscar Wilde in the lobby of the Russell Hotel. There were many invitations to dinner — at Rideau Hall, at the Blakes', and at the mansions of other shakers and wheelers. Zoë came to visit him during almost every session and, while she was there, they entertained at the hotel or at some fashionable restaurant. He went to balls and *soirées,* and the ladies smiled their satisfaction at being in the company of this elegant man, courteous, courtly, and ever so entertaining.

In March 1883 Laurier and Zoë went to Montréal to hear a concert by the *Canadien* Emma Albani, one of the greatest sopranos of their time. The tickets were five dollars each and, after the performance, there was a magnificent reception at the Hôtel de Ville. They spoke to her for a few minutes, and Louis Fréchette read a long poem he had composed in her honour.

~

Between the defeat of the Mackenzie administration in September 1878 and the Riel agitation of 1885, the political demands made on Laurier were not onerous — and he did little to make them so. However, events sometimes overtook him.

When he came back to Arthabaska from his sojourn in Ottawa, he could not always escape politics, much as he desired to, especially provincial politics. He needed a friendly voice in Québec, and, in 1880, he associated himself with Ernest Pacaud and others to establish a Liberal newspaper in Québec City called *L'Electeur.* Pacaud was the editor, but Laurier wrote for it and raised money. *L'Electeur* was a lively newspaper, forcefully written, polemical, and unafraid. In a seven-year period, it had fifty libel suits to answer. Not once was it found guilty. Pacaud was a shrewd man.

It was, therefore, just part of the game when, on 20 April 1881, it published an unsigned article entitled "La caverne des 40 voleurs" — The Den of the Forty Thieves. It caused a sensation. Whoever had written it indicted the premier, Adolphe Chapleau, the contractor, railway financier, and Conservative bagman Louis-Adélard Sénécal, and Arthur Dansereau, editor of the Montréal newspaper *La Minerve* and Chapleau's patronage agent. According to the article, these "robbers" were not any "Tom, Dick, and Harry" but important men "who have been entrusted with a glorious task, the task of restoring the finances of the Province of Québec." The chief of the band was none other than "Louis-Adélard Sénécal." There followed a series of accusations, one worse than the other, demonstrating a corruption so vast and so inbred that it was nothing else but "robbery erected into a system." The "thieves," particularly Sénécal, had to be driven out of the temple. Another article followed the next day in which Sénécal was compared with Intendant Bigot of New France fame. Sénécal, furious but unbowed, sued the newspaper for libel. He asked for $100,000.

The trial opened in Montréal a month later. Laurier acted as the lawyer for the business manager of the paper. No one in and around *L'Electeur* could identify the author of the supposedly libellous article. A few days into the trial, Laurier admitted that he knew the author. And the trial ended — for the moment. In the fall, when it was clear that his client was to be found guilty, Laurier admitted his authorship. He became the accused and his trial opened on 5 October 1881. He was ready. He had given to his lawyers, Honoré Mercier and George Irvine, the Liberal member for Mégantic in the provincial legislature, a memorandum that contained all the evidence against Sénécal that he had amassed over the years. Irvine himself had also accumulated much documentation on Sénécal in the course of the fifty-three trials in which he had acted against the railroad man. The trial dragged on and on with a provincial election campaign throughout November. Juggling both the trial and the elections, Laurier rushed from one to the other, more eager, however, for the lawsuit. Finally, on 2 December, the day the province elected Chapleau and his Conservative government by a vast majority, the judge declared a mistrial: the jury was hopelessly divided, with nine for an acquittal and three for a conviction. No further proceedings were instituted. Laurier was vindicated, even though there was no clear decision. Most certainly, he accomplished what he had set out to do — to settle his score with Sénécal, whom he had never forgiven for helping to drive *Le Défricheur* into bankruptcy and for engineering his defeat in Drummond-Arthabaska in 1877.

After that episode, he became less visible in provincial politics. The continued attempt between 1879 and 1883 to forge a coalition between Chapleau's Conservatives and the provincial Liberal Party annoyed him, even though he understood that the divisions between the extreme and moderate wings in both parties made governing for either almost impossible as the province progressed relentlessly towards bankruptcy. The *Progammistes* who had transformed themselves into *Castors* — "that detestable and fanatic, that seditious and intolerant sect," as Tarte called them, vowed to destroy Chapleau, eliminate all moderates, and place politics at the service of the bishops and the racial interests. The few "extreme" Liberals who were still around, men like Honoré Beaugrand, editor of *La Patrie*, were determined to finish the work begun by the *Rouges* some forty years before. This situation led Chapleau, Mercier, Dansereau, David, Pacaud, and others to favour the formation of a coalition of the moderate elements within the two parties.

Laurier's views changed as the talks progressed and the difficulties increased. In the beginning of the discussion, he opposed any talk of a coalition, arguing that it would blur party lines at the federal level and would not stop the priests hurling insults at the Liberals. However, following the provincial election of 1881 and the federal election of 1882 in which the Liberals were trounced, he favoured the union of the moderate Conservatives — the school of Cartier — with the moderates of the Liberal Party, among whom he counted himself, into one political formation. In the fall of 1882 he wrote to Blake to that effect. It was too late to turn back, he said, and "I now desire to see the coalition effected at the earliest moment." He hoped that when it was a fait accompli, the party would be strengthened. Yet he kept the door open: if it were possible to get both wings of the Liberal Party to speak with one voice on crucial issues, then "I would not speak thus." He didn't have much hope for that, however. Two months later, in November, he changed his mind again. No alliance was possible with the provincial Conservatives because they were "corrupt to the core." Moreover, it would not be in the public interest: too many Liberals had also been contaminated and they favoured the projected coalition only because of the patronage that would come their way as office holders. The talks went on, but they came to nothing. It would not be until 1896, with the help of Tarte and the silence of Chapleau, that Laurier would bring the Cartier-Chapleau Conservative group into the fold of the Liberal Party.

Meanwhile, the first order of business in Ottawa was to settle the leadership issue within the party, and this meant another duel between Mackenzie and Blake. It took a couple of years to resolve it. Immediately after the 1878 electoral reverse, Mackenzie had been depressed and had offered to resign, so as to give his caucus the opportunity either to confirm him in the leadership or to elect someone in whom they had greater confidence. As the session wore on, however, he abandoned his plan and didn't mention it again. In October 1879 Blake had returned to the House of Commons in a by-election, but Mackenzie made no overtures to him to take on the leadership. Indeed, Mackenzie consulted no one, never met his colleagues in caucus, and operated as if he were a one-man party. Disenchantment bred rebellion. Towards the end of April 1880 matters finally came to a head. The party whip called a caucus meeting without inviting his leader. Laurier was ill at the Russell Hotel, but was able to receive three of his colleagues who needed his support in their attempt to dethrone Mackenzie in favour of Blake. In sympathy with their aims, Laurier agreed to go with them to Mackenzie's office in the House of Commons on the morning of the 27th.

It was a most unpleasant experience. He had dreaded it and hardly slept during the preceding night, his relentless coughing keeping him awake. But it had to be done. Five of them went to Mackenzie's door. The atmosphere was tense, and, after an awkward exchange, Laurier went straight to the point:

"Mr. Mackenzie, we have been defeated. You have been defeated. And it is only human nature that a defeated army should seek another general. There is not a man who has not high regard for your services, but there is a general feeling ..."

Here he was interrupted by his tight-lipped superior: "Very well, if that is so, I shall soon cease to lead the Liberal party."

And Mackenzie showed them out. Around 2:00 that night and just before the House of Commons was to adjourn for the day, he rose and announced that he was withdrawing as leader of the opposition: "From this time forth I will speak and act for no person but myself." In May, Blake became leader of the Liberal Party, with Laurier as his Québec lieutenant. He was always a reluctant leader and talked often of resigning, though Laurier managed to convince him to remain. In December 1882, for example, he wrote Blake a long letter that divulged his own personal expectations in the exercise of political leadership. "I have often thought," he revealed, "that to such a nature as yours the position of leader, in our coarse political atmosphere, was a dragging down instead of a lifting up." Followers were bound to a leader not merely by "ties of political fealty," but "by a strong personal attachment" that made it impossible for them to accept being led by anyone else. It was also the moral responsibility of a leader to stay in office until he was certain there was someone to "take the leadership." He gave Blake a challenge. "Instead of resigning," he stated categorically, the party should be "reconstituted with higher and nobler aims." Those aims? To bring the party to a more elevated standard: "I have told you before, & I can only repeat, that in my judgment, there is no more urgent reform than educating public and private opinion to unselfishness, & until that reform is achieved all other reforms are impossible."

While Blake was leader of the Liberal Party and leader of the opposition, the Conservatives inaugurated the National Policy and realized the national dream. Macdonald built a transcontinental railroad, gave Canada a high protective tariff, and tried to people the West.

Laurier contributed little to the discussions on these issues. He contented himself with learning as much as he could from Blake. It was as part of that training that, in the summer of 1881, he undertook his first trip outside Ontario and Québec. With Blake and Pacaud, he visited Nova Scotia, arriving in New Glasgow on 5 August. Three days later, in the pouring rain, he attended his first meeting along with four thousand people. The next day, he spoke in Port Hawkesbury — too long according to some! Then it was St. Peter's, Windsor, Kentville, Bridgetown, Digby, Clark, and Yarmouth. Everywhere he and the Blakes went, there were large crowds and much cheering. Laurier spoke mainly about the tribulations of the Canadian Pacific Railway: its enormous cost, its opportunities for corruption, and its "odious monopolies." He was elegant, charming, but not altogether inspiring. He suddenly abandoned the tour after the Yarmouth engagement and returned to Arthabaska on 18 August. It had rained too often for him. He felt dizzy and weak, so Pacaud took him home. Zoë put him to bed for a few days. He had enjoyed the trip, however, and was pleased with the reception they had received. He was impressed by the ocean, which he had never seen before.

Throughout the first half of the 1880s, the only issues being debated in Ottawa to which he put his powerful mind and established principles were provincial rights and provincial autonomy. Laurier was the first politician to state categorically that Canadian federalism demanded a consistent policy for the maintenance of a balance of power between the federal and the provincial governments. Any scheme that tipped the balance in favour of the one at the expense of the other was to be avoided; otherwise, Canadian unity could not be maintained.

His first sortie in this regard occurred over the Letellier matter. Luc Letellier-de-Saint-Just, a *Rouge* and an unreformed Liberal, was the lieutenant governor of Québec, having been appointed by Mackenzie in 1876. Two years into his mandate, he chose to dismiss his lawfully elected premier and the Conservative administration of Charles-Eugène Boucher de Bourcheville, a *Programmiste* and the servant of the bishops. When he heard of Letellier's coup d'état, Laurier wrote to Pacaud: "We are all convinced here that Letellier has spoiled it all; it is hardly possible to defend his action and it is certainly unconstitutional, unless he has certain facts that we do not know of." Dejected, he added: "There is nothing we can do." However, after the return of the Conservatives to power in the federal elections of 1878, the Québec wing of the party moved for Letellier's dismissal in the session of 1879. The whole matter was engineered by Tarte, aided by Chapleau, Dansereau, and Sénécal. They all moved to Ottawa for the duration. Sénécal mortgaged his life insurance and bought a house on Metcalfe Street, which became known as *la maison bleue*, in which they lived as they prepared their strategies.

In the debate that ensued, Laurier, while not defending Letellier, opted for the primacy of provincial rights. An election had been held in Québec and the people had elected a Liberal government — albeit one that could only govern by the vote of the Speaker. There the matter should rest, for the federal authority had no power, no legitimacy, to interfere in what was essentially a provincial matter. Laurier expressed at that time the federal-provincial philosophy that would guide him throughout the years: the federal powers of intervention in matters provincial — reservation and veto — may only be exercised "for the protection of imperial or federal rights" and "never to afford relief to any section of [the provincial] community that may deem itself aggrieved by that legislation." Federal interference in such circumstances "would be a violation of the federal principle." Where, then, could the "aggrieved portion of the community" seek redress? According to him, it must "seek and can find its relief in the application of the principle of responsible government."

Letellier was duly dismissed and a Conservative appointed. The Legislative Council created a crisis, an election followed in 1881, and Chapleau became premier of Québec with a vast majority. Laurier didn't take it well. He wrote to Blake: "I never anticipated a victory, but I had always thought that we would carry between 20 & 25 seats," which constituted the Liberal core. The provincial results did not augur well for the federal elections that were to take place in 1882.

Laurier was not looking forward to them. Corruption still pervaded every tissue of Québec society. And the English population wasn't any better. It discouraged him. With a corrupt public opinion, with all kinds of money against the Liberals, with the clergy still ready for a fight, as if Conroy had never been there, he warned Blake: "We must always be defeated." He didn't know what to do. At the beginning of his career he was convinced that the Liberals' greatest obstacle was clerical influence. It was still there, but they could now argue — at least with intelligent and conscientious Catholics — that, by the authority of the pope, the people were free.

However, he came to be persuaded that corruption was the greatest obstacle in Québec to a sound democratic life. "*La corruption* is almost universal among us, *Canadiens*, because of the way in which we are educated. The young, like I, learn from priests who are good men, but who are also prejudiced, biased, and, except in Theology and Philosophy, very ignorant, especially of modern history. The books they have read, all the sources of information to which they have access, are the continental Ultramontane books and press. They have predisposed us to a horror of liberalism and liberty. Thus, they have created a dependency on ignorance and tradition. And from there comes the corruption."

In the federal elections held on 20 June 1882, Laurier played his usual role of getting himself elected and supporting candidates here and there in Québec, but he didn't take charge of the campaign in the province. That annoyed Blake, who as early as January had begged Laurier to start organizing. But Laurier did not. He had his legal practice to attend to, his books to read, Zoë and the "children," a harsh winter to contend with, and he was tired and often not well. He found the electorate apathetic, there was no money, and he was loath to impose his leadership. By May, little had been done. To add insult to injury, several candidates had the gall to demand thousands of dollars to run in difficult constituencies. "C'est absolument intolérable!" he complained to Zoë. When the results were in, Macdonald's Conservatives had won 139 seats; Blake's Liberals, 72. In Québec the party division remained the same: 52 Conservatives and 13 Liberals. Laurier was re-elected in Québec-Est, but with a reduced majority.

He was blamed for the poor results. To some degree, the criticisms were valid. He was too prone to exaggerate the difficulties he encountered; his natural fatalism followed him everywhere; and he developed a tendency to think that everybody was out to get him. His inclination to postpone to tomorrow what had to be done today caused him endless trouble. It was, however, his aversion to the exercise of power which gave his political friends their greatest worry. Pacaud often chided him for what he considered a weakness in Laurier's character. Pacaud went at it so hard that, at one point, he feared he was doing irreparable harm to their friendship. With his usual good grace, Laurier soothed him: "I am upset that you think I can be angry with you. I have no reason to be annoyed. We have different opinions on many subjects; that does not prevent us from being friends."

Beyond that, he was generally silent. William Dafoe, who was barely beginning his journalistic career in the 1880s as the Ottawa political correspondent of the *Montreal Star*, recalled much later that, by 1884, Laurier's career was over. His interest in politics was, apparently, "of the slightest," and his political activities consisted "chiefly of being an acting secretary of sorts" to Blake. Few remembered his eloquence, as he was almost always silent. His main activity was to ensconce himself in "some genial alcove" of the library and read. A hard-hitting Liberal political organizer once told Dafoe: "Laurier will never make a leader; he has not enough of the devil in him."

7

THE NORTH-WEST TRAGEDY
OF 1885

On Wednesday, 2 July 1884, Laurier received a telegram that Louis Riel had arrived at Batoche in the North-West Territories. The first thing Laurier had to do was to learn, to teach himself, what he didn't know about the West. He knew it was large, that it contained a diverse population but was mostly Indian and Métis, that the buffalo had disappeared, that the railway was going through it, that the white population was increasing — and that was about all. His ignorance was broad, his concern narrow and sporadic, his attention unfocused. He had never travelled to Manitoba or beyond and hardly knew anyone from those parts. In that way, he was a typical central Canadian politician. Canada was fixed on the axis of Toronto-Montréal, with bypasses to Ottawa and Québec City. The rest was there, but of little importance. Laurier had not yet acquired *le sens du pays* — the feeling for the whole country. *Mare usque ad mare.*

He had, of course, been involved in the debate surrounding the Riel amnesty question in 1875. His first speech in the House of Commons in English had been on that subject. At the time, though, he had fallen under the spell of some form of *nationalisme*, which made him temporarily accept as valid that *Canadiens* should consider federal, or Canada-wide, issues in the light of their national — racial — interests. He had broken his vow to consider national or pan-Canadian issues in the light of equity and justice, and not to be influenced by race and religion. He had helped to transform an issue of justice and human rights into a question of race and religion. It had been wrong and he knew it. He should have stuck to his original script, which was to argue for amnesty on the grounds that Riel and his people in the Rebellion of 1869–70 wished only to be treated like British subjects, not "bartered away like common cattle." Was this problem still relevant in 1884? Had Riel come back to lead another popular movement because the situation had not changed? Were men, women, and children still being denied their rights as British subjects? He would find out and, he hoped, keep race and religion out of it.

He spent the year between Riel's return and his speech in the House of Commons on 7 July 1885 doing his homework. He searched the documents, read the reports, became cognizant of the petitions, consulted far and wide, and ended up with a vast command of what had happened since the Canadian government took over the lands of the Hudson's Bay Company in 1870. He also followed closely all the tragic events that were happening in the West, around Batoche and later in Regina, starting in the middle of March 1885 and ending on a bleak November day of that year. He was determined that he would not be caught unknowing and uncaring.

~

Louis Riel is the most paradoxical and perplexing person in Canadian history. Born on 22 October 1844 in the Red River Settlement of what is now Manitoba, he was the eldest child of Louis Riel, a fur trader, farmer, and defender of the Métis, and of Julie Lagimodière, the daughter of the first white woman in the West, Marie-Anne Gaboury. His paternal grandmother was a Franco-Chipewyan *Métisse;* consequently, Riel was part Indian. He belonged to a large and loving family — there were eleven children — for whom the Catholic religion was the centre of life. He was bright, and his bishop arranged for him to go to the Petit Séminaire de Montréal in 1858 to study for the priesthood. The death of his father in January 1864 affected him greatly, and he abandoned his studies a year before he was to graduate. He tried law — interestingly, in Rodolphe Laflamme's office — but, when it didn't suit his personality, any more than the priesthood would have, he made his way back west, arriving in Saint-Boniface in the summer of 1868. He found his people destitute, owing to a grasshopper plague the previous year and harassment by the white settlers and surveyors who had come from Ontario — the infamous Canadian party. The vast majority of them, particularly Charles Mair, a poet of sorts; John Christian

Schultz, a doctor and a lieutenant governor-to-be; and the tempestuous and arrogant Thomas Scott, were bigots whose essential mission was to establish the power and might of the English race in the former lands of the Hudson's Bay Company. They would stop at nothing to achieve that goal, establishing a precedent that plagued Laurier after he became leader of the Liberal Party in 1887.

The transfer of those lands between Ontario and the Rockies was accomplished without any thought of, or consultation with, the inhabitants of those territories. No doubt, according to some interpretations of international law, it was also unnecessary to confer with them about the type of government that should be established and the way land would be held in the future — a landholding pattern that conflicted with the one established before the coming of the white man. When the representatives of the government of Canada, official and non-official, arrived to assume Canadian suzerainty over those vast lands, they found it inhabited by two groups of people who were not prepared to be pushed around in the name of the higher interests of the Canadian state: the First Nations and the Métis.

In the Red River Colony, white settlers were the minority. They included the descendants of the Scots whom Lord Selkirk had sponsored in the early nineteenth century, farmers, land speculators, and merchants, a mixture of French-speakers, English-speakers, Catholics and Protestants, Americans looking for manifest destiny, Orangemen, and missionaries of various sorts. Among them lived ten thousand sons and daughters of a new nation, the *nation métisse*. The fathers of that nation were the *coureurs de bois* of New France and the *voyageurs* of the post-Conquest era; the mothers were Native women. The children of that alliance were Catholic and French-speaking, but raised in their maternal culture. They constituted the majority in the colony. A few Métis were English-speaking Protestants, their fathers having been Selkirk settlers.

The Métis were a semi-nomadic people, pursuing their own life apart from the whites and the Natives who surrounded them. They earned their living trapping, supplying furs and other goods to white settlers and Indians, performing odd jobs, and farming. They held their lands in long strips with a small frontage on the river, a method of landholding incompatible with the surveying regulations imposed by Ottawa. At the beginning, their entire livelihood and survival depended on the buffalo, but by 1885 that animal had been hunted practically to extinction.

As the white man's invasion progressed, particularly around the time of Confederation, the Métis became restive about their rights and liberties, fearful of being dispossessed, and concerned about their way of life, language, and religion. When no one told them what was happening and where they fit in the scheme of nation building, they found themselves a leader in the twenty-five-year-old Louis Riel, established a provisional government, and eventually took up arms to defend their existence and survival. This so-called First Riel Rebellion (August 1869–August 1870) was put down by an army sent for the purpose from central Canada, but not before the Métis had wrenched concessions from Macdonald and Cartier: security for the French language and the Catholic religion, land grants in accordance with the Aboriginal rights of the Métis, and the entry of the Red River Colony into Confederation as the fifth province of Canada under the name "Manitoba." Before that had been achieved, however, the most tiresome death in Canadian history occurred, that of the adventurer Thomas Scott.

Scott had arrived in Upper Fort Garry, now Winnipeg, probably in November 1869 and quickly made friends with the Canadian party. He supported Mair, Schultz, and others in opposing Riel and his plans for the Red River Colony. Scott and fifty-three others were arrested on 7 December 1869. A month later, he escaped and did considerable mischief before he was rearrested on 18 February 1870. During his incarceration, he insulted the Métis, calling them all sorts of racist names. Unable to control him, even after they had come to blows, the Métis who guarded him demanded that he be court martialled in accordance with their traditions. Found guilty and condemned to death, he was executed by firing squad on 4 March 1870. He did not, however, rest in peace. His execution — murder to some — was a blunder of great magnitude that for decades would plague Canada-in-the-making. It caused Riel's death.

Laurier was particularly interested to find out what had happened between 15 July 1870, when Manitoba became a bilingual province with the power to safeguard the interests of the Métis as guaranteed to them in the settlement, and Riel's return in the summer of 1884. What he found out was not encouraging.

Riel was by then forty years old, an American citizen, married with two children, and living in St. Peter's Mission in central Montana, some eight hundred miles from Batoche, where he taught school. After his exile from Canada, he had wandered in the United States, was in and out of sanatoriums, and had done nothing of any significance. However, the Métis remembered him, especially what he had accomplished in Red River. They hoped he would repeat his miracle and save the *nation métisse* one more time. That is why they sent for him.

When Gabriel Dumont, one of the best military leaders Canada ever produced, made the journey to Montana to find Riel in June 1884, the situation of the Métis had deteriorated yet again. It had not been possible for them to live harmoniously with the men and women of another culture and language who had invaded their lands and often robbed them of their entitlement — their own improvidence not helping. They became a minority, and they found themselves harassed once more and their survival threatened. But instead of taking up arms, they moved, some to the United States and a greater number to the banks of the meandering Saskatchewan River. There they squatted until the arrival of the government's agents — surveyors, mounted policemen, and magistrates — in the late 1870s. Again, with these others in their midsts, they experienced the old anxiety, the gripping fear, and the ever-present danger of disappearance. The Indians, too, were aroused: their crops a failure, their life on the reserves bleak, and the encroachment of the white man devastating. In the winter of 1884–85 they needed food, blankets, and clothing, or else misery and starvation would follow. But government officials dismissed the desperation of both the Indians and the Métis.

What did they want, these "insignificant" people? In 1884–85, on the banks of the Saskatchewan, the Métis wanted what their fathers had fought for on the banks of the Red River in 1869–70: to stop being bartered away like common cattle. That was the conclusion Laurier came to. The Macdonald government, which had bungled the first encounter with the Métis, was doing it again. The Métis asked that the lands they occupied be recognized as theirs; that their traditional system of surveying be adopted in their settlements rather than the American rectangular one favoured by the administration; that, in recognition of their Indian entitlement, each Métis be granted title to approximately a quarter-section of land, as had been the case in Manitoba; and that they be adequately represented and consulted. Laurier was convinced that these demands were just and that they should be met within an adequate period of time.

They were not. Petitions were sent to Ottawa, delegations arrived, bishops and priests mailed letters and reports, and police officers and government officials warned of the gathering storm. But still the mighty slumbered in the nation's capital. When Riel returned in July 1884 he tried to negotiate. He even offered to be bought off, but was unsuccessful on both counts. He held meetings, argued with the missionaries, and prayed. Meanwhile, the agitation was growing. Laurier, who didn't trust and care for Riel, saw in his actions the manipulation of naked power for his own purposes. But that did not lessen the validity of the grievances of the 26,000 Indians and the 7000 Métis who lived in the North-West Territories. Despair led to anger, and Ottawa replied with an increase in the size of the police force. By the beginning of October 1884 Riel had a draft of the people's petition to the authorities thousands of miles away. It was discussed and refined in many assemblies, and, on 16 December, it was sent to the governor general. Three weeks later, a note arrived acknowledging its receipt. The people waited for redress. To pacify them, the federal government awarded some government jobs to a few Métis leaders; a commission was appointed to conduct a demographic survey; and again the police force was augmented while plans were being made to move troops quickly and efficiently should rebellion break out. At the same time, the Cabinet announced that the Métis in Saskatchewan were not entitled to claim land through their Indian blood because most of them had already received a scrip in Manitoba after 1870. Ten days later this policy was reversed and what had been begged for over many years finally became acceptable. But by then the Métis cause had been transformed from a political matter into a religious crusade.

When he began to keep a diary in the early fall of 1884, Riel displayed the religious megalomania that Laurier had observed in his conversation with him ten years before. Riel saw himself as the prophet sent by God to establish the "Catholic, Apostolic, and Living Church of the New World." He heard voices telling him what to do. From then on, Riel's decisions, which Dumont and the other followers accepted, as their customs demanded, were all motivated by his apostolic mission and dictated by the voices. In the process, Riel hindered the cause he was meant to defend.

By the end of February 1885 it was obvious that there would be no hurry to satisfy the Indians and the Métis. On 17 March, on Dumont's advice, a provisional government was formed, with Riel as president and Dumont as adjutant-general. To enhance his position, and again with the effect that it belittled his cause, Riel had himself called "David" or "Exovede," which means "he, picked out of the flock." Eight days later, the new regime conducted its first battle. For the next two months the insurrection dragged on, the insurrection in which 3500 troops from central Canada — transported on sleighs provided by the Canadian Pacific Railway — and 850 Métis participated; in which a Gatling gun (a sort of machine-gun) spewed forth a deluge of bullets; in which priests refused absolution to women who dared see their husbands, while they themselves passed on strategic information to the Red Coats; in which Dumont proved he was a great tactician; in which old men fought with bullets made of nails; in which the white man's general ordered the use of exploding bullets, an act against the basic principles of war at that time; in which Riel carried his crucifix, prayed to his voices, and encouraged his men; and in which the "Canadian" army went on a rampage and plundered as it wished. When it was over, two hundred Métis and soldiers had died, many more were wounded, six million dollars in cash was spent, and the country was launched in its first "racial" confrontation. And all for a dispute over forty or fifty thousand acres of land in "a wilderness of tens of millions of acres," as someone observed at the time.

On 15 May Riel surrendered to the "English general." He was taken to Regina, where he was tried for treason and found guilty on 1 August, though the six-man jury recommended mercy because it was convinced of the merit of the Métis cause. The government had been negligent and, in more ways than one, had caused the insurrection. But the Criminal Code at the time did not permit mercy, even if the judge had been inclined to it. On 18 September 1885, therefore, he condemned Riel to hang. The sentence was delayed while appeals were lodged with the Court of Queen's Bench in Manitoba and with the Privy Council in London. Neither was successful, and Macdonald's government decided to allow the sentence to proceed. To pacify the three *Canadiens* in the Cabinet, however, a board of inquiry of three government doctors investigated Riel's sanity, which had been an issue in his trial. The doctors found him sane, even though he had delusions when the subjects of politics and religion came up. On 16 November 1885 Riel was hanged. Canada was never the same after that.

~

While these momentous events were taking place, the House of Commons, which had supported the government during the insurrection, turned its attention to what had gone wrong. On 6 July 1885 Edward Blake moved a motion of censure citing "grave neglect, delay, and mismanagement." Laurier spoke the next day and delivered a precise speech in which he indicted the Macdonald administration:

> This I do charge upon the government; that they have for years and years ignored the just claims of the half-breeds of the Saskatchewan, that for years and years these people have been petitioning the government and always in vain. I say that they have been treated by this government with an indifference amounting to undisguised contempt, that they have been goaded into the unfortunate course they have adopted, and if this rebellion be a crime, I say the responsibility for that crime weighs as much upon the men who, by their conduct, have caused the rebellion, as upon those who engaged in it.

For six years, the government had delayed and refused to grant what rightfully belonged to the Métis; Riel came back, and again the Métis were scorned; but the bullets of Duck Lake awakened the sleepy giant in Ottawa. At the last minute, the administration found merit in what was being asked. As Macdonald said, he did it for the sake of peace. Laurier had a hard time with that line of argument: "For the sake of peace, when we were in the midst of a war! For the sake of peace, when insurgents were in the field and blood had been shed." No, it would not do — nor would it do for the government to hide, as it was doing, behind the animosity and anger against Riel which was pretty general in Ontario. It was all Riel's fault, it was alleged. "No, it was not," he snapped. And it certainly would not do to arouse the prejudices found in the country against Riel to camouflage the ineptitude of the Ministry of the Interior:

> We are not yet so built up a nation as to forget our respective origins, and I say frankly that the people of my own province, who have a

community of origin with the insurgents, sympathize with them, just as the sympathies of the people of Ontario would go altogether in the other direction.

I am of French origin, and I confess, that if I were to act only from the blood that runs in my veins, it would carry me strongly in favour of these people.

But, above all I claim to be in favour of what is just and right and fair.

What was right and fair was that justice be done, and "let the consequences fall upon the guilty ones, whether on the head of Louis Riel or on the shoulders of the government." Laurier was convinced that Riel, Dumont, and the others didn't rebel against the queen; rather, "they rebelled against the tyranny of the Canadian government." Throughout all the agitation that followed, he didn't depart from this conviction and from this line of argument. Blake's motion of censure was defeated and, on the same day that Riel's trial began, the House adjourned until 25 February 1886. In the meantime, Riel's shadow would rule the streets.

~

On receiving the news of the insurrection at Red River, the *Canadiens*, like everyone else in Canada, deplored it and demanded that the authority of the law and of the country be restored. In the ceremonies dispatching Québec's Ninth Battalion in April 1885, most agreed that the mission of these soldiers was to uphold law and order and to serve as agents of peace. The prayers of the people went with them.

Then insecurity set in! Every day the newspapers were filled with reports of unanswered petitions, dismal poverty, and the precarious position of a people who had developed a country, only to see it become foreign to them. When the rebellion was over, discordant voices were heard throughout the land, and different and opposite interpretations were given to events. In Québec, Riel surrendered, while in Ontario he was captured. In Ontario there was a demand for punishment, while in Québec there was one for mercy.

When Laurier admitted in the House on 7 July to a natural sympathy for "these people," he expressed what was in effect a general condition in the province of Québec. *Déchirement* — a tearing apart of the heart — was the accurate word to describe the powerful emotion that seized the *Canadiens*. Shocked by the revelations of tyranny and incompetence, and by reports of the behaviour of the Ontario soldiers against the civilian population, they demanded mercy, especially after Riel was condemned to death. There was more than that simple emotion, however. "Riel was one of us!" Riel was family — *parenté!* For him to hang: they too would be on the gallows! Added to this, of course, was the perennial and aggravating problem of being a minority. The issue was not only that Riel was to be saved because he was a *Canadien;* but that his fate was an indication of *Canadien* power and influence in Confederation.

Laurier, guarded as he might try to be, was caught up in this sentiment — "entraîné par le courant," as Tarte put it. But, just like Tarte and others, he tried to resist it. He had no empathy for Riel, and he didn't care much for rebellions and insurrections. Any loss of blood frightened and repelled him. He was more than satisfied, however, that the people living on the Saskatchewan had been wronged. The injustice filled him with anger, and he argued that those responsible had to pay. He would bring the power of his words to what was now *his* cause. At the same time, Laurier recognized that the issue was a godsend in Québec for the Liberals, at both the provincial and the federal level. They sensed blood! They could benefit! But the pitfalls were also there.

Riel est mort! At 8:15 this morning, Regina time, he was taken from his cell and hanged in the prison courtyard. The shock is unbelievable. Zoë is in tears and, with many of her friends, has been to church to pray for the repose of his soul. Émilie, who is as fragile as Zoë, went with her.

It is now quite late and, still, telegrams are pouring in, demanding justice.

It is unbelievable that a civilized nation like ours should stoop so low. Morally, it is indefensible what my country has just done in the name of law and order. Riel did not die for law and order; he died because of Thomas Scott. Now, finally, Scott's death has been avenged.

What will our people do, on both sides of this issue? Already, here the cry is "Mon frère, Riel!" and over there, in Ontario and elsewhere, it is "Let him die!" What will it be tomorrow?

Zoë and I have talked long about the repercussions of this act. Our country shall be divided more than ever before. All the prejudices, the old wounds, the slights — only Zoë's God knows what else will appear and dictate our course of action.

Race and religion are about to dominate the politics of Canada. Not justice, not mercy, not liberty — race and religion. And with that, an abyss will separate our two peoples.

My course must be clear. Riel is not the issue here. That he be of *Canadien* blood is not the issue. That he be a Catholic, brought up among us, is not the issue. The issue is the *incurie* — the criminal negligence — of the Macdonald government. On that ground alone, I will take my stand.

Part of that will mean identifying with the pain of the half-breeds. Part of that will be stating clearly that British subjects cannot be arbitrarily deprived of their rights and treated unfairly. When that happens, they have to defend themselves. Part of that will be stressing that mercy is a more ennobling act than revenge.

But how feasible is this course? How misunderstood will I become? Can I withstand the tumult?

Zoë tells me she will pray.

On 17 November 1885 the province of Québec went into mourning. Since May, the people had poured their emotion, their money, and their energy into saving Riel, despite the smallpox epidemic that was raging in Montréal. They had failed. A part of them died on the scaffold of Regina with Riel. Municipal offices flew their flags at half-mast; shopkeepers displayed Riel's picture in windows that were dressed in black; the Montréal transit system came to a halt; men and women went to pray before and after work; teachers described in vivid detail the horror of dying by hanging; shocked students vowed their hatred of "les maudits anglais"; the bishops refused the consolation of masses and other religious ceremonies for the repose of Riel's soul; and parishioners retaliated by burning bishops and their political allies in effigy and even threatening to burn down episcopal residences. Politicians called meeting after meeting.

During the summer months between his intervention in the House of

Commons in July and Riel's death, Laurier participated in meetings in the various parts of the province. He stressed the government's culpabilité, or guilt, in the "troubles dans l'Ouest." He objected that the award of titles and decorations only perpetuated the memory of a civil war, a "fratricidal conflict." Not once, however, did he suggest that Riel had been executed because he was "notre frère," though many of his countrymen believed that was the real reason for Riel's execution.

Riel was hardly dead when a *Mouvement national* was formed out of the committees that had been established throughout the province to raise funds for Riel's defence and to obtain signatures on petitions asking for clemency. Laurier didn't participate in its formation, though he did agree to attend the main Montréal demonstration that was held on the Champ de Mars on 22 November. It was a Sunday.

In the morning he met with Honoré Mercier, who had taken lead of the nationalist movement and was about to form a political party, the *Parti national*, and with other participants to draft a set of resolutions. They followed the line Laurier had pursued: the government was at fault and must be defeated; in that pursuit, the province must be united. An agreement must be forged with many of the Conservatives who, he was told, were prepared to abandon their party.

After the drafting of the resolutions came the speeches. Three platforms were set up, around which were grouped fifty thousand people. Everybody who was French-speaking and could make it was there. Politicians, regardless of their affiliation, came in large numbers. Only the *Canadien* ministers in Ottawa — Hector Langevin, Joseph-Adolphe Chapleau, and Joseph-Philippe-René-Adolphe Caron, were missing.

"Where are they?" Laurier asked from the centre platform to which he had been assigned. "Why did Chapleau not go to Regina to defend his compatriot, Louis Riel?" He ended by answering the question he had raised in 1875 when speaking about amnesty for Riel over the incidents of 1869–70 in the Red River Colony: when the rights of British subjects are abused by arbitrary power, "where is the one amongst us who, if he had happened to have been with them, would not have been rebels as they were?" Since the principles of justice and liberty that led him to speak on Riel's behalf in 1875 were the same in 1885, he saw no reason why: "Had I been born on the banks of the Saskatchewan, I would myself have shouldered a musket to fight against the neglect of governments and the shameless greed of speculators."

He was not to be allowed to forget those words.

~

By the end of the year, Blake was back in Canada. He didn't like what he heard about the agitation in Québec and the part Laurier had played in it. No doubt he received his information from Ontario Liberals like Richard Cartwright who had encouraged Laurier to vigorous action so that the Conservative Party in Québec could be split in two. Blake came to the conclusion that Laurier and other Québec Liberals had kept silent all summer and then, when Riel was dead, stirred up agitation about the execution. On the last day of 1885, Laurier decided to explain his actions to Blake, and the justification for the strategy he had adopted.

After the House adjourned on 20 July and until Riel's death in November, the personality of Riel was a secondary matter. The chief issue was the grievances of the North-West. We attacked the government over and over again for its misconduct.

Then, came the execution — and a general commotion in the province. I thought we could rally all the branches of our party in unanimously condemning Riel's hanging. I was wrong. The Ontario press tells me that this course of action is not tenable. If that is the case, then that course must be abandoned.

I was firmly convinced — and still am — that if we could break the unity of the Conservative Party in the province, we should then have a majority in the next general election, which is bound to come by 1887. It would be easier to achieve that goal if we could rally Liberals everywhere in Canada to condemn Riel's execution. I may still be able to pull it off. Many in Québec see the Liberals as the defenders of the rights of minorities and, as such, the defenders of the interests of the *Canadiens* within the federation.

Immediately after Riel's hanging, however, there was a general upheaval in Québec. In some ways, I encouraged it. I am prepared to admit that, as I am to acknowledge that there was a great flood of passion, of unthinking anger, of blind prejudices.

Riel was not executed for leading an insurrection. He was hanged for Scott's murder — that is the simple truth. I have just found out that the Regina sheriff, Jack Henderson, had been imprisoned in Fort Garry in 1870. He is said to have whispered to Riel as he was placing the hood and noose around his neck: "Louis Riel, you had me once and I got away from you. I have you now and you will not get away from me."

I am certain that, in holding the government responsible not only for the rebellion but for all the consequences of it, including Riel's death, we are quite right.

~

On 25 February 1886 Laurier was back in Ottawa for the session. There he found fifty-two Conservatives from Québec and thirteen Liberals. By this time, Blake had made his position clear in a speech he had given in London, Ontario, in the middle of January: "I do not desire a party conflict on the Regina tragedy; I do not propose to construct a political platform on the Regina scaffold; or to create or cement party ties with the blood of the condemned." Laurier had given much thought to the meaning of Blake's remarks. Did it mean that Blake would fall behind the Ontario Liberals in condemning the government's administration in the North-West, but not what flowed inevitably from it — Riel's trial and execution? Since their rapport was intimate, they had no qualms about discussing the issue in a dark alcove of the Parliamentary Library. They must have come to an understanding. Unlike a good number of Ontario Liberals, Blake would include Riel's hanging in his censure of the government.

By clever manoeuvring, however, the government limited the debate on the matter. The opposition was left with no recourse but to debate the entire issue of the North-West insurrection and its aftermath on a simple motion: "This House feels it its duty to express its deep regret that the sentence of death passed upon Louis Riel, convicted of high treason, was allowed to be carried into execution." The Liberals had been outmanoeuvred. Then came Tuesday, 16 March 1886. History was about to be made.

It was late, almost 11 p.m. Zoë had arrived in Ottawa a few days earlier. She was sitting in the Speaker's Gallery, waiting and knitting. She didn't know it was actually to happen that night. The exact day and time had been left to the vicissitudes of the debate. The House was practically empty and the members were restive. From the front row on the left side of the Speaker, Laurier stood up. Zoë dropped her knitting and leaned forward in her seat. She saw several members on both sides, including Blake and Chapleau, enter and take their seats. The galleries also filled up, and officers of the governor general's guard and members of his household arrived unannounced. Laurier, pale and coughing lightly, began to speak.

"Mr. Speaker," he said, as he shuffled the papers on his desk and waited for the latecomers to take their seats. When he was satisfied that he had everyone's attention, he declared that Riel's death had been a judicial murder and that the *Canadiens* had not lost their heads. He admitted that if an injustice was committed against a fellow being, the blow fell deeper into his heart if it involved one of his kith and kin.

He reviewed the government's record and the procedure at Riel's trial. He found the former inexcusable and the latter unjust. Then, in prose unparalleled in the annals of Canadian parliamentary debate, he had the courage to continue:

> I appeal now to my friends of liberty in this House; I appeal not only to the Liberals who sit beside me, but to any man who has a British heart in his breast, and I ask, when subjects of Her Majesty have been petitioning for years for their rights, and these rights have not only been ignored, but have been denied, and when these men take their lives in their hands and rebel, will any one in this House say that these men, when they got their rights, should not have saved their heads as well, and that the criminals, if criminals there were in this rebellion, are not those who fought and bled and died, but the men who sit on these Treasury benches?

As for those who attacked him for his notorious remark — the shouldering of his musket — on the Champ de Mars on that Sunday in November, he attempted to explain the powerful reaction in his province to Riel's execution. He knew he wouldn't have an easy time of it but he felt impelled to do it just the same. The men who took up arms on the Saskatchewan, he pointed out, were in the wrong and their rebellion had to be put down. However, the men who waged that rebellion were "excusable," for they were the victims of hateful men who, having the "enjoyment of power, do not discharge the duties of power; who, having the power to redress wrongs, refuse to listen to the petitions that are sent to them; who, when they are asked for a loaf, give a stone." In light of that reality, he said, staring at Chapleau across the aisle and, not far from him, at a leader of the Orange Order of Ontario: "I ask any friend of liberty, is there not a feeling rising in his heart, stronger than all reasoning to the contrary, that those men were excusable?"

As for Riel himself, he was no hero to Laurier. "At his worst, he was a subject fit for an asylum; at his best he was a religious and political monomaniac." That he was insane was "beyond the possibility of controversy." But he was not a "bad man." So, if he was insane, why was he put to death? The easy answer — because he was found guilty of treason. Laurier scoffed at that. He declared Riel's trial unfair and unjust, dismissed the medical commission sent to examine Riel as a sham, and wondered out loud why Riel's secretary, William Jackson, was found insane after a short hearing, while Riel was not. Like many in his province, he asked: "Was it because one was of English blood and the other of French blood?" That was an important question, and the answer was difficult to come by. But there was no denying that "Jackson is free today; Riel is in his grave."

Those were his sentiments and he shared them with his people. He would not apologize. Nor would he retract the words spoken on the Champ de Mars. Was he being disloyal? Certainly not. If the hypocrites of the Conservative Party expected him to allow fellow-countrymen like the Métis, "unfriended, undefended, unprotected, and unrepresented in this House to be trampled under foot by this government," they had the wrong man. "That is not what I understand by loyalty; I would call it slavery."

To Laurier, Riel was executed to avenge the death of Thomas Scott. The same administration that had refused to act — to punish the crime — in 1870 was now, fifteen years later, making up for its omission. Honourable members were shocked and annoyed at this remark. But he found the words to quell his anger and, at the same time, go beyond the politics of the moment: "Sir, we are a new nation, we are attempting to unite the different conflicting elements

which we have into a nation. Shall we ever succeed if the bond of union is to be —
revenge?"

He had spoken for over an hour and a half, but his words had a power that
was compelling attention. Zoë sensed that the whole House was aware of it, for
not a sound could be heard but the ticking of the clock. He looked in her direction, then he turned to the Speaker and, with great emotion and love, said:

> Today, not to speak of those who have lost their lives, our prisons are
> full of men who, despairing ever to get justice by peace, sought to
> obtain it by war; who, despairing of ever being treated like free men,
> took their lives in their hands, rather than be treated as slaves. They
> have suffered a great deal, they are suffering still; yet their sacrifices
> will not be without reward. Their leader is in the grave, they are in
> durance, but from their prisons they can see that that justice, that
> liberty which they sought in vain, and for which they fought not in
> vain, has at last dawned upon their country. Their fate well illustrates
> the truth of Byron's invocation to liberty, in the introduction to the
> "Prisoner of Chillon":

> > Eternal Spirit of the chainless mind!
> > Brightest in dungeons, Liberty thou art!
> > For there thy habitation is the heart —
> > The heart which love of thee alone can bind;
> > And when thy sons to fetters are consigned —
> > To fetters and the damp vault's dayless gloom,
> > Their country conquers with their martyrdom.

Zoë wiped a tear, as many more did the same. Beyond that, there was no
movement.

> Yes, their country has conquered with their martyrdom. They are in
> durance today; but the rights for which they were fighting have been
> acknowledged. Two thousand claims so long denied have been at
> last granted. And more — still more. We have it in the Speech from

the Throne that at last representation is to be granted to those Territories.

Turning to his colleagues on the left of the Speaker's chair, he reminded them that they had been vindicated: "This side of the House long sought, but sought in vain, to obtain that measure of justice." He looked at Blake, who had stood solidly with him among the Liberals in condemning Riel's execution, and added, as if speaking only to his leader: "It could not come then, but it came after the war; it came as the last conquest of that insurrection." He turned back again to the Speaker and, in a clear, loud, and proud voice, he sealed his fate:

And again I say that their country has conquered with their martyr-dom, and if we look at that one fact alone there was cause sufficient, independent of all others, to extend mercy to the one who is dead and to those who live.

He sat down. The applause when it came from both sides of the House was deafening. Blake shook his hand; the Speaker adjourned the debate; Chapleau crossed the floor to bid him well; others crowded in. Zoë picked up her knitting and walked slowly to Laurier's office, where she waited for him to bundle him up before the walk to the Russell. It was close to two when they went to bed. A day or so later, she returned to Arthabaska with the realization that something irrevocable had happened that night. What it was, she could not fully discern; but another major change in their existence — their life together — would happen soon. She was not as uncomfortable as before with that possibility.

Others had the same premonition. Many in his party began to look at Laurier in a different way. They admired his courage to adhere to his own line of conduct, his vitality in the defence of what he called justice and liberty, his courtesy in meeting opposition, his intellectual grasp of issues, and his aston-ishing capacity to put in words the highest ideals of citizenship and the redefi-nition of their country. They were in the presence of a leader. How far that leadership could be taken remained to be seen. However, sooner rather than later, it would be put to the test.

Blake, whose health was giving grave concern to his family, had talked again of resigning at the end of the session of 1885 and was still thinking about it seriously. On 16 March 1886 he was confirmed in what he had concluded many years before: in Laurier there was a leader made for Canada. He would have a say in determining when that leadership was assumed. For the moment, and at the start of a five-hour speech to the House of Commons, he said that Laurier's address had given the "crowning proof of French domination," that French domination so feared by the Tories, the Orangemen, and their newspapers in Ontario. Laurier had invaded the English tongue and, "in that field has pronounced a speech, which in my humble opinion, merits this compliment, because it is the truth, that it was the finest parliamentary speech ever pronounced in the Parliament of Canada since Confederation." And the sick man bided his time!

It was a significant night on the government side, too. When Chapleau crossed the floor of the House to speak to Laurier, he realized that any thoughts of ambition were over for him. He had refused to assume the leadership of Québec which Mercier had offered him before the Champ de Mars meeting, and he had not been able to silence the opposition against him ever since. Later, during a federal by-election in Longueuil, for example, when he was on the same platform as Laurier, he was constantly interrupted, and bits of rope — symbol of the noose around Riel's neck — were thrown at him. He stopped speaking and Laurier, advancing to the front of the platform, said, in a voice full of anger: "I will consider it a personal insult if Monsieur Chapleau is not allowed to finish his address." Chapleau was certain that he had taken the right course, but whatever he had aspired to in the woods behind the Collège de L'Assomption would now not be fulfilled.

In the middle of the night of 24 May 1886 the government's motion of regret on Riel's execution came to a vote. The administration of Sir John A. Macdonald was sustained by a massive majority: 146 to 52. Twenty-four English-speaking Liberals supported it — over half of the caucus.

∼

Meanwhile, on 19 May 1886 in Saint-Lin, Laurier's father, Carolus, died.

~

Laurier spent the summer and the fall in Arthabaska and, mostly, on the hustings preparing for the provincial election of 14 October. Honoré Mercier was the leader and Ernest Pacaud the organizer, as the provincial Liberals tried hard to transform the elements of the *Mouvement national* of the post-Riel era into a *Parti national*. Laurier was in charge of getting the English vote out for the Liberals, particularly in the Eastern Townships, where he talked much about the government's handling of the crisis in the North-West. Often this brought him to Riel, even though he had nothing new to add to what he had been saying all along. To Blake, who disapproved of that emphasis, Laurier maintained that he had to devote much time to the matter of the North-West and, therefore, to Riel: "What ground we have gained, and are still gaining, is gained upon that question, and upon that question alone. Were we to suppress it, we would stand exactly as we stood before, or nearly so." Stressing the incidents of 1885 in the Saskatchewan valley didn't mean, however, that he gave any support at all to what Mercier was attempting to do: the formation of a purely nationalist party rising up from Riel's corpse.

Depending on the ebb and flow of political allegiances, Mercier was recognized as having won the election — he would be premier three months later. Laurier, however, was not as successful as he had hoped in the English-speaking ridings of the province. No English-speaking Liberal was elected either in the Eastern Townships or in Montréal on 14 October 1886.

~

After the provincial election, it was time to get ready for the federal contest. The momentum had to be kept up. Pacaud was still in charge and he arranged a huge rally in Saint-Roch, in the midst of Laurier's Québec-Est constituency, on 4 November. To the enthusiastic crowd, he stressed what would be his theme through the campaign: the North-West and Riel. Again he was careful not to associate himself too closely with the *Mouvement national*, even though he allowed his political friends to be more categorical. After that there was Trois-Rivières, Montréal, a trip to Saint-Lin, and one to Toronto on 10 December.

The Toronto appearance came about because he was dared to go to that most Tory of cities and state his position on the execution of Louis Riel. He wanted to go, but Blake and others were not so keen. They feared incidents that would harm them in the forthcoming elections, and they were concerned that Laurier's position would cost them many votes. The Toronto Young Men's Liberal Club was on Laurier's side and they invited him. He accepted. Blake met him at the train station — along with a body-guard. There was a crowded reception at a large hotel, and then he was whisked off to the Horticultural Pavilion, where he found it full to the rafters. As he mounted the stage with Blake, there were a few jeers and he gave a nervous smile. He walked with his head held high to his chair and sat peacefully, his hands on his knees and his eyes closed, waiting to be introduced. With that done, he stood up and advanced. There were no jeers, but there was no applause, either. He began to speak.

It was not a great speech. He had thought that the Scots, the Irish, and the English in this audience would prefer the logic in his documents to his eloquent interpretation of them, and he chose to be cerebral. It was a mistake he would not repeat in his future encounters with the Anglo-Saxon mind. He reiterated in Toronto what he had been saying since July 1885: the Tory government had bungled its stewardship of the North-West. "I charge against them that they have treated the half-breeds with contempt, with undisguised disdain," he began. "I charge against them that they would not listen to their prayers; I charge against them that they drove them to despair, that they drove them to the rashness, to the madness, to the crime which they afterwards committed." Having stated his position, he challenged them with accepting his fundamental creed and the *raison d'être* of his being in politics: "When we find a government ill-treating a poor people, simply because they are poor and ignorant, I say that it behooves us to fight with all the means that the constitution places in our hands."

He marshalled his words as carefully as he could, as he professed his faith in British institutions. He didn't bore his audience, but he failed to move them — except once. Twenty-two years before, he had said in his valedictory speech at McGill; "The union of the people is the secret of the future." Now he defined the nature of that unity and the content of that secret:

We are Canadians. Below the island of Montréal the water that comes from the north, the Ottawa, unites with the waters that come from the Western lakes; but uniting they do not mix. There they run parallel, separate, distinguishable, and yet are on stream, flowing within the same banks, the mighty St. Lawrence, rolling on towards the sea bearing the commerce of a nation upon its bosom — a perfect image of our nation.

We may not assimilate, we may not blend, but for all that we are the component parts of the same country. We may be French in our origin — and I do not deny my origin, I pride myself on it — we may be English or Scotch, or whatever it may be, but we are Canadians, one in aim and purpose.

He thanked them for their courtesy in listening to him attentively and he begged their indulgence for speaking so long. Exhausted, as he always was after such exercises, he sat down with the conviction that again he had pushed the frontiers of men's minds and hearts. He was applauded and cheered by even those who had come to scoff. Blake was effusive in his thanks. He spoke for half an hour. Many considered it the most powerful public address Blake had ever given. So pleased was Blake that he took Laurier immediately to London, Stratford, and Windsor, with the same result. Some did jeer, others planned to harm him physically, editorialists condemned him as a traitor, and young people were sent to deliver wooden muskets to him on the platform. The majority, however, acknowledged this man of courage and vision, and they did not forget.

Nor did he. At the end of the year he wrote to Blake to thank him. He was glad he had gone to Ontario: "It is you, my dear friend, that I am most indebted to, for you have risked more than anybody else. I feel much more than I can express how generous your conduct has been."

Laurier came back to Arthabaska for Christmas and a short rest. It was a nice holiday for him, as the attention of the province was riveted on the provincial legislature that opened towards the end of January 1887. Laurier stayed well away as Mercier manoeuvred himself into the premiership of Québec. February would bring the federal elections.

The Liberals were ready. Laurier had worked the province; Pacaud had organized his battalions; Mercier was fit and eager to help — repaying the favour Laurier had done him. The winter, though, was harsh; the Conservatives, under

Chapleau and Tarte, and with Sénécal's money, wouldn't let go; a few bishops and priests intervened here and there in favour of the Conservatives; and those Ultramontanes who had abandoned their party over the Riel affair returned to their fold. In spite of these *contretemps*, Laurier was optimistic about the results. His health and vigour had never been better; victory was in his grasp.

On 22 February 1887 it escaped both him and Blake. Even though the Liberals gained two seats in Ontario and seventeen in Québec, Macdonald still had a smaller but comfortable majority of thirty-seven seats in a House of 215 members. The Québec results — thirty-two Conservatives, thirty-two Liberals — were gratifying, however, and ensured Laurier's position as the Québec leader of the federal Liberal Party. He had a good majority in his own constituency of Québec-Est and he managed to defeat almost every Conservative in the Québec electoral district. His law partner, Joseph Lavergne, was elected in Drummond-Arthabaska, a gain from the Conservatives.

Blake decided to stay on as leader of the opposition, provided that Laurier, Richard Cartwright, and others helped him with the work of the session. But his health declined further and, by the end of May, he was forbidden to leave his house to return to the Commons. On 1 June he announced that he would resign. That same afternoon the caucus sent a small delegation to ascertain his views about a possible successor. Tired and visibly shaken, he replied: "There is only one possible choice — Laurier." To Laurier himself, Blake said: "It is because you are a French-Canadian — among your other qualifications — that you must lead our party. Our opportunity lies in Québec. Without Québec, we will never hold office. Besides, my dear friend, there is no one else to whom I can transfer the burden of office. I know you well and you are up to it."

The days following were filled with talk and more talk, consultation after consultation. The caucus struck a committee on which Laurier sat to find a solution, there being no time to waste. Gradually, the caucus members came to recognize that, indeed, there was no other man. At the Liberal caucus meeting of 7 June, Cartwright moved that Laurier be offered the leadership. Without Laurier's vote, the motion passed unanimously.

Politely, he thanked them for the honour, but declined. They pleaded with him to consider the party, but again his answer was the same.

For the next twelve days he had hardly any rest. The consultations continued in earnest, and telegrams to Zoë flew back and forth. To his surprise, she agreed with the Blakes: he was the only man for it. Finally, on a beautiful and sunny Saturday, 18 June, he decided that he had to accept for the good of the party and "perhaps of the country." He told the caucus that his leadership would last only until Blake was ready to come back. On 23 June 1887 it was officially announced that Wilfrid Laurier was the new leader of the Liberal Party of Canada.

Laurier had reached his Rubicon.

8

THE CROSSING OF THE RUBICON
1887–1891

Ottawa, le 29 juin 1897

Mon cher Ernest:

The repeated attacks of Québec citizens upon the Salvation Army
must cease. They are unworthy of the liberal society which I pride
myself in representing. The Army must be able to hold its parades
without interference — in full liberty and in peace.

If necessary, I am prepared to march at their head to protect
them.

Laurier's first official act as leader of the Liberal Party of Canada and of Her
Majesty's loyal opposition was to defend the rights and liberties of a small
group of people in the capital city of the province of Québec. It spoke
well for the next thirty-two years.

Becoming leader, however, had made him miss Zoë's birthday. She welcomed the gift he brought at the beginning of July when he returned from
Ottawa, accepting his apologies by telling him that birthdays didn't matter much
to her. But he found her anxious. She had not yet taken full measure of what
the leadership meant in her life. He would be in Ottawa longer than before, but
he already spent one-third of the year there. She would have to go up more often.
There would be tours and meetings and speaking engagements — that she was
familiar with. The stenographer and other political people would intrude and,
at times, invade her home. She would have no problem with that, either — she
was a spontaneous and hospitable person and her house was always crowded.

One or three more wouldn't matter very much. Besides, living with the Gauthiers had taught her about whirlwinds. However, her practical mind needed to sort out all these people and activities, and she had to find her way to do what she wanted to do: to protect him, make his life less burdensome, keep in touch with family and friends, and care for the "children." That caused her some anxiety.

So did the financial factor. When he practised law, Laurier made good money. His name and reputation attracted clients to his and Lavergne's office. She estimated that he spent about half his time practising his profession. With his fees and his parliamentary indemnity of $1500, it was enough for them to live on gracefully, in spite of the many expenses occasioned by his being in politics. For some of these, though, he was reimbursed. With his being the leader, circumstances would change. There would be less time for law, and his two new posts of Party leader and leader of the opposition did not carry a stipend. Lavergne would have to work longer and harder, but he, too, as a member of Parliament, now passed many months in Ottawa. Where would the money come from to replace that income? What about the additional expenses of clothes, better rooms in Ottawa or even a house, entertainment, travel, and whatever else she was forgetting? She feared that the lack of money to meet his obligations would make him disheartened and desperate. This concern would affect his health and hasten his death. On the other hand, she had agreed to his new position. He had the ability to convince her that what he wanted was the best. Having found out early in their life together that his well-being consisted of a combination of things, only some of which she could offer, she had to let him be. She would pray, but she was fully aware that the next few years would not be easy.

July was a hectic month, with little of the rest they had both anticipated. Everyone, every district and constituency, wanted a piece of him. Invitations poured in from all over the province. In desperation, he accepted one from the little town of Somerset in the constituency of Mégantic. Pacaud was furious: his first appearance as leader should have been in Québec-Est. He was right, of course, but Laurier laboured under the assumption that he went where he was invited. So Somerset it was, on Thursday, 2 August. He would use the meeting to enumerate the three main objectives that would preside over his leadership.

Sadly for him, he hadn't much time to define them. There were things to think about and look after: visits from family and friends, by-elections, patronage questions, and party organization. His legal offices were filled with clients and people requiring attention, and the stenographer had to be kept busy to justify his keep. In between, he found a minute here, an hour there, a day alone to mull over his *projet de pays*, his grand design. There was hardly any time for Émilie.

~

When he became leader of the Liberal Party in 1887, Canada was not in a healthy state. British Columbia, temporarily pacified by Macdonald and the Canadian Pacific, was always on the verge of rebellion; the Riel affair was still simmering in the North-West, instigating demands for even more autonomy; Manitoba was building railways in defiance of the contract with the Canadian Pacific Railway; Ontario was barely recuperating from Macdonald's and Oliver Mowat's skirmishes over the disallowance of provincial legislation; Québec, under Mercier, was pursuing a policy of greater *nationaliste* autonomy; and the Maritimes, particularly Nova Scotia, were on the verge of pulling out. How long could the "present fabric of Canada" last? Laurier had to find an answer.

Canada's population at that time was fewer than five million, the vast majority concentrated in Ontario and Québec. Few immigrants came in, and Canadians and *Canadiens* left in droves for the United States. In practically every region of Canada, Richard Cartwright once pointed out, "you cannot find one single solitary Canadian family which has not a son or a daughter or a brother or a sister or some near and dear relative now inhabiting the United States." Canada could not grow and prosper in such circumstances. Again: How long could the present fabric last?

Everywhere lay the seeds of racial and religious discord. Riel had seen to that. Buried under the prairie earth, he still threatened the well-being of the country. Québec thundered against the intolerance of Ontario, and Ontario denounced papal influence and French domination. It would be easy in such an atmosphere for a demagogue to appear and smash the union to bits.

The unity that Confederation had guaranteed some twenty years before was not much in evidence. The national sentiment it had been asked to foster was present in some people, but not in the majority. Canadians thought of themselves as citizens of regions divided into provinces, some more powerful and more equal than others. Ignorance was bliss; prejudice against one another was rampant; and the fabric appeared to be held together by the will of one man — Macdonald — and the sheer force of bribery.

The economic situation was also unsatisfactory — due, some said, to Macdonald's National Policy of protectionism and transcontinental railways. The farmers bitched, as did coal and lumber merchants and other exporters. A grassroots movement arose in many places across Canada for a liberalization of trade with the United States and the harnessing of the CPR — particularly given the current recession. The promise of protectionism had not been fulfilled in rural areas and in the West, and internal markets were no longer growing.

In addition, many wondered about the place of Canada in world affairs. Where did Canada fit in the master plan of the British Empire, where it was recognized as the senior dominion? And how should Canada adapt to the ever-expanding agenda of its neighbour to the south, the United States of America?

In his Somerset speech on 2 August, Laurier did not mince words. If truth be told, he said, "the Maritime provinces submit to Confederation, but do not love it; the province of Manitoba is in open revolt; the province of Nova Scotia demands its separation from Confederation; in fact, carry your gaze from east to west and from north to south and everywhere the prevailing feeling will be found to be one of unrest and uneasiness, of discontent and irritation." He went on to blast the Conservative government in Ottawa for its failure to comprehend the country, for its obsession with control, and its unbridled use of the veto power, "by far the most arbitrary weapon with which tyranny has ever armed a federal government." Confederation could survive only if the federal union — the only union possible "that can secure civil and political liberty and national unity" — was respected. For Laurier, national unity lay with provincial autonomy, in those spheres that belonged to the provinces.

But there was something beyond regions and provinces. There was Canada. In his speech, he addressed the *Canadiens,* but through them he reached out to every area, region, and province in the country:

> I ask you one thing, that, while remembering that I, a French-
> Canadian, have been elected leader of the Liberal Party of Canada,
> you will not lose sight of the fact that the limits of our common

country are not confined to the province of Québec, but that they extend to all the territory of Canada, and that our country is wherever the British flag waves in America. I ask you to remember this in order to remind you that your duty is simply and above all to be Canadians.

To be Canadians! That was the object of Confederation in the intention of its authors. The aim and end of Confederation was to bring the different races closer together, to soften the asperities of their mutual relations, and to connect the scattered groups of British subjects.

What occupied Laurier's mind the most, though, between his accession to the leadership in June 1887 and his Somerset speech at the beginning of August was the economic stagnation that prevailed over the land. Laurier and his party were determined to find a remedy for it and, at the same time, to offer the electorate an imaginative policy that would counteract Macdonald's National Policy. In the pursuit of that objective, he first consulted Blake: "Is it time to endeavour to strike for a bold policy, or shall we abstain, or shall we wait?"

Laurier had the choice of two courses of action — one in the direction of the empire, the other towards the United States. The former was known as Imperial Federation, and, since 1885, had been spearheaded in Canada through the Imperial Federation League. It aimed to meld all components of the British Empire together through an imperial parliament, a single military force, and imperial preferential trade. The British race would expand yet again. "An idle dream," scoffed Macdonald; "the dream of yesterday," dismissed Blake. Laurier, who had thought very little about the empire, said nothing — for the moment.

The second route was closer to home. It lay via Washington and it took the form of direct annexation, commercial union, unrestricted reciprocity, and many other names. Annexation, although it found many devotees, would not catch the Canadian imagination. But what about "commercial union"? That, to Laurier, meant one tariff for both countries, with the proceeds to be divided on a per capita basis, and no customs duties at all between the two. It was not such a far-fetched idea. Ever since the abrogation of the Reciprocity Treaty in 1864, Canada had been wanting closer economic ties with the Americans. In 1887 there was a chance that the idea could be pursued, for in negotiations over the fisheries with the United States that year, Canada proposed a larger treaty covering both the fisheries and unrestricted trade between the two countries.

Laurier sought the advice of a few men in his party, and he found enough support for commercial union to continue exploring the issue. Blake, however, did not reply to his inquiry. In the elections of 1887 he had declared that the tariff was not an issue, and now he was too ill to participate in what would become a point of division between him and Laurier. Nor did he respond to Laurier's enthusiastic note of 14 July announcing his "bold policy" of commercial union. Laurier was so taken with it that he planned to go to La Malbaie, where Blake was vacationing, to discuss it with him. He would bring Zoë. However, family pressures kept the Lauriers at home. Consequently, by the time of Laurier's Somerset speech, Blake had not validated the policy. Nor had there been any serious indication from the American government that it was willing to "treat with us," as Cartwright put it. At Somerset, then, Laurier was vague on the subject, stressing the need to end the Conservative policy of retaliation, as he called protectionism, and to show the American people that "we are brothers, and to hold out our hands to them, with a due regard for the duties we owe to our mother country. We must not forget that any kind of reciprocity with the United States would be to the advantage of Canada." It was hardly a clear or specific statement. Laurier was groping for a policy that would make every inhabitant feel positive about belonging to Canada.

He spent the fall continuing his consultations. Blake had little enthusiasm for commercial union. Mackenzie was revolted; but Cartwright favoured it. Others were struck with mortal terror, fearing to be branded as traitors to the mother country. Laurier received all these views in Arthabaska and wondered if he would ever get anything off the ground. Instead of uniting the party and the country, was he about to divide them irrevocably? He needed something to rally his caucus, ignite the imagination of Canadians, and make a bold stroke. With Blake, he argued that "we must be prepared to take up the subject not only for discussion but for action," but the ailing man was soon on his way to Europe to recuperate and was, therefore, of little help. Laurier's inclination was to strike as quickly as possible and "casser les vitres" if necessary. All that bravado was more political than economic.

~

Laurier had no rest at all. He became impatient with Ernest Pacaud and those around him. The party lost crucial by-elections and he had no time for his legal practice. The bills mounted, with no hope in sight. His bold policy had brought only distress and discouragement. He didn't know where to turn, except to Blake. In two quite intimate letters, one before the session of 1888 and the other in its midst, he poured his heart out.

He wanted Blake to reassume the leadership so that he could fulfil his own goal — to live in this quiet place, in the company of his books and a few select friends. He did not want to shirk his duty, but the responsibilities and the burdens of leadership were too much for him. If Blake would not return, the party would have to find someone else. He spoke to a few members of the caucus about his resigning at the end of the session of 1888. This was not a question of choice, he told Blake in March. It was that he had "no taste for the position. I find no pleasure in it." Financially, he was hard-pressed, too, and would soon be seriously embarrassed.

Blake was sympathetic and suggested that he tell the party he couldn't give all his time to the leadership. "My opinion is that our party would gladly accede to this view. I cannot look forward without the greatest apprehension to your resignation & trust that calamity may be averted; but not at the cost of an embarrassment to you which no friend has the right to impose."

The calamity didn't happen and no resignation was forthcoming. Laurier was well satisfied with the 1888 session, which began on 23 February and ended on 22 May. He was busy through it all. "Commercial union" as an expression was superseded by "unrestricted reciprocity." The bold policy had become a purely commercial one, and he intended to keep it strictly on that line, he advised Blake, who was still in Italy. He hoped it would sell well in the country, be of interest to the Americans, and cause no patriotic heart to break.

In the summer of 1888 Laurier and Zoë took a ship from Québec and sailed to La Malbaie to see the Blakes. They found Blake in good health and pleasant form. They spent hours discussing the questions of CU and UR, as Blake called them, but the old leader was not prepared to debate the Liberal economic policy in public. He was still opposed to reciprocity, and he asked Laurier to drop the matter, as others had, too, in Ontario. Those Americans, he said, who had favoured some form of CU, now appeared to clamour for annexation pure and simple. But Laurier believed his idea was a good one and he was not prepared to abandon it. He was sure that Blake would not speak out against him. "If I cannot help you," Blake had remarked with some passion, "I will not hurt you. Be sure of that!"

~

On 26 March 1889 an obscure Conservative member of Parliament, William Edward O'Brien, set off a pernicious war of intolerance that was to last for several decades and to make Laurier question whether a *Canadien* or a Roman Catholic could ever serve as leader of a political party in Canada. The main inspirer and handler of this racial conflict was D'Alton McCarthy, a narrow-minded Protestant, Conservative member of Parliament for Simcoe North in Ontario, founder of the Imperial League in Canada, high priest of the Equal Rights Association, and éminence grise behind the Orange Order. McCarthy's mission was to abolish every vestige of the French language, *Canadien* culture, and Roman Catholic educational rights outside Québec. Indeed, if the noble Anglo-Saxon race could conquer the French again, he would have his day. His philosophy was simple: "One Québec was more than enough." He disapproved of what he saw as the basic policy of both parties: "wooing the French." "The French," as he called the *Canadiens*, were "the great danger to the Confederacy." French "nationalism" had to be checked wherever it found life. If the ballot box couldn't bring it about in this generation then "bayonets will supply it in the next."

What had enraged McCarthy and his followers were the Jesuits' Estates, or the "Biens des Jésuites." These were vast tracts of land given to the Jesuits before the Conquest of 1760. The British confiscated these lands so they could be transferred to Lower Canada in 1832 and to the province of Québec in 1867. In between these dates, the Jesuit Order was suppressed by the pope and later reinstated. In 1887 the Jesuits demanded either the return of their estates or compensation. Premier Mercier offered $400,000 — a sum far lower than the $2-million value placed on the properties — to put an end to the squabbling. But the actual division of the money remained the crucial question. Mercier stepped around that political minefield by asking the pope, Leo XIII, to distribute the money. He put it all in a law that was passed on 28 June 1888. The provisions in the Jesuits' Estates Act were only one page long, but the preamble covered several pages and contained all the correspondence exchanged between the pope, the government, and the Jesuits.

The "old" Liberals of Laurier's generation were not in favour of Mercier's action. Louis-Amable Jetté, writing to Laurier at the time the bill became law, accused Mercier of acting imprudently, with dire consequences for the liberties of the *Canadiens*. He predicted that the Jesuits would use the money to establish a university in Montréal, with the result that, in ten years' time, "there will not be a single educated French-Canadian who will dare call himself a Liberal." Laurier was not indifferent, but he saw it as purely a provincial matter. Therefore, it was none of his affair — until it entered the national arena.

The Jesuits' Estates Act aroused a violent Protestant reaction, encouraged and supported by opportunists like McCarthy. So agitated were some Protestants that a couple of their ministers preached from the pulpit that to assassinate a Jesuit would be an act welcomed in heaven. A campaign was launched to force the Macdonald government to disallow the Québec legislation on the grounds that a foreign power had supplanted the authority of the British Crown; that the public treasury was being used to compensate individuals who had no legal right to restitution; that it infringed upon the separation of church and state; and that the secularization of the clergy reserves a generation earlier had settled the question of clerical estates.

The debate on O'Brien's motion to disallow the Québec law lasted three days. Laurier spoke on 28 March. Satisfied that Mercier was redressing a wrong that had lasted too long and that the legislature of Québec was in full accord with what he was doing, Laurier said that Mercier's offer should be the end of it. As for the racial antagonism that permeated the whole debate, he asserted that, in his Canada, "there can be more than one race, but there shall be but one nation." He reiterated what he had said before: "I do not intend to forget my origin, but I am a Canadian before anything." The following day, the motion was defeated 188 to 13, but the mischief continued its inexorable march.

At the grandiose Saint-Jean-Baptiste Day celebrations in Québec that year, Laurier turned his attention to the *Canadiens*. It was not possible to go on in Canada without generosity on everyone's part. To those like the *Castors*, the far right wing of the Conservative Party, or even Mercier, given his exclusive *Canadien* nationalism, Laurier had this to say:

> We are French-Canadians, but our country is not confined to the territory overshadowed by the Citadelle of Québec; our country is Canada.
>
> Our fellow-countrymen are not only those in whose veins runs the blood of France. They are all those, whatever their race or whatever their language, whom the fortune of war, the chances of fate, or their own choice have brought among us and who acknowledge the sovereignty of the British Crown. The rights of my fellow-countrymen are as dear to me, as sacred to me, as the rights of my own race.
>
> What I claim for ourselves is an equal place in the sun, an equal share of justice, of liberty; that share we have; and what we claim for ourselves we are anxious to grant to others.

In more ways than one, his words were a warning and an appeal: a warning of the need for moderation and an appeal for consideration; a warning to remember that no one, no community, no race, was an island; and an appeal for tolerance and acceptance of others as they were. Everyone had an equal place in the sun.

But did they? On 9 August 1889 Cartwright wrote to say that Manitoba would move to abolish separate schools and the French language in that province. Where would the madness end?

Six weeks later, on 30 September, Laurier took his same message to Toronto. It was a risk. He was relatively unknown in the province and in its capital city, and he had not as yet won the enthusiastic support of the Liberals. The Ontario Liberal leaders didn't want any part of him there. His position during the debate on the Jesuits and their properties had caused quite a stir in the kingdom of the Tories. Practically everywhere in Ontario, he was described as an agent of the Jesuits, and his people were represented as the enemies of Confederation. He had to challenge those scurrilous charges.

The audience was hostile and had come to put this *Canadien* in his place. They liked a good fight, and they remembered from his speech in 1886 that he had courage. So they listened, but interrupted him along the way. For five minutes at his mention of McCarthy's name a tumult almost erupted. However, he didn't flinch. And they quietened down as he told them in plain English that he had no lesson to receive from anyone about standing up to priests and bishops, or anyone else, in the defence of civil liberty and religious freedom. He had been there and, should the attempt be made again, "we shall do as in the past; we shall fight them."

But much more was to come. If there were people in Québec, as the Toronto newspapers and McCarthy's clique continued to assert, who "dreamed of forming themselves into a small community of Frenchmen on the banks of the St. Lawrence," he was not one of them. If the pope's name had not been mentioned in the Jesuits' Estates Act, it — he had to stop here for the wild uproar to end — would have passed easily. If any legislature tried to "substitute the authority of the pope for the authority of the queen," that would be treason and would have to be dealt with as treason. If anyone thought that the Jesuits — again the uproar — could be refused liberty "because they might abuse it," then that would be an abuse in itself, an abuse of the principles of British Liberalism. And if anyone in the hall believed that use of the French language was a danger to Confederation, he had this to say: "I am a French-Canadian; I was brought up on the knees of a French mother, and my first recollections are those recollections which no man ever forgets. And shall it be denied to me, the privilege of addressing the same language to those who are dear to me?" He had not given them an inch.

With astounding courage, "directness of purpose," as the *Canadian Gazette* put it, and high statesmanship, he had offset his enemies, renewed the spirit and fibre of his fellow Liberals, and rendered "a great national service." According to John Willison of the *Globe*, it was that speech that established his authority over the Liberal Party and made him its undisputed leader. He showed that he would not be "turned from his purpose. This man would be a giant in some great national crisis."

∼

A month later, Zoë, Laurier, and the Pacauds spent five days in New York. They stayed at the Park Avenue Hotel, visited St. Patrick's Cathedral, stared at the mansions of the rich, saw Cora Tanner in *Fascination* at the Grand Opera House, and ate at Delmonico's. The ladies shopped along Fifth Avenue while Laurier read in the Astor Library on Lafayette Place or talked endlessly with Pacaud about things to come. They had a good time, and Pacaud paid for it all. Laurier was cheerful.

No sooner had he returned to Arthabaska, however, than he became quite ill. Zoë bolted the door of her house, barred everyone from his presence, especially the stenographer, and proceeded to make him well and whole. She had succeeded by the end of the year.

~

In the parliamentary session that opened on 1 February 1890, Blake returned to the House — he had kept his seat through his two-year absence. Cartwright was now Laurier's seatmate, so Blake sat a few benches down. But he was his old self — combative, brilliant, and determined to influence national policy. The situation could have been quite difficult for both of them had Laurier allowed it to be. He was genuinely happy Blake was there. Every now and then they talked in the Parliamentary Library as they had done before, and Laurier swept under the rug the sneers and innuendoes that he was to be replaced as leader. At the same time, he had to be ever vigilant. Did that mean that he had reconciled himself to being leader of the Liberal Party? The time to answer that question had not yet arrived.

The House had been in session only five days when McCarthy introduced a bill to abolish the use of the French language in the legislature and courts of the North-West Territories. "In the interest of the national unity of the Dominion," he said, "there should be a community of language among the people of Canada." The language option had been allowed since the mid-1870s and it cost the taxpayers of the Territories about four hundred dollars a year. It proved of direct use to only a few people, since there were hardly any *Canadiens* in that vast sweep of land between the western frontier of Manitoba and the Rocky Mountains. There were, however, Métis. The debate on McCarthy's motion lasted for one week in February. It was a week of highly strung emotion devoted to a perilously divisive discussion of a minor issue — an issue filled with the potential of racial violence, not so much in the House of Commons as in the country.

McCarthy had prepared his public well. Before the session, he had dismissed the *Canadiens* as a "bastard nationality" and encouraged his followers to fight. After all, he argued, "this is a British country, and the sooner we take up our French-Canadians and make them British, the less trouble will we leave to posterity." French ought to be banned across the country.

It was a most anxious time. Tension was in the air. Prejudice lived so near the surface of cordiality that many feared that irreparable damage could be done to political loyalty and racial harmony. Violence lurked in the galleries and on the streets, perhaps even on the floor of the House of Commons. The day before Laurier was to speak in the debate, he wrote to Émilie that his office was crowded all day by "anxious men, rushing in with long faces, men with advice, men with a prayer and then again with different advice and a different prayer." He took it in his stride. His colleagues were always nervous before he made an important speech. They didn't totally trust his "French-ness" and his "Catholic-ness." But they had nothing to fear.

Many members from both sides of the House spoke eloquently to undo the mischief as much as possible. Laurier was moved by John A. Macdonald's entreaty for tolerance, and was particularly proud of the contribution made by so many in his party. Cartwright delivered the most formidable rebuke of all to McCarthy: "I say that no good has come of this Bill; I say that no good can come of it; and I am sorry to have to add that, in my judgment, speaking without prejudice or malice, I cannot but believe that no good was intended to come out of the proposal."

By the time Laurier stood up to speak, he had come to realize that this debate was only the first shot in a war to deprive his people of "everything which constitutes their distinct individuality" in Canada. That war would take a long time to work itself out. With fire in his eyes and resolve in his voice he said:

> I denounce this policy as anti-Canadian.
> I denounce it as fatal to the hope we at one time entertained, and which I, for one, am not disposed to give up, of forming a nation on this continent.
> I denounce it as a crime, a national crime.

What then was the solution? It was only by extending the principles of provincial autonomy to the North-West Territories that the issue could be resolved. The institutions of the North-West were still in their formative stage. The future would, therefore, determine the various forms they would take. But provincial autonomy was a cold and dry fish with no bones, no flesh, no heart, no soul. A nation, however, was alive: it had vitality and passion; it was what he was about. And so:

> We are here a nation, or we want to be a nation. The honourable gentleman will revert to the cold, dry argument that, after all, a duality of race will produce friction, and that friction will produce danger. But where is the remedy? The true remedy is mutual forbearance and respect.

Macdonald had made the question a free vote, but he was not about to have McCarthy's absurd racist views vindicated by a majority in the House of Commons he cared so much about. Nor was Laurier, even though the potential for mischief was less on his side of the House than on Macdonald's. With Blake's help, the Macdonald government framed a motion that allowed the North-West Assembly to be master of the language in which it published its deliberations; the federal government, however, would continue to publish ordinances in both English and French, and both languages would still be used in judicial proceedings. The amendment also denied McCarthy's main objective: uniformity of language would not be pursued as a national objective. Laurier was among the 149 members of the House who accepted it — though fifty voted against it, including a few Québec Liberal members.

This division in his ranks vexed Laurier, and he made his feelings known to Pacaud. "It is important," he wrote to him the day after the vote, "that you mention in your articles that the principle of provincial autonomy is vital to our province." In the final analysis, he reminded Pacaud, "we have no other means to protect ourselves." His strong sense of equity made him apply the principle even if it ran counter to the interests of "notre cause." In the case of the North-West Territories, it would be unjust and not very perceptive to impose two languages when the people living there desired only one.

There wasn't much time, however, for the luxury of introspection. There were provincial elections to be fought: Nova Scotia and Ontario in May, and Québec in June. New Brunswick had already elected a Liberal administration in January. Laurier's role outside Québec was limited, but in his own province he was willing to work to achieve a triumph for Mercier. "You can use me wherever you like," he wrote to Pacaud. Such intimacy didn't please Blake very much. Laurier admitted that Mercier's methods were "repugnant to my convictions," but argued that those of the Conservatives were worse. Besides, he understood quite well that a provincial base was a good foundation on which to build a federal victory. He did, however, warn both Pacaud and Mercier about railroaders bearing gifts — advice neither of them took. On 17 June Mercier won with a large majority. In the shadows stood the men of the railways and Joseph-Israël Tarte.

~

Tarte had played a part in provincial and federal politics since the early 1870s. He was small in stature, sported a goatee, and was always immaculately dressed. His energy was astounding; his mind, fertile; his capacity for polemics, unparalleled; his organizational skills, unsurpassed; and he was incorruptible. He was the conduit for millions of dollars in election funds: not one penny ever found its way into his bank account. Mercurial, he changed his mind regularly and his political affiliation often. Attached to the Ultramontanes at the beginning of his journalistic career, he had moved away from them to the Chapleau-Sénécal wing of the Conservative Party after Chapleau entered the federal Cabinet in 1882. Eight years later, he was ready to migrate again — this time to Laurier's Liberals. In his baggage was the documentation on a scandal the likes of which had not been seen since the days of the Pacific Scandal. By the time the satchel was empty, a Father of Confederation was destroyed, a member of Parliament expelled, and Tarte had become the architect of Laurier's victory in 1896. The scandal is known as the McGreevy-Langevin Scandal.

Interestingly, Tarte had begun to reveal his allegations during the provincial elections of May-June 1890 as part of the Conservative strategy to defeat Mercier. The information had come to him through Robert McGreevy, the brother of the well-known contractor and Conservative fundraiser, Thomas

McGreevy, who was also the member for Québec-Ouest in the federal Parliament. In 1888 the brothers had a falling-out: Thomas, for unknown reasons, sued Robert for the recovery of loans amounting to $354,000. Robert swore revenge and began accumulating documents while Thomas's suit meandered its way through the courts. At the beginning of the session of 1890, Robert took his documents to Ottawa, where they were shown to Macdonald, Sir Hector Langevin, and McGreevy. Robert received no satisfaction in that quarter. He therefore turned to Tarte in March. Tarte showed the documents to Chapleau, Caron, and the lieutenant governor of Québec, Auguste-Réal Angers, before contacting Macdonald twice. The prime minister dismissed the charges as lies. With the tacit approval of Chapleau and Caron, who were both at odds with McGreevy and Langevin, Tarte began to incriminate Thomas in his newspaper, *Le Canadien*, on 18 April 1890. At Chapleau's request, Langevin's name was not mentioned in these early articles. Tarte had three objectives in mind: to force Macdonald and Langevin to abandon McGreevy; to implicate Mercier's Liberals, who were about to hand over $800,000 to Thomas for his participation in the building of a railway in Québec, $300,000 of which was to go to Liberal provincial election coffers; and to exact his personal revenge against Thomas, who had foiled some of Tarte's pet projects in the previous years.

Tarte's revelations during the provincial campaign shocked Laurier, Blake, Cartwright, and many other federal Liberals. Laurier had cautioned Pacaud not to get involved, but it was inevitable that he would be. He was the chief of Mercier's men. As for Mercier, he kept reassuring Laurier. Do not lend credence to Tarte's accusations, he urged; order our friends to keep quiet; and remember that Thomas McGreevy has been most useful to us, and can be so again in the forthcoming provincial and federal elections. Laurier was not reassured, but he maintained his reluctant alliance with Mercier. Tarte wrote that Laurier's continued assistance to Mercier was not honourable and not compatible with his views on political honesty and morality. That Laurier was not more forceful would cost him dearly down the road.

Thomas McGreevy was no man to be put asunder. He sued. On 5 May he had Tarte arrested for libel and, nine days later, filed suit against the editor of *Le Canadien* for $50,000. This didn't frighten Tarte, who continued, with the help of Robert, to collect documents. What had been a political cause became a private one. When Laurier saw all of Tarte's documents, he realized their political implications and ramifications. The scandal had to be followed through to its logical conclusions. The Conservatives would be considerably hurt; the Liberals, much less so. It was a fair price to pay. He agreed to be Tarte's lawyer and to incorporate him slowly into the party. The case, though, went nowhere. It was postponed and, when the matter was brought before Parliament after the federal election of 1891, it was dropped entirely. Meanwhile, Mercier was triumphant in the Québec election of 1890.

$\sim$

In 1891 the time had come for a general election. Tarte had accused the treasurer of the Conservative Party in Québec, who was also a member of Parliament, of corruption and had implicated a senior Cabinet minister; the Americans were moving to lower tariffs and introduce some form of reciprocity; and the Canadian Pacific — that Tory government on wheels, as the *Globe* called it — needed another federal guarantee. Such conditions were conducive to the call for a general election sooner than later. Tarte was politically dangerous, but his impact could be minimized if the Liberals were fighting an election rather than demanding committees of inquiry in the House. The Liberal thunder over better trade relations with the Americans could be stolen if the government could announce that a form of reciprocal trade could be worked out with the Americans without contravening the national policy of protection and loyalty to the empire. And since the Conservatives couldn't possibly go to the people without CPR money — which was not forthcoming — they had to frighten the company to "shell out" as never before to Macdonald. In that last part of the scenario, Laurier was the innocent catalyst.

At the beginning of February he was on his way to New York to speak at a dinner organized by the Board of Trade. He discovered that William Cornelius Van Horne, the president and chairman of the board of directors of the CPR, was on the same train. Laurier went to Van Horne's car and talked with him about various political and economic matters. Before leaving, he remarked, "I suppose, since you are in on the secrets of the government, you can tell when the elections will be held." Van Horne, to whom Macdonald had confided in November 1990 that there would not be an election for at least ten months, answered without a hint of guilt: "I am not in on the secrets of the government. Ask Sir John." Laurier looked at him for a minute or so and replied: "Well, then, I may give you some news: Parliament will be dissolved before we return from New York." Laurier was not in the councils of the government, but his reading of the implications of what was going on enabled him to make an educated guess.

Van Horne was astounded: it might mean a Liberal victory. As soon as he could, he telegraphed Laurier's prediction to his colleagues. On 3 February, Macdonald dissolved Parliament and set the elections for 5 March. Two weeks later, the old chieftain, with the CPR on his side, opened his campaign and uttered the famous cry: "A British subject I was born; a British subject I will die." At the same time, the Conservative slogan, "The old man, the old flag, and the old policy," was launched. With that battle hymn, Macdonald planned to assure his victory. He was dying, his Québec wing was in tatters, reciprocity was popular, and his party was racked with scandals and discredited. But he was certain he would pull it off one last time. "My course is clear," he intoned. "With my last breath will I oppose the veiled treason which attempts by sordid means and mercenary proffers to lure our people from their allegiance; and I appeal with equal confidence to the men who have trusted me in the past, and to the young hope of the country, with whom rest its destinies for the future, to give me their united and strenuous aid in this my last effort for the unity of the Empire and the preservation of our commercial and political freedom."

Laurier's political manifesto was less a cry for patriotic fervour than a clear statement of Liberal policy: "The reform suggested is absolute reciprocal freedom of trade between Canada and the United States." It would not impair Canada's links with the empire or make traitors of Canadians. Still, it was well to remember that "the day must come when, from no other cause than the development of national life in the colony, there must be a clashing of interests with the mother land, and, in any such case, much as I would regret the necessity, I would stand by my native land." Such reasoning was not as compelling as Macdonald's ringing slogans with the electorate, and it was soon superseded by the fallout from the theft of a pamphlet in an obscure printing plant in Toronto.

The pamphlet in question was by Edward Farrer, the chief editorial writer of the *Globe*, the most important Liberal newspaper in Ontario. In his booklet, which he had drafted before his appointment, Farrer, in a moment of astounding stupidity, showed the Americans how to annex Canada by making Canadians vulnerable through a variety of economic measures. From Macdonald on down, the government cried "Treason! Collusion!" The Liberals could do nothing about the unfortunate association, try as they might.

They fought on, however. The Maritimes had more or less to be left to themselves. Sir Charles Tupper had returned from London, where he served as the high commissioner, to take command and buy every vote he could. In the West and in British Columbia, the fifteen seats were also in the hands of local politicians. Ontario and Québec were the major battlegrounds. No one but Laurier controlled the campaign in these two provinces. Cartwright, whose enthusiastic support for reciprocity suited the mood in rural areas but antagonized city folks was let loose where he could do most good. Laurier was everywhere in Québec, preceded by Pacaud. When Laurier launched his campaign in his own constituency on 17 February, Mercier led the phalanx of provincial Liberals and promised him a fifteen-seat majority; Tarte made his intention known to be an independent candidate in Montmagny; the Grand Trunk Railway helped the Liberal cause, but not to the same extent that the CPR supported the Conservatives; and the bishops feared annexation. Wholesalers and traders, manufacturers and stock promoters, bankers and railroaders followed Laurier everywhere he went to threaten, to cajole, and to purchase support for the Conservatives. And there was Edward Blake.

Blake had never reconciled himself to the fiscal and economic policy of his party. That Laurier knew; they had discussed it often over the previous two or three years. Even the movement from the "commercial union" of 1887 to the "unrestricted reciprocity" of 1891 didn't impress him. Since Blake's conscience always compelled him to speak his mind, he planned to do so before the elections. Accordingly, at the end of January, he drafted a manifesto to his electors: the famous West Durham letter. But when the election was announced, Blake had not yet sent it. Laurier's immediate concern was to convince Blake to keep silent. A planned Ontario Liberal Convention was cancelled so he would not have an opportunity to speak.

Laurier was successful in obtaining Blake's consent to "die dumb," as Blake confided to a friend. He didn't ask that Blake not run. He and other Liberals were quite willing to have him stand as "a candidate for freer trade relations with the United States," not as a proponent of the official Liberal policy of unrestricted reciprocity, as long as he didn't criticize it. Blake, however, decided that his silence necessitated withdrawal. Consequently, he wrote to his electors that he was not to be a candidate, and that his letter would be published after the election. It was a heavy sacrifice on his part and Laurier sympathized. Unfortunately, Blake's silence provided ammunition to the Conservatives, who interpreted it as tacit support for their position.

On 5 March 1891, in spite of all these contretemps, Laurier and the Liberals did quite well. In fact, they almost pulled it off. They had a larger share of the popular vote than in 1887; Macdonald's majority was reduced to twenty-seven seats; Ontario Liberals stole seven seats from the Conservatives; the results in the Maritimes and in the West, including British Columbia, were the same as in 1887; and in Québec Laurier secured five additional seats, even though the majority of the popular vote in that province went to the Conservatives. Then came the "stab in the back."

It was the West Durham letter. Blake was determined to publish it the day after the election. Laurier attempted to prevent that. "Undoubtedly," he wrote to Blake on 3 March, "your utterance coming when the bitterness of the campaign will be at its highest pitch, will not be received with the calm temper, by either side, which the public welfare would require." Blake, however, was adamant that he would go ahead. "I am very sorry," he replied, "to find myself unable to adopt your views." On 6 March the West Durham letter captured the headlines across the country.

Its publication weakened the Liberal Party. It lost every by-election between March 1891 and January 1893 — fifty-five in all — increasing the Conservative majority in the House to close to sixty seats. Most Liberals were quite angry; some of them, like Cartwright, never spoke to Blake again. He was totally ostracized and his political career in Canada was over.

The defeat, Blake's betrayal, rampant electoral corruption, and Laurier's massive efforts during a campaign marred by rain, sleet, and snow took their toll. For several weeks following the election, Laurier took to his bed. He was often feverish and he hardly ate. He did, however, read a little and, without rancour, thought of his future. He was not in the House when, on 11 May, Tarte opened the little bag he always kept attached to his person and took out the *petits papiers* that contained his evidence for the most important political scandal since 1873. This time it involved, not the construction of a railway, but the federal Department of Public Works. After making sixty-three charges against Langevin, McGreevy, and the department, he demanded a parliamentary investigation by the Select Standing Committee on Privileges and Elections. The hearing began on 26 May.

~

On the evening of Saturday, 6 June 1891, Sir John A. Macdonald died at his residence in Ottawa. On the next Monday afternoon, in the House of Commons, Laurier spoke on behalf of his caucus, his party, and himself. "His loss overwhelms us," he said in one of his most moving speeches in Parliament. Macdonald's place was "so large and so absorbing that it is almost impossible to conceive that the politics of this country — the fate of this country — will continue without him." This was not the time for political partisanship; rather, it was the time to sink all differences and "to remember only the great services he has performed for his country — to remember that his actions displayed unbounded fertility of resources, a high level of intellectual conception, and, above all, a far-reaching vision beyond the event of the day, and still higher, permeating the whole, a broad patriotism, a devotion to Canada's welfare, Canada's advancement, and Canada's glory."

He was moved by the tributes, the thousands of people who assembled to watch the funeral procession, and by the genuine grief he saw all around him. An institutional man by tradition, Laurier saw in Macdonald one of the institutions of his country. He had watched the old man for seventeen years superbly managing his Cabinet, his caucus, and his followers. At the same time, he saw Macdonald as the chief architect of the political immorality he found everywhere. "For Sir John A., politics was a game — with no rules," he once admitted. But he never questioned Macdonald's life-long interest in the welfare of Canada.

~

After the state funeral and the official mourning period, the Tarte drama continued. The country was shocked to hear of trap doors into inner offices, of contracts awarded to fictitious contractors, of estimates removed from departmental offices to be shown to friendly contracting firms, and of gifts of silver and jewellery given to engineers in return for padding contracts to cover electoral expenses. The hearings in the Select Committee ended on 19 August and, eventually, two reports were issued. The Liberals found both McGreevy and Langevin guilty as charged, and the Conservatives exonerated Langevin. The debate on the findings began on 21 September and, when Laurier spoke, he insisted that the Conservative Party in Québec had benefited from McGreevy's crimes. Tarte denied that and, early on the morning of the 24th, the House adopted the majority report by a vote of 101 to 86.

As a direct result of the scandal, a bill was passed which made it a criminal offence for anyone who was either dealing with the government or expecting to deal with it to give, or to promise to give, any money for electoral purposes. Thomas McGreevy was expelled from the House and was later sentenced to a few months in jail. Langevin was not called to succeed Macdonald as prime minister, although he was the senior minister and had been promised the succession. He had no alternative but to resign, which he did on 11 August 1891. The Conservative Party stood discredited and its disunity in Québec was further accentuated. When Chapleau left Ottawa to become lieutenant governor of Québec in 1892, it was left leaderless, a situation that would favour Laurier in 1896.

Unfortunately, no sooner had Tarte finished with his scandal than Mercier, Pacaud, and the Québec provincial Liberals became embroiled in the Baie des Chaleurs Scandal, named for a railway in the Gaspé peninsula of Québec. The railway began construction in 1882 but had hardly progressed by 1891, even though it had received both provincial and federal subsidies. It was a provincial project, but the revelations associated with it weakened the position of the federal Liberals across the country, particularly in Ontario.

In the summer of 1891, the Senate's Railway Committee heard that out of a payment of $175,000 to a claimant involved in the original company, $100,000 was paid to Pacaud as the intermediary between the claimant and Mercier's provincial government. Pacaud was said to have used the money for electoral purposes, and $10,000 had been used to replenish the coffers of the federal Liberal Party. On 11 September 1891 the committee concluded that the Québec Liberal government had, in effect, given itself a subsidy.

The matter didn't end there. Mercier was incommunicado at his farm at Sainte-Anne-de-la-Pérade, the senior Cabinet minister who had signed the order to pay the $175,000 was recuperating at La Malbaie, and Pacaud was on his way to Europe. It seemed that the only official who took the Senate's report seriously was the lieutenant governor, Auguste-Réal Angers. He proposed a royal commission composed of three judges to inquire into all matters pertaining to the railway. He also ordered the government to limit its decisions and actions to urgent matters. A constitutional crisis was brewing.

The commission issued two reports, one in December 1891 and the other in February 1892. The first one by two of the judges implicated Mercier, Pacaud, and Charles Langelier, a provincial Cabinet minister and the brother of Laurier's colleague in the House of Commons, François Langelier. The report of the third commissioner also incriminated Pacaud and Langelier, but not Mercier. No sooner had Angers received the first report than he fired Mercier and called the Ultramontane senator, Charles-Eugène Boucher de Boucherville, to form a new government. The legislature was dissolved and an election was called for 8 March 1892. De Boucherville won it handsomely, with fifty-two Conservatives to eighteen Liberals and one Independent.

The revelations of a scandal involving his provincial friends traumatized Laurier. He feared becoming implicated — he, personally, as a friend of Pacaud's; and his party, politically, because Pacaud served as treasurer of the federal Liberal Party in Québec. When the accusations were first made in the Senate in August, Laurier wrote to Beaugrand, the editor of the Montréal Liberal newspaper *La Patrie*: "Tell me whether there is not some fatality pursuing our party; it is just at the moment that we are showing up the full extent of the corruption of the Conservative Party that a similar revelation comes upon ourselves." The strategy he first proposed to deal with the scandal was naive, cerebral, and ineffective. Later, a couple of weeks before the first report of the Royal Commission was made public on 15 December 1891, he saw Mercier and arranged for a reconstruction of the ministry that would include men, like Joly de Lotbinière, whose integrity was unquestionable. Joly was willing, but Mercier's dismissal pre-empted any attempt to salvage the situation. Beyond that initiative, Laurier didn't do anything publicly until January 1892, when he condemned Angers's decision as arbitrary and unconstitutional and stated categorically that the transaction between the claimant and the provincial government was indefensible. He hoped that those implicated would clear their names and re-establish their honour to the satisfaction of the people.

He was not so reticent in private. In letters to Émilie, he made reference to Pacaud. He was mystified, he told her, and "I look to the near future with apprehension." He mentioned that Pacaud's problems weighed on him. "I cannot approve of him, I cannot stand by him; this is what makes me ache." He asked her to see Pacaud, to assure the "unfortunate boy" of his "unalterable affection," even though "I cannot defend his action in public, nor approve his course in private." Pacaud should not be dejected; "he must keep a dignified silence; he must now bow before the storm: that is the only way for him to resume his old place, & when he has come again to that, I do hope that from that moment he will act & only act from the best impulses of his nature."

Pacaud finally broke his silence in March 1892, after the provincial elections in which neither he nor Laurier played any significant role and a month before he was charged, along with Mercier, for defrauding the queen. He wrote Laurier a long letter explaining his position. In reporting it to Émilie, Laurier said that Pacaud's position was not as desperate as he had feared. "He speaks very hopefully. I firmly believe that he can yet retrieve his position, if he only will be careful." A month or so later, Pacaud, after much reticence so as not to embarrass Laurier, came to Ottawa. Laurier met him at the train station and took him to the Russell, in view of everyone. Their conversation was satisfactory on both sides. Pacaud resumed his activities within the federal wing of the Liberal Party, and the Baie des Chaleurs Scandal was not discussed by Laurier again. There were several trials and many different charges. In the first one, in October–November 1892, both Mercier and Pacaud were found "not guilty" after the jury had deliberated for five minutes. In another trial in which Pacaud was tried alone, he was found guilty and condemned to repay the $100,000. The Supreme Court, however, eventually exonerated him totally.

~

Meanwhile, Blake's isolation had continued unabated. Then, suddenly out of the blue, Laurier wrote to him.

Le lundi, le 20 juillet, 1891

My dear Blake:

I hope divergences in political views will not affect our personal friendship. You know how often and how sincerely I have offered you the opportunity of resuming the leadership of the party. My heart is no more in the position I occupy than it was four years ago, but since I am in it I must discharge its responsibilities to the best of my judgment. May I not rely on your indulgence and friendship to give me help and assistance whenever you can, consistent with your own views of public duty? Apart from the trade question, I know of nothing in which we could not act as in the past.

Wilfrid Laurier

What prompted Laurier? He had sought no contact with Blake since that day in March when the West Durham letter was published. Why in July did he reopen the dialogue and reach out, four months after the "stab in the back," a blow that had cost him and the party he led considerable difficulties, internally as well as externally? The reason was that he had wanted to do so all along, but that he had not known how to do so and on what terms. He also felt that it was up to Blake to make the first advance. When Blake tarried, Laurier took the initiative. On the surface, he consulted Blake on a constitutional question, but the request for the resumption of their friendship arose out of Laurier's magnanimity of spirit and the generosity that marked his relationship with almost everyone he cared about. Beyond that, Laurier, unlike Blake, was a political leader of remarkable courage who held no grudges, and who constantly sought harmony. He was not weak; he was valiant.

Laurier's letter moved Blake, and he responded with two letters of his own. The first one confused Laurier. Blake reproached him for not having written sooner and admitted to being sad, hurt, and bitter about Laurier's silence. Nor did he want anything to do with the leadership. "You say truly," he wrote to Laurier from La Malbaie where he was vacationing, "that you have often and sincerely offered me the resumption of the lead. You know that the position has always been most distasteful to me. Neither of us has ever wanted the crown of thorns and no question can ever arise on that head." However, Laurier had opened the door; Blake walked through it in another letter.

At the beginning of August they were good friends again. As Laurier reported to Émilie, who was also vacationing at La Malbaie with her children: "I received from him two days ago a most affectionate letter, in which the mis-understandings of the last few months are all waved aside." Other prominent Liberals also resumed their contacts with Blake. The "Oracle," as he was called, was no longer isolated.

Laurier confided his feelings for Blake in two or three letters he sent around that time to Émilie at La Malbaie. She was bound to see the Blakes. He wanted her to know how he felt, "because I am sure when you meet him, I must come in for a share of your conversation, but under no circumstances, & for no reason, never show him a letter from me." The reason for that instruction was that Laurier didn't want Blake to know through Émilie "how his action seems unjust to me and that how I feel his conduct towards me, unjustifiable." In spite of Blake's "slap in the face of the party & of me particularly," Laurier couldn't be angry with him: "I know him too well, & love him too well." His reconcili-ation with Blake was "a great burden from off my heart," and it provided Laurier with the opportunity to ponder again his resignation as leader. "I must now press him to come to the front. Apart from all other reasons, he is wealthy, & I am poor, he can bear the sacrifice & I hardly can." Until that could be arranged, "I must plod along for some time more but I do not give up the hope of release." He was determined to follow an even course: "I see the goal & towards the goal I direct my efforts, discarding the impetuous frowns of the rash, the cautious advice of the timid."

Émilie did see the Blakes and was entertained by them. She bragged to Laurier that Blake neglected all his other guests to concentrate totally on her. She feigned surprise. Laurier reproached her with false modesty. "You know your own powers too well, my dear friend. Tell me frankly, is it not true that you would

Laurier, as portrayed by Marc-Aurèle de Foy Suzor-Côté

Laurier the member of parliament for
Drummond-Arthabaska in 1874

Zoë Laurier in 1878

Le Collège de L'Assomption

The Laurier home among the maples in Arthabaska

Laurier House in Ottawa

The Honourable Wilfrid Laurier,
leader of the opposition, 1891

An elegant Zoë in 1900

The Lauriers in their chauffeur-driven automobile with unidentified friends

Wilfrid and Zoë on their golden wedding day, 13 May 1918

Sir Wilfrid Laurier   Lady Zoë Laurier in 1911

Laurier entering the Parliament Buildings in Ottawa

Laurier's office in the Parliament Buildings around 1902

Laurier relaxing at the races

Laurier lying in state in the Victoria Memorial Museum in Ottawa,
21 February 1919

Laurier's funeral procession passing the Château Laurier,
with the Parliament Buildings in the background

The Laurier memorial in Notre Dame Cemetery in Ottawa

have been surprised, if the reverse had taken place?" Laurier knew his Émilie!

In the succeeding months following their reconciliation, Blake and Laurier often communicated with each other by letter and in lengthy visits in which others joined, trying to catch the spirit of the past, to find ways whereby Blake could re-enter public life in Canada as a Liberal, and to reach a mutual under-standing of what unrestricted reciprocity entailed — one both Blake and the party could live with. Unfortunately, they could not succeed, and in May 1892 Blake went off to Ireland, where he was elected to the British House of Commons and took up the cause of Irish Home Rule. He kept in contact with Laurier and other Liberals as they moved, over the years, away from unrestricted reciprocity with the United States to a trade policy that favoured British pref-erence at the expense of American goods.

Blake rejoiced at this development. The split in the party was bridged.

~

Laurier's letters to Émilie at this time were also in the nature of a reconciliation. Over the years since they had known each other, they had kept up their rela-tionship without changing its form and content. Joseph Lavergne was Laurier's law partner and, since 1887, he had been a member of Laurier's caucus; he also lodged at the Russell Hotel. Until Armand entered the Petit Séminaire in Québec City in 1890 and Gabrielle went to the Convent of Jésus-Marie in Sillery to finish her studies, Émilie hardly came to Ottawa at all.

Absence, and a round of malicious gossip, had led to a crisis between them. Rumours abounded that their relationship was one of adultery and infidelity. Zoë, Joseph, and Laurier refused to pay any attention to them, but Émilie did. In 1890 she had wanted Laurier to deny them publicly. In her frustration she had been harsh with him: she had reproached him with indifference, callous-ness, and neglect; she had threatened him with a thousand questions and tended to think the worst of him. He, in turn, had reproached her.

His letters between 1891 and 1893, with their effusive sentimentality, their romantic wanderings, and their emotional declarations, were meant to reassure her both of his affection and of her place in his life. She was despondent in those years and often ill, illnesses brought about by the deep depression she was in.

She complained all the time about one thing or another; the absence of her children at school drove her to desperate loneliness; and Arthabaska provided no solace, no relief. Laurier was away, Joseph was away, the children were away, and she was left all alone. Even when Laurier came to Arthabaska, he was often too busy to see her, to meet as in the old days. She didn't know where to turn to appease her loneliness and her pain. Consequently, Laurier tried to comfort her by gushing over her. Since the weight of the leadership on his shoulders rendered him morose, he sought to lessen the burden by confiding in her.

When they met each other, even when alone — which was not often — Émilie and Laurier never used the familiar *tu*, preferring the formal *vous*. The same practice continued in their correspondence. He wrote to Émilie mainly in English and she, always, in French, since her knowledge of English was poor. That lack of fluency caused her to misunderstand him often and to reproach him accordingly. His letters began with "My dearest friend" and ended with words like "Of all your friends the truest," or "God bless you and your own, friend so dear." There was nothing in them that could injure Zoë or Joseph, who knew of their existence. Émilie was constantly ordered to tell Joseph this and that, and Armand and his cousin often brought in the mail. They talked of books in the letters, but most were filled with thoughts and news about her children.

One of the most touching moments in that correspondence was the *compte rendu* Laurier gave her of Armand's visit to his father and him at the Russell Hotel in the middle of July 1891. Armand arrived "rather fagged," but he soon recovered and ate "four, yes four mutton chops," the following morning. Laurier found him enchanting, "full of magnetism, winning & attractive, & at the same time so frank, so outspoken, so clever also, & so ready witted." Laurier was familiar with Armand's qualities, but what struck him was the boy's range of information: "He has an amount of general knowledge upon most subjects, which is astonishing in a child of his age." He also had the gift of repartee: "this is his mother all over!" Laurier ended his report to Émilie with the words: "Well, my dearest friend, let me again tell you, what we so often remarked together, that you have every reason to be a proud mother."

Armand was a charming boy, bright, refreshing, somewhat moody and intemperate, indolent like Laurier, and ever so loving: "Bonjour ma maman aimée. Kiss papa et Minnie, the dogs, the cats and the pigeons for me and my big cow. As for the rooster, I would fear to insult him. Tell him that I am his humble servant." At one time, Laurier feared that Armand, living with the priests, would want to become one. He was in Ottawa and had just attended a religious ceremony where a Dominican priest preached. He concluded that "la prêtrise ne raffine pas son homme" — the priesthood doesn't necessarily refine a man. He related the incident to Émilie and added: "I saw your dear Armand in that cassock and surplice and my heart rebelled." How better would it be for him to make of Armand "a man of the world, capable of fighting, of loving, and of suffering."

Gabrielle was as much in his thoughts as Armand. He worried about her studies and her loneliness: "I learned," he wrote to Gabrielle in October 1891, "how difficult it has been for you to be separated from your parents, and that you cried. I understand, ma chère Gabrielle. It is difficult to leave one's parents; especially a good father and a good mother like your parents are. I also learned with joy and pride, I who love you, how brave, courageous, you were and determined to do your duty. This is why I am writing you, to tell you how very proud I am of you and to ask you not to forget me and to keep me in your memory."

Wilfrid and Émilie were both lonely people. The years 1890–93 were probably the worst of Laurier's life, both politically and personally, and they were not good for her, either. Consequently, they hung on to each other, both fed at times by a natural feeling that destiny might have plotted a different course for their lives.

~

By the 1890s the Russell Hotel had been totally refurbished, though Laurier continued to consider it vulgar — especially when he was ill and lonely. The Rotunda had a huge dome, decorated with frescoes of pastel nymphs cavorting in various stages of undress, marble columns arising from the mosaics of the floor, and a majestic staircase with a large stained-glass window on the first landing. From the Rotunda, Zoë and Laurier would access the reading room, the café, and — if ever — the bar. Everything was well proportioned and most elegant. The café was bright, the tables far apart, the service discreet, and the food "capable of tempting the palate of even the epicurean monk." The newspaper and magazine stands were said to have the largest collection after the Parliamentary Library. Before luncheon or dinner, the guests would congregate in the upstairs drawing room, a large room with two fireplaces, a grand piano, sparkling chandeliers and tall windows that provided a fine view of the Parliament Buildings. Laurier's bedroom was one of the best in the hotel: large, sunny, and cheerful, with its own bathroom and fireplace, and several chairs and tables. Attached to the hotel was a theatre and elegant rooms for entertaining. During the session, the Lauriers would receive caucus members and their wives, visiting politicians from other provinces, business contacts and members of the diplomatic corps, ladies and gentlemen of their acquaintance, and friends and relatives. On the whole, they both liked living there. Zoë would have preferred a house, but they couldn't afford one.

Laurier was still reserved in his appreciation for Ottawa, except when the sun was shining, the flowers were in bloom, and the Outaouais sparkled. Unfortunately, he visited the capital only during the sessions of Parliament, when it was cold in the winter and raw in the spring. Also, he didn't know Ottawa. For the most part, he kept to the House and his hotel, and the short walk between them. Occasionally, he ventured out to attend functions, make courtesy calls, and dine in a few of the grand houses of Sandy Hill. He rarely walked by the Rideau Canal, or on the two wide stone bridges that linked the Upper Town with the Lower Town. When he went to church, he took a horse-driven cab to the cathedral, but hardly ever went into the Lower Town, where most *Canadiens* lived. The Gatineau Hills were unknown to him. Only in time would he come to know Ottawa and yearn to transform it into a fitting capital city for Canada.

⁓

On Tuesday, 17 November 1891, the *Canadiens* of New England entertained Laurier at a banquet at the Hotel Vendome in Boston, a function attended by hundreds of people and many dignitaries, including the governor of Massachussetts. François Langelier accompanied him. The ballroom was decorated with Canadian scenes such as Niagara Falls, flags of both countries, and flowers in abundance. The menu was astonishing, and included oysters on the shell, turbot, fillet of beef with béarnaise sauce, sweetbreads and "nageoire de tortue en caisse" (turtle fin in pastry?), duck, lettuce salad, crème chantilly, ice cream pudding, assorted cakes, fruits and cheeses, olives and coffee. Fifteen different toasts were drunk, including one to the ladies.

In his speech, Laurier reviewed the history of Canada, its struggles for emancipation, its status as a self-governing colony within the British Empire, and the policies of the Liberal Party, including reciprocity. He spoke in both English and French, and the most notable passage in English was his denunciation of Imperial Federation, a subject dear to the heart of McCarthy and his cohorts. It would be suicide for Canada, Laurier said, to be involved in a structure that would force the country to participate in the wars Great Britain was forever waging all over the world. Imperial Federation was an absurd idea, both in international relations and in trade. In trade, he said, "I prefer the Yankee dollar to the British shilling, especially when the dollar is so near and the shilling so far away."

In French, he mentioned how sad he was to address his audience on foreign soil "dans notre langue maternelle à tous." He would have preferred to do so "sur notre terre natal du Canada." He had never understood the need for French Canadians to exile themselves in the United States when there was so much land in Canada, so much wealth, on which to build a fine future. He didn't reproach them for their decision; he was just sorry it had happened. He wished them well as American citizens.

Three days later he was back in Arthabaska to celebrate his fiftieth birthday.

9

THE LONG JOURNEY TO POWER
1892–1896

The years 1892–96 were devoted to three main concerns for Laurier: the Manitoba Schools Question, the organization of the Liberal Party through the convention of June 1893 and his western tour in the fall of 1894, and the elections of June 1896. In between, he dealt with other weighty matters, particularly the future independence of Canada.

These were years of turmoil. After Macdonald's death, a crisis arose over who should succeed him as prime minister. The McGreevy-Langevin scandal had made Langevin's succession impossible; John Thompson, the able minister of justice, refused on the grounds that as a Catholic, or a "pervert" as the Protestants called him, he would never be acceptable; and no one else could be found in the Cabinet of suitable calibre. To bridge the gap, Laurier's former dean of law at McGill University, Senator John Abbott, was called. He was the least obnoxious to the many factions within the Conservative Party. He served two years, and then Thompson was persuaded to accept. Thompson formed his government at the beginning of December 1892. He died, two years later, at Windsor Castle. Who would replace him? Mackenzie Bowell, a senator and a past Grand Master of the Orange Order, got the nod and remained in office through crisis after crisis, until April 1896, when he was supplanted by Sir Charles Tupper. In the space of five years, Canada had four prime ministers.

The issue that caused these crises was the Manitoba Schools Question, a matter that was to dominate the Canadian political agenda for more than six years.

When the province of Manitoba was created in 1870, the federal government allowed the legislature of that province to make laws governing education, provided the rights of denominational schools were not disturbed. If any minority ever felt deprived of its rights, it could appeal to the Governor General in Council for redress. The federal government also reserved itself the authority to ask Parliament to make remedial laws for the due execution of this provision should the provincial legislature ever interfere with the rights of a minority in this matter. The Manitoba Act, therefore, gave unqualified protection to the French-speaking and Catholic minorities of Manitoba — and to their separate schools.

By 1890 the population of the province had altered considerably and the Protestant majority had serious reservations about the separate schools, arguing that they were expensive to maintain and that they fostered religious divisions inimical to the unity of Manitoba. Though the majority did not agitate in favour of the abolition of these schools, their opposition lay very near the surface and could easily be aroused.

The furore over the Jesuits' Estates Act provided the sparks that ignited the Manitoba Schools controversy, aided by McCarthy's fiery anti-Catholic crusade and the enthusiastic support in the Manitoba Orange lodges. In May 1889 the campaign began when the *Brandon Sun* demanded the abolition of the separate school system, and in June and July the cry was taken up in other news-papers. The Liberal government of Thomas Greenway, which had been involved in a series of political scandals, seized on the issue with surprising alacrity in order to divert public attention from its irresponsible management of the affairs of the province. In August it announced that a non-denominational school system would be established, with a single department of education and a responsible minister. McCarthy followed with his usual racist and anti-Catholic speech at Portage la Prairie on 5 August. At the same meeting, Joseph Martin, the silly attorney general of Manitoba, promised that the French language would be obliterated as an official language. In the session of 1890 the Manitoba Legislative Assembly passed a law that abolished the official use of the French language, denied *Canadiens* the right to a French jury in provincial courts, and replaced the dual school system that had existed since 1870 with a nondenom-inational one. Roman Catholic schools could still function as private schools, but they would receive no subsidies from the public treasury and all Manitobans would pay a school tax to support the public school system.

Outside the province, these draconian measures received scant attention in the federal election of 1891. Both the Conservative Party and the Roman

Catholic episcopacy agreed to ignore the issue so as to deprive the Liberals of any ammunition. Chapleau, in the name of Macdonald and his government, promised the archbishop of Saint-Boniface, Alexandre Taché, that redress would be forthcoming once the election was past. For their part, the Liberals encouraged Macdonald and his government to postpone any action until the courts had rendered judgment. Blake's motion to that effect passed unanimously. The federal government, which had until 11 April 1891 to disallow the Manitoba legislation, was relieved and the long and interminable journey of the issue through the courts began, with the full concurrence of the episcopacy and the Ultramontanes.

In February 1891 the Manitoba Court of Queen's Bench declared the Manitoba legislation constitutional. Immediately, the federal government appealed the case to the Supreme Court, which on 28 October 1891 reversed the judgment of the Manitoba court. Manitoba appealed to the Judicial Committee of the Privy Council in Great Britain, the court of last resort. Its decision came down on 30 June 1892: the legislation was *intra vires* — constitutional. That decision left the Roman Catholics and *Canadiens* of Manitoba one resource left: federal remedial action in accordance with section 3 of clause 22 of the Manitoba Act of 1870. Petitions poured into Ottawa and the Manitoba Schools' crisis began in earnest.

The federal government didn't know what to do and it chose to evade its political responsibilities. It argued that since the Manitoba legislation was within the jurisdiction of the province and hadn't, according to the Privy Council, deprived the Catholic minority of any rights, could the Canadian Privy Council (the government) entertain the minority's appeal? Only the Supreme Court could answer that question. Naturally, the Court said no, on 24 February 1894. Fearing negative political repercussions if it acted, the government went to the Privy Council in London. Naturally, their Lordships said yes, provided the government didn't repeal the 1890 legislation. After five years' delay, the Canadian government had no way out but to act.

Meanwhile, late in 1892, encouraged by the Manitoba spectacle, the Council of the North-West Territories in effect abolished the separate school system and limited the teaching of French in the schools. No disallowance was entertained. And in 1894 the Manitoba legislature reinforced and refined its 1890 legislation, without any opposition.

While this judicial rigmarole was going on, the bishops were getting more and more impatient. In 1891 they didn't intervene in the elections, preferring, as Bishop Laflèche wrote to Taché, to appeal to the government after the election rather than before. When no action was taken, the Québec bishops considered issuing a *mandement* in 1894. They were unable to obtain the consent of their non-Québec colleagues, however, and, on the advice of the Ultramontane ministers in the federal Cabinet, they abandoned the idea in favour of a collective letter to the Governor General in Council. They persuaded Father Albert Lacombe, a respected Oblate missionary and unofficial ambassador of the CPR to the western Native peoples, to present the letter on 9 May 1894. In it, the Canadian bishops complained that the educational legislation in Manitoba and the ordinances in the North-West Territories were unjust, and they requested that the rights of the minority be re-established through remedial action. The Thompson government forwarded the letter to the provincial and territorial authorities concerned, and the bishops waited. Both Manitoba and the North-West Territories did not bother to reply.

Ten months later, on 21 March 1895, the Mackenzie Bowell government issued a remedial order to Manitoba, commanding that the government there restore the full educational rights of the minority. Should Manitoba refuse, the federal government would use its constitutional authority to legislate.

There wasn't any doubt in anybody's mind that the remedial order was a bluff. It permitted the Conservatives to portray themselves in Québec as defenders of the *Canadiens* and the Catholics; and, in Ontario, to assert that no federal interference would be forthcoming — it being only an administrative act to which there would be no follow-up.

On 19 June 1895, the Manitoba Legislative Assembly refused to be intimidated. Manitoba would not obey.

~

Laurier learned to be a politician and to manage men and issues with the Manitoba Schools Question. His party stood divided: some *Canadien* members wanted redress at all costs, while some Canadians from all provinces insisted that provincial autonomy should prevail. The sentiment in Québec favoured justice for the minority; that in Ontario was directed to the creation of a British country, with one language, and one identity from sea to sea. Hovering in the periphery waiting to act were the Roman Catholic bishops, who feared that separate schools would disappear within the melting pot. Laurier had to steer a course that avoided all the pitfalls placed in his path and that reconciled two conflicting principles he had always expounded: justice to the minority and provincial autonomy. To achieve that goal, he had to have the power to do so. Only a victory in the next election would give him that power. He must, then, unite as many as possible around his banner and combat his opponents. During the five years in which the subject was at the very centre of the affairs of Canada, he refused to reveal his hand.

Joseph-Israël Tarte felt no such inhibitions. In March 1890 *Le Canadien* advocated the disallowance of the Manitoba legislation. A year later when it was not disallowed, he wrote that French Canada was entering a period of persecution. At that time, he also rejected all attempts to resolve the issue through the courts — he was never of the opinion that judges, who were named to their posts because they were the political friends of the party in power, were necessarily apolitical. By 6 March 1893, when he opened the first full-fledged debate on the schools question in the House of Commons, he attacked the cowardice of the government in taking refuge under the skirts of the judges. With his no-confidence motion, Tarte managed to force Laurier into the arena.

Laurier's preference was for a Canada where Canadians and *Canadiens* lived peacefully together and in the full exercise of their rights. He therefore rejected all attempts to create a melting pot. He abhorred all religious and racial conflicts, and was sensitive to the fact that Canada, in both federal and provincial politics, must avoid issues which deliberately inflamed passions and which could only be resolved at the expense of the minority position. Divisive matters could not be ignored, but they had to be resolved through compromise. This conciliatory approach was the basis of his national philosophy. It appeared naive to many and unworkable to others. Laurier himself frequently had to work around it and, in the process, he was always abandoned by one side or the other. Still, it remained a constant throughout his forty-five years in public life.

In the Manitoba Schools affair, he preferred the clear and unequivocal restoration of the separate school system of that province. When John Willison of the *Globe* insisted that the position of the Liberal Party should be based on the principle of provincial rights even if it meant sacrificing the minority, Laurier thundered back at him with some impatience: "How is it possible to talk of Provincial Rights when by the very letter of the constitution, jurisdiction is given to the federal authorities to review and to override provincial legislation?" Provincial rights were not absolute.

On the other hand, what could the federal government do if its "restoration" wasn't acceptable to the provincial authorities? The minority couldn't be abandoned to its devices — of that he was certain. In some way the federal government had to play its constitutional role. What it was he wasn't certain in 1890; consequently, he supported the first round of judicial references, while at the same time he inclined to the side of the minority. By 1893 he had made up his mind what the Liberal Party's policy would be, but he didn't make it public for three years.

As the courts decided and redecided, the possibilities for restoration of redress changed considerably. The key judicial decision for Laurier was that of the Privy Council in June 1892: the 1890 Manitoba Schools legislation was constitutional. Unless Manitoba could be cajoled or coerced into restoring the separate school system it had abolished, nothing could be done for the minority in terms of full restoration through legislation. Another way had to be found.

Laurier indicated his way in a private letter to the editor of the Ottawa newspaper, *Canada,* in 1893. It all depended on the final outcome of the judicial appeals. If their Lordships decided that the minority could not lodge an appeal with the federal government, "the only remedy which would remain to [them] would be to request an amendment to the constitution." Since "such a policy would entail a similar demand on the part of the McCarthy group to abolish the French language in Parliament and separate schools in Ontario," the fabric of Confederation could not hold. "Such consequences ought to make all sensible men reflect."

If, however, the courts decided, as they did, that the federal government could entertain the request of the minority, he would pursue a settlement similar to that made in New Brunswick in 1871 after the separate school crisis there. The solution had been to create one subsidized and non-sectarian school system. However, children could be grouped by religion and, where numbers permitted — as in L'Acadie — the schools were both Catholic and bilingual, textbooks reflected denominational sensibilities, and teachers trained in Roman Catholic normal schools could obtain provincial teachers' certificates. That was Laurier's policy, and it would be the policy of his party — if he could reconcile Ontario's demands for full provincial rights with Québec's insistence on separate schools.

It took Laurier three years to achieve that reconciliation. In the meantime, he kept his own counsel, stuck to his principles, unleashed Tarte, and let Willison wallow in provincial rights. It was good politics. If Tarte went too far, he could be reined in; if Willison became too cantankerous, he could be admonished. Besides, Laurier didn't think they would cause him much trouble even if they took each other to task in public, as they often did. Without ever saying publicly how he, Wilfrid Laurier, would solve the problem, he was seen as the upholder of provincial autonomy in Ontario and the defender of separate schools in Québec. There, it was taken for granted that Tarte spoke for Laurier. As Pacaud wrote in *L'Électeur:* "The position which M. Tarte holds in the party of M. Laurier, for which he is the chief organizer in this province," revealed Laurier's mind.

However, this tactic had its drawbacks. Keeping quiet was not in Tarte's character. He attacked bishops and Conservatives, chastised Liberals privately, and almost drowned Laurier in words. Tarte felt deeply about the Manitoba Schools issue, for, to him, it was defining the place *Canadiens* would occupy in Confederation and the shape of their future in North America. He was sometimes impatient with Laurier, wanting him to condemn publicly the slanders of the *Globe* and its position. Laurier did no such thing, but he told Willison privately that his newspaper had taken the "ridiculous position" that though the right of appeal existed, "the appeal is never to be granted; it is always to be denied, because, if granted, it would mean an abridgement of provincial rights." In dealing with both men — both being vital to any Liberal success — Laurier managed to convince Willison to concentrate on attacking the Conservatives and to associate provincial rights with justice to the minority. He was also able to persuade Tarte that coercion, through a remedial order or legislation, was not the solution. The means to render some justice to the minority had to be more "rational" and more likely to maintain the legitimate rights of the minority. What Tarte had to do, they finally agreed, was to attack the Conservatives for their inaction, while letting it be known that with Laurier in power right and justice would triumph.

To secure the place of *Canadiens* in Confederation more securely, Tarte seized the opportunity of the school affair to bring about a new political alignment in Québec and a vigorous *force de frappe* in Ottawa. "If you commanded fifty members from Québec," he once asked Laurier, "you would be master of the situation, n'est-ce-pas?" He advocated not a *Canadien*, Catholic party, but a political realignment formed from the Liberals and the moderate Conservative followers of Chapleau in Québec, from Mowat's party in Ontario, and from sympathetic Maritimers. Laurier encouraged him.

Laurier's first major speech on the school question was in supporting Tarte's vague motion of censure of the government in March 1893. He took the opportunity to remind the honourable members that the separate schools of Québec and the Catholic schools of Ontario were protected under the British North America Act. This protection had been instigated by the Protestants in Québec. If the Catholic majority abolished those schools, would members claim that the federal government could or should not intervene? He knew the answer. What he didn't understand was the double standard so far as Manitoba was concerned. He then turned to Archbishop Taché's contention that Manitoba had created not a public school system in 1890 but a Protestant one, thereby forcing Catholics to attend Protestant schools. Laurier didn't know if this charge was true or not, but he served notice that, if it were the case:

> I say this, and let my words be heard by friend and foe, let them publish it in the press throughout the length of the land, that the strongest case has been made for interference by this government.
>
> If that statement of His Excellency be true, though my life as a political man should be ended forever, what I say now I shall be prepared to repeat, and would repeat on every platform in Ontario, every platform in Manitoba, nay, every Orange lodge throughout the land, that the Catholic minority has been subjected to a most infamous tyranny.

He asked for facts; he chastised the government for floundering and, in the process, allowing racial and religious passions to rise to a dangerous level; and he exhorted everyone to be calm. Tarte's motion was defeated, and the comedy continued.

~

At two o'clock in the afternoon of Tuesday, 20 June 1893, some two thousand Liberal delegates who had arrived by train from all over the country, including "a sprinkling of the fair sex," convened in the Rideau Rink in Ottawa for the first national convention of any political party in Canada. It was Willison's idea, one endorsed by Laurier, and it had taken six months to prepare. In every province, committees had been formed to establish Liberal organizations where there were none and to strengthen the existing ones. The members, many of them new to the party, discussed and passed resolutions and elected delegates. In Québec, Tarte was in charge, and he founded Liberal associations in every district and in every constituency.

Laurier, looking healthy and fit and joyful, and Zoë, proud and confident, arrived on the 19th from Montréal on a special train all decorated with bunting in the colours of the party; the station itself was festooned with flags, and a large crowd had gathered. He received an address of welcome, and he replied by predicting that a Liberal government would soon be installed in Ottawa, a remark much appreciated by the enthusiastic crowd. When that happened, he continued, "it will be a great pleasure to me to make Ottawa as attractive a city as possible, to make it the centre of intellectual development in this country, and have it known as the Washington of the North." His carriage was taken in procession to the Russell, where the Whip of the party and one of the chief organizers of the convention had reserved a suite of rooms in which he could receive guests, meet with delegates, entertain, and spend private time with Zoë. At night he opened the Reform Club of Ottawa on Elgin Street and agreed to become its "godfather." He was pleased to see so many Liberals in the capital of Canada who valued principles, democracy, and the equal footing of creeds and races. "But we must have organization. Principles without organization might win; but organization without principles has been known to have often succeeded."

The next day marked the official opening of the Great Liberal Convention.

At 3 p.m. sharp Laurier and Zoë entered the Rideau Rink to an overwhelming and long-lasting ovation. The rink was, according to the *Daily Citizen*, tastefully and joyfully decorated with flags and large mottoes stating the party's principles. At the eastern side, a large platform had been constructed. It was, unfortunately, intensely hot. Laurier moved that Oliver Mowat, the premier of Ontario, be made chairman of the convention. Vice-presidents were elected and resolution committees formed to prepare the platform of the party. It was, after all, a Liberal and democratic convention. Laurier's main address came in the evening. He dismissed the Conservatives' National Policy as "a fraud, a failure, and dangerous," and he asked for the delegates' help in ridding the country of it. Their applause and cheers expressed their assent. Turning to the tariff, he changed in one short sentence what had been the policy of the party since 1887: the only tariff that was necessary was a revenue tariff, and the trade policy of the party was free trade. He spoke of his loyalty to the British Empire, but he was quite blunt: he would never sacrifice the interests of Canada to those of the empire. Canada came first. To those who wanted to stand up for England first and Canada second, he advised them to "go back and live in England." His loyalty was to stand up for Canada, and from that he would not deviate. Again, there were loud cheers and stomping of feet in accord. Macdonald's Franchise Act was duly condemned and the temperance issue put on the back burner, even though he had his mind made up and would act when the time arrived. As for the Manitoba Schools Question, he wished that the matter had not arisen. But it had and it would have to be dealt with. For now, he agreed with Tarte that the government was made up of cowards who had shifted the entire issue to the courts and, thus, prevented the Liberals from acting until the judicial process was over. The partisans didn't want to see the clever evasion there and they applauded him for his statesmanlike remarks.

In between private meetings with delegates and social gatherings, he listened to the presentation of the resolutions. Organization was tightened and a chief organizer was appointed in each province. Tarte, who officially entered the Liberal fold during the convention and attracted an enormous amount of attentions, was confirmed as the chief organizer in Québec. The enthusiasm for Laurier made him the invincible leader. There were no concrete and formal resolutions on the Manitoba Schools Question — at Laurier's request.

However, in a session held entirely in French, he was less evasive than his normal self. He took no responsibility for what had happened. His was not to govern, nor was it to parade his religion in public. If he had been in power, "J'aurais rendu justice." He would not have sought refuge behind the judiciary. "J'aurais eu le courage de mes actes." He would have had courage in his actions. He gave no details.

Émilie was not there.

~

After 1893 the relationship between Émilie and Laurier began to ebb. Their need for each other became less pronounced. She acknowledged that her children now had lives of their own, and she spent most of her time away in Québec City or in Ottawa. She returned to Arthabaska in between sessions and in the holidays. As for Laurier, the continuing collapse of the Conservative Party and the confirmation of his leadership made him want to avoid any possible hint of scandal. Power was then within his grasp. And, frankly, he had tired of Émilie's constant litany of reproaches.

Furthermore, Zoë came to Ottawa more often. She and Laurier entertained, she learned more English, and together they entered high society in the capital. At first Émilie was restive. She had expectations of being a "grande dame extraordinaire" and of eclipsing Zoë. But Zoë had acquired a friend — one who arrived in Ottawa on 25 September 1893 to take up residence at the centre of political and social power in the country, Rideau Hall, the residence of the governor general.

Lord John Campbell Hamilton, the seventh Earl of Aberdeen, was forty-six years old when he was appointed governor general of Canada. He was a diminutive man, absurdly rich, intelligent enough, and willing to share his office with his wife, Ishbel. She was a woman of intense energy, great passion, strong convictions, and determined zeal; she was also a Presbyterian Liberal with a social conscience, an organizer par excellence, a meddler in political affairs, a feminist, a perfect accomplice with her husband, and a friend of the Lauriers. Ishbel Aberdeen was probably the most interesting woman in nineteenth-century Canadian history. The Aberdeens stayed in Canada with their four children until 12 November 1898.

They liked Rideau Hall. Lady Aberdeen found the servants' quarters "ample and very comfortably arranged," the ballroom "v. good," the drawing rooms "roomy," but the ordinary dining room "not a good room, gloomy and smells of kitchen." She complained that there were only a few rooms for visitors and that the carpets were the worse for wear. However, "we think we shall be very comfy," and she immediately began to make plans for a "little chapel" on the grounds. She had it completed by the time Christmas came around. She also went around the house and placed pictures of the British prime minister and Liberal leader, William Ewart Gladstone, everywhere she could.

When they entertained at dinner, the guests dined in a room that could seat thirty. It was a pleasant room with the ceiling and walls stained in terra-cotta, and mouldings of black and gold. A stuffed black bear stood in one of the corners. For state occasions, the ballroom, with its much-admired white and gold mouldings and corniches, was adorned with a dais and thrones for Their Excellencies, above which hung a large oil painting of the governor general painted by Robert Harris, famous for his painting *The Fathers of Confederation*.

On Saturday, 18 May 1894, the Aberdeens had the Lauriers to dinner for the first time since their arrival. Lady Aberdeen recorded in her diary: "He is a brilliant man, & very agreeable socially — talks English v. well — is an immense admirer of the Scotch. Mme Laurier is shy, & prefers talking French — but is v. Pleasant when one comes to talk to her — she looks sad, feels having no children." A year later, on Monday, 13 May, there was a "dinner party for 30 tonight — very bright." Laurier took Her Excellency in and they had a great talk, while "H.E. had Mme Laurier and Mme Lavergne." The socialites' tongues wagged incessantly about the meaning of that, not to mention Émilie's elegance and Zoë's dowdiness. It meant nothing. Émilie's elegance was all contrived, and Zoë's fashions were more than adequate and were in keeping with the kind of person she was.

By the middle of the 1890s, both the Lauriers had embraced fashion, though he was more determined than Zoë. Over the years, Laurier had not gained any weight at all. He was tall, his hair a little greyer and less bountiful but still curly and cut close to his head, his face well shaved and pale, his eyes more penetrating and kind. He was always impeccably and immaculately dressed.

Like all proper gentlemen of that time, Laurier wore four kinds of armour:

the morning suit, the frock-coat suit, the lounge suit, and the formal evening suit. His morning coat was single-breasted and had tails at the back. It was worn also with a single-breasted waistcoat over a starched shirt, with a wing or butterfly collar and a long black knotted necktie. The trousers were narrow and broke over the boots. When it was time for a frock coat, Laurier favoured a high starched winged collar with a black bow tie, to which was attached the horseshoe tie pin that the Gauthiers had given him while he was at McGill, a high-buttoning waistcoat, narrow trousers, and a knee-length frock coat. His lounge suit had a short single-breasted jacket, waistcoat and trousers to match, starched wing-collar shirt, and a long knotted tie. His evening suits were traditional: cut-in tail coat, black trousers and waistcoat, a white shirt with a starched front and stiff winged collar, and a white bow tie. Links fastening his shirt cuffs had to be visible at his wrists. His boots were pointed and, from 1893 onwards, he wore spats. He carried grey suede gloves and, from time to time, a cane. A top hat was de rigueur with the morning suit and frock-coat attire, while the Homburg served him well with the lounge suit.

Not to be outdone, Zoë had also over the years developed a feeling for fashion. She became less severe in her attire and discovered colour and ribbons. She had a weight problem and couldn't, like Émilie, wear clothes that exaggerated or accentuated her matronly shape. She tended to be conservative, but remained "très soignée" in garments that were loose and avoided too much décolleté. When she came to Ottawa, she arrived with day dresses, tea dresses, house dresses, and evening dresses, along with coats and furs and frocks and muffs and purses. She always wore a hat and gloves in her "public appearances," and carried a parasol or umbrella. Her hair, which was also growing grey, was generally knotted at the back of her head. She favoured lace, frills, bows, and other such adornments, and jewellery bought at Birks in Montréal or which Laurier gave her as gifts. In her hair, there was a jewelled ornament of some sort; on her bosom, a corsage; and when etiquette demanded it, she added a folding ostrich-feather fan.

∼

Two centrifugal forces — Canadian nationalism, with its emphasis on closer ties with the British Empire and on building a British country in North America,

and *nationalisme canadien*, with its emphasis on affirmation and protection —
plagued Laurier all through his political life. He sought to reconcile them, to
merge them into one Canadian nationality without destroying their inner core.
Too often, Canadians of both "races" tended to be paranoid and fearful of the
intentions of the other. Threats were issued and mischief was done. Laurier
believed in a Canada of two "races," the dominant forces of which were Québec
and Ontario. He didn't give much thought to what happened to those who were
of neither British nor French origin. The concept of multiculturalism didn't exist,
but dualism did, and its coexistence was too often challenged.

Laurier's pursuit of the "independence" of Canada was based on his pro-
found acceptance not only that it was inevitable but that it was vital to the survival of the Canada he foresaw in his dreams and in his heart. He never doubted
that the content or nature of that independence would be unique to Canada and,
as such, would fulfil the wish he had expressed when he graduated from McGill
University: "Mighty nations, indeed, may well come to us to seek a lesson in
justice and humanity." Without independence, Canada might fall into the throes
of civil war at worst, or fail to achieve unity at best. Both would be fatal. Whether
independence was achieved in his lifetime or not, it didn't matter. What mattered was that nothing should make it more difficult to attain.

To prepare Canadians and *Canadiens* for that inevitable day of independence, he argued that the rights and aspirations of each "race" should be recognized and respected and that Canada should loosen its ties with Great Britain.
Above all, it should not commit itself to a policy of greater involvement in the
empire. Moderation, conciliation, Canadianism — these were the keys to the
future.

~

The gains made at the Liberal Convention had to be consolidated, so Laurier
embarked on his first trip to the West in the fall of 1894. Zoë accompanied him,
along with his brother Henri, who served as his secretary; Philippe-Auguste
Choquette, the Liberal member for Montmagny; William Gibson, the young
Liberal member for Lincoln, Ontario, and his wife; Charles Hyman, the Liberal
Party treasurer; Duncan Cameron Fraser, the giant of the Maritimes; Sydney
Fisher from the Eastern Townships of Québec; and James Sutherland, the chief

Whip of the party. It was a well-balanced delegation, and it was meant to demonstrate the diversity within the Liberal Party.

Laurier, Zoë, and Henri prepared themselves well, reading everything they could and asking questions of members of Parliament; in Laurier's case, missionaries, who were Zoë's acquaintances; and lawyers, whom Henri met in his work as an official of the court in Arthabaska. They pored over maps and statistics, particularly those of the 1891 census. They discovered a fragmented Canada, linked by rail and telegraph, and on the edge of becoming what geographers called "a modern, urbanized, industrial nation," with Manitoba serving as the gateway to the prairies and British Columbia fast becoming an important resource economy. While the total population of Canada was close to 5 million, not more than 350,000 lived in the regions they were about to visit: 153,000 in Manitoba, 99,000 in the North-West Territories, and 98,000 in British Columbia.

By the fall of 1894 the tide had turned in Laurier's favour and that of his party. A week or so before he left, there was a large meeting in Saint-Lin, organized by Tarte to wish him *bon voyage*. It was the first time Maman Adeline had seen him in public, so sure of himself, so eloquent, so admired by her neighbours and the thousands who came from all around. Carolus would have been pleased, she thought to herself. Recent by-elections in Québec had favoured the Liberals, as they did in Manitoba; and Mowat had been re-elected in Ontario. Indeed, the tide was turning. The Liberal message was about to reverberate through the Cambrian Shield, the endless prairies, the chains of mountains that guarded the door to British Columbia, and down to the Pacific Ocean.

Laurier and his party would traverse one of the largest countries in the world and travel more than three thousand miles over a land they had never visited before. On his way, they would encounter the Canadian Shield, that vast area of nearly two million square miles — over half of Canada — which forms an enormous *U* on both sides of Hudson Bay. The Canadian Pacific Railway had penetrated it in the 1880s, but the rewards were yet to come. At the western end of the Shield, the party would pass through a triangle that extended from eastern Manitoba to the foothills of the Rockies. In it, they would find a sparse population but the largest area of cultivable land in Canada: the western prairies, where the horizon falls into the sky. After that, the Pacific Ocean would beckon, but to reach it they would have to cross the mountain ranges known as the Rockies, the Selkirks, the Coast, and the Cascade. Barriers everywhere.

They left in a private railway car from Toronto on 22 August. The first stop was North Bay, followed by a day in Mattawa, then on to Sault Ste. Marie, Sudbury, and Port Arthur. On 3 September, they arrived in Winnipeg an hour late. The crowd at the station was so dense that the reception had to be cancelled. Instead, Laurier made a pleasant and short speech, which was well received. They stayed in a private house, and went by carriage to visit the chief places of interest in the city. At the Manitoba Hotel they encountered Pauline Johnson, the famous Mohawk poet who was also visiting Winnipeg. At night there was a meeting at Brydon's Skating Ring, which had a seating capacity of three thousand.

By 7:00 p.m. six thousand people had filled the place to the rafters, occupying all the seats, standing in the aisles, perching on the window sills, and even dangling from the roof. The ladies more than filled the ample space allotted for their exclusive use, and hundreds of people were turned away. It was, according to the *Manitoba Free Press*, "the greatest mass meeting ever held in the West." Laurier talked again of the nefarious effects of the National Policy and promised remedy along the lines that had been adopted at the Liberal Convention of 1893. He remade the pledge about the prohibition plebiscite, agreed to study the feasibility of the Hudson Bay Railway, and, on the schools issue, added nothing to what he had already said. He was a provincial rights man and, "in the Dominion House of Commons, I have stood up for the authority of the province." This he would continue to do. That was the policy of the party, as agreed to among Liberals the previous June. It was also his policy. On the other hand, he wanted it clearly understood that if it were shown, as the archbishop of Saint-Boniface had claimed, that Catholic children were forced to go to what was in effect Protestant schools, he would stand up against that tyranny and injustice, regardless of the cost to him personally. He took the opportunity as well to repeat his political credo: "I would spurn to appeal to the feelings of any race or to the passions of my creed or race. On the present occasion, let me say that the one aim that I have is to unite all the races on this continent into a Canadian nation, to develop this confederation upon the lines that once impelled Sir John Macdonald and George Brown to cease a life-long struggle and unite for the common good." As for the future, he predicted that if "we will but stand true" to the Liberal principles of freedom and justice, "it seems to me that the day will not be far distant when these fertile plains shall be teeming with population — with millions of population, happy, contented and progressive." The papers reported that the honourable gentleman resumed his seat amidst loud applause and cheering.

Later, while Zoë had tea with the ladies, the mayor of Saint-Boniface arrived with a group of supporters of separate schools. With Joseph Martin sitting there, they accused the Greenway government of Manitoba of having established a Protestant school system that Catholics were forced to attend and pay for. There was no doubt, they insisted, that Archbishop Taché had told the truth. Laurier heard them, made copious notes, and was surprised to hear their allegations, since the government had briefed him to the contrary. He would again ask the federal government to ascertain the facts before taking any further action. As for their main question — whether he would support redress to their grievances — he assured them that, should the Catholics be coerced into attending Protestant schools, he certainly would entertain that the Catholic school question be brought before the Parliament of Canada. What he meant by his answer they were not sure, but they left his presence convinced that he would act in their best interests.

He relived his Winnipeg triumph in Portage la Prairie and Brandon. The *Brandon Mail* described him as a political acrobat rather than a statesman, unwilling to give the lie to the Catholics or to the Greenway government. Then the train headed for British Columbia.

On 10 September Laurier and his party were on Vancouver Island. His tour began in Victoria with an "immense" meeting of five thousand people, or one-third of the population of the city, at the Market Building, where the ladies "had vied with the gentlemen" to decorate the hall with bunting, flags, pictures, branches, flowers, and slogans inscribed on enormous wooden planks. When he rose to speak, the ovation lasted for some time. At first his voice was too soft to be heard in such a large hall, and the people advanced — dangerously, according to Zoë — towards the platform. He soon adjusted, and he preached the sermon he had come to give them: the gospel of free trade, the development of resources, and Canadianism. He kept them spellbound. They had never before heard such grand flights of eloquence, such fine language so devoid of bitterness, and words so rapidly delivered. They cheered and applauded.

A day later, he was in Saanich on Vancouver Island's east coast. He went there by the Victoria and Sidney Railway, filled the Agricultural Hall, and kept his audience until 11 p.m., a late hour in those parts. He mentioned the school controversy, without adding substantially to what he had already said. From there, it was on to Nanaimo, where he was a guest of the Nanaimo Reform Club, visited the most important coal mine of the region, and spoke that evening at another large meeting at the Opera House, which was full to the point of bursting.

Laurier and his party arrived in Vancouver on the morning of the 13th on the steamer *City of Nanaimo*. A large crowd was present to cheer him at both the dock and the Hotel Vancouver. After lunch, he visited Stanley Park with the organizers. Later that afternoon, there was a reception hosted by the mayor's wife. Over 200 people attended, including visitors from Fiji, Honolulu, and Australia who wanted to meet Laurier and, especially, hear his voice. Both Zoë and Laurier were at their charming best and much admired by the guests, who consumed vast quantities of chocolate cake and ice cream along with tea and coffee. At 8 p.m., Laurier was scheduled to speak at Market Hall. Zoë sat with the ladies in the front rows. Again, the hall was tastefully decorated, and the overflow crowd was attentive, enthusiastic, and well behaved. Laurier waxed poetic about British Columbia: "Of all the wonders we found in British Columbia, the greatest was not your Rocky Mountains, capped as they are with the snow of eternal ages, your mighty rivers, your minerals, your wealth — perhaps the greatest wonder to be found in this province is the new City of Vancouver." Turning to the mayor sitting not too far from him, he added: "Sir, to think that only ten years ago this very place on which we are now standing was still a primeval forest, and that where ten years ago there was a primeval forest and gigantic trees, now you see a city of some 18,000 people with all the appliances of modern civilization, which bids fair to become one of the mighty cities of Canada."

There seemed to be no time for rest — and Zoë worried. On the 14th, he spoke to two thousand people in New Westminster, met with fishermen and cannery workers in the Fraser Delta, and went on to Kamloops and Revelstoke to hold yet more meetings.

Then he was off to Edmonton — a town of fewer than five thousand people — where he spoke on Thursday, 20 September. As he visited what would become the capital of a new province he would create, he was told of its pre-historic origin as a meeting place for Indian gatherers and hunters, its roots within the Hudson's Bay Company, and its rivalry with Calgary, which received the railway in 1883 while Edmonton had to be satisfied with a branch line in 1891. On Saturday he arrived in Calgary, a town of hardly four thousand people, yet practically every one of them came to hear him. It was an important centre for the CPR and for the fast-growing cattle industry, but the economy was poor, transportation costs high, and the American tariff had created an almost impenetrable wall. No wonder his message of free trade was well received, as was his plea "Let us be Canadians." In spite of the economic downturn, he was amazed by the potential of these two centres and of their hinterland. In Saskatchewan, he made a brief stop in what the CPR had created in 1882 — Regina, the capital of the North-West Territories, where there were fewer than two thousand people.

In the course of his travels out west, Laurier must have shaken 5000 hands, taken off his hat in greeting 500 times, kissed dozens of babies and small girls who gave him bouquets, received a hundred delegations of various kinds, heard addresses of welcome in every place he went, mentioned the words "free trade" and accused the Conservatives of nefarious deeds a thousand times, presented his views on the Manitoba Schools issue at least fifteen times, attended forty-five official functions, eaten too much food he wasn't used to, and been seen or heard by approximately sixty-five thousand people. Zoë was particularly surprised to find that a good number of *Canadiens* were living in most of the places she visited.

While he was in Vancouver, Laurier didn't pay a visit to Chinatown. It wasn't the proper thing to do. The Chinese, the Japanese, and the "East Indians," though they made up 11 percent of the population of the city, were not acceptable to the majority of their white co-citizens. There had been clashes and riots — the last ones in 1886–87 — and no self-respecting Britisher would be seen in the company of these "aliens" unless they built the white man's railways or performed other menial tasks. Laurier met none of these people, and none of them attended his meetings. Similarly, he saw, but hardly met, only a few of the First Peoples, though they made up probably the majority of residents of the West. Delegations in Manitoba and in the North-West Territories were ushered into his presence. He didn't know how to deal with them, so he handed their chiefs ten-dollar bills.

It was as if they had no particular place in the Canada he wanted to invent, except for the one they already occupied as wards of the Crown.

On the journey back to Montréal, and with the help of Henri, Laurier made copious notes, and discussed the political ramifications of the tour with the politicians in his party. All were satisfied. He was tired but in good spirits. He had accomplished what he had set out to do: to present himself to westerners and to touch them profoundly with his personality, his charm, his eloquence, and, he hoped, his message. He had been told that the people had heard of him and had great expectations. They were not disappointed. Even though he spoke mainly of his "new gospel of Free Trade," he realized that he was at his best when he communicated his deep love for Canada, "the freest land that is to be found on earth," and the need for harmony "between all the races and religions" on the land. Without that cooperation, there would be no Canada.

Coming back east at the beginning of October, Laurier had a new sense of purpose and a better awareness of the tasks that lay ahead in the country. He had travelled over a land of incredible beauty, of awesome dimension, and of unparalleled possibility. He now appreciated the sheer distance from place to place that would have to be bridged, the enormous prairie lands that would have to be occupied, the plentiful resources that would have to be harnessed, the majesty of the mountains that would have to be preserved for generations to come, and that far-flung Pacific province that would have to be developed. If he wrote speeches on the way over, he spent the return journey day-dreaming about the country he had just discovered. Was he the man to undertake those tasks, or the leader to invent a country? He still had doubts.

~

Laurier had no sooner arrived in British Columbia than he received a telegram from Pacaud: Mercier was dying. He might not survive the month. Laurier asked Choquette to go to Montréal as soon as possible to see his old friend on his behalf. On Thursday, the 27th, a telegram came from Choquette that he had seen Mercier that day. The dying man had whispered that he was sorry he would not see Laurier as prime minister of Canada and would not be able to contribute to his victory. Laurier was moved and wished he could have gone in person.

Le mardi, 30 octobre 1894

Mercier died today. Upon my return from the West, I immediately went to him. He didn't recognize me. It is most tragic. Politics killed him at fifty-four — a little more than a year older than I. He was a diabetic. His illness had made him blind. He was totally destitute and bankrupt and the Conservatives have, until quite recently, persecuted him with a cruelty and vengeance unheard of before in the annals of our political life.

Chapleau visited him in September and begged forgiveness for the harm politics do to friends.

Mercier was a man of great intelligence, astounding energy and flair, and a patriot. Unlike me and so many of us who fought clerical domination in our youth, he, like David, had maintained close links with the church of his ancestors. I didn't approve of his methods, and his tactics and his temperament were far different from mine. He was a Liberal, though of a different shade from me, and he managed to break the monopoly of the Conservatives. He demonstrated that the Liberal Party could be as much the defender of *Canadien* interests and aspirations as the Conservative Party. In that sense, he helped our cause considerably.

~

The year 1895 began with a new prime minister — Mackenzie Bowell. With his appointment, the Manitoba Schools Question entered the first of its last phases. It began with the Privy Council deciding that the minority, after all, could appeal to the federal government for redress in accordance with the constitution. Two months later, after much wrangling among the ministers, an order was given to Manitoba to restore to the minority what it had taken away: Catholic schools, a share of the provincial grants to education, and exemption from paying taxes to support another system. If the Manitoba government refused, it would be divested of its right or power to control education in the province. A month later, the parliamentary session opened. Laurier, who had been ill for three weeks, was well enough to be in Ottawa. The session dragged on and, on 19 June 1895, Manitoba replied with a firm no. What would the federal government do?

Introduce remedial legislation immediately, or wait for the next session or even the next Parliament? The Cabinet was badly divided, with the three *Canadiens* insisting on immediate action and the others preferring to wait and fight the inevitable elections on the remedial order rather than on a special bill. It decided to temporize, and the three *Canadiens* resigned, along with Sir Charles Tupper's son; soon, however, two of the *Canadiens* and Tupper's son returned to the fold. No replacement, though, was found for Angers, the most prominent of the *Canadiens*. Finally, on 6 July, and after an incredible *marchandage* or haggling and unbelievable plots and counter-plots, Bowell announced that if no accommodation could be arrived at with Manitoba, a remedial bill would be introduced in Parliament not later than 2 January 1896.

"They are in the den of lions," Tarte told Laurier. And it was so. Laurier had anticipated the decision of the Privy Council and welcomed it: the minority had certain constitutional rights that had to be entertained. He chose, however, not to say that publicly. Caution was the keyword. He did what he did best: criticize the government and lecture its members: "I wish," he said in the House on 15 July, that "the minority in Manitoba may be allowed the privilege of teaching in their schools, to their children, their duties to God and man as they understand those duties, and as their duties are taught to them by their church." To do that, the country needed the facts and then conciliation: "If that object is to be attained, it is not to be attained by imperious dictation nor by administrative coercion. The hand must be firm and the touch must be soft; hitherto the touch has been rude and the hand has been weak." He would have the courage to act, he said, for his courage consisted not in making "hasty promises and then ignominiously to break them. My courage is to speak softly, but once I have spoken to stand or fall by my words." His aim was to keep the party united while the government was hopelessly divided. To Fielding in Nova Scotia, who was not enamoured of separate schools, he added another reason for his public silence about what he would do if he were in power: a remedial order and remedial legislation would not re-establish the separate school system of Manitoba; rather, they would "lead us into an agitation that will demand the abolition of all separate schools in every province."

The pressure, though, was so great that he wondered if he should stay on as leader. His health, his lack of ready cash, his being a *Canadien* and a Roman

Catholic, and the constant vacillation of the party led him, if not to discouragement, at least to insecurity. His law practice was non-existent: in 1894 he was in court only once. He was about to run into debt, even though, as he was quite willing to acknowledge, the party had been generous in helping him since 1887. It was difficult to go on, especially with the postponent of the elections until 1896. Still, he was loath to leave his party under the conditions that prevailed in 1895.

In the fall, he undertook another tour of Ontario. It lasted for almost two months and took in fifty-six different locations. He praised free trade, was aware of the movement for prohibition, and expressed his aversion to Macdonald's franchise bill. Once he had paid his homage to the planks of the Liberal Party platform, he turned to the school issue. All his speeches on that subject in Ontario were based on the remarks he made at the beginning of the tour in Morrisburg, on 8 October:

> I have expressed an opinion more than once upon this question, but
> I have not yet expressed the opinion which the ministerial press
> would like me to express. I am not responsible for that question, but
> I do not want to shirk it; I want to give you my views, but remem-
> ber that war has to be waged in a certain way. When the Duke of
> Wellington was in Portugal, he withdrew at one time within the lines
> of Torres Vedras, and there for months he remained, watching the
> movements of the enemy. I am in the lines of Torres Vedras. I will
> get out of them when it suits me and not before.

He reminded his audiences that he had always wanted the honourable course of action to be taken: that meant investigating the subject at once, bringing the parties together to hear them, and having the facts brought out so as to see whether a case had been made for interference or not. That was the fair, the just, the equitable, the statesmanlike way to deal with the issue of the Manitoba schools. His ploy or policy was not like that of the government, a most windy government: "They have blown and raged and threatened and the more they have raged and blown," Greenway has not budged. Here is what he would do: "If it were in my power, I would try the sunny way. I would approach that man Greenway with the sunny way of patriotism, asking him to be just and to be fair, asking him to be generous to the minority, in order that we may have peace among all the creeds and races which it has pleased God to bring upon this corner of our common country." In conclusion he asked the audience a question: "Do you not believe that there is more to be gained by appealing to the heart and soul of men rather than by trying to compel them to do a thing?" They agreed — and even allowed him to remain within the lines of Torres Verdas and come out in his good time.

When he left Ontario in November, his good time had not yet come — but there was something brewing in Ottawa, he told Pacaud. By then, the government was pretty well irrevocably weakened, with even its newspapers in Québec distrustful of its shenanigans and its incapacity to replace Angers. "At present," he wrote to Willison in November 1895, "in this province, we could sweep everything." A few weeks before the session, two by-elections gave him two constituencies in Québec that had voted Conservative for almost a generation. He attributed the victories not only to the bungling of the Conservatives but to the growing impression in Québec that, "were we in office, I personally could do more to settle the question." Tarte was doing his work well.

The skies, however, were not totally without clouds. In his letters to Willison and in his conversations with Tarte before the session, he was convinced that Bowell would introduce a remedial bill. His prediction was confirmed when Clark Wallace, perhaps the most important Orangeman in the country, resigned from the Cabinet in December. What else would force him to do that if it were not remedial legislation? If that were the case, what then of Québec? Might not the Conservatives regain their lost ground? He would have to wait and see. The politics of conciliation, of the sunny ways, were at the top of his agenda. The next session would tell the tale.

~

It was late, almost midnight. The household was quiet, almost everyone being in bed. In her full-length damask dressing gown, her hair falling loose on her shoulders, her face glowing in the light of the fire in the marble fireplace, Ishbel Aberdeen looked younger than her thirty-nine years. The room she was in was well proportioned and pleasant, with its crimson Brussels carpet, pale green wallpaper, darker green chintz chairs and sofas, fine paintings from Canada and from her estate in Scotland, European and Canadian furniture, and Gladstone smiling at her from his position above the mantel. She sat at her writing table while she wrote the day's entry into her diary:

January 2nd 1896

Parliament was duly opened to-day in accordance with the pledge given that it would re-assemble before the 3rd of January in order to provide remedial legislation for the minority in Manitoba in answer to their appeal, should the Provincial Legislature still refuse to provide the same themselves.

It being so soon after New Year's Day, a festival much observed in Canada, it was decided to adjourn any business till the 7th & only to do the formal opening to-day. A little snow had fallen in the night, but not enough to prevent wheels, & the postilions wore their usual livery & not furs. I wore my blue velvet, made to look very pretty combined with my white & gold embroidered poplin, & the pages were in white & gold & very much admired.

H.E. got through both English & French versions of his Speech very well, although it was rather long. It is always a trying performance to have to shout this from the throne. But to-day the people were very quiet, special arrangements having been made with the head of the police to place detectives in plain clothes about to ask people to be quiet, especially the M.P.s, while the French version was being read. For this always was the difficulty. They were quiet enough while the English was being read & then fell to discussing the contents as soon as the French began.

We retired to the Speaker's room & received the Ministers wives & others & then drove home. We had a very successful State Dinner of between 80 & 90 to-night, I dining as the only lady. This seemed to be approved of & tended to keep things right. Afterwards we had a crowded State Reception, which went with a good deal of go, the Ministers staying late & making themselves generally agreeable.

When the House reconvened on the 7th, there was no remedial bill. Instead, seven ministers had resigned on the 5th, prompting Laurier to write to Émilie in Arthabaska: "It is evident, nothing can save the government." All he had to do was to give Bowell and his gang enough rope to hang themselves. In the midst of the crisis, Lady Aberdeen kept in touch with Laurier through an emissary belonging to one of her organizations. In this way, she discovered that he should be sent for to form the government. She thought there was much merit in that, but it was not to be, even though at the skating party on the 11th at Rideau Hall, which both Laurier and Zoë attended, he went off for a walk with a "confidential friend" and talked about what would happen if he were appointed: there would be immediate dissolution, formation of a new Cabinet in three days, and, if the Liberals were in power at dissolution, they would sweep the country. He repeated most of that to Her Excellency when he took her in to tea. The next day, aides to the governor general prepared a memorandum that if Bowell could not regain mastery over his Cabinet, with the "Bolters," as the ministers who had resigned were called, returning to the fold, Laurier should be sent for. "H.E.'s mind is pretty well made up." Laurier made a good impression on Lady Aberdeen: "He certainly seems to look more into the future & to take a more statesmanlike view of things than the others — & he does not grasp at power." But the Bolters returned to Cabinet when Bowell agreed to resign at dissolution and it was understood that Sir Charles Tupper would take his place. Instead of forming the government then, Laurier succumbed to indigestion and a cold, and Ishbel and Zoë nursed him back to health.

With the government whole again, the remedial legislation was introduced on 11 February 1896, five weeks after the opening of Parliament. It proposed to set up a separate school board that would administer all Catholic schools, appoint qualified teachers and inspectors, and select textbooks from the list authorized for either the public schools of Manitoba or the separate schools of Ontario. It made no financial provisions for the maintenance of these schools, except to say that Roman Catholics could elect to pay their municipal school tax to support their schools. Those who did would be exempt from contributing to the maintenance of the public school system.

In the midst of the debate that followed, the governor general and Sir

Donald Smith, a high-powered Conservative, convinced the government that an attempt should be made to solve the crisis without recourse to remedial legislation. Accordingly, Smith went off to Manitoba to see what could be done and to prepare the way for a more formal negotiation.

Meanwhile, the remedial bill made its way through the House of Commons. The time had arrived for second reading. On 3 March Laurier, who had spent considerable time hesitating, considering, and consulting, was ready to announce the Liberal policy. He did so in one of the shortest speeches he ever made and which Cartwright described to Lady Aberdeen in the words: "a piece of history had been made, the gauntlet had been thrown down & we should not hear the last of that speech for many years." Pale, with his stomach rumbling and Zoë knitting in the gallery, Laurier realized that he was playing his last card. He rose and, in one sentence that took thirty lines in *Hansard,* he told all those who would oppose him — bishops, priests, Conservatives, recalcitrant Liberals, newspaper editors —to go to hell:

> Mr. Speaker, if in a debate of such moment it were not out of place for me to make a personal reference to myself — a reference, however, which may perhaps be justified, not so much on account of the feelings which may not unnaturally be attributed to me, being of the race and of the creed of which I am, but still more in consideration of the great responsibility which has been placed on my shoulders by the too kind regard of the friends by whom I am surrounded here — I would say that, in the course of my parliamentary career, during which it has been my duty on more than one occasion to take part in the discussion of those dangerous questions which too often have come before the parliament of Canada, never did I rise, sir, with a greater sense of security; never did I feel so strong in the consciousness of right, as I do now, at this anxious moment; when, in the name of the constitution so outrageously misinterpreted by the government, in the name of peace and harmony in this land; when in the name of the minority which this bill seeks or pretends to help, in the name of this young nation on which so many hopes are centred, I rise to ask this parliament not to proceed any further with this bill.

Zoë, who knew what he was going to say, was still surprised at the power of his words. His friends on the precinct of the House were on their feet, as they were in the packed galleries. When the Speaker had managed to restore order, Laurier continued making his points with an awesome logic: provincial independence was guaranteed in the powers granted by the constitution, and intervention was to be employed only after an exhaustive inquiry and sincere attempts at conciliation.

There was a moment of silence, as he marshalled his thoughts for the most important message he could convey to members in the House and to Canadians outside:

> Sir, I cannot forget at this moment that the policy which I have advocated and maintained all along has not been favourably received in all quarters. Not many weeks ago I was told from high quarters in the Church to which I belong that unless I supported the school bill which was then being prepared by the government and which we now have before us, I would incur the hostility of a great and powerful body.

Before he spoke, he had been told that representatives of the Roman Catholic Church were in the chamber, even Father Lacombe, who had written him an open letter on 20 January 1896. That letter delivered the episcopal ultimatum: submit, accept the legislation, or "the episcopacy, united with the clergy, will rise to support those who may have fallen in supporting us."

> Sir, this is too grave a phase of this question for me to pass over in silence. I have only this to say: even though I have threats held over me, coming, as I am told, from high dignitaries in the Church to which I belong, no word of bitterness shall ever pass my lips as against that Church. I respect it and I love it.

Briefly he remembered the vast crowd in the Salle de Musique on 26 June 1877. What he said then, he was about to repeat now:

> Sir, I am not of that school which has long been dominant in France

and other countries of continental Europe, which refuses ecclesiastics the right of a voice in public affairs. No, I am a Liberal of the English school. I believe in that school which has long claimed that it is the privilege of all subjects, whether high or low, whether rich or poor, whether ecclesiastics or laymen, to participate in the administration of public affairs, to discuss, to influence, to persuade, to convince — but which has always denied even to the highest the right to dictate even to the lowest.

He took a sip of water, relaxed, closed his eyes for a second before telling them all who he was: the acknowledged leader of a great party — *Canadien* and Roman Catholic though he was — made up of Protestants and Catholics, French and English, of all the diversity of Canada. Consequently, let it be known to all that

So long as I have a seat in this House, so long as I occupy the position I do now, whenever it shall become my duty to take a stand upon any question whatever, that stand I will take not upon grounds of Roman Catholicism, not upon grounds of Protestantism, but upon grounds which can appeal to the conscience of all men, irrespective of their particular faith, upon grounds which can be occupied by all men who love justice, freedom and toleration.

That said it all. He had come to the end of what he wanted to say, what he wanted Conservatives, Liberals, bishops and ecclesiastics, and all Canadians people to know. It was time to close:

So far as this bill is concerned, I have given you my views. I know, I acknowledge, that there is in this government the power to interfere, there is in this parliament the power to interfere; but that power should not be exercised until all the facts bearing upon the case have been investigated and all means of conciliation exhausted. Holding these opinions, I move that the bill be not now read the second time but that it be read the second time this day six months.

Courageously and firmly, he had challenged the government and the bishops. Should he win the next federal election, there would be no remedial legislation to solve the Manitoba Schools issue. As Cartwright said, he had thrown the gauntlet. It was now up to those others. He sat down amidst ovation after ovation from his party. Zoë, who had put down her knitting towards the end of the speech, took it up again and smiled in his direction. It was going to be all right — in the long run.

Now, however, his motion had to be dealt with, and the vote was taken at 5:30 in the morning of Friday, 20 March. He came into his office with Zoë and his secretary an hour before. His face was swollen with a toothache — "grippe in the gums," Lady Aberdeen diagnosed it — when he entered the chamber a few minutes before the vote. Upon being called by name, he voted "yes" and waited for the results. They were about the same as his Whip had predicted. Laurier's motion not to proceed was defeated, but the government's majority was cut in half, and seven of his Liberals (six from Québec and one from Nova Scotia) voted with the Conservatives. With difficulty he asked for an adjournment of the House until Monday, but to no avail. Tupper was determined that the bill would go to the committee that afternoon. Laurier went back to bed.

The bill was destined never to become law. There was just no time left. The constitution gave a maximum of five years for the life of a Parliament. The seventh, which had convened on 29 April 1891, had, therefore, to end by 26 April 1896. The first reading of the bill had taken place on 11 February, and the debate on the second reading lasted from 3 to 20 March. Then there was a crisis of sorts, when Smith returned from Manitoba with a window of opportunity. On 2 April, however, the Manitoba government refused to consider the government's proposal. By Easter the bill was in the Committee of the Whole. The members, who slept in their offices or in the reception rooms, consuming vast quantities of liquor and food, spent 223 hours discussing only a few of the 112 clauses of the legislation. On 15 April the committee had to discontinue its discussion, when the attention of the House was needed to pass an important financial measure. On Thursday, 23 April 1896, Lady Aberdeen was able to write in her *Journal*:

The prorogation of the longest Parliament ever held took place this evening. This too was unusual as the ceremony generally takes place in the afternoon. But they had a lot of business to finish up & at the last moment at 8 o'clock asked H. E. to delay his coming for twenty minutes. There was a great turn out. We retired to the Speaker's Rooms afterwards & received any who wished to see us.

The Elections have been fixed for June 23 & the meeting of the new Parliament for July 16. So a summer Session is now a certainty & H.E. will have to be here anyway.

We had supper upon our return.

TUESDAY, 23 JUNE 1896

On the day after Parliament was dissolved and the election called for 23 June, Laurier was with Tarte and the entire Québec Liberal delegation in the House at the opening of the campaign in Montréal. It was at night, and an immense throng, with torches lighting their way, came to escort him from David's house to Sohmer Park, where another huge crowd had assembled at the entrance to the hall. On the way they stopped at the Champ de Mars and the Place Viger to see the fireworks, and in the hall, where ten thousand could be seated, there were at least twelve thousand people. He spoke on all the issues, was duly applauded, and everyone went away feeling good, hopeful, and proud that among them there was such a man.

He spent the weekend with Zoë at Charlemagne's house in Saint-Lin, where he sat quietly near Maman Adeline remembering the past and visiting Carolus's grave. He was caught up in the emotion of his memories, and he wept with her for all he had left behind. While there, he also had long conversations with the parish priest, the remarkable Jean-Baptiste Proulx, the former rector of the branch plant of Laval University in Montréal. Proulx knew everybody in Rome, in Québec, and in Manitoba, where he had served as a missionary. He favoured Laurier's solutions to the school and language problems. "Be firm," Proulx advised, and "make a general but formal promise to act in the best interests of both the minority and the majority." He even hinted that Rome wouldn't smile favourably on the resurrection of the "influence indue cléricale" of the 1870s. Proulx also supplied the Liberal leader with information and advice throughout the campaign under the pseudonym of Joannes. The following Monday, refreshed, Laurier set out to conquer Québec, without which there could be no victory.

His challenge there was not so much from the Conservatives or from the Tory press. The real contest was between him and the bishops. In spite of their disappointment over the Conservative government's handling of the school question, the bishops were still in sympathy with the Conservative Party, for they distrusted the Liberals more. By that time, the leadership of the episcopacy of Québec was in the hands of Bishop Laflèche of Trois-Rivières. It did not bode well for Laurier.

As the remedial bill made its way through the House, Laflèche and his episcopal allies, among whom was the new archbishop of Saint-Boniface, Louis-Philippe-Adélard Langevin, had tried to intimidate Laurier, going so far as to threaten him. But he had stood firm. With the failure of the legislation in April, Laflèche proposed that the bishops of Québec should prepare a *mandement* to guide the electorate, which had become the court of last resort. They had promised the Conservatives their help if remedial legislation was introduced. The Conservatives had done their part; now the bishops had to deliver.

The *mandement* was read in all the churches on 16 May. In it, the twelve bishops who signed it — the entire episcopacy of Québec and the archbishop of Ottawa, whose diocese straddled Québec and Ontario — declared themselves the natural judges of the Manitoba Schools Question, those empowered by God to stipulate what solution was best. Given the lack of episcopal unanimity, the bishops did not condemn the Liberal Party or endorse the Conservatives. Rather, they zeroed in on the candidates. Only those candidates who formally and solemnly affirmed that they would vote in Parliament for a law that restored the rights of the minority in Manitoba could be supported by a Catholic elector. There was no way out of that "obligation."

In the secret *Circular* to the clergy which accompanied the *mandement*, the bishops went much further. The priests of Québec were told that only remedial legislation could meet the episcopal objective. It was understood that Laurier, who had promised that there would be no remedial legislation if he became prime minister, should be opposed. Furthermore, with one exception, the bishops insisted on written declarations from the candidates that would support a law acceptable to the episcopacy in Parliament. All the Liberal candidates in Québec, save Laurier and seven others, signed on the dotted line.

Then Laflèche went on the offensive against Laurier personally. In a sermon delivered after reading the *mandement* — he didn't feel himself bound by the order not to comment on it — he censured Laurier, citing his famous speech of 3 March. He called him a "libéral rationaliste" and, as such, an enemy of the church. To vote for Laurier was a mortal sin; to work for him, give money to his party, or stand as his candidate were also mortal sins.

Laurier was now fair game. He was a *Rouge* again, the enemy of God and the church. Those who supported him were on their way to hell. Attempts to persuade the archbishop of Québec, Louis-Nazaire Bégin, to follow the "liberal" attitude of his predecessor, Cardinal Taschereau, failed. Laurier bore the abuse rather well, even though at times during the two-month campaign, exhausted and with his voice in a shambles, he wanted to strike back. But he didn't. Only Zoë knew what it cost.

~

It was not by arguing with bishops that Tarte hoped to make Laurier prime minister of Canada. With his characteristic frankness, he admitted that he had been treasurer of the Conservative Party during three elections and, he confided, "I must tell you that elections are not won by prayers." What he did for the Conservatives, he now set out to do for the Liberals. Without the "resources of power" — the spoils of patronage — he relied on careful organization, publicity, and personal contact.

Before 1893, when Tarte formally entered the party, there was no permanent Liberal organization in Québec. With Pacaud, he set about creating one. By July 1894 there was a central office and, during the next two years, Liberal political clubs were founded all over the province. An army of young men were ready to hold the constituency associations together, revise the electoral lists, distribute literature, invade every constituency to preach the gospel according to Laurier, and go from door to door inviting electors to hear Laurier speak and, above all, to vote for him. Tarte also developed a Liberal press to spread the word: a new newspaper, *Le Soir*, was founded in Montréal in April 1896, and *Le Cultivateur*, which Tarte owned and which had a circulation of 40,000, became a sort of official Liberal organ. *La Patrie* also had a good circulation, but it was often considered too radical to be of much use.

And Tarte found the money. He was a protectionist in a free-trade camp. He told the doubting industrialists and businessmen: "Look, Laurier will be the next prime minister of Canada; there is no doubt about that. I will be in the Cabinet and I tell you that the tariff will be reformed to everybody's benefit, without hurting in any way the interests of the business community. I am your friend; I am your guarantor." It worked — and the *caisse* of the party was in good condition.

By the beginning of the election campaign, Laurier was ready. He was now a household name and the seed had been planted: a *Canadien* and a Roman Catholic was more likely to help the Catholic minority in Manitoba than a party that had failed to do so during five long years. Tarte was confident; so was Laurier — and Tarte estimated that Laurier would carry forty to fifty seats in Québec alone.

The Conservatives were also ready. Their forces were impressive, even if the party had lost much of its appeal. They made full use of their financial resources and had extensive help from their well-financed press. In addition, the bishops and the clergy were in open sympathy with them. With all this assistance, the Conservatives had good reason to hope they would obtain the same results as in the past.

During the two-month campaign, Laurier stayed mostly in Québec. In the West, he relied on the good will he had created during his triumphant tour in 1894 and, in Ontario, on the speeches and visits he had made in fifty-six constituencies in the fall of 1895. Tarte took him everywhere in the province and he organized large meetings and huge *assemblées contradictoires*. Tarte estimated that between 1895 and the election in June 1896, there must have been three hundred such meetings; prominent Liberals like Mowat and Fielding often spoke at them, and Laurier shook the hands of probably 200,000 voters. Everywhere he went, people were impressed and inspired; his rhetoric moved them and his charm captivated them. They were also amused by the little man, Tarte, with his speech impediment and wild gestures, who urged them to vote for his leader.

Nomination day was on 16 June, a week before the election. Laurier was in Québec City, as were the Aberdeens. He was duly nominated, gave his usual speech, and Tarte took him to yet another meeting in another constituency. At

Zoë's insistence, he went to Arthabaska for a day or so to recuperate from a sore throat and some digestive malaise. He voted there on 23 June.

~

On that beautiful Tuesday evening, the province of Québec gave him forty-nine seats, leaving the Conservatives with sixteen. Laurier was more powerful than the bishops. In the rest of the country, the vote was about evenly divided: Nova Scotia, ten Liberals to ten Conservatives; New Brunswick, five to nine; Prince Edward Island, five to three; Manitoba, two to four; North-West Territories, five to one; British Columbia, four to two; and Ontario, forty-three each to the Liberals and the Conservatives, three McCarthyites, two Patrons of Industry, and one Independent. Laurier could count on a majority of thirty in the House of Commons.

The next day was Saint-Jean-Baptiste Day and, early in the morning, a special train brought Laurier and Zoë to Québec City for the victory parade. It was a triumphant journey through the main streets of Old Québec, which were decorated with flags and bunting and large pictures of the hero. His carriage was filled with flowers; people lined the streets and gave way to their delight; bands played; and fireworks detonated. There was so much jubilation that the parish priest of Saint-Sauveur led the crowd in three hurrahs for Laurier as the young men of his constituency unharnessed the horses, lifted up his carriage, and carried him in triumph on their shoulders. It was a great day, marred only by the racist editorial in the Toronto *Mail* that the country was being sold to the French and that "Quebec will demand her pound of flesh." Lady Aberdeen was not amused.

While he was in Québec, Laurier telephoned the principal aide to the governor general to ask that no appointments to the Senate or to the courts be made. His Excellency was of the same opinion and, satisfied on that point, Laurier returned to Arthabaska to celebrate Zoë's fifty-fifth birthday on 26 June. Meanwhile, Sir Charles Tupper, who had become prime minister upon dissolution, was fuming: the governor general, pleading previous engagements, could not meet him until 3 p.m. on 2 July. When Tupper arrived at Rideau Hall for the interview, Lady Aberdeen marvelled at his composure: "The plucky old thing came down blooming in a white waistcoat & seemingly as pleased with himself as ever. He did not at all appear as the defeated Premier come to render an account of his defeat & of its causes to the representative of the Sovereign. Not he! Down he sat & for an hour & a half harangued H.E." Tupper was annoyed that Aberdeen expected him to resign forthwith, but he wasn't prepared to co-operate. The electoral recounts would not be in until 7 July, and he would wait. Aberdeen didn't say much, though he refused to sanction the appointments Tupper wanted to make and he directed him to deal only with ordinary admin-istrative matters until the 7th. Tupper was not pleased. He hinted strongly that Aberdeen was not following precedents and was infringing upon the principle of self-government.

On the 8th Tupper arrived at Rideau Hall at 11:00 a.m., but didn't resign. He came back at 6 in the evening and tendered his formal resignation. By that time, Laurier was on a train between Québec City and Montréal. Telegrams were dispatched, and he replied that he would be in Ottawa the next day.

Thursday, 9 July, was an exceedingly hot and humid day. Laurier arrived at the Russell in the late afternoon and immediately received Captain Sinclair, who came in the name of the governor general to ask him to read over the mem-orandum describing His Excellency's decisions — and the reasons for them — since the election. He and Sinclair talked everything over, and Laurier agreed to take full responsibility for Aberdeen's "despotic" acts.

The next day, at 11:00 a.m., he was at Rideau Hall. Alone in the office of the governor general of Canada, he was asked to form a government. He accepted, and undertook to do so by Monday morning, the 13th, at the latest. On his way out, Lady Aberdeen sent a lady of her entourage to present him with a note "enclosing a piece of heather sent from Scotland last year & a pin of enamelled white heather with an ivy leaf, "to help fulfil a prophecy that if "a girl meets a man & gives him a piece of white heather as he leaves the house on any quest, she brings him good luck."

On Saturday, 11 July 1896, he was sworn in as president of the Privy Council. As of that moment, Wilfrid Laurier became the seventh prime min-ister of Canada since Confederation, and the first *Canadien* to do so. It had been a long journey from the farm in Saint-Lin to the highest elected office in the land.

~

The moment of Wilfrid Laurier has arrived. It will last fifteen years. When it ends in 1911, his country will be totally transformed. Some of that will be his doing; much of it, though, will be in reaction to events and circumstances over which he has no control. Often what he wishes cannot be; and more often what he dreads will happen, forcing him to contain both it and himself. But that he knows. It has all been part of his life.

His health is a problem that time has not tamed. Every year, and often more than once a year, it badgers him, leaving him usually weak and disoriented. Bronchitis, gastritis, difficulties in breathing, sweating, general lassitude, impatience: these are the characteristics. Over the years, though, he has learned to anticipate whatever bout is coming and to adjust himself accordingly.

When he arrives at his moment in 1896, he realizes that he will have to be careful to pace himself and to do the work he has to do in an atmosphere that is as free of tension as possible. That implies, he tells himself, a strong Cabinet to which much can be delegated, a loyal caucus that will not hamper him, an effective control over the machinery of government, a keen and accurate perception of what is possible, and the craftiness of Machiavelli combined with the idealism of Sir Galahad.

Émilie Lavergne is still his friend, but his relationship with her needs to be clarified so as to avoid stressful incidents, not so much in his private life as in his public milieu. As for Zoë, a long talk is overdue. Adjusting will not be easy for her: there will be increasing political and social demands made on her, along with appeals for her assistance; high society may well frighten her; and her lack of fluency in English is certainly a stumbling block. But she has courage and has often demonstrated her *grandeur d'âme* to him and to others. He knows her to be intelligent, a good judge of people, and almost prophetic in her assessment of events. She has an abiding interest in what he does and in the things that affect him. She is, after all, his guardian. And he prizes that, happily seeking her advice. She has never embarrassed him with her judgments; she is the soul of discretion; and that will not change. He is certain, though, that she will badger him for her causes and for the artists she is bound to adopt.

He has outstanding qualities of mind and soul to be an effective leader: he revealed those characteristics in his youth at L'Assomption. Circumstances and chance have often tested him since, and seldom have they found him wanting. He can put into words the deepest aspirations of his soul. He can express attainable goals in the conduct of human affairs in a language that is noble and exalting. Herein lies his strength.

Canada relishes who he is — and he intends to take it as far as he can. His life is a theatre, played on a set he has designed but often hesitated to mount. Now he is upon it, but he has no illusions. The people will cheer him; they will show him warmth and respect; but they will not necessarily agree with him or always vote for him. Too often, they will taunt and deliberately misjudge him and misconstrue his policies and his words. He knows that.

Another hurdle is his bossiness, tyrannical even at times. Zoë can vouch for that. Once he has decided on a course, it is almost impossible to move him forward. For a Liberal who holds "change" to be the natural condition of democracy, he is quite set in his ways, sunny as they may be. When he doesn't get his way, however, he wastes no time analysing and punishing: he has learned to be satisfied with what can be. In this regard, he is helped by his strong inclination never to allow political criticism or rejection to impair his personal relations.

Then, there is Canada, an entity sacred and essential to his being. "The unity of the people is the secret of the future — L'union entre les peuples, le secret de l'avenir," he had declared in 1864. No sooner was he installed in Ottawa ten years later than he proceeded to fashion that unity. He has had no easy time of it. Now that his moment has arrived, he has no illusions that it will be any easier. Under the thin top soil of nationalism lies the hard rock of race and religion, of regionalism, and of political partisanship. And there are too many around willing to do mischief to achieve their ends. How is he to control them and the events they may unleash?

If national unity exacts compromise, is it always to be his people who will pay the largest part of it? If revenge is no way to build a country, can constant denial not breed revenge? Or abdication? Or withdrawal? Can he fashion the unity of all the people out of elements that do not trust one another and that are paranoid about the domination of one over the other? Can he, a *Canadien* and a Roman Catholic, be accepted as the impartial umpire of all? Or will he be the first and the last of his kind to be prime minister of Canada?

Unity! Moderation! Conciliation! These are the tools. These are the constituents of his national policy. If he fails, there will be no Canada at worst, and no future *Canadien* prime minister at best. The task, then, is to transform two nationalisms — a Canadian nationalism that looks outward to find its aspirations, and a *Canadien nationalisme* that looks inward to ensure its survival — into one, just like the rivers that empty into the St. Lawrence. Is his dream all a mirage? Or is it rather a pillar of fire by night and a pillar of a cloud by day?

What of God? He wants to have faith, to pray, but he seems incapable of either. Oh! He believes in a Supreme Being, the Creator to whom all humans owe everything they have. He also accepts the justice and mercy of His laws. But more than that is not possible. He wishes he could find consolation at the loss of his cherished illusions. With no faith, there is no hope, and he grows indifferent to the blows that all his efforts have not succeeded in averting. Where is God at this, Wilfrid Laurier's, moment?

PART II

"FOLLOW MY WHITE PLUME"
1896–1919

11

THE INAUGURATION OF POWER
1896–1898

Because he had already made certain arrangements before the election, Laurier was able to name his Cabinet in two days. It had been agreed that Oliver Mowat would leave the premiership of Ontario to become a senator and minister of justice; William Stevens Fielding would relinquish a similar role in Nova Scotia to be minister of finance; and Andrew George Blair would do the same in New Brunswick and come to Ottawa as minister of railways and canals. It was obvious, as early as 1895, that should Laurier win, Tarte, indispensable as he was as an organizer, would enter the Cabinet as minister of public works. The post of minister of the interior and superintendent general of Indian affairs was reserved for Clifford Sifton from Manitoba, should he behave over the Manitoba Schools affair. After those key nominations, the others fell into place. From Prince Edward Island came Louis Henry Davies, a member of Parliament since 1882, as minister of marine and fisheries; from Nova Scotia, Frederick William Borden, as minister of militia and defence; and from Ontario, Richard Cartwright in trade and commerce, William Mulock in the Post Office, Senator Richard W. Scott (representing the Catholics of that province) as secretary of state, and William Paterson as comptroller of customs. From Québec, beside Tarte, came Henri-Gustave Joly de Lotbinière, a former premier and a respected Liberal, as controller of inland revenue; Christophe-Alphonse Geoffrion, a *Rouge* with ancient credentials, as minister without portfolio, as was Richard Reid Dobell, a rich lumber merchant from Québec City and a newcomer to the party; and Sydney Arthur Fisher, Laurier's old friend and a gentleman farmer from the Eastern Townships as minister of agriculture. In addition, Charles Fitzpatrick, a prominent

Québec lawyer who had defended Riel, became solicitor general, but without Cabinet rank.

Laurier had a larger Cabinet than Macdonald had appointed: seventeen members, including himself. The demands of regional representation were met with four from the Maritimes; five from Ontario; one from the West; and seven, including himself, from Québec. The reason Québec had the most places was that Laurier was convinced he could never be re-elected unless Québec was solidly behind him. Lady Aberdeen approved of the Cabinet: "a very strong one it is."

Laurier made it known that he was the boss. The ministers were to administer their departments with integrity and efficiency, and without embarrassing the government. They could make plans and set objectives, but major matters had to receive the approval of the Cabinet after being vetted by him. As for patronage, they were permitted to initiate it and do pretty much as they pleased, but there were two rules: he was the first and last judge, and could veto their appointments; and he asked to sign as many letters of designation as possible. In that way he was sure to have a group of organizers across the land who were directly loyal to him. He was not able to include many, particularly in Ontario and Québec, who had claims to office. He found jobs for some, promised posts to others, and charmed most of the disappointed with his "sunny ways." The *Rouges*, though, feeling slighted, gave him a hard time, holding Tarte responsible.

On the morning of 20 August, the Aberdeens, with all their retinue of children, nannies, aides and secretaries, servants, horses, mattresses, pots and pans, arrived back in Ottawa from Stanley House in Nova Scotia and the Citadelle in Québec City. Lady Aberdeen had had quite a time of it. A most awkward move, she wrote in her diary, "as it was a sort of three-cornered affair and it was a problem how to sleep at the three places on three successive nights on the same mattresses which had to be conveyed from place to place." But she was on time for the beginning of the new régime.

The Opening of Parliament went off very well & was very largely attended. Being at this time of year we did not think that there would have been many ladies, but the place was crammed. I made an attempt to be allowed to come in morning dress, but there seemed to be a doubt about whether the change would be liked, so it was dropped for this time. But I find that Madame Laurier is all for the change. It is too ridiculous to be driving through this very colonial town dressed up in diamonds & evening dress in full daylight.

The speech was very brief. Sir Oliver Mowat told me that the paragraph foreshadowing the settlement of the Manitoba Schools Question might have been worded more strongly & that he thought it would probably be arranged amicably without a Commission. He is rather sorry for this, as he & Sir Henri Joly would have been on the Commission & were very keen to bring the settlement about. It will be a great feather in Laurier's cap if a solution can be arrived at so early in the régime.

The Eighth Parliament of Canada was duly in session, and the Laurier era was under way.

~

With Laurier's victory in 1896, the battle for the political supremacy of Québec, begun with the *Programme catholique* in 1871, entered its final phase. The first item on the agenda was Manitoba's separate schools. Discussions between the Liberals and the Manitoba government had been going on for some time, and they continued after 23 June. At the end of July, Joseph Martin, the first of Laurier's intermediaries, reported that Attorney General Sifton was willing to receive a private and confidential memorandum from the federal government outlining proposals for an honourable compromise. The Manitoba government, which was, according to Martin, committed "to go as far as they possibly can to meet your views on the School Question without departing from any of the principles which they have laid down in the past, would then advise if Laurier's suggestions could be implemented, and if so, the legislature would act upon it." In August, before the opening of Parliament, Laurier, with Mowat, Fitzpatrick, and Tarte, prepared such a memorandum, and it was discussed with Sifton and other members of the Greenway government when they visited Ottawa later that month. Mowat acted as chief negotiator for the federal government, and the discussions went well.

Before any settlement could be concluded, however, or made public, it was necessary to feel the pulse of the minority. For that reason, Justice Routhier, a Laurier supporter, a former *Programmiste,* and the judge in the famous Charlevoix case of "influence indue spirituelle," went to Winnipeg to see his daughter. He found opinions divided, but concluded that a settlement — without remedial legislation — would be acceptable to the minority.

By the middle of October a settlement of sorts was ready. It was then time to test it with the minority and, especially, with Archbishop Langevin. No one was better equipped to do this than Tarte. By 24 October he and Henri Bourassa were in Winnipeg on a supposed tour of inspection of government projects in the West and in British Columbia. Tarte was appalled at Langevin's cavalier insouciance about the condition to which Catholic and French-language education in Manitoba had been reduced: with half the schools closed, about 1500 children were left without instruction. He was determined to remedy the situation. Since he held the entire Roman Catholic episcopacy of Canada responsible for the mess in Manitoba, he visited Langevin four times to inform him that the settlement would be a matter between governments and that Langevin would not be shown the document before its publication. Nor could most of the items on the episcopal wish-list be implemented; they demanded the complete and full restoration of the separate school system that existed prior to 1890, and that was impossible. Tarte met with Greenway and, more often, with Sifton, who was most cooperative. Everyone realized "the necessity of understanding and conciliatory action." He also had some advice for Laurier:

> There is no reason why the Federal government should express satisfaction or dissatisfaction. Let the legislature adopt the proposed amendments; let them be put in force. If, as I have no doubt, the Catholics express themselves as satisfied, the last word will have been said. But it would be extremely imprudent to tie ourselves now, and thereby to give our adversaries in Parliament ground for attack. Our role hitherto has been to act as amici curiae. Let us stick to that. This is the position which I have taken with the Catholics here. I have promised them to continue our good offices in the application of the law.

Sifton will ask you for an order-in-council approving the set-tlement. Let him wait, telling him that it will not be advisable to do anything before my return.

Tarte's instructions were followed. On 17 November Sifton entered the Laurier Cabinet, and on the 18th Laurier wrote to Pacaud letting him know that a set-tlement was about to be made official and that a copy would be dispatched from Ottawa in a day or so. The next day, Laurier forwarded the text, though Pacaud was cautioned not to publish it until he received further instructons. On that day as well, 19 November, the Manitoba government passed the necessary legisla-tive instruments to implement the settlement. On the 20th, Laurier wired Pacaud: "Publish document forwarded yesterday." The publication of the Laurier-Greenway Settlement coincided with Laurier's fifty-fifth birthday.

The *Laurier-Greenway Règlement* did not re-establish the separate school system as it had existed before 1890 in Manitoba. It did not organize Catholic schools into Catholic districts, nor did it permit pupils to be segregated by reli-gious denomination for secular schoolwork. However, it attempted to mitigate the most offensive grievances of the Roman Catholic and French-speaking pop-ulation. It permitted separate religious instruction between the hours of 3:30 and 4:00 in the afternoon when the parents or guardians of ten children attending a rural school, or 25 in a city, town, or village, petitioned the Board of School Trustees to that effect. Catholic schoolteachers would be hired when the Roman Catholic enrolment of a school in urban districts listed forty or more Catholic students, or twenty-five in rural districts, again if the parents petitioned the board. Finally, on parental request, instruction could be given in French or any other minority language when ten or more children of the language group in question were in attendance.

Greenway gave his word to Tarte that Catholics would be represented on the board and that a Roman Catholic French-speaking inspector would be appointed — though he had to be threatened, cajoled, and bribed into keeping it. Teachers with a Québec diploma would be accepted within the system, and books Catholics objected to would not be used in teaching Catholic children. These points were not to be implemented immediately, but Tarte was firm in his opinion that they would be: Laurier would see to it through the magic of subsidies.

Laurier was satisfied. The agreement was not as advantageous as he had desired, but after six years of quarrels and agitations that bordered on civil war, "it was not possible to obtain more." It would have to do. He directed the caucus to be calm and unprovocative, with the result that in the 1897 session of Parliament there was little discussion of the settlement. He would have to keep at it, though. In time, concessions could be wrung out of the Manitobans.

But Laurier had another reason for accepting the settlement: provincial autonomy, the cornerstone of Confederation, the foundation of Canada's political system, and the key to his national harmony agenda. In a country like Canada, a country with different races and creeds and the inevitable passions they gave rise to, only provincial autonomy could guard "the safety of Confederation and the interests particularly of the province of Québec." That didn't mean that federal intervention should never be exercised. Quite the contrary. But it should be implemented "only as a last resort, when every other means has been exhausted, and when all hope of conciliation and of understanding with the provincial authorities have been found vain." The reason Laurier found Canada so difficult to govern was that these principles — provincial autonomy and centralization — lived side by side in a state of antagonism.

Still, with a stroke of his pen, Laurier was party to an arrangement that altered the constitution of Manitoba irrevocably. George-Étienne Cartier had created it in 1870 as a bilingual province, with guarantees of language and of religious schools for the French-speaking population of the Red River Colony. In 1890, unilaterally, a Manitoba Liberal government smashed that arrangement and got away with it. And, in the fall of 1896, Laurier had reduced his own language to a secondary status in Manitoba. No longer the equal of English, French was now one of many. Did he not in that process extinguish the dual Canada that was at the centre of his vision for the Canada-to-be?

When colleagues and others remonstrated with him about it, he found safety in arguing that he had not created the situation in Manitoba: he had inherited it. And so he was satisfied that he had done the best possible in a bad situation. He was also convinced that the settlement was an opportunity — an opportunity to solidify the survival of the French "race." For him, the salvation of the French race was not in isolation, but in struggle. "Give our children the best education possible," he used to say, "put them on an equal footing with those of the other race, and give them the legitimate pride which they will have in such a struggle. There is salvation. There is autonomy."

Langevin didn't see it that way at all. From his cathedral in Saint-Boniface, he countered for all Canadians to hear: "I tell you there will be a revolt in Québec which will ring throughout Canada and these men who today are triumphant will be cast down. The settlement is a farce. The fight has only begun." In a by-election in Saint-Boniface in 1897, Langevin announced that Catholics who voted for the Liberal candidate were not to be given absolution and that their case was to be reserved for the archbishop. On the eve of the election, the Blessed Sacrament was exposed all day in the cathedral, and parish priests went from door to door to warn voters that should they vote Liberal they would not be buried in consecrated ground. Not suprisingly, the Liberal was defeated.

In Québec, all the bishops except one encouraged Langevin in his opposition. They banned newspapers that extolled the virtues of the settlement. David's pamphlet *Le Clergé canadien, sa mission, son oeuvre* [*The Canadian Clergy, Their Mission, and Their Work*] was banned and sent to Rome. In it, David stated that in the 1896 election the actions of the bishops, particularly Laflèche, amounted to "the denial of all political freedom, the overturning of the basic principles of the constitution; it is a heresy as dangerous for the Church as for the State." In January 1897 the Sacred Congregation of the Index Expurgatorius placed it on the list of forbidden books. On Sunday, 27 December 1896, Ernest Pacaud was in the Basilica in Québec City attending High Mass when an episcopal letter was read forbidding Catholics to read *L'Électeur*. In November it had "insulted" the bishops by criticizing their conduct during the June elections and had then published David's pamphlet. Pacaud squirmed: Had not a pope blessed him and his issue to the third generation? That very afternoon, he met with some of his financial advisers and, the next day, the Feast of the Holy Innocents, he issued his paper under the new name of *Le Soleil*.

Internally, Laurier raged at the humiliation of his two friends. At the same time, he wouldn't be drawn into a war with the bishops either — a war that could easily be interpreted as one against the church. Catholics had the same civil rights as other men in Canada. He would appeal to the authorities of his church to recognize that the Catholics of his province and his country could exercise their civil rights freely and, at the same time, remain faithful to their church. He ordered Pacaud, and suggested to others over whom he had less control, to be respectful towards the clergy. Victory was bound to come. "We must wait and, above all, wait in silence."

Three days after the archbishop of Québec had placed an interdict on *L'Électeur*, Laurier was in Montréal attending a banquet in his and Greenway's honour. Again he opened his heart for all to see what was on his mind:

> I have devoted my career to the realization of an idea. I have taken the work of Confederation where I found it when I entered political life, and determined to give it my life.
>
> Nothing will deter me from continuing to the end in my task of preserving at all cost our civil liberty.
>
> Nothing will prevent me from continuing my efforts to preserve that state of society conquered by our fathers at the price of so many years and so much blood.
>
> It may be that the result of my efforts will be the Tarpeian Rock, but if that be the case I will fall without murmur or recrimination or complaint, certain that from my tomb will rise the immortal idea for which I have always fought.

~

In the meantime, there was a miracle in Saint-Lin. In July 1896, as Charlemagne recounted to Zoë, grasshoppers had invaded the farmland. The infestation was worse than ever before and threatened to destroy all the crops. The parish priest, l'abbé Proulx, would have none of it. In early August he commanded his archbishop to visit his parish and summoned his parishioners to the cemetery, where he had Charlemagne and other strong men erect a large cross. The archbishop said some prayers, and Proulx made the longest sermon ever heard in those parts. He promised to build a chapel at the foot of the cross should God in his mercy rid his parish of the pest. He went further. To the horror of the archbishop and the faithful, he ordered the authorities of heaven to obey him forthwith. Realizing what he had done, he became confused and dismissed his people.

Charlemagne, having installed Maman Adeline and his wife in his *calèche*, climbed to his seat. He picked up the reins, which were covered with grasshoppers, and he shook them off as he had been doing constantly for over a month. However, this time it was different. Instead of jumping away, the irritating creatures fell dead at his feet. Everywhere, on the trees, on the fences, in the fields, on the crops, on the animals, it was the same, and millions of the corpses were carried to Montréal by the waters of the Achigan River.

Proulx had his miracle. It was time for him to go to Rome — but not before carpenters had begun to lay the foundation of the chapel.

∼

To Rome. Obviously, Laurier could have no peace with the bishops and the priests unless Rome intervened. After the election, Fitzpatrick, Tarte, and others were charged with preparing a document for the Holy See which would be a formal protest against episcopal and clerical intervention in politics and an appeal to Leo XIII to restate clearly the directives promulgated by his predecessor, Pius IX, that had protected the liberties of Catholic electors and the peace of the country. Fitzpatrick asked Gustave-Adolphe Drolet to take the statement of the members of Parliament to Rome on their behalf. It was a stroke of genius. Drolet was fifty-two years old, a Conservative by temperament, an obedient servant of the church by conviction and love, a lawyer, a *Chevalier*, a veteran, and the author of *Zouaviana*. In the last half of the 1860s, when Pius IX was having difficulties with Garibaldi and his Red Shirts, Drolet had become a pontifical Zouave, one of the soldiers whose mission it was to guard the pope. That credential, it was hoped, would open doors for him. He left at the beginning of September 1896. When the negotiations with Greenway's government were well under way and Laurier could see some light at the end of the tunnel, he arranged for Proulx, who was well known and respected in Vatican circles, to go to Rome on some pretext or other to state the government's case, reminding the cardinals and the pope that many Catholics in Canada — who only sought "to exercise their duties as citizens in accord with the recognized principles of the British Constitution" — felt wronged by the actions of certain of their bishops. Proulx was also to try to obtain "a statement of doctrine which would have the effect of bringing regrettable abuses to an end, maintaining peace and harmony in our country and reassuring the consciences of Catholics."

Proulx left on 10 September and was back in Canada by 17 January. Both he and Drolet failed in their missions. In fact, they had a hard time of it. Half the Québec episcopacy went to Rome in the summer and fall of 1896, and those who didn't go sent copious memoranda. They did everything they could to undermine Drolet and Proulx and to libel and slander the prime minister. Once again, he became an anti-Catholic, a Free Mason, a free-thinker, and an anti-clerical. The bishops deliberately misrepresented the judicial decisions involved in the Manitoba Schools dispute, knowing full well that they were quite safe in doing so. The Vatican's ignorance of the constitutional and political workings of a country like Canada was astronomical.

Laurier did not give up. He knew what he wanted — the appointment of a papal delegate. The idea would be hard to sell. The Canadian bishops, both within and outside Québec, were opposed to the idea, fearing that it would be interpreted as a rebuke to Laflèche and his cohorts. It would also antagonize the Protestants, who would see it as another papal intervention in the affairs of Canada.

In January, Solicitor General Charles Fitzpatrick went to Rome. Unlike his predecessors, he was successful. He was a close colleague of Laurier and was seen as representing his voice. He came with legal opinions prepared by both Edward Blake and the cardinal archbishop of Westminster. He was accompanied by Charles Russell, the son of an eminent British Lord, who was well connected and had a flair for Roman politics. They were both charming, diplomatic, and pious; indeed, Fitzpatrick prayed so much that he had calluses on his knees. And they had impressive letters of introduction: Russell was a friend of the thirty-two-year-old Spanish favourite of the pope, Monsignor Raphaël Merry Del Val, and Leo XIII, received them in audience, listening attentively and sympathetically. Shortly thereafter, His Holiness named a special commission of cardinals to investigate and, on 8 March 1897, Canadian newspapers announced Del Val's nomination as papal legate. Laurier breathed a sigh of relief.

Del Val spent three months in Canada. Like those who had been sent before him, the Vatican diplomat listened attentively to the various points of view being hurled at him, to elaborate justifications, to endless assertions of principles, to conflicting episcopal opinions, and attended interminable religious ceremonies. His first act on his arrival on 31 March was to order the bishops to behave; his second, to investigate Langevin's complaints.

Laurier undestood how fragile was Del Val's mission. The young legate had to end the episcopal quarrels between the bishops of Québec and bring about unity among all the bishops of Canada, without any of them losing face. It was not an easy matter. Furthermore, he had Langevin to contend with. Was the archbishop intransigent? Or did he have a case? Laurier had better be on his guard, for Del Val was bound to test his and Greenway's good faith. In the middle of his mission, he sent Laurier a memorandum that contained a list of administrative concessions that, he said, would make the settlement more palatable and bring about "a less hostile attitude on the part of the Catholics." If neither Laurier nor Greenway was prepared to cooperate, he warned the prime minister that Rome would decide in favour of the bishops.

Laurier was determined that Del Val would succeed. He set about to purchase concessions from Greenway by introducing a motion in the House of Commons to grant Manitoba $300,000 from the "School Fund." Unfortunately, Tarte reported to him that "the Catholic M.P.'s oppose it absolutely." Laurier was in despair. But not the papal legate.

In Rome, Del Val set about to convince the pope and the cardinals that Laurier was on the right path. He recognized that the bishops were correct in their basic arguments: in 1890 the Catholics of Manitoba were indeed deprived of the rights granted them by the Canadian constitution; and the federal Parliament had the power to redress the situation. However, Del Val looked to the future and realized that, as a matter of practical politics, Ottawa could not pass a remedial law, regardless of which party was in power. Consequently, mixed schools, or some arrangement like the proposed settlement, was the only solution.

Del Val won his point and the bishops lost theirs. On Sunday, 9 January 1898, congregations in every Catholic church in Canada heard an encyclical that the pope addressed to the Canadian episcopacy and the faithful. *Affari Vos* [Your Affairs] reiterated Rome's condemnation of nondenominational schools and emphasized the obligation for Catholic parents to send their children to Catholic schools. Therefore, Leo XIII stated, the bishops had acted well in accordance with the teachings of the church when they protested Manitoba's "blow at Catholic education." The episcopacy had the blessing of the pope "for the things which you sought and still seek to protect and defend." At the same time, the pope spoke of the Laurier-Greenway Settlement as a beginning, even though it was still "defective, unsuitable, and insufficient." Limited as it might be, though, he urged everyone to accept this "partial satisfaction," to work within it, and to derive from it "as much benefit and advantage as possible." Again Laurier was satisfied. It was as much as he had hoped for. As far as he was concerned, the incident of the Manitoba separate schools was over.

But not the war with the bishops. It would go on for at least another year after *Affari Vos*. Laurier had an ally in the new archbishop of Montréal, Paul Bruchési. As he wrote to Laurier at the end of January 1898: "Leo XIII asked me, Mr. Minister, to work with all my strength to obtain it (religious and political peace through improvement to the Laurier-Greenway Settlement). I shall so labour." If Bruchési was more or less capable of containing Langevin, he had no success with his colleague Bégin in the Archdiocese of Québec or in the dioceses of Rimouski and Chicoutimi. "The warfare which went on there," he reported to Del Val in November, "goes on still, with this difference, that it has become undercover in place of open." In his letters to Del Val, he used words like "persecution" in describing what was done to priests who didn't toe the episcopal line.

Laurier's solution was for Rome to send a permanent apostolic delegate to Canada. After much pressure on Del Val, and a return visit by Charles Russell to Rome to represent the Canadian government's case, Archbishop Diomedus Falconio was appointed to the position in June 1899.

At last, Laurier had his peace with the bishops — and a way of dealing with whatever episcopal disputes lay in the future.

~

After the opening of the session on 25 March 1897, Zoë went house-hunting. She found one to their liking at 335 Theodore Street, a pleasant enough avenue in Sandy Hill. A jeweller by the name of John Leslie had built Laurier House, as it came to be called, in the 1870s. The well-known Ottawa architect James Mather designed a three-storey brick house in the fashionable Second Empire style, with round-headed windows, iron cresting, fancy dormer windows, and a mansard roof atop the yellow brick walls. The Liberal Party bought the house for the Lauriers for $9,500. They made some renovations, bought carpets, drapes, and furniture, and expected to move in during the fall.

The session occasioned dozens of receptions and dinners and "at homes." The Aberdeens gave lavish dinner parties, generally for about eighty people, and more intimate ones for twenty or thirty guests. When the Lauriers were invited to Rideau Hall on formal occasions, they dressed in all their finery and were driven there in style. On their arrival, they were taken to a private salon, where the Aberdeens and their house guests and aides joined them for a glass of wine and lively conversation. Meanwhile, the other guests assembled in the racquet court, a large room with a gallery, where an aide sorted them all out. For the occasion, the court was covered with Belgian rugs, good sofas and armchairs, some straight-backed chairs, and tables of various sizes. Once paired off, the guests chit-chatted among themselves, eating hors d'oeuvres and drinking punch, wine, or fruit juice. Eventually, the Lauriers entered and mingled with their fellow guests. Ten minutes later, the Aberdeens were announced. Ishbel was always accompanied by a couple of pages, usually her sons, dressed in Louis XIV costumes. They carried her train and, during dinner, ran around delivering messages and notes. Their Excellencies walked around the room in full regalia, greeting everyone. When dinner was announced, the governor general led Zoë to the ballroom, which had been trans-formed into a dining room, followed by Her Excellency, who had given her arm to Laurier. The table ran on three sides of the large room, though, later, Ishbel switched to round tables. The Aberdeens sat opposite each other in the middle, with the Lauriers on their immediate right. The food was always quite good, the wine excellent but not plentiful — the colonials had a tendency not to be abstemious — and the service discreet and effective. Many guests over the years complained about the piper, who, clad in the official tartan of the Aberdeens, walked around the room at least three times during dessert "making that infernal noise."

Until they moved into their own house, the Lauriers didn't entertain as often as they would come to do. However, they did what they had to and more, inviting old friends, political allies of all shades and periods, and members of the Cabinet, the caucus, and the diplomatic corps — with wives, of course. Zoë brought to these luncheons, teas, and dinners no pretences of any kind; the food was excellent, the small staff was cooperative, and the conversation was quite enticing, especially when Laurier was present. Many of their friends stayed with them as guests. They were a hospitable couple; on the whole they gave probably two receptions a week and attended two more.

Émilie Lavergne had been coming to Ottawa every now and then during the sessions since 1893. She always stayed at the Russell Hotel with her husband, in a room on a different floor from the Lauriers'. She quickly became quite popular with the socialite set. The Lauriers were her patrons and introduced her in circles where she, as the wife of an unknown backbencher, would not have had a chance on her own, especially Rideau Hall. Nor did Laurier hide his friendship for her. She was always proper with him and deferential to Zoë, though her body language and affectations had a way of hinting that there was something mysterious — an intimacy bordering on the sinful, perhaps — between Laurier and her. The poor and simple folk of Ottawa bought it, especially the gossip columnist immortalized as Amaryllis — as have most of those who have written about Laurier and Émilie ever since.

In the summer of 1897 Joseph Lavergne resigned his seat in the House of Commons to assume the duties of a judge of the Superior Court in the district of Ottawa. It had all been arranged towards the end of the session. Lavergne was never at home in the House of Commons — he was simply not very good at being a member of Parliament. A judgeship was permanent and it paid better.

The Lavergnes lived in Ottawa from 1897 until the summer of 1901, when Laurier appointed him a judge in Montréal. By then, the relationship between Laurier and Émilie had been over for quite some time. Their paths seldom crossed each other and, even though they lived just a few doors apart, Émilie and Zoë didn't fraternize as in the old days of Arthabaska. After the move to Montréal, there were hardly any contacts between the four of them. In their hearts, though, they regretted the "good old times."

~

It was a tired Laurier who disembarked in England with Zoë on 12 June to attend Queen Victoria's Diamond Jubilee. The seven-day voyage had been pleasant enough, with the sea mostly calm. Unfortunately, Laurier wasn't a good sailor and he spent much of the time feeling miserable and wrapped up in shawls.

Immediately on their arrival, there was work to do and no time for a satisfactory rest. They were taken to London, to the largest suite the Cecil Hotel could provide, and all at the cost of the British government. Carriages were placed at his disposal, Zoë's, and his aides'. The courting for Laurier's heart and soul began immediately on his arrival.

~

It is Tuesday, 22 June 1897, in the sixtieth year of the reign of Her Majesty Queen Victoria, queen of Great Britain, Ireland, and her dominions beyond the seas and empress of India. It is also the day of her Diamond Jubilee celebrations.

With the help of the valet, Laurier puts on the official dress of a member of Her Majesty's Most Honourable Privy Council, which gives him the title of Right Honourable: white socks, pointed shoes, white breeches, golden lace, dark formal jacket, and cocked hat. With great ceremony, the valet brings him the plush leather box with its velvet cushion. From it, he removes the seven-pointed star of a Knight Grand Cross in the Most Distinguished Order of St. Michael and St. George and affixes it to Laurier's chest. The prime minister of Canada, the Right Honourable Sir Wilfrid Laurier, is ready.

As he waits for Zoë, his Canadian military attaché, Captain Bates, and the British representative of the Colonial Office go over the program and all the other details of the long day ahead. When Lady Laurier is ready — that is, when her maid is satisfied — she comes in. They stand and admire her in her pearl-grey silk gown and with diamonds in her hair. He finds her regal and her eyes the same as they were when he first met her. He senses her nervousness and pats her hand as he kisses her cheek. The carriage awaits them at the entrance of the hotel. It is time to go. She takes her full-length cloak, and the officious civil servant informs her she will not be able to wear it in the procession at St. Paul's Cathedral. She knows and smiles. She puts on the cloak and they leave with Captain Bates in attendance. It is 7 a.m.

They reach the portico of the hotel, where there is a grand open carriage with four fine horses and coachmen and postilions in livery. They take their place in it. She finds it damp and sits close to him. Slowly and majestically they make their way to the Victoria Embankment, through the streets of a

London scrubbed clean and gleaming with flags and flowers from all over the empire. Fifty thousand soldiers, sailors, marines, and cadets, not to mention detachment upon detachment of police, guard the six-mile route of the procession to the cathedral. Thousands of people are already on the streets; there will be millions by the time the queen passes by. Officials and ticket-holders are slowly taking their assigned places on scaffolds of benches. The rooftops, balconies, and windows of private houses, government buildings, office towers, and hotels are also filling up. Trotting at a good speed, they proceed. Some people in the crowd — Laurier has been in the papers almost daily for the past twelve days — recognize him and cheer happily. He waves enthusiastically; Zoë is more guarded.

It is now 8 a.m. and they have reached the Victoria Embankment. Shortly thereafter, the Governor General's Guards of Canada move in front of his carriage, while the Toronto Grenadiers and the Royal Canadian Highlanders line up behind. He is in the lead of the colonial officials.

There are people everywhere. Each foothold on the facade of the cathedral is occupied, and the roof is filled with diminutive persons looking down. On the stands, seat-holders are there by invitation: ambassadors and dignitaries with their families from the colonies occupy the right-hand side, and the colours of their national dress shimmer like a thousand rainbows. On the left are the European ambasadors, *chargés d'affaires*, legates, and other foreign representatives, also with their wives. The crowd of dignitaries does not recognize the Governor General's Guards, but when they see Laurier and Zoë they instantly identify him and the applause is deafening. He smiles and waves; Zoë sits beside him, enjoying his triumph. His carriage drives around the cathedral and comes to a standstill on the north side. Ushers and clerics escort them to their reserved places, where they await the queen and chat with those around them. Zoë has left her cloak in the carriage, but she doesn't need it. It is much warmer now that the sun has won over the clouds.

At noon, there is a sudden movement as the queen's finest carriage appears, drawn by eight cream-coloured horses adorned with trappings of gold and brilliant ribbons. The people are taken unawares, but when they see the queen in her simple black and grey costume, her black and white bonnet, and her white parasol protecting her from the sun, the sound of their happiness rattles the windows of the cathedral. She is sitting alone on the rear banquette, with two princesses in front. To the thundering cheering of thousands of voices, she disembarks and, preceded by the Princess of Wales and the Princess Christian of Schleswig-Holstein, she ascends the steps of the cathedral towards the prime minister of Great Britain, the colonial secretary, and, at the top, the archbishop of Canterbury. The open-air ceremony begins with the *Te Deum,* followed by prayers and the benediction. The choir sings the closing hymn, but the people do not appear to have had enough. Spontaneously, the vast crowd breaks into "God Save the Queen." Laurier finds the response most moving. He joins the throng when the archbishop, overtaken by the moment, breaks with protocol and leads his flock in three lusty cheers for the queen. After that, Laurier and the other dignitaries regain their carriages, as the queen receives the archbishop of Canterbury and the bishop of London in hers. The service has lasted just twenty minutes.

The procession starts again. First come the troops, then the sixteen carriages of the princes, princesses, and envoys; more troops, the queen, her sons and various aides on horseback, more troops, the Governor General's Guards, and Laurier's carriage, followed by the rest of the colonial representatives. All along the route, past Carlton House Terrace, the gardens of St. James's Palace, Marlborough House, Clarence House, and so many other famous places, the cheering never stops, much of it directed at Laurier, so close behind the queen. By 2 p.m., Victoria is back in her castle.

As Laurier and Zoë return to their hotel, he realizes that in cheering him, the crowd roared for Canada. As prime minister of the senior dominion, he has used the day to place his country on the roster of nations. He feels the wind of "independence" flowing into him, mingled with an overwhelming pride that he, a *Canadien* from Saint-Lin, Québec, is a leading member of this astonishing empire. If these are contradictory emotions, he is not totally aware of it.

∼

Laurier was the key player in the imperial tournament in London. If they could get him to agree to their plans, Joseph Chamberlain and the imperialists would have an easy time with the other colonial representatives. To them he was the centre-piece, but on his own he became the centre of attraction. Some said that after the queen, he was the most popular person at the Jubilee. He was a *Canadien,* the son of a conquered race; he was the prime minister of the senior dominion; he was gracious; he knew which fork to use; his lady was well dressed and spoke English; he put words together in a way the imperials were not used to; he drank wine and was even more eloquent; and he was all puffed up with pride — and anxiety about the audiences at home. "For the first time on record," some said, "a politician of our New World has been recognized as the equal of the great men of the Old Country." Condescending — but the British were like that.

The queen received him in audience both in Buckingham Palace and at Windsor Castle. He, Zoë, and the other premiers and their wives had lunch there on 6 July in the Waterloo Room. He returned the next day to be sworn in as a member of Her Majesty's Most Honourable Privy Council. They attended the queen's garden party and the state ball, both at Buckingham Palace. And Victoria created him a Knight Grand Cross in the Most Distinguished Order of St. Michael and St. George. He had not wanted it. Early in the New Year he had turned down a knighthood and he thought the matter had been dealt with. But he had not counted on the kindnesses of his friends. Lord Aberdeen and Donald Smith the Canadian high commissioner, had lobbied for him and, shortly after he arrived in England, he discovered that he was on the Jubilee honours list. He sent his refusal to the Colonial Office, but Chamberlain was scandalized: the queen had already agreed, a public announcement had been made, he just couldn't refuse. What would she say? It was discourteous, verging on the treasonous. It would mar her enjoyment of her Jubilee. Zoë, who in jest had said she might like being Lady Laurier, sympathized with him and encouraged him in his stand. For almost a week he held out, but finally he capitulated. Sir Wilfrid he became. Lady Laurier she would be.

He was dined and wined in London, in Wales, in Edinburgh and Glasgow, in country houses, in banquet halls, and in hotels. There were balls and dinners, luncheons and receptions, garden parties and teas, march pasts and troopings of the colours, a naval review at Spithead, honorary degrees from Oxford and Cambridge, and the Cobden Club's gold medal for "distinguished services to the cause of international free trade." In dozens of conversations, in his palatial suite, in corridors and in drawing rooms, he spoke a million words. On 10 July he fulfilled a lifelong ambition: he went to see Gladstone at Hawarden Castle in Wales. He arrived for tea at about 4 o'clock, they had their picture taken, and he enjoyed a long discussion.

The whole process of adulation, the pleasure at being the centre of attraction, and the object of loud and continuous cheers caused him some trouble. It all began with the speech at the Mansion House. To remarks of the mayor that all seated at dinner were Englishmen, Laurier stressed that he was of "French descent" and was proud of it. He then added that he was "British to the core!" On 2 July the Colonial Institute gave a banquet in honour of the visiting premiers at which the Duke of Connaught presided. After interminable toasts, it was his turn to reply to the one His Royal Highness had just proposed to the "United Empire." It was not the champagne that made him remark that the basis on which the British Empire rested was not force or violence, but freedom and justice, and "it was to the eternal credit of the English nation that wherever they have extended their Empire, they have always respected the religion of their new subjects and, when the concession of political freedom was made, it was made freely and generously." He really believed that. The next day at the luncheon of the Liberal Club, he was even more blunt in his appreciation: "It would be the proudest moment of my life if I could see a Canadian of French descent affirming the principles of freedom in the Parliament of Great Britain." Of course, he "could not hope to live long enough to see it," but some of those who were in Canada that day might live to see it. In a committee room of the House of Commons, where most of the members had gathered to hear him, he spoke for forty-five minutes — and again he repeated what he would come to regret. The time had arrived when self-governing colonies like Canada should be represented either in the British Parliament or "in some grand national council or federal legislative body genuinely representative of the Empire as an organized entity."

Had he gone mad? Or was it Sir Donald Smith's champagne? In all probability he was addressing the electors of Ontario more than the members assembled before him in London. He went on to admit that the national sentiment for Canadian representation in the councils of the empire was growing stronger every day and could not be overlooked. It would have to be faced. He followed with an even more atypical remark: "Let the watch-fires be lit on the hills, and

Canada will be the first to respond." Did that mean his consent to participate in the wars of the empire? Or was it just the euphoria of the moment?

These remarks about Canada's place in the empire were always accompanied by eloquent phrases and sentences about his pride in Canada's achievement and the future of his country. To the Fishmongers' Company, he objected to the use of the word *colony* ("I dislike that word!") when speaking of Canada. Canada had a population of five million, he pointed out, but had a territory "sufficient to give food and shelter to 100 million." He invited British men to immigrate. He already had one thousand jobs to hand out, since he was planning to build a railway in the Yukon. Women were welcome too. He spent much time explaining to his hosts that "Canada is a nation. Colonies are born to become nations. Canada is free and freedom is its nationality. Canada is practically independent. The first place in our hearts is filled by Canada." When he pleased them by saying, "in a few years the earth will be encircled by a series of independent nations, recognizing, however, the suzerainty of England," or that there should be an Empire Parliament, he hoped they understood that such constitutional arrangements were only for the day after tomorrow. For the moment, he and the rest of his countrymen were satisfied with arrangements as they were.

It was understandable that he was misunderstood on both sides of the Atlantic — and across the Channel, too. At the beginning of July, he explained to Pacaud that all he had meant to say by his famous remark, "I am British to the core" was that he was attached to British institutions. Unfortunately, there was no easy translation in French for what he had actually said. Later, when he addressed the British Chamber of Commerce in Paris, he was clearer in his views of imperial constitutional organization. The "great principle of imperial representation," as French colonies were represented in her parliament, might be the solution, but he doubted it: "Our situation is very different." Canada was quasi-independent. Consequently, "if, as the price of imperial representation, we had to renounce our autonomy, our legislative independence, we would have none of it. If imperial representation is to be the solution, it can only be as the complement and not as the negation of that which exists today." Whether that was enough explanation and clarification remained to be seen.

Much of what he said during the Jubilee celebrations was rhetoric, some of which washed well at home, some of which floundered. It was, however, in the five sessions of the Colonial Conference that the real Laurier — or at least one more in keeping with his past — appeared. Beginning on Saint-Jean-Baptiste Day, 24 June, Chamberlain and the colonial representatives met at intervals until 29 July. There were eleven prime ministers or premiers, all members of the Imperial Privy Council. Was this government speaking to government? Was this the prototype of a potential Imperial Cabinet? Hardly. When Chamberlain brought forward the possibility of such an Imperial or Federal Council to coordinate affairs that the members had in common, Laurier and most of his colleagues said no — even though he thought he might consider it at a later date.

On the matter of cooperation in defence, either by "contributions to sea power" or a possible exchange of regular troops between the colonies and Great Britain, Laurier didn't even bother to reply. As for freer trade within the empire, Canada had already made its point with its "preferential tariff" and saw no reason for an imperial *Zollverein*. In his view, and without asking for it, what England had to do was to renounce its commercial treaties with Belgium and Germany, which it did on 30 July. The only tangible result of the conference was a resolution that they should meet again at regular intervals, preferably every three years. With that accomplished, Laurier and Zoë left for the continent.

In France, where they went in the middle of July, there were also a few traps to avoid. France and Great Britian were not on the best of terms, and the French intelligentsia hadn't appreciated Laurier's declaration that he was British to the core. There he stood among them, a Frenchman of 1789 — or so it was said: "His lofty stature, his well-built and solid frame, his clean-shaven face, his rather long hair turning grey, his clear and penetrating eyes, firmly cut lips, powerful shoulders and straight neck, and his well-dressed air and easy bearing evoke the memory of the members of the Assembly of 1789. It is as if one of them who had lived a life of thought had suddenly emerged from his retreat to plead in sonorous and vigorous terms the cause of the rights of man and liberty." A curious sight, it was.

After he had made peace with his critics, his sojourn there with Zoë was most pleasant. Sightseeing in Paris was almost a daily occupation, as was making speeches. And he made good ones:

Separated from France, we have never forgotten the honour of our origin; separated from France, we have always treasured its culture;

separated from France, if we have lost our share of its glories, we have made a conquest always dear to French hearts: we have to-day in Canada Liberty, Equality, and Fraternity: that is our conquest.

Or:

> If there is anything that the story of France has taught me to regard as an attribute of the French race, it is loyalty, it is the heart's memories. I recall, gentlemen, those fine lines which Victor Hugo applied to himself, as explaining the inspiration of his life:
>
> > Fidèle au double sang qu'ont versé dans ma veine,
> > Mon père vieux soldat, ma mère vendéenne.
>
> That double fidelity to ideas and aspirations quite distinct is our glory in Canada. We are faithful to the great nation which gave us life, we are faithful to the great nation which has given us liberty.

Or again:

> A day will come, in a future more or less distant, when by the mere fact of our growth in numbers, the colonial tie, light and tenuous though it may be, will become heavy because it will no longer correspond to our national aspirations.

And he talked about Montcalm and Lévis!

In Paris, he received the ribbon of the *grand officer de la Légion d'honneur* from the president himself. In conversations with him and other illustrious and important men, he gave a simple message: France and England should make efforts to understand each other, to reach out to each other, and to do good for mankind. In that way he, Laurier, would be better able to ensure more securely the racial harmony and unity he craved for his country.

By then exhausted and even tired of words, he and Zoë escaped to the cognac country of Charente and to the country of his ancestors. He saw much of the Canada of his youth: houses that looked like many in Québec; a fortification that ressembled the Porte Saint-Louis, with cannons mounted in the walls as in Québec City; furniture and pictures that reminded him of Saint-Lin; and an accent and *tournure de phrases* — way of saying things — that he and Zoë were familiar with. They shared with these people an identity. They had roots there. No wonder he was moved to say:

> Quand je m'éloignerai de ses rives bénies, quand, monté sur le navire qui m'emportera, je verrai graduellement les côtes s'effacer et disparaître à l'horizon, c'est de toute mon âme, c'est du plus profond de mon coeur, que je dirai et que je répéterai: 'Dieu protège la France!'

Leaving France, they stopped in Switzerland on their way to Rome. Laurier consulted a doctor about the state of his health and was told there was nothing to worry him unduly. In Rome he met Charles Russell and dined with Del Val. Zoë visited churches, museums, and convents. They had an audience with the pope: she all dressed in black as was demanded by the protocol; he in the uniform of an imperial privy councillor, with the insignia of the Order of St. Michael and St. George and the *Légion d'honneur*. For an hour he and His Holiness talked of Canada; the need for religous peace and harmony through conciliation, moderation, and compromise; and the future of a land that could feed and house a hundred million people. It was a most cordial meeting and he came away from it convinced that his points had been well received.

After that, they returned to France to tie some loose ends, to England to say goodbye, and to Ireland because Zoë wished it. Anxious to see their "children," Arthabaska, and the new house, they returned home on the *Labrador*.

~

When the *Labrador*, all decked out with flags and pennants, entered the St. Lawrence towards the end of August 1897, Zoë noticed that many of the inhabitants were lined up on both shores waving and yelling and chanting. After sundown, they saw the first of the immense bonfires, *feux de joie* they called them, lit to herald their arrival. As the ship proceeded upstream, one fire after the next lit the way. When the vessel approached Québec City, the fog was thick, but, as if by enchantment, it dissipated as Laurier arrived on the shores of the ancient capital. Twenty thousand of his compatriots were there to greet him, to cheer him, to hear him: "Today Canada has taken its place among the nations of the world." Often he left the official entourage and walked among the crowd to shake a hand here and there, smile at an old man leaning on his daughter, cuddle a child, gently tap the cheek of an adolescent, and accept bouquets of flowers. With Zoë on his arm, he visited the Basilica and signed the visitors' book at the archbishop's palace. At various receptions, she was given a piano and a dining-room set. Both were so large that she joked she would have to build another addition to her new house.

A couple of days later they embarked on the *Druid.* On their way to Montréal, they stopped in Trois-Rivières. "I went to Rome to place at the foot of His Holiness, the Supreme Pontiff of the religion in which my fathers died and in which I was born, I live, and want to die, my respect and my *soumission.*" He didn't meet or see Bishop Laflèche.

In Montréal, half the population — men, women, children — was on the Champ de Mars to greet them. Half of them couldn't hear a word when he said: "I am not one of those who pretend to a patriotism that relies on the revival of old antagonisms. I am not of those who believe that God has placed us here, men of all races, to continue the battles of our fathers. *Non. Je ne suis pas de ceux-là.*" He lunched with the governor general while Zoë and Madame David — they were staying at the Davids' — went shopping. There were more gifts for their new house — expensive ones! A couple of times, Wilfrid needed to rest, so Zoë went in his place to smile, accept flowers, utter general thank yous, and bring his regret. She did that rather well.

The Montréal visit finished, they boarded the train for Arthabaska. The vice-regal car was attached to theirs. Both he and the governor general had a long conversation, and Aberdeen reported to his wife: "The Lauriers are naturally very pleased & very gratified by all their European experiences but they do not seem the least spoilt & they are genuinely glad to be home." When the train stopped in Arthabaska, there was a large crowd waiting for him, "le plus grand des Canadiens." From his car, the governor general watched the demonstration of genuine affection for and pride in his first minister. He smiled, but didn't leave his car. It was Laurier's day. The Lavergnes, though, were not there.

After a short rest, they were off to Toronto and finally Ottawa. All along the way, people waved as though a royal train was passing by. In Toronto, there was joy and pride. He made the same speeches; she received more gifts. Joseph Pope recorded that Laurier was "the lion of the hour."

After a long rest in Arthabaska, he returned to Ottawa on Friday, 24 September 1897. There, waiting for him, were the Klondike and the gold. Sifton was sent out to investigate and came back in November determined that, unless Canada built a railway to the Pacific, the United States would inherit it all. There were rumblings of corruption, and some of it involved Tarte and the Intercolonial Railway that Laurier had determined would be extended from Lévis to Montréal by purchasing the Drummond County Railway in which Tarte had been involved. The partnership with Tarte would be difficult, Laurier had no doubt. But, for the moment, he had to be defended and supported.

The return to administrative duties tired Laurier out. When he went to Halifax for the Provincial Exhibition at the beginning of October, he was quite weak. It was his first visit to Nova Scotia as prime minister of Canada. There were, of course, a dinner and an address. Then, according to Ishbel and her faithful diary, "he was lunched at the Exhibition & spoke afterwards out of doors to a huge concourse of people. We thought of going too, & sitting in the Grand Stand, but it was decided that it was better not. The poor man was v. seedy, having had a very rackety journey by train to get here in time & having been v. sea sick. He nearly fainted during his reception, but had quite plucked up in the evening."

On his return to Ottawa, he decided that the time had come for the Americans. Over the years, there had been trouble, large troubles, that extended to the rights — or was it privileges? — of American and Canadian fishermen in each other's waters, to problems about Canadian sealers in the Bering Sea, and to transportation, trade, workmen under contract, gold, the boundary with Alaska, and much else — the list seemed endless. In the past the Americans had discussed Canadian questions with the British first, but Laurier didn't want any more of that. While he was in England in 1897, he had convinced Chamberlain that Canada must have a free hand with Washington. Technically they had agreed. All he needed now was to put that arrangement into practice.

In November he went to Washington. The president was cordial and agreed with Laurier to submit all outstanding questions to a Joint Commission that would meet as early as possible. Laurier had doubts that it would accomplish anything substantial: "We have had a warm welcome and some cool proposals. I confess, though, that I have very serious doubts as to any practical results to be expected from the Commission." But since his pessimism was his way of accustoming himself to the worst — a lesson taught him by his frequent illnesses and brushes with death — he waited peacefully to be proven wrong.

In the meantime, he and Zoë moved into their new house. And the year ended.

12

CANADA REBORN
1898–1905

To achieve his dream of building a country, John A. Macdonald had his National Policy. It consisted of an industrial-manufacturing heartland protected by high tariffs; a large farming community in the plains of the West; and a transcontinental railway that linked these two regions together, taking the tools manufactured in the East to the farmer in the West and conveying the grain of western Canada to ports and markets.

To achieve his vision of Canada, Wilfrid Laurier also had a national policy, one that could well be called the "Stamp of Canadian Nationality." In addition to the maintenance of national unity, which was his primary concern, it consisted of five main headings: Tariff and Trade; Settlement of the West; Transportation and Communication; Autonomy of Canada vis-à-vis the empire; and Canada and the United States. The matters that fell under each heading tended to overlap and to become confused with other pursuits and political circumstances. However, the agenda was clear and it was launched as soon as he was in office. On tariff, the moderate protectionist John Charlton put it best: "We may as well tell a Yankee to go to Hades and we will go to England." Sifton would be given carte blanche to people the West. Transcontinental railways would be built to get the gold out of the Yukon, the minerals out of northern Ontario, and the wheat out of the prairies, and Tarte and Dobell would improve the St. Lawrence to make it navigable all year round. Laurier gave himself the responsibility to cut as much of the umbilical cord to the empire as possible, and he would also supervise relations with the Americans.

If Laurier was to have any chance of implementing his stamp of Canadian nationality, he knew what he needed to do. He had to be master of his administration, win as many terms as possible, prevent civil war over racial and religious disputes, promote national harmony, and keep Québec under his control, since it was the main source of his power.

He began with the economy, which meant the tariff. Laurier inherited a Canada that was economically depressed with low prices and wages, few and small markets for home products, little immigration, an exodus to the United States which was devastating to the growth of the country, and a belligerent United States that was erecting destructive tariff walls wherever possible. Fortunately, economic indicators prophesied better times. In rapid succession, the international economy improved with price and wage increases; mining developed in southern British Columbia and in Alberta, helped by the CPR; gold was discovered in the Klondike district of the Yukon Territory, and the gold rush was on; the momentum to settle the West was launched in the United States; and Laurier's confidence in the limitless success of Canada, "the country of the twentieth century," provided the psychological boost to greater improvement.

What was Laurier to do with the tariff? The Liberal policy as established at the Great Liberal Convention of 1893 and built upon since was the promotion of free trade everywhere on the planet, but more particularly with Great Britain and the United States, and "a tariff for revenue only." When Laurier came to power, the total revenues of the state were in the order of $39 million and expenses, $45 million. The only sources of taxation were excise duties on things such as tobacco and spirits, and receipts from the tariff.

In order to set the proper rate, Laurier had to answer a few questions. He sent Charlton to the United States to ascertain if the Americans were prepared to "trade with us." If they didn't want to, Canada would have to do without. In the spirit of the time, Laurier was certain that "we can do without it very successfully." Charlton reported back that the Americans weren't interested. Meanwhile, Laurier named a tariff commission headed by Fielding, with Paterson representing the protectionist interests in the party and Cartwright the free trade ones. They travelled across the country and heard from farmers and industrialists, manufacturers and bankers, and from representatives of every possible interest group — all in open sessions. Their findings formed the basis of the first Fielding budget.

On 23 April 1897 Fielding was ready. He delivered what critics described as a "masterly achievement." It was also a wily one. Protection if necessary, but not necessarily protection; free trade if necessary, but not necessarily free trade. Fielding was certain, though, that he was on the right track. He added to the free list, reduced rates, and changed specific duties, with the overall effect, the financial Conservative critic said, "there is to-day, as between the two sides, practically no difference upon the expediency of the principle of protection as the guiding principle of our fiscal system." Perhaps; but the budget did begin to launch Canada on the road to free trade.

Since the Americans would not "trade with us," Canada would trade with the British and the rest of the world. That is how the country got a two-tier tariff: high protectionist rates against those countries that applied the same to Canadian goods; and preferential rates ($12\frac{1}{2}$ percent preference in 1897 and 25 percent in 1898) to those that were friendlier in trade. Fielding made certain that everyone knew, particularly in Ontario, that what he was granting was an "imperial preference" and that Great Britain would be the main beneficiary. Great Britain and the Colonial Office were not consulted.

What Fielding proposed in April 1897 was accepted by Parliament and by the country, and formed the basis of all his budgets until 1911, when reciprocity with the United States reared its head again. That was a long way away, though. For the moment of 1897, the question was: Would the tariff stand in England?

∼

It had a good chance. For it was the age of imperialism. It was also the moment of jingoism, that dreadful bellicose patriotism that was the trademark of scoundrels, if not racists.

Both came about because the major countries of Europe had not enough to do at home, or they didn't want to do what should be done. Their people were prosperous, with a high level of productivity. But they were bored. The social fabric of the mother country demanded that the people have new challenges, new markets for their products, new locations for their surplus population. The imperial powers invaded the lands of others who were weaker than they. To justify their actions, they gave themselves airs, pretending it was all in the cause of the white man's burden, or "la mission civilisatrice de la France," or the Prussian know-how, and, above all, in the superiority of the white man over the other miserable creatures of the planet. It was the divine mission of the European and the Anglo-Saxon to rule over the barbarians, to civilize them, to convert them, and to exploit them in the name of God and of the empire.

As for jingoism, the bastard child of imperialism, it was born in the pool halls, the factories, and the music halls; it found its way in slum parishes and Gothic cathedrals, and it soon gained entrance into the legislatures and the chambers of deputies, in the posts of the military high command, in the inner sanctum of governments, and in Buckingham Palace. And it sold newspapers.

Great Britain was the leader of the imperialist movement. In the person of the colonial secretary, Joseph Chamberlain, the empire had its vindicator. Chamberlain was a queer fish at best; at worst, he was hard to decipher. He was a businessman who became a social reformer, a Liberal politician and supporter of Gladstone, the colonial secretary in Conservative governments, an imperialist, and a pain in Laurier's side. He wanted to revamp the empire, unite its diverse parts, and see that the sun never stopped shining on the British Empire. Had it not been for Laurier, he may very well have pulled it off.

English Canadians saw their involvement in the empire as a positive adjunct to their Canadian patriotism and nationalism. To deny the empire was to deny Canada. After all, as George Monro Grant, the principal of Queen's University who was also an ardent imperialist and a Canadian nationalist, explained: "We are Canadian, and in order to be Canadian we must be British."

This schizophrenic nationalism meant that for Canada to grow up with confidence and with the proper attitude, the umbilical cord could not be cut as yet, or even in the near future. But that was not destructive of the ideals of Canadian nationhood and independence. The time had not yet arrived for either of them. Until it did, the best way to move forward was to help establish an imperial partnership of the various elements of the British Empire. In that partnership, Canada would play a distinct role. It could take its place among the nations of the world, though it would remain substantially "English." All things considered, being a vocal and participatory constituent of the empire was a damn sight better than being a colonial.

Canadiens, the second part of the equation of Canada, didn't fit at all in this scenario. They had only one country — Canada; they had only one nationality — *Canadienne.* They accepted Canada's "Britishness" without too much difficulty since they understood it to mean an allegiance to a monarch, a set of liberties and rights, membership in an exclusive club, and a kind of unwritten-but-accepted Canadian independence. They certainly didn't see it as the superiority of the Anglo-Saxon race to which they had to be assimilated, an imperialism that would deprive Canada of its capacity to make independent judgments and decisions as to its future welfare, and a statement that Canada was bound to participate in the wars that Great Britain might wage all over the globe. They had also been too often the victims of that superior race the Anglo-Saxons thought they were, not only in their past, but also close to the present. Consequently, they viewed imperial partnership as gross and incomprehensible nonsense.

What of Sir Wilfrid?

When Laurier left Canada for his first voyage to Europe on that bright June day in 1897, he had limited understanding of what imperialism might imply. There had been talk of the empire, of an Imperial Federation, of being ready when the mother country called, and a great deal of rhetoric to which he himself had contributed. He favoured Canadian nationhood, based on a cultural and linguistic duality and independence. To achieve these goals was the single objective of his political life. On the other hand, he too at times was schizophrenic. He was an English Liberal; he admired British institutions; he was an anglophile; and he sincerely believed that the collective and individual liberties and rights that his people enjoyed had come from the British. As he said at an official dinner in London, he and his fellow-countrymen had learned to appreciate British rule because "there was not a man in Canada today of French origin who did not realize that he found under the flag of England far more freedom than he would have enjoyed under the flag of France." To have been a part of the British way of life, which after his coming to power expressed itself more and more as an imperial way of life, had been good for Canada. He had doubts, however, as to how long the connection could be, or had to be, maintained. The time would come for the break. His policy was not to bring it about, but to pave the way without sacrificing his ideals of Canadian nationhood and independence.

In being true to his ideals, Laurier encountered two contradictory currents — Ontario and Québec — the one favouring an almost unlimited partnership, the other the independence of Canada. He shared Québec's view, and wrestled with it constantly. The colonial bond, if maintained for a long time, would be "a cause of atrophy," an obstacle to the "development of the country"; it would stifle initiative and subordinate "all our aspirations to the consideration of the interests of the metropolis." But the time had not yet come for change. If there were only *Canadiens* in the confederation, he would not hesitate to bring independence about. However, "the idea is not yet ripe enough for the English population." He had to wait or he would "put the two races in conflict" with each other. The test of his leadership would be how well he could manoeuvre between the two "races," without sacrificing national harmony.

~

In his tenure as prime minister of Canada, Laurier attended four Imperial Conferences — 1897, 1902, 1907, and 1911. As the years advanced, newcomers challenged the imperial supremacy of Great Britain and imperialists increased the pressure on Laurier to lead the colonies to a greater centralization of the empire. The three issues he faced at succeeding conferences were the same as in 1897: political and constitutional reorganization of the empire through either representation in the British House of Commons or, even better to Chamberlain's mind, "a real Council of the Empire to which all questions of imperial interest might be referred"; increased trade between the colonies and exclusive tariff privileges to bring about economic centralization; and the sharing of the cost of imperial defence through colonial contributions of money and men and the exchange of military personnel. On the last two issues, Laurier's views were consistent throughout the years: "no" to economic centralization and, above all, "no" to military integration.

The United States was Canada's natural trading partner, not Great Britain and not the countries of the empire. Consequently, Laurier's policy throughout his tenure was to oppose free trade within the empire as "impractical." Canada would continue to grant a preference on British goods if Great Britain did the same, and, as for the colonies, reciprocal arrangements could be negotiated with those countries that were interested. Laurier was most focused on the neighbour to the south, however, and he struggled to free Canada from treaties and other arrangements that impinged on better trade relations with the United States. By 1911 he had won his point.

In regard to military matters, Canada was not to become involved in the European penchant for war. "There is a school abroad," he once said in the House of Commons, "there is a school in England and in Canada, a school which is perhaps represented on the floor of this Parliament, a school which wants to bring Canada into the vortex of militarism which is the curse and the blight of Europe. I am not prepared to endorse any such policy." On the other hand, Canada was part of the empire; Canadians were British subjects; the majority in Canada agreed with him that "the supremacy of the British Empire is absolutely essential, not only to the maintenance of the Empire but to the civilization of the world." It was therefore Canada's duty to help defend it. The best way to do so was not by paying tributes of money and men, but by becoming totally responsible for the defence of Canada. That was the true Canadian policy, and he tried to implement it both in decision-making and in action. It cost him dearly.

How was Canada to belong to the empire? That question was always present. Was the empire to be one centralized entity? Or was it to become a federation of quasi-independent countries that were really colonies? Or was it to develop as a union of independent nations cooperating with one another on matters that were of mutual interest? Laurier admitted that "we are making for a harbour which was not the harbour I foresaw twenty-five years ago, but it is a good harbour." The first harbour for him had been a sort of imperial Parliament. No sooner had he uttered the notion than he abandoned it. It went counter to his long-cherished view that Canada was bound to be independent one day; therefore, nothing should be done that might limit that independence. Moreover, there was always the goal of national harmony and unity. Imperial shenanigans might endanger the fabric of Canada.

The harbour Laurier chose placed Canada as a nation that voluntarily accepted to be part of the British Empire. There would be no more reference to Canada as a colony: it was a self-governing dominion. There would be no more Colonial Conferences — only Imperial Conferences to deal with matters of interest "between His Majesty's Government [Edward VII was by then on the throne] and His Governments of self-governing Dominions beyond the Seas."

To achieve what he did was no easy matter. Chamberlain in 1902 considered Laurier's obstruction to his pet ideas as coming from a man who was not a total Englishman, but one with too much French blood. Instead of sailing back home in a huff, Laurier arranged a dinner between Chamberlain and the other four members of the Canadian delegation: Fielding, Borden, Mulock, and Paterson. The colonial secretary received the same response from these pure Anglo-Saxons: "We are loyal subjects of His Majesty; we wish to remain a member of the British Empire; but we are Canadians."

The greatest difficulty, though, was to resist the pressure from the British social set. At all the conferences Laurier attended, he was dined and wined by "royalty and aristocracy and plutocracy and always the talk was of Empire, Empire, Empire." It was hard not to succumb to the flatteries of a beautiful, magnificently gowned and jewelled duchess. Even strong men had been known to lose their heads. Laurier didn't, though, lose his completely. Instead, he, Canada, Great Britain and the Empire — they all altered their positions slightly and compromised. Canada came of age, within the family.

~

Laurier soon found that governing wasn't an easy matter. Ministers were jealous of each other; the *Rouges* continued to view Tarte as an upstart who had no place in their party; the Senate, where the Conservatives had a majority, impeded the passage of his legislation; and the Tuppers, father and son, continued their vendetta against the Aberdeens, who they felt had robbed them of power. For all these reasons, the session, from 3 February to 13 June 1898, was tiresome and tedious for him. At the beginning of May, the Aberdeens announced their return to the United Kingdom before the expiration of their term "for private and family claims and interests." It was a blow, both to him and to Zoë. He spoke of their "warm heart and unresting energy," and he promised that they would not be forgotten in Canada. And it seemed that everyone of his generation was dying off. He would soon be alone.

The first death was that of Cardinal Taschereau on 12 April 1898. He had been ill for some time, and his moderating influence was not present during the politico-religious quarrel of the middle 1890s. His coadjutor, Louis-Nazaire Bégin, succeeded him and was named cardinal in 1914. Bégin was a mediocre man, full of intrigues and pretensions. He was not one of Laurier's favourite churchmen.

A month later, on 11 May, D'Alton McCarthy fell off his horse and died. Laurier had planned eventually to name him minister of justice. McCarthy had come a long way from the mischief of the early 1890s. His death was premature. Lady Aberdeen confided in her diary: "Mr. McCarthy's death was much felt. He was universally respected & was a most charming and able man. He contemplated joining the Liberals for good & all & had talked it over with Laurier very recently."

Lady Aberdeen's last appearance on the floor of the House of Commons, in her "accustomed seat" to the right of the Speaker, was to hear Sir Wilfrid's eulogy of Gladstone on 26 May to mark his death:

It is no exaggeration to say that he has raised the standard of civilization.

I would say that the one trait which was dominant in his nature, which marked the man more distinctly than any other, was his intense humanity, his paramount sense of right, his abhorrence of injustice, wrong, and oppression wherever to be found or in whatever shape they might show themselves.

Injustice, wrong, oppression acted upon him as it were mechanically, aroused every fibre of his being, and from that moment to the repairing of the injury, the undoing of the wrong, the destruction of the oppression, he gave his mind, his heart, his soul, his whole life with an energy, with an intensity, with a vigour paralleled in no man unless it be the first Napoleon.

She found it a "v. fine" speech.

On 13 June Chapleau died in his apartment at the Windsor Hotel in Montréal. "The death of Sir Adolphe is a national loss!" he telegraphed Lady Chapleau. He was a pallbearer at the funeral. He and Chapleau went far back in the history of Québec. Of the triumvirate that had dominated Québec's political life — Honoré Mercier, Joseph-Adolphe Chapleau, and Wilfrid Laurier — he was the only survivor. It was a moment for some reflection.

Almost to the day, a month later, it was the turn of Bishop Laflèche to be summoned to his Maker. When Henri's wife asked Laurier where he was going all dressed up in his ceremonial costume and his silk hat, he replied: "I am going to the funeral of Bishop Laflèche. He was a fanatic, but a holy priest."

Then, closer to home, his half-brother Ubald died at the end of August. He was a doctor who had lived in the United States. His health had always been precarious and he suffered from one of the many lung diseases that afflicted practically all of the Lauriers. Laurier and other members of the family had been supporting him for many years. They had sent him to California, where Zoë went to visit him in the fall of 1896; later, he lived in British Columbia. Three weeks before he died, Henri went to fetch him and his family and brought them back to Arthabaska. He died in Laurier's house and was buried in Saint-Lin.

A few days before, the Aberdeens and their children had come to visit for the afternoon. They spent a "most enjoyable and quiet" five hours with the Lauriers. The lunch was simple; they photographed and were photographed; and they walked up to the church and then to the boys' school, with Laurier admitting that "he had not walked so far for months." And they talked about Canada, the school settlement, and the forthcoming meetings of the Joint High Commission. Laurier asked the Aberdeens to be in Québec City in September to lend a hand. Before they left, he promised them, yet once again, that "famous suckling-pig expedition to a French farmhouse." Ishbel found Arthabaska "much prettier than we had imagined," with its hilly wooded country and its location "along some heights overlooking the Nicolet River winding through the valley below." At 6 p.m. they reboarded their train on their way to Stanley House.

After the Aberdeens left, there were only a few days for Laurier to get ready for the meetings of the Joint High Commission that had been established between Canada and the United States to resolve unsettled issues. It had been scheduled earlier, but the Spanish-American War of April-August 1898 had intervened and the first session of the commission was not convened in Québec City until 23 August. It was to last until 10 October; the second session would be held from 9 November 1898 until 20 February 1899 in Washington. When Chapleau's death precluded his appointment as chairman of the commission, Laurier took it on, despite misgivings about his absence from Ottawa and the conduct of public affairs for such a long period of time. The other members of the Canadian delegation were Richard Cartwright, Louis Davies, and John

Charlton, with Joseph Pope and Henri Bourassa as secretaries. In addition, the lone British representative was the Lord Chancellor, while Sir James Winter, premier of Newfoundland, represented that colony. Six Americans were appointed to the commission.

At first the meetings went well: "There is no doubt that there is a new and general good-will observable here." The Aberdeens helped to make that happen. They arrived in Québec on 13 September. For the next three weeks, they didn't stop entertaining, and the commissioners participated in all the activities: farewell parties for the Aberdeens, a dinner Zoë gave for Lady Aberdeen and the wives or daughters of the members of the commission at the Parent Park Hotel, lunches and dinners for the American and Canadian delegates. "It was difficult to see how those poor Commissioners were to get any time for their work with all the social entertainments they were expected to get through."

They did a good deal of work, but no firm decisions could be taken until after the American election on 8 November. The Republicans won and, a day later, Laurier and the Canadian delegation were in Washington. Things didn't go so well there. On 8 February Laurier wrote to Zoë that "nous n'avançons pas." They were making no progress. One day they agreed on something; the next day complications set in; and the day after that they had to start all over again. It was most discouraging. But he would persevere, monotonous as it might be.

By the time the second session ended on 20 February 1899, Laurier had not been very successful. There were twelve contentious issues between Canada and the United States which the Joint High Commission had to deal with. Laurier considered four of them to be of the greatest importance. On the Bering Sea seal fisheries controversy, progress was achieved and the matter was substantially solved; but the solution had to be part of a general treaty and, when that was not forthcoming, the sealing arrangements were not finalized. With regard to the Atlantic fisheries and to lumber, "we made no progress whatever." The final stumbling block was the Alaska-Canadian boundary. No compromise could be reached that was satisfactory to both sides, and the commission never met again. The boundary problem would fester until it was arbitrated in the fall of 1903.

The Joint High Commission sat sporadically during its term. There were many breaks and rest periods, and there was government business to attend to. One such business was the prohibition plebiscite held on 29 September 1898.

Liquor has been an integral part of Canadian life since the arrival of the white man in the early sixteenth century. *L'eau de vie* was an indispensable instrument in the settlement of New France; it kept the *coureurs de bois* and the *voyageurs* warm on their lengthy journeys; it was used as cash by the traders of the Hudson's Bay Company; it relaxed the farmer, the miner, and the shopkeeper; it provided solace for the soul and an escape from the great and small tragedies of life.

Since the days of New France, unsuccessful attempts had been made to curb its use. After Confederation, the Dominion Alliance for the Total Suppression of the Liquor Traffic was founded in 1875. Three years later, the Scott Act, a mild prohibition measure, was in effect. Plebiscites were held in Manitoba in 1892, Prince Edward Island in 1893, and Ontario and Nova Scotia in 1894. In all, the majority of voters decided in favour of prohibition. Every year Parliament was besieged with petitions and motions to enact a prohibitory law, but the British North America Act had not defined the powers of the provincial and federal governments in this matter and nothing was done that was satisfactory to the prohibitionists. Most of the agitators and supporters were women. Indeed, the entire women's movement of the twentieth century has its roots in the anti-liquor movement.

By the time of the Liberal Convention of 1893, it seemed clear that the federal government had power over both the manufacture and the import/export of hard liquor and that the provinces were responsible for its control and retail sale. When the matter came up on the convention floor, Laurier decided that a plebiscite would be held to determine the issue. It was scheduled for the end of September.

Most of the provinces other than Québec had favoured prohibition at some time, but Laurier, who seldom drank, was not sympathetic to prohibition. The government would lose revenues of around $8 million annually; the cost of applying the law would be another $22 million, so there would be higher taxes; the ban would constitute a massive interference in the private lives of citizens; and the people of Québec would oppose prohibition because the concept was foreign to them and against "all their conception of right." Tarte took charge of the campaign both in Québec and in New Brunswick.

On 29 September the men of the country voted. In all, some half million votes were cast — about 44 percent of eligible voters — a considerably lower percentage than in regular elections. Of the total ballots cast, only 23 percent were in favour of prohibition. In Québec, where 74,259 electors took the trouble to vote, 13,706 were in favour and 60,553 opposed. "Only a trifle over one-fifth affirmed their conviction of the principles of prohibition." Given these results, Laurier was not inclined to act. Besides, why disturb Québec unduly?

There was also time out from the Joint High Commission to bid adieu to the Aberdeens. On 29 October, a month after the plebiscite, the Aberdeens, making "a special exception to ordinary rules," dined with the Lauriers at their residence in Ottawa. To compensate for the farm-house dinner Laurier had promised them so often, Zoë had a suckling pig prepared in the proper *Canadien* manner. And "very good it was," proclaimed Ishbel. They all had a great time. They liked and respected one another. Zoë was by then much involved in Lady Aberdeen's good works as vice-president or honorary patron of various societies. Towards the end of the soirée, Lord Aberdeen "produced an old French loving cup copied from one of the time of Henri II with fleur-de-lis etc. & engraved with an inscription from us to Sir Wilfrid & Lady Laurier & 'Oublier nous ne le pouvons' & having filled it with a splendid loving cup concoction it was passed round solemnly. Sir Wilfrid said a few charming words of acknowledgement in French & so all passed off very nicely." As a parting gift, the Lauriers gave them "one of those dear little red Québec berlot sleighs."

Lady Aberdeen, like Laurier, took a deep interest in the beautification of Ottawa — "the grand improvement," she called it. What she proposed was to get a plan made and adopted

> whereby a beautiful stately drive or esplanade would be constructed from Major's Park right down Sussex Street, along which only build- ings of an approved type would be allowed & that only on one side, leaving the river side free & open & terminating at Government House grounds with a new & worthy Government House overlook- ing that lovely view on the river which may be had from the Governor General's bay — then throwing a bridge over to Gâtineau, which would enable a drive to be made all round the other side of the river & coming back by Hull. Of course the same drive would have to be continued West of the Parliament Buildings to the

Chaudière Falls. It would make a glorious place of it & there is nothing now to prevent it.

She had first thought that Government House should be located at that spectacular place known as Nepean Point. However, the dreadful government Printing Bureau and the ugly CPR bridge, "which is mauling it to pieces and which Sir Wilfrid laments as much as anybody," made that impossible. But she had plans for the site: an open-air skating rink, a tobogganing slide right across the river, a sports centre as a "rendez-vous for all the sports for which Ottawa is famous both in winter & summer" — and a new geological museum to be constructed as the first beautiful building.

Laurier was much interested and she dragged him, along with Tarte and Fielding, to inspect her plan. To Ishbel's admonition, "Look fifty years ahead," the three of them responded that perhaps it could be done earlier. It was Fielding who came up with the idea of putting Ottawa "under a Commission like Washington." Mrs. Fielding, Zoë, and other Cabinet wives got involved and, in due course, the Bill Respecting the City of Ottawa was introduced in the House of Commons. It proposed setting up an Ottawa Improvement Commission, with four commissioners and an initial budget of $60,000 (later expanded by Laurier to $100,000). Passage of the legislation in the Commons and the Senate was far from easy, marked by the same negative attitude that Canadians have exhibited towards their capital city since Confederation. Laurier, Tarte, and Fielding persevered and, a year after the Aberdeens had left Canada, the four commissioners were named and the Improvement Commission (which would become the National Capital Commission in due course) was in action.

The Aberdeens left Canada on 19 November and the Mintos (Gilbert John Murray Kynynmond Elliot, 4th Earl of Minto, and Mary Grey, Countess of Minto) arrived the same day.

Then it was time for God to work His wonders.

~

On 6 April 1899 the archbishop of Montréal wrote to Laurier: "Je viens de vous faire part d'une grande joie." The great joy was that Christophe-Alphonse

Geoffrion, an old *Rouge*, one of Laurier's confidants for many years and a minister without portfolio in his Cabinet, had performed his Easter duties and thereby reconciled himself to the church. The archbishop went to Geoffrion's house to say Mass, "a beautiful victory of God's grace." By this time, Geoffrion was ill and he died the following July.

Not satisfied with converting Geoffrion, the archbishop turned his attention to Laurier: "And you, cher Monsieur Laurier, allow me to ask you the question in the name of the affection that I have for you: Have you performed your Easter duties? You need to be completely with us. You desire it, why wait?" If Laurier has done them, so much the better; if not, he should as quickly as possible. "Do not refuse me that: I would be happier than if you arranged for Lord Strathcona to give $5,000. But the two *bonheurs* will go hand in hand."

Three days later, the deal was done. Laurier re-entered the portals of the church of his birth, his family, and his ancestors. The archbishop was overjoyed — even if it took him three months to acknowledge the event. Why the conversion? Only God and Laurier — and, perhaps, Zoë — knew.

With that part of his life in order, Laurier was ready to confront the Boers of South Africa, who were about to invade the psyche of Canadians.

~

In South Africa, two peoples confronted each other: the Boers and the British. The Boers resented the newcomers, the foreigners, who were invading their land and treating them like cattle. The British were not at their best when they were challenged about their record, their arrogance being what it was. The forces of empire building played their part and, inevitably, war came between the Boers and the British on 12 October 1899, when the Boers fired the first shot. It was heard all over Canada, and it provoked a racial conflict that divided the country even more severely than Riel and the school and language questions had.

While the crisis was brewing, Laurier and Canada paid little attention. It was all so far away. At first he tended to sympathize with the Boers. It never entered his head that any demands would be made on Canada. He was wrong.

In July 1899 Chamberlain wrote to Lord Minto to ascertain if the Canadian Militia Act could be interpreted as justifying the use of Canadian troops outside Canada "in case of war with a European power." Laurier replied that the Militia Act was concerned only with the defence of Canada and that the theatre of war had little to do with it. Minto, who declared himself "an old friend of Canada" because he had served as chief of staff to General Middleton, commander of the troops during the Riel Rebellion in 1885, plaintively asked Laurier to consider sending troops immediately. But Laurier contented himself with moving a resolution of support in the House and by leading MPs in a rousing rendition of "God Save the Queen."

An agitation to send troops, engineered by Hugh Graham, the jingoist owner of the *Montreal Star*, swept the country in August and September. Thousands of positive replies were received, but the negative ones were all destroyed.

On 21 September, when Tarte returned from Europe, he met with Laurier and Bourassa. Tarte was adamant: not a penny for South Africa without the consent of Parliament. If Canadians wished to equip regiments and make other contributions at their own expense, that was fine by him. "But not a penny without the direct authority of Parliament." Bourassa was in total agreement with Tarte. "I am prepared," he said in his pontifical way, "to resign my seat on that stand."

The following month the military got into the act through the person of the British commander of the Canadian Militia, Major-General Edward Hutton. Directed by him, an article appeared in the *Canadian Militia Gazette* which stated categorically that if there were a war, Canada would send a force. And he proceeded to print the overall contingency plan.

Laurier dismissed the plan as "pure invention." He added something that he was going to regret: "Though we may be willing to contribute troops, I do not see how we can. There is no menace to Canada." As he was making his denial, Chamberlain — never at a loss for ways of doing mischief — cabled Minto to thank Hutton and the Canadian people for their patriotism by offering "to serve in South Africa." Chamberlain's dispatch didn't mention that only Colonel Sam Hughes, a member of Parliament, had offered to raise troops at his own expense.

When war was at last declared, the Cabinet met to discuss Canada's position. David Mills, Frederick Borden, and William Mulock favoured sending a contingent at Canadian expense. Richard Cartwright, Henri Joly de Lotbinière, Richard Scott, William Paterson, Clifford Sifton, William Fielding, and Charles

Fitzpatrick were more restrained and sought to reconcile the two groups. Tarte was unyielding. Not a cent! It would be a betrayal of a sacred trust and a dangerous precedent. Canada would always have to participate in imperial or empire wars. Québec would be irreconcilable. It could well be lost in the next general election. "Be Canadians," he yelled at his colleagues. More quietly, he turned to Laurier and almost whispered: "I may well have to resign." Laurier listened and didn't say a word.

That night, Tarte called a meeting at his house. Henri Bourassa was present, along with Jean-Lomer Gouin, the Liberal member of the Québec Legislative Assembly who was to become premier of Québec during the First World War, and Rodolphe Lemieux; all three opposed any form of Canadian participation. On the other side were Napoléon Champagne, the member for Wright, and Napoléon-Antoine Belcourt, the member for Ottawa. Laurier opened the meeting by stating that the government had been asked to send 10,000 troops to South Africa. "Many in the Cabinet favour that position; a few, 'comme notre ami Tarte,' do not. The country is being divided on racial lines. If we do not act responsibly we may tear the fragile fabric of our country apart."

He rejected the suggestion that Parliament be called in session: "The government may be defeated. Please, gentlemen, do not laugh. It is a serious matter. The Whip has counted his people and he cannot guarantee a victory. The pressure is immense. Willison has told me that I must send troops or resign." No one spoke. When he had let that sink in, Laurier went on: "In light of this situation, we are left with the need to forge a compromise, *une voie moyenne.*"

At that Bourassa stood up and cried in a rage: "I don't want any part of that compromise. You have given your word privately and publicly that not one Canadian soldier will be sent without the consent of Parliament. You said that . . ."

Laurier interrupted him: "No, Henri. What I said was I did not see how it could be done. There is a large difference."

"It's sophistry. You have even informed the colonial secretary to that effect. Besides, how can you possibly effect a compromise? What would it contain?"

"I do not know yet. I have more consulting to do this night and tomorrow. But I have to tell you that a compromise there will be."

"Does that compromise pay any attention to the opinions of the province of Québec?"

"Mon cher Henri, the province of Québec has no opinions; it has only sentiments."

"No different from any other province," Belcourt said, while Bourassa added: "We may have only sentiments, but they are noble ones!"

"Henri, the circumstances are very difficult for us all."

"Well, Sir Wilfrid, it is because the circumstances are difficult that I am asking you to remain faithful to your word." Bourassa looked at Laurier for a moment and wondered whether he should say what he thought. Tarte, who knew both well, prayed silently for the miracle that he would not. But Bourassa forged ahead:

"To govern, Right Honourable Sir, is to have enough heart, at one difficult moment, to risk losing power to save a principle."

There was an intake of breath, but the smile remained on Laurier's face. He wouldn't take the remarks as an insult. Nor would he taunt the younger man.

"We must be practical," he said, simply.

Lemieux burst out laughing. He looked at Laurier and saw the deep concern in his eyes. He was pale and his hand trembled. His pain was obvious. To alleviate his own sadness, he thought of a pun: "Puisque le vin est tiré, il faut le Boer."

Laurier smiled and wondered how he would translate that untranslatable expression to his unilingual colleagues the next day.

They went home, but he stayed with Tarte to attempt one more time to convince him. "Mon cher Tarte," he said, "we have to compromise. We have no other alternative." Tarte didn't answer that statement directly. Instead he asked:

"Bourassa, who has studied the question from beginning to end, believes this war to be unjust. Do you?"

"To me it is clearly and manifestly a war for religious liberty, political equality, and civil rights. It is a just war — perhaps even the most just of all the wars England has ever fought. But, important as that question is, we must not lose sight of our purpose. The interest of Canada demands that we maintain national unity. Public feeling in the English provinces is too strong to be opposed. We cannot afford to challenge the sentiments of the country."

"But Québec, Sir Wilfrid?"

"You know as well as I do that many support Canadian participation. The mayor of Montréal is on our side; so are *Le Soleil* and *La Presse*. But, on the whole, you are right: sending troops to South Africa is not popular in our province. That is why I need you. You cannot resign. Québec must be with us or we shall not form the next government of Canada. By resigning, you may well endanger *Canadiens*. They will be accused of greater disloyalty. It is a most dangerous situation for everything we have worked for. Will you give yourself the night to think it over? The Cabinet meets again tomorrow morning. In the meantime, think of the minimum you can live with. I will ponder the maximum I can get away with. Bonsoir."

And Laurier walked the short distance to his house, to his library, and his meditation on a possible *via media*.

The next day, a compromise was forged. It took the form of an order in council. No contingent would be sent; no 10,000 troops either. All the government was prepared to do was to equip a force of one thousand volunteers and transport them to South Africa. The "moderate expenditure" involved "may well be undertaken by the Government of Canada without summoning Parliament, especially" — and here one could see the hand of Tarte writing and erasing and writing — "as such an expenditure under such circumstances cannot be regarded as a departure from the well-known principles of constitutional government and colonial practice, nor construed as a precedent for future action."

Five days later, Bourassa resigned his seat in the Parliament of Canada. At the end of October the men promised to the empire in its great need left Canada for South Africa. By the time the fifth session of the eighth Parliament opened on 1 February 1900, Bourassa had been re-elected as an independent in his constituency of Labelle. Laurier ordered that he be unopposed. A month later there were riots in the streets of Montréal.

On 1 March the news of the deliverance of the British garrison at Ladysmith, which had been under siege for three months, provoked the first outburst. In a "practical demonstration of their loyalty," as the *Montreal Star* described it, the English-speaking population of Montréal celebrated the victory by drinking toasts and singing patriotic songs, particularly "God Save the Queen" and "Rule Britannia." Many offices and factories were given a half-holiday, and the same privilege was extended to the students at McGill.

At 10 a.m., a crowd of about two thousand first visited the *Star*'s offices and then proceeded to Tarte's newspaper *La Patrie*, *Le Journal*, and *La Presse*, where they insisted on hoisting the Union Jack after molesting several employees and breaking a door at *La Patrie*. The procession then marched to the City Hall, where a frightened mayor met them, hoisted the Union Jack himself, made a patriotic speech about the solidarity of the empire and its glories, a nd gave all the civic employees a half-holiday. From Dominion Square, where the *Star* distributed flags and supplied free beer, the crowd marched off to the Université Laval de Montréal, where again they broke doors and furniture and raised the British flag. A *Canadien* student, however, cut the rope on the pole, and the fallen flag provoked a general mêlée and further destruction of property.

A few hours later the *Canadien* students retaliated. Waving French flags and singing "La Marseillaise," they made their way to the three French newspapers that the McGill students had charged in the morning and asked that the Union Jack be lowered, since it was then nightfall. The McGill students suddenly returned, armed with guns, sticks, iron bars, and frozen potatoes. The *Canadien* students and a few policemen repressed the mob by hosing them down with cold water, encasing many of them in ice on that cold winter night. Shots were fired, a few were wounded, and the mob broke every window in the university building. The crowd was finally dispersed.

Next day, the newspapers picked up where the students left off — and they turned out to be more irresponsible in their commentary than the young pranksters had been in their behaviour. Monseigneur Bruchési ordered the Laval students not to retaliate; the principal of McGill apologized and offered to pay for the damages. That evening, there were more demonstrations on both sides, though sanity prevailed. After some four days of rioting, everybody went home to bed, some too drunk to remember what had happened. Then the agitation moved to the House of Commons.

Laurier, however, was vindicated. His *via media* saved the day. Hotheads, like the students, Bourassa, and the ever irrational media, endangered what he had set out to do: "What would be the condition of this country today if we had refused to obey the voice of public opinion?" he asked rhetorically. A most dangerous agitation would have ensued, ending with "a cleavage in the population of this country upon racial lines. A greater calamity could never take place in

Canada." Laurier wanted to avoid division; and his entire political life, dedicated as it was "to try to promote unity, harmony and amity between the diverse elements of this country," dictated that he compromise as he must. And so:

> The work of union and harmony between the chief races of this country is not yet complete. We know by the unfortunate occurrences that took place only last week that there is much to do in that way. But there is no bond of union so strong as the bond created by common dangers faced in common. Today there are men in South Africa representing the two branches of the Canadian family, fighting side by side for the honour of Canada. Already some of them have fallen, giving to their country the last full measure of devotion. Their remains have been laid in the same grave, there to rest to the end of time in that last fraternal embrace. Can we not hope that in that grave shall be buried the last vestiges of our former antagonism? If such shall be the result, if we can indulge that hope, if we can believe that in that grave shall be buried the former contentions, the sending of contingents would be the greatest service ever rendered Canada since Confederation.

Before this horrible war was over with the Treaty of Vereeniging on 31 May 1902, 7300 Canadians participated in it at a cost of approximately $2,800,000. In South Africa, the troops demonstrated courage and stability. It was unfortunate that those qualities could not be applied to many in Canada.

~

As Canadians and *Canadiens* were surrendering to the fires of passion over South Africa, Ottawa and Hull were burning. On Thursday, 26 April 1900, a fire started in Hull early in the morning. Within three hours it had destroyed almost everything standing on Rue Principale from Brewery Creek to the Rivière des Outaouais. It practically wiped out the city. Not more than five people died, mercifully, but hundreds lost their homes, their belongings, and their jobs. The city of Hull had no large building in which to place the homeless. Churches and convents were used, but they were not sufficient. Many, hundreds even, spent that night huddled up on the streets.

By noon a fierce wind caused the flames to leap across the river, where they ignited the lumber piles at the end of Victoria Island and spread, half a mile wide, to Carling Avenue over seventy city blocks, covering 440 acres. The fire killed seven people in Ottawa, left 8370 residents homeless, and destroyed 1900 buildings. The west end of the capital was totally destroyed. The damages were in the millions. The homeless were taken to the Exhibition Grounds and housed there, while LeBreton flats, Rochesterville, and Sherwood southward to Dow's Lake were buried in fiery ruins.

Laurier immediately appointed Scott, the secretary of state, to coordinate federal help, and Fielding issued a cheque for $10,000 for relief purposes and announced that when the House reconvened the following Tuesday, the government would introduce a motion to allocate $100,000. The money was to be spent on both sides of the river: "The river must not be a line of demarcation," Laurier had ordered. The governor general sent $1000 to the Relief Committee, Laurier $100, Mulock $500, and within a few days $1 million had been raised. Borden ordered the Militia out to prevent looting, and issued blankets and other equipment from the government's military stores.

Laurier and Zoë inspected the damage, visited the victims, and expressed their condolences and prayers. The Council of Women appointed a liaison committee, with Zoë the most influential member. She had considerable experience in raising money and organizing relief. She set to work, counting on Laurier to do his part. By the end of 1900 much had been accomplished to rebuild both cities, in spite of the skyrocketing insurance rates.

There was also another election. The results were most interesting.

~

Tarte spent the summer of 1900 as Canada's commissioner to the Paris Exhibition. He embarrassed Laurier and the government by making speeches that were interpreted at home and abroad as being disloyal to the British connection. In August he returned to Canada to prepare for the election on 7 November. Inevitably, he became the central contentious issue in Ontario, but in Québec and in the Acadian parts of New Brunswick he was worth his weight in gold. In French-speaking places his strategy was the same as in 1896: Laurier was the only possible protector of *Canadien* interests. Against Laurier were arrayed the nefarious forces of Toryism, determined to destroy the duality of Canada. The Boer War crisis was proof of that. With great intuition, Tarte knew that *Canadiens* and *Acadiens* would forget about the contingent to South Africa if he could show them that he and Laurier were being attacked by the Tories for only one reason: they were both *Canadiens*. But he also knew that arguments didn't win elections any more than prayers do. Organization did. Tarte put an efficient organization in place in every constituency. He arranged large meetings, *assemblées contradictoires*, door-to-door campaigns — and everywhere he went Laurier was the hero of the day. The prime minister also took on the role of an educator, "enlightening the population on imperial questions," as he confided to Lord Minto. He was proud of what he had accomplished during the Boer crisis: "In 1899 we had the responsibility, we shouldered it bravely, publicly; and privately, I asked our compatriots to uphold the honour of our race." As for Bourassa, he allowed his name to stand in the list of official Liberal candidates, but refused to take any money from the party.

In Ontario, the main opposition strategy was to discredit Laurier through Tarte. Willison warned Laurier of that: the Protestant Protective Association, the St. George Society, the Orange Order, and other racist organizations had decided to attack a government headed by a *Canadien* and a Roman Catholic and largely supported by people of the same race and religion. However, to disguise their prejudice, they used Tarte's supposed disloyalty to the empire as the focus of their attack. While their tactic was successful in many ways, Zoë and Laurier were triumphantly received everywhere they went.

The West was left to Sifton, and the Maritimes to Blair, Davies, and Fielding, though Laurier did make a quick tour of the Atlantic seaboard. Everywhere his message was the same: the Liberals were good for Canada. There was general prosperity, a surplus in the treasury, improved transportation and communication, a preferential tariff for the mother country, prudent assistance to the empire, and the promise of ever more prosperity. But Laurier was wary of newspaper reporters. He found them "dangerous." "They take a thought on the wing and develop it in the direction of their own opinion." Dangerous indeed!

In the end, though, the media didn't matter very much. On 7 November 1900 Laurier won a splendid victory. The results were close to what Tarte had predicted. In the three Maritime provinces, where imperialism was not a prominent issue, he had 27 seats to the Conservatives' 12 — and in the sweep Tupper was defeated. In Québec, where his imperial policies were most unpopular, the victory was complete: 58 out of 65 seats. His own majority of 2850 votes in Québec-Est was the largest in Canada. In Ontario, the Liberals lost 14 seats (they had 37, compared with 55 Conservatives and 3 Independents); they split the West, including British Columbia, with 11 for the Liberals and 6 for the Conservatives. Overall, the Liberals elected 133 candidates; the Conservatives, 80.

A nice way to begin a new century.

∼

On Monday, 1 January 1900, Victoria is queen of England; Lord Minto is governor general of Canada, and Sir Wilfrid Laurier is his first minister. Confederation is thirty-four years old.

There are 5,369,666 of us on this immense land that is our country. Ten years before, we numbered 4,833,239, giving an increase of 536,427. Not enough, if we are ever to reach the 100 million that Canada can feed and house. The largest gains are in Québec, about 200,000; in Manitoba, 100,000; in the North-West Territories, 112,682; and in British Columbia, around 80,000. Both Montréal and Toronto have grown, as has every other city except Kingston. Roman Catholics far outnumber any other religious group, but Protestants together outnumber Catholics by almost one million. In addition, we have 16,432 Jews and 122 sects ranging from Confucians to Fire-Worshippers. The male population is 2,751,473, of whom 1,747,622 are unmarried. More than 1,200,000 women are also unmarried, out of a female population of 2,619,578. Divorce is uncommon: only 322 females and 339 males. As to origins, we are a mixed lot: 56 percent of our population is British (English, Irish, Scottish, and Welsh) and 31 percent is French. The remaining 13 percent is spread among Germans, Austrians, Belgians, Chinese, Dutch, Finns, Galicians, (East) Indians, Italians, Japanese, Negroes, Poles, Jews, Russians, Scandinavians, Swiss, Syrians — and 10,892 Métis, 93,319

Aboriginals, and 43,398 Americans. Precisely 1,181,778 Canadians live in the United States.

We don't much like the Chinese, the Japanese, the (East) Indians, the Negroes, or anyone else who isn't exactly like us. That amounts to a great number of people. The revenues to the federal treasury from the "Head Tax" — paid by "Asians" before entry into Canada — is $1,632,942.

The flow of immigration has begun, but Sifton will have to do better if the twentieth century is to belong to Canada.

~

In the first year of the new century, Queen Victoria died on the evening of Tuesday, 22 January 1901. The buildings were draped in black; flags flew at half mast; archbishops and bishops issued *mandements;* politicians made speeches; clergymen pronounced themselves at the mercy of the Deity; organizations passed resolutions; newspapers edged with black borders proclaimed their grief; Lady Aberdeen waited upon the new royal consort, Queen Alexandra, to present an address signed by 25,000 women of Canada; the House of Commons was decked in black and purple; and, during the period of mourning, there was no entertaining.

The House opened a new session on 3 February and, five days later, Laurier moved an "Address to the King," Edward VII, in which he said of the new monarch's mother: "She is now no more — no more? Nay, I boldly say she lives in the hearts of her subjects; lives in the pages of history. And as the ages revolve, as her pure profile stands more marked against the horizon of time, the verdict of posterity will ratify the judgment of those who were her subjects. She ennobled mankind; she exalted royalty — the world is better for her life."

One of the first acts of Canada's new sovereign was to announce that the Duke of York (later to become George V) and his wife Mary would visit Canada in September. Canadians rejoiced.

The war in South Africa continued. Men were killed or wounded or went missing. Some returned home; others were sent to replace them. Bourassa, sanctimonious as ever, demonstrated how tedious he could be. The session that began in early February dragged on into May. Zoë often accompanied Laurier to the

House, and sat in the gallery knitting away and watching over him. He always brought a couple of books with him and read as the debate dragged on. Joly de Lotbinière had gone to Victoria as lieutenant governor; Mulock had become minister of labour before the election and kept his job as postmaster general; Sir Charles Tupper retired as leader of the Conservative Party and was replaced by Robert Laird Borden, member of Parliament for Halifax; the economy continued to prosper; Sifton energetically peopled the West; and there was serious talk of bringing Newfoundland into Confederation. For his part, Laurier made speeches, mostly on Canada's relations with the empire. In early June he escaped to visit the Collège de L'Assomption, as he had done three times before, in 1873, 1883, and 1893.

On Monday, 11 June, at 9:30 a.m., Laurier and Zoë, Tarte, Dansereau, the Jettés, Senators Gasgrain and Dandurand, the mayor of Montréal, and a few others embarked at the Windsor Hotel in magnificently refurbished streetcars which the Compagnie des Tramways de Montréal had put at their disposal. It took them about seven hours to get to L'Assomption, for there were many stops along the way to receive addresses, make promises to build a bridge here or a road there, receive flowers, sign visitors' books, and meet the people while Tarte conferred with the political lieutenants of the region. At L'Assomption, a large crowd was waiting. He tried to speak, managed for a few minutes, then burst into tears, remembering all that the place had meant to him. The Archambaults, numerous as the stars in the heavens, smiled at him from the front rows — but there was no Oscar; he saw Charlemagne and his wife standing close to his mother's people, the Martineau family — but not Maman Adeline: she was too old to attend. Not far from where he spoke was the place where Joseph Papin had taught him to be a *Rouge* — after sneaking out of the college — and where Carolus sometimes met him to deliver forbidden books. Also the church he attended every Sunday. It was too much.

At night there was a celebration. The *salle académique* was filled with students, parents, former students — many from around his time — and the citizenry for miles around. He arrived in a splendid carriage. The superior presented an address and he replied: It was here that he became a man; that he learned to read widely, think, and debate; that he met the men who were his allies and his friends, and who had remained so through the turns and twists of life. He remembered his former teachers, particularly Barret; and he admonished the students to work hard.

The next day, while Zoë was entertaining the family at the Archambaults', he attended a lunch in the *salle de récréation*. There were eight hundred in the room, mostly former students. There were no toasts, no addresses, no speeches — only the exchange of memories. He decided to stay an extra day. In the afternoon, he held a political rally in the yard. Thousands of men and women attended.

He went all over the college, room by room, walked to where Madame Guilbault's *pension* used to be, and was driven to the *Bois des écoliers* to relive the good times he had enjoyed with Marion, Riopel and, particularly, Oscar. Before he left, he strolled among the students waiting to say goodbye to him. He "invited" them to "love our parents and our teachers, our Church, and our *patrie*." With tears in his eyes, he told them he didn't know if he would ever be this way again and, taking the edge of the school flag in his hands, he kissed it reverently and lovingly as he muttered: "Ad Majorem Dei Gloriam."

He and Zoë went to Saint-Lin to see Maman Adeline and the rest of the family. He had a long chat with his friend, l'abbé Proulx, and he managed to make a few political points while visiting the neighbourhood. By Saint-Jean-Baptiste Day they were back in Montréal and, on the 25th, he spoke at an outdoor rally in honour of the patron saint of the *Canadiens*: Canada was no longer a colony "but a nation" — a nation where there is "fraternity without absorption, union without fusion." Then:

> I love my country because it resembles no other. I love my country because even in the difficulties which arise it calls forth the noblest resolutions, the strongest, the most generous qualities of man. I love my country above all because it is unique in the world, because it is founded on respect for rights, on pride of origin, on harmony and concord between the races who inhabit it.
>
> Our pride refuses to follow longer the beaten paths. Henceforth we must march along other roads and towards other horizons. Let us have in view only the development, the prosperity, the grandeur of our country. Let us keep in our heart this thought: "Canada first, Canada forever, nothing but Canada."

After that, the time had arrived for the royals.

~

The Duke and Duchess of York, who were to ascend the throne of England in due course, arrived in Québec City aboard the *Orphir* on 15 September. Thousands of people greeted them. For the next six weeks they had hardly a moment to themselves as they lived aboard the luxurious royal train provided by the Canadian Pacific. Their itinerary was charged with state dinners, processions, lunches, addresses — even though the prince was said to find them boring — investitures, unveiling of statues to Victoria, garden parties, church services, gifts, concerts, bronco busting, cowboy riding, Indian powwows, inspections of troops and guards of honour, hunting, lunch with lumberjacks, and shooting the Chaudière rapids. Everywhere they went, whether it was Québec City, Montréal, Ottawa, Winnipeg, Regina, Calgary, Banff, Vancouver, Victoria, Toronto, Hamilton, Belleville, Kingston, Brockville, Cornwall, Sherbrooke, Saint John, Halifax, or points in between, thousands came out to greet them, to shout their love for the empire, and to wish them well. From Halifax, the royal couple left for home on 19 October, to become the Prince and Princess of Wales. After their departure, the Canadian people picked up the bill. The half-million dollars the visit had cost was well worth it.

Laurier accompanied the duke and duchess in their procession across Canada in a private car — made in the United States, to the disgust of many — attached to a special train that always preceded the royal train. From Victoria he wrote to Zoë on 1 October: it has been a great trip, beautiful weather all the way ("un temps des dieux"), and everybody is behaving nicely and receiving the royal guests with great civility, taste, and kindness. He was proud of his people. "Au revoir, ma chère bonne amie. Je t'embrasse de tout coeur."

~

In 1902, Laurier turned sixty-one. He was ready to take on Chamberlain once again.

The occasion was the coronation of Edward VII and Queen Alexandra in the summer of 1902. Almost every day of the past five years, someone, some-where in London, was making plans to reorganize the empire by making the colonies more or less appendages of Great Britain's prestige and power. The year 1902 was no exception. A new king and queen were to be crowned: what a splen-did opportunity to invite everyone from the colonies to forge a new unity. Of the three main items on the agenda — constitutional reorganization, economic reorga-nization, and military reorganization — Laurier had little interest. His only concern was to increase Canadian trade with Australia and to secure, if possible, "preferen-tial treatment for the goods of Canada in the British market."

The coronation was to take place on 26 June 1902, and the king invited Laurier and Zoë to be guests of the British government "for a fortnight from the time of their arrival" in England. While the political heads of the domin-ions and colonies were in England, Chamberlain determined that it would be a fine opportunity to hold a Colonial Conference in parts of June and July. Laurier accepted and, on 14 June, he and Zoë sailed from New York for Great Britain. On the same day, Fielding, Borden, Mulock, and Paterson, who were to be part of the Canadian delegation, left from Montréal. The Lauriers stayed again at the Hotel Cecil in a larger suite than in 1897, with one of the king's carriages manned by two of his footmen in royal livery at the door. Soldiers from the Coronation Contingent took turns guarding his door.

No sooner had they arrived on 21 June than the king fell ill and the coro-nation was postponed. He was operated on and, after a tranquil rest aboard his yacht, he was well enough to announce that he and his queen would be crowned on 8 August. Meanwhile, Chamberlain's conference opened on 30 June. He didn't accomplish any of his purposes. Laurier, "the icy wind from Canadian snows," had seen to that.

There was, therefore, time for speeches. Laurier gave his first at the Dominion Day dinner with some 520 guests, including Zoë and the Aberdeens. It was a splendid affair: "Canada is the brightest gem in the Crown of the British Empire. It is not a colony, but a nation with a nation's history." The Duke of Marlborough gave a dinner: "The Empire can be well defended by the arts of peace." At the Coronation Banquet held at the Guildhall on 11 July, Laurier warned Chamberlain, who was recuperating from a fall at the Canadian arch: "It would be a fatal mistake to try and force events." At the Canada Club, five days later, he painted a bright picture of the future of his country: "We have a population of five million; we have room and land for 100 million. So send us your surplus population." On the 26th he was in Edinburgh with the other premiers to receive an honorary LL.D: "To build up an empire, they must conquer the hearts and the intelligence of the people of the empire."

Then came the coronation at Westminster Abbey. Laurier dressed in his Privy Council uniform with a blue velvet robe over it; Zoë in a chic silk gown and a tiara made with 175 "selected" diamonds (the gift of the Liberal senators). The ceremony was long and tiring, but uplifting in its pageantry and symbolism. During the days that followed, there were state dinners and, in a private audience with Queen Alexandra, Zoë received the silver Coronation Medal. Laurier again refused a peerage. Before they left England, the Lauriers gave a "grand" banquet at the Hotel Cecil for their friends and acquaintances and, practically, every Canadian and *Canadien* in London.

By the time Laurier left London for Jersey, in the Channel Islands, he was exhausted. Zoë wanted them to come home so he could recuperate in the clean air of Arthabaska. He, however, thought it best to remain in Europe and to pretend that everything was as normal as possible. Through sheer will-power, he had hidden his tiredness, the weakness in his legs and arms, and the terrible pain in his chest. Only Zoë and the valet knew. He had to go on with it. "C'est mieux comme çà."

In France, where they arrived on 19 August, Laurier met with President Émile-François Loubet for two hours, during which he stressed the value of a rapprochement with Great Britain and an *entente cordiale* between the two countries. There was a fabulous lunch at the Élysée; both and he and Zoë saw Archbishop Bruchési; he went to Lille for a commercial and industrial exhibition, and he made more speeches. Zoë spent her time in the galleries, met artists, entertained Canadians and *Canadiens* in his name, did some shopping, and looked after his every need, physically and psychologically. Together they consulted specialists in Paris, who prescribed various drugs and treatments and diets, all of which made him only weaker.

On 5 September they were in Geneva, where Laurier conferred again with the doctor he had seen in 1897. Laurier thought he had cancer of the stomach, that his tuberculosis was reappearing, and that he was about to die. He was diagnosed with asthma complicated by chronic bronchitis and asthenia, a general weakness of the whole system. He stayed in Switzerland for a couple of weeks and it did him so much good that he was able to write to Dansereau: "My health has been deplorable, but the Swiss climate is doing wonders. I shall return to Canada in good form and ready for the battle."

He spent some time recuperating in Italy and, by 7 October, after a brief stop in Paris, he was in Liverpool waiting to sail home on the *Lake Erie*. First, though, he opened the Produce Exchange of Liverpool. He made seven speeches that day. Then he took to his bed and stayed there as he crossed the Atlantic. Arriving in Rimouski on the 16th, he was so weak that he was taken off the ship and sent to Québec City in a special train. To David and Senator Dandurand, he looked awful and ready to die. Zoë was in tears. She had almost lost him during the voyage. But, as he said, "I am not dead yet."

David and Dandurand made plans to inform the newspapers that Laurier was not dying and that there was nothing organically wrong with him. Rather, the prime minister had returned tired after fighting a long battle abroad to maintain the interests of Canada. He had suffered much and he needed rest. The strategy was sent to Dansereau for publication in *La Presse* and to Pacaud for *Le Soleil*, and from these two newspapers it would spread across the country.

Thousands came to greet them at the train station in Québec City and at City Hall, where the mayor presented an address in which both Laurier and Zoë were praised for their devotion, grace, and service to Canada. He replied briefly, regretting that it was not possible for him at this time to take the rest His Worship and others wished upon him. That night, thousands more cheered them at the Gare Viger in Montréal. The next day, there were more tributes, more words, and more gifts. After a night's rest, Laurier went straight to Ottawa for his day with Tarte.

Tarte, useful as he might be in the winning of elections, was a thorn in Laurier's side. He meddled in the departmental affairs of the other ministers; he was outspoken to a fault, enraging the jingoists and the imperialists at every opportunity; and he continued to confront the *Rouges*, unable to forgive them for their relentless attacks against him. Tarte was also a protectionist and, from the day he became minister of public works, he never missed an opportunity to remind everyone of that. His disenchantment with the Fielding tariff of 1897 grew steadily as the Americans maintained their high tariff on Canada's agricultural products while selling Canadians an enormous amount of manufactured goods that entered the country at a much lower rate. Increasingly, public opinion indicated that if reciprocity was impossible with the United States, Canada should retaliate. Tarte shared that view and campaigned openly in 1902 for "a tariff that will protect our national industries and waterways, and that will protect our national trade."

During Laurier's absence in the summer, Tarte intensified his crusade for a readjustment of the tariff in favour of protection. He made speeches all over the place, "going from bad to worse" and doing "furious mischief." Ministers began to bicker, worrying the governor general intensely. Minto didn't approve of his ministers fighting over policies in public. He summoned Tarte and demanded an explanation for his breach of Cabinet solidarity. Tarte refused to admit that he was guilty of anything: "Your Excellency, I will continue to speak what I must and if it costs me my resignation, so be it."

No sooner had Laurier arrived in Ottawa on the 19th than he read newspaper accounts of Tarte's "mischief." He didn't like what he read at all. Tarte had challenged his leadership, his control of his administration. Above all, Tarte had been disloyal to the government, to the party, and to him personally. He would have to go. Yet it was not going to be easy, and the consequences might turn out badly for Laurier and the Liberals. Tarte had been most useful for almost ten years and was the brain behind the victories of 1896 and 1900 in Québec. They had gone to school together, had fought countless battles, and had become friends. His forced departure might drive him back into the arms of the Tories. Secure in his power base, though, Laurier was willing to take that risk. He summoned Tarte for a chat. When the little man came in, Laurier was sitting very straight in his chair, behind his desk. After the *plaisanteries d'usage*, he refused to be drawn into lengthy explanations. He had read the speeches and he understood that something had to be done about the United States, but the time was not ripe: Canada was "experiencing a moment of great prosperity. We should not risk upsetting the economic climate." But that was not the issue. "You have acted disloyally to your colleagues in announcing a policy of your own, without in the first place consulting them." Therefore, "as soon as I have seen the Governor General when he returns from Toronto on the 21st, I will have to ask for your resignation." Tarte did not wait to be formally asked. On the 20th he resigned, and his letter was delivered while Laurier and Zoë were at City Hall for their official welcoming ceremony. The next day, however, Laurier replied to Tarte, telling him in effect that he had fired him. In a personal note, he expressed his sadness at what had happened: "I thank you for your good wishes; and you may be certain that I regret very sincerely that our official relations are ending in this manner, but the separation was inevitable." They continued to remain friends, and Laurier even advised Pacaud — who didn't like Tarte at all — that there were to be no personal attacks on him. Laurier then made some modifications to his Cabinet before he wrote his own letter of resignation.

As Laurier crossed the ocean returning to Canada, his resignation was not far in the back of his mind. Ill, lethargic, and depressed, he didn't see how he could go on. Back in Ottawa, he mulled over it for two weeks finding some energy to catch up on his work. One day, however, he wasn't able to get out of bed. He could hardly breathe. The doctor was called and Laurier was prescribed tranquilizers, another diet, and much rest. He did what he was told, but the despondency remained, especially when he contemplated what had to be done with the West, with the Americans, and with the country in general. One day in November in a Cabinet meeting he felt so bad that he excused himself and rushed to his office to rest. He decided he couldn't go on, so he picked up his pen and wrote a letter to his colleagues announcing his resignation. As he was about to ring for a messenger, Fielding came by to see how he was. "Here," he said, handing Fielding the letter. The minister of finance could be prime minister by the end of the day. Fielding, after reading the letter, folded it neatly and returned it to Laurier: "Do not do that today. Wait until tomorrow. Think about it and about the consequences that your departure will have on our country and on our party. Your health is not that bad. I have taken the liberty to speak to Lady Laurier. She assures me that with some rest, complete rest, you will recuperate and continue to serve as Canada's prime minister with great distinction. Please, do not send this letter."

Fielding, as the most respected and admired Liberal after Laurier, refused to be anointed. His advice was worth taking. Laurier summoned his carriage and went home. Two weeks later, the Lauriers were comfortably installed in the best hotel in Hot Springs, Virginia. By the middle of December he felt well enough to accept a summons from President Theodore Roosevelt and Secretary of State John Milton Hay. He went to Washington and their talks on the Alaska boundary and other matters went relatively well, but they exhausted him. On his return to Virginia, he and Zoë journeyed by train to St. Augustine, Florida, where they stayed at the Hotel Alcazar. Periodically, he sent reports on his progress to friends. To Dansereau, on 30 December 1902:

> The weather continues to be beautiful; my health improves every day; and next Monday, I return to the country of snow. Before I do that, though, I have decided to spend the last three days of this week in Palm Beach. We miss you, especially my wife since she has no one to humour her out of her moroseness.

And to Pacaud, 1 on January 1903:

> We both thank you for your good wishes. After David, you are the oldest friend I have. As for 1902, I see it disappearing with relief. It leaves behind only painful memories. I have been quite ill and, at one moment, I thought it was all over for me. The seven weeks I have passed here in total rest have done wonders. It remains to be seen, though, if my cure will last. I think so.

And to Joseph Lavergne, on 3 January:

> During the night, the windows remain opened; during the day, we swim in the sun. The gardens are filled with flowers, birds, and butterflies. I, who love the sun, am cheered by all of it.

On 6 January, they were back in Ottawa in "very good health" and with "no burning question, no irritating problem" to deal with. All that needed to be done "was to push forward as fast as possible the development of the country." He and Zoë settled back in their house on Laurier Street.

~

They had been living there for five years now. The house had taken on their style and their personality. They replaced the wooden steps in the front with cement ones, added large flower containers, lengthened the verandah, attached decorative iron cresting to the roof, replaced the wooden fence with an iron one, put up a flag pole, and planted shrubberies and several large sugar maples. The property was commodious and comfortable, but not in the least grand or pretentious.

It was a home rather than an official residence. On the ground floor was the drawing room or "salon," as Zoë called the large space into which she crammed Louis XVI furniture, expensive gilt chairs, a rosewood baby grand piano, tables overflowing with knicknacks, ornaments, small sculptures, and photographs, and potted plants. The floor was covered with a pink carpet, a large chandelier hung from the ceiling, and the walls were covered with paintings from her favourite Canadian artists, particularly Marc-Aurèle de Foy Suzor-Côté. The dominant colours were a soft mixture of green, rose, and écru.

The salon was connected to the dining room by a "pair of elegant leaded-glass panelled doors" made in London and costing $357.08. It was also a large room, with crimson wallpaper and dark mahogany furniture. A tall cabinet in one of the corners held mementoes of Laurier's career, and a portrait of Lord Strathcona hung on the walls.

Not far down the hall was one of their favourite places: the morning room. It was small, cosy, and filled with sun from a southwest exposure. Zoë had a player-piano in the room, along with her aviary of canaries and finches, her favourite chair to knit in, some pieces of sculpture by Louis-Philippe Hébert, and a card table on which to play poker and keep her accounts. Kewpie and Peter, the Pomeranian dogs; Gyp, the fox terrier; Fritz, of unknown ancestry; a Persian cat and other assorted felines loved the morning room, but had the run of the house.

Laurier's special room was his library on the second floor. It was a large room with a good exposure to the sun, airy and bright. It contained five thousand books and he spent an enormous amount of time there, reading, meditating, receiving visitors and colleagues, and working with his secretary, Rodolphe

Boudreau (and later Lucien Giguère), who occupied a small office next to it. He often burned the midnight oil, sitting in his comfortable chair by the window in summer and by the fire in winter.

The servant quarters provided ample space for the cook, the valet, the Irish lady's maid, and two other maids. A laundress and assorted cleaning staff came as required. Until they bought a car in 1909 for $1268.49, and for which they built a garage to house it, the chauffeur, and his wife, the Lauriers used a horse carriage hired from a local livery. In 1897, while Laurier was in England, Mulock raised $100,000 — the Jubilee Fund — to provide the money to run the house, pay the servants, eliminate a backlog of debts, and build up an annuity.

The routine of the house revolved around Laurier himself. He got up at eight and, by nine, he was eating breakfast and perusing the Ottawa *Citizen*. His secretary, meanwhile, was arranging the correspondence that had been delivered from the parliamentary post office. At 10:15 he took the streetcar, which passed right in front of his house, and went, alone, to his office in the East Block, where he saw visitors and assorted deputations. His lunch was generally brought to him from his home, since there was no parliamentary restaurant while he was prime minister. In the early afternoon, before the House met, he had informal meetings with his Cabinet. At 6:15 p.m. he generally took the streetcar back home. Dinner followed, or whatever official function, either at home or in the capital, he had to attend. He often brought MPs home for dinner "sans cérémonie," telephoning Boudreau, in whose office was one of the three telephones in the house, that so many were expected. Laurier himself hated the telephone and he used it only when necessary. (In 1898, for instance, he went to Montréal and took refuge at David's house. Unfortunately, he didn't telephone David in advance and, before long, he received a nasty letter from his friend: "You come to Montréal; you go to my house; you don't tell me or anyone else, with the result that I and my family miss your visit. Obviously you don't believe in the telephone.")

When the House had night sessions, Laurier and Zoë would go again by streetcar (before the purchase of the automobile) and he would sit patiently, reading most of the time in his seat. He never read, though, when a young member, from either side of the House, rose to speak. He cupped his hand behind his right ear and listened attentively, often leaving his desk to shake the hand of the orator. Zoë, meanwhile, sat in the gallery knitting. At the end of the sitting, they would go home in the carriage (or the chauffeured car) that Boudreau had arranged for. As Laurier grew older, he went less and less to evening sessions of the Commons and, if he did, he seldom stayed longer than an hour.

When the House wasn't in session, Laurier stayed at home most mornings, invading Zoë's card parties, writing speeches, reading, and dealing with his immense correspondence. Sometimes, guests who were in Ottawa only until the afternoon trains came to lunch.

On Monday, Thursday, and Saturday afternoons, Zoë entertained her friends: luncheon and poker, sometimes bridge. There were formal dinners on Wednesdays and Saturdays; informal luncheons of twelve or fourteen on Sundays; at-homes every Sunday afternoon; and intimate affairs on Sunday evenings involving bridge, music, dancing, good food, and the best of wines.

The house was constantly filled with young people and children, friends and relatives, nieces and nephews. Both Laurier and Zoë cared about their family: they paid bills — dental work for one, tuition for another; Laurier arranged for jobs; and they provided accommodation. There was always a relative of some sort in residence.

Zoë was an accomplished cook. She bossed her husband around, kept the accounts, and paid the bills. Every now and then she complained that he left her with no money. "I know," he replied, "but you are richer than I at this particular moment. Give me credit. And I'll repay you." She watched over his health, acted as his best political adviser, and was a good listener and gossip. She had her own welfare department, and he called her the "Minister of Public Charity": her monthly accounts listed every cent she gave out helping this one or that. Sympathetic and kind, she served on many committees to raise money for all sorts of causes, and, as the prime minister's wife, she became the patron of organizations as different as the Sons of Scotland and the Salvation Army Rescue Home. She entertained with grace and polish, knowing intuitively the right social mix. Many found love in their house. An artist herself, she had, since the days of Arthabaska befriended poets, musicians, sculptors, and painters. She was tireless in her efforts to help them financially, to introduce them to those who had money, and to encourage them to greater heights. She was a great patron of the arts. She also taught herself English so she could communicate with the majority of the people around her. Very few returned the kindness.

And she looked after Laurier. She cuddled him in his misery, dined and wined his friends and associates, and was by him day and night. She anticipated his mood, encouraged him, and loved him. She was fiercely partisan and would not entertain a word of criticism about Wilfrid. She knew when to give advice and when not to. Often she was morose. Life was not always easy. The greatest sadness in her life — even though she would never admit to it — was not having children of her own. She would have made a good mother.

~

The 1903 session of Parliament was the longest in Canadian history up to that time. It began on 12 March and ended on 24 October. During the session, the poll tax on Chinese immigrants was raised to $500; the mixing of margarine with butter was forbidden; arbitration would henceforth settle railway disputes; Oliver Mowat died; Albani toured Canada; Blair was fired; Chamberlain resigned; Laurier gave two new Senate seats to the North-West Territories; more than 650,000 were now living in the West, which did not then include British Columbia, an increase of 190,000 since the census of 1901; the Chambers of Commerce of the Empire met in Montréal; Laurier created a new transcontinental railway; and the Americans foiled him. Through it all, he showed no sign of weakness or bad humour, but Zoë knew that his health was not as good as he pretended. It was good enough, though, to do some nation building.

Canada was booming: between 1897 and 1911, a total of 1,833,527 newcomers arrived in Canada, and many of these immigrants settled in the North-West Territories; wheat production was close to a hundred million bushels a year; the timber and minerals of northern Ontario and Québec were waiting to be exploited; eastern manufactured goods had to reach the prairies; the people had to be enticed to settle farther north than in the southern band along the border with the United States; and the binding of the country even more closely together continued to be Laurier's primary objective. He felt the need for a *projet de pays*, a gigantic undertaking that would be a work of national magnitude. Like Macdonald, he found it in railways.

It has been said that "Americans build railroads to develop their country; Germans, for purposes of war; but Canadians, apparently, just for the fun of

building them." Laurier didn't see himself in that class. He was, though, a vision-
ary, more interested in the grand scheme than in the hundreds of details that
went into it. What did he want by 1903? Another transcontinental railway. Who
was to build it? Early on, the CPR was ruled out because of the fear Liberals had
of monopolies. Laurier, however, had already helped the CPR construct a branch
line to the mining territories of the Crowsnest Pass in return for a reduction of
charges in the shipment of wheat. Another potential player, the Intercolonial, was
unsuitable because it was a state-owned operation. There were two other possibilities. Since 1896, two railway entrepreneurs of astonishing deviousness and
capacity for taking risks, William Mackenzie and Donald Mann, were everywhere in Canada constructing lines that in 1902 made them the controllers of a
network, the Canadian Northern, with a port on the Great Lakes at Port Arthur.
They sensed that the time had come for them to expand to the St. Lawrence and
the Atlantic and, as well, reach the Pacific. At about the same time, the Grand
Trunk awoke from its lethargy. It had refused to be a part of Macdonald's
transcontinental rail system, thus "missing the boat," as it were, as the Canadian
Pacific syndicate took on the task. At the beginning of the twentieth century, the
Grand Trunk decided that it too desired a railway from sea to sea. Consequently,
in the fall of 1902, its officials petitioned the government for subsidies to build
a line from North Bay to the Pacific coast. Laurier turned them down.

The Grand Trunk proposal was unacceptable because it didn't fit Laurier's
scheme. He wanted an all-Canadian route that would take Canadian goods to
ports on both oceans, that would serve sectional interests, and that would give
access to the mining deposits of the north through Québec City — which he
represented in Parliament — and northern Ontario. The Grand Trunk plan met
hardly any of those objectives.

Laurier spent most of 1903 in long and tiring negotiations with the railway
people, the Cabinet, the caucus, and every pressure group interested: some
wanted it here; others there; many were frightened of the cost; others thought
it better to build feeder lines and link them to water transportation; many argued
that it was irresponsible and economically unviable to build a railway that would
pass for the most part through an economic wilderness; a few thought it should
be handed over to the Americans. In addition, there was Mackenzie and Mann.
Many of Laurier's interlocutors were of the opinion that he should marry the

Grand Trunk and the Canadian Northern. Jealousies between them were so great that Laurier wasn't willing to spend the time arranging such a match. Besides, he was an optimist about the country: "The flood-tide is upon us that leads to fortune." His government would cause one transcontinental to be built and if others, because of the great prosperity he was presiding over, were willing to risk their private capital to build railroads, so be it.

To meet the objectives he had in mind, he came to the conclusion that the best course was to build a new transcontinental railway, on Canadian soil, from Moncton in New Brunswick to Prince Rupert on the Pacific coast, via Québec City, northern Québec and Ontario, Winnipeg, and Edmonton. A subsidiary of the Grand Trunk — a new company, the Grand Trunk Pacific — would build the western portion of the line from Winnipeg to the coast. The government would be directly involved and would build the 1800-mile eastern portion, from Moncton to Winnipeg, to be known as the National Transcontinental, and would lease it to the Grand Trunk Pacific. There would be no grants of vast tracts of land to the railway builders, as had been done in Macdonald's day for the CPR. An independent railway commission, the Board of Railway Commissioners, would supervise the development of transportation in Canada and control railway rates. Laurier never questioned his railway policy: it was the right thing to do.

Blair, the minister of railways and canals and a close ally of Mackenzie and Mann, was opposed to the government policy, preferring an alliance with the Canadian Northern. He was also miffed that he had not been properly informed and consulted, even though he was present at the Cabinet meeting that endorsed the scheme and voted against it. He resigned two weeks before the bill was to be presented in Parliament. It was a serious blow to the government, but Laurier took his chances and accepted Blair's resignation.

On 30 July 1903 Laurier was ready for Parliament. The galleries were full; every member was in his seat, and the scribes were alert. From her place almost facing him, Zoë thought he looked pale — but he always did before such encounters. She knew that he would speak for three hours. He began with the end — a sort of peroration — in which he laid down all the objections he had heard over the past seven months:

To those who urge upon us the policy of tomorrow and tomorrow
and tomorrow; to those who tell us wait, wait, wait; to those who
advise us to pause, to consider, to reflect, to calculate and to inquire:
our answer is No! This is not a time for deliberation; this is a time
for action.

History was upon Canada. We had embarked on a great voyage that brooked no
delay; the West, the Canadian West, was waiting for an exit onto the Pacific;
and those who toiled in the forests, in the mines, fields, and shops "of the older
provinces" needed an outlet, too. It was imperative that he proceed. "It is not
of tomorrow but of this day, of this hour, and of this minute." To those who
admonished him to go via the United States: he answered with a firm no. What
he was after was a fully Canadian route secured and leading to Canadian ports
on two oceans. "I have found," he said, "that the best and the most effective
way to maintain friendship with our American neighbours is to be absolutely
independent of them."

He went on to analyse the bill he was presenting in all its details, leaving
nothing to chance. He had an answer for every criticism: he had heard them all.
He moved a little to his right and put his left hand on the back of his chair as
he came to the end:

I am well aware that this plan may scare the timid and frighten the
irresolute; but, Sir, I may claim that every man who has in his bosom
a stout Canadian heart will welcome it as worthy of this young
nation, for whom a heavy task has no terrors, which has the strength
to face grave duties and grave responsibilities.

He sat down to a thunderous ovation.

The debate dragged on until the end of September, when the legislation
passed in the House of Commons, and, in October, in the Senate. However, that
wasn't the end of it. It came up again in the session of 1904 as new arrangements
had to be made to the contract to lighten the financial load of the builders.
And still that wasn't enough, as the years dragged on and the dream became
mired in bankruptcies, mismanagement, lost opportunities, greed, and political

extravagance. By the time Laurier left office, little of his railway policy remained intact. Moreover, Mackenzie and Mann had managed to build beyond the Great Lakes to Montréal — with the help of the government — giving Canada a third transcontinental. Something had gone terribly wrong. Why?

Over the years, many explanations have been given. Some cite the lame excuse that Laurier was not able to foresee every eventuality; others claim that he paid too little attention to practical and especially economic matters, thereby confirming the criticism that "the only figures he understood were figures of speech." Perhaps! But the source of the difficulties with his railway policy lay much deeper than the numbers on a piece of paper. He believed that individuals were animated by lofty ideals to pursue the good of all. He championed a magnificent optimism in Canada and her people. Canada was on the march, and nothing could stop it. "Carpe Diem!" If the day wasn't seized, the opportunity for Canada "may never recur again." It was that vision that inspired him to say at Massey Hall in Toronto in the fall of 1904: "Let me tell you, my fellow countrymen, that all the signs point this way, that the twentieth century shall be the century of Canada and of Canadian development."

~

As Laurier was caught in the throes of his transcontinental dream, word reached him at the beginning of July that Pacaud was quite ill with some form of tuberculosis. He lay at home, wrote his articles, and worried about the future of his newspaper and his succession. Laurier hoped he would recover: "Prends courage! I had the same illness as you have. I got better, followed by many years of good health." By September he was frantic to go to Québec City to see his friend. "Follow my example. I am now fully recovered. Yet we are no longer young; we cannot hope to have the same strength as in the days of yesteryear. And now: courage and patience! You have always had plenty of courage; I cannot say the same of patience, since it was never one of your favourite virtues."

As soon as the session was over, he and Zoë left Ottawa to see Pacaud and his family. Laurier made arrangements for the reorganization of *Le Soleil* on behalf of Pacaud's children. He died on 19 April 1904.

~

[The Alaska Boundary Question] reached during 1903 a stage which involved settlement, and, meanwhile, caused keener discussion in Canada than any event since the outbreak of the War in South Africa.

This comment was published in the *Canadian Annual Review* of 1903 and introduced the question: Who owned what? Where was the line of demarcation between Canada and the United States, which had bought Alaska in 1867? What had the crest of the mountains to do with a Canadian access to the Pacific Ocean? Would the rich minerals of the Yukon have to go through American territory to reach the sea? These important questions had no satisfactory answer — yet one was desperately needed, especially during the Yukon gold rush.

What Canada wanted was not additional territory, but direct access from the sea — through the coastal inlet known as Lynn Canal, where the ports of Dyea and Shagway were situated, and across the passes to the Yukon River. If the head of Lynn Canal "lay within Canadian territory, goods from Vancouver to the Yukon could enter freely; otherwise they must pass through American custom houses, to the greatest advantage of Seattle." To fulfil his national-building purposes, Laurier needed an answer.

In attempting to provide one — at least one favourable to Canada — Laurier tried to surmount the weakness of the Canadian case. For seventy years, apathy had reigned as Canada had accepted the status quo and allowed the squatting Americans to become settlers. They therefore had rights. During the meetings of the Joint High Commission in 1898 and 1899, the matter of the boundary was discussed, but to no satisfactory conclusion. Canada proposed that the matter be settled by an arbitration tribunal, but the Americans and the Canadians couldn't agree on its composition.

For the next four years, the matter festered. President Theodore Roosevelt had his eye on South America and, to be successful there, he needed the consent of Great Britain. To achieve that, he was prepared to make concessions in Alaska. Britain allowed the president to have carte blanche where he wanted it, but failed to obtain any deal on Alaska. By December 1902, Roosevelt and Laurier had agreed during their talks in Washington that a tribunal would decide the issue. It would be composed of six eminent jurists, three from each side. Laurier was concerned about a possible deadlock, with the result that the Americans would continue to keep the land and restrict Canada. However, nothing better could be hoped for. He consented and put his faith in the spirit of the treaty they had made. Roosevelt fooled him.

The American "impartial jurists" were undoubtedly honourable men, but they were senators who had fought Canada's claims all along; one represented the state of Washington in the Senate, the state that benefited the most from the Yukon trade. Laurier was stunned, as were the Canadian people. He thought seriously of withdrawing Canada from the whole dishonest mess, but Great Britain, without having the courtesy to wait for Canada's answer, ratified the treaty in the name of the empire. It was the first betrayal of Canada on the altar of Anglo-American relations. The next crucial one was to come soon after.

Who should the three impartial jurists be on the British-Canadian side? Laurier was under great pressure to take a leaf out of Roosevelt's book and name active politicians — all they had to be, obviously, were lawyers. He declined. He had made a treaty in good faith: he would honour it. Consequently, Canada was represented by the Lord Chief Justice of England, Lord Alverstone; by Mr. Justice Armour of the Canadian Supreme Court, who died during the proceedings and was replaced by Allen Bristol Aylesworth of the Ontario bar; and by Sir Louis-Amable Jetté, lieutenant governor of Québec and a former puisne judge of the Supreme Court of Québec.

During the summer, the tribunal met in Great Britain to hear arguments and read a mountain of briefs. In September and October, it heard oral arguments — and Blake was one of the Canadian counsel. By then, the Canadians began to wonder if they had not been had. Alverstone was really not a member of their side: he saw himself more as an umpire. Sifton, who served as the British agent, wrote to Laurier in October: "I think the Chief Justice intends joining the Americans, deciding in such a way as to defeat us on every point." Why? "A predetermination to avoid trouble with the United States." Jetté and Aylesworth "are much exasperated and considering withdrawing from the

Commission." Laurier's answer was a command: "Our Commissioners must not withdraw. If we are thrown over by the Chief Justice, he will give the last blow to British diplomacy in Canada. He should be plainly told this by our Commissioners."

On 17 October, Laurier waited anxiously for the announcement of the decision. Canada lost by the vote of the Englishman. Roosevelt was jubilant: "It is the greatest diplomatic victory of our time."

It was a subdued and sad Laurier who spoke about the award on the last day of the session. He was deeply disappointed, he said. He stopped, overwhelmed by an emotion arising deep from inside him, but he refused to control it: "I have often regretted that while the United States is a great and powerful nation, we are only a small colony, a growing colony, but still a colony. I have often regretted also that we have not in our hands the treaty-making power which would enable us to dispose of our own affairs." And he ended with a strong declaration: "So long as Canada remains a dependency of the British Crown, the present powers which we have are not sufficient for the maintenance of our rights." Canada had to have more extensive powers, "so that if ever we have to deal with matters of a similar nature again, we shall deal with them in our way, in our own fashion, according to the best light we have."

To attain these treaty-making powers, he would wait. He would build Canada's freedom of action case by case.

~

After that long and tiresome session, Laurier and Zoë were suddenly summoned to Saint-Lin. Maman Adeline had died. They left immediately by special train with Henri and Carolus. She had been Laurier's mother since the death of his birth mother in 1848. With her remaining children Charlemagne, Henri, Carolus, and Doctorée, her grandchildren and great-grandchildren, he answered the prayers of the Rosary led by the abbé Proulx. Many of his political friends came from Ottawa, Montréal, and Québec; Émilie and Joseph were there; as were priests from the Collège de L'Assomption and a representative of the Young Liberals' Club of the Université Laval. He was the chief pallbearer and, as he walked behind the *cortège*, he was moved by the villagers in large numbers lining the streets and blessing themselves as the magnificent hearse went by, drawn by four black and decorated horses and hundreds of bouquets of flowers. Proulx received them at the church, and the superior of the college said the Mass. She was laid beside Carolus and next to Laurier's mother and sister. Zoë and the other ladies of the family stayed at Charlemagne's — women didn't attend funerals in those days.

They spent the night reminiscing and the next day, they returned to Arthabaska via Montréal. It was the end of an era. Saint-Lin would never be the same for him without her.

13

THE UNEASY TRUCE
1905—1911

O n 21 February 1905 conditions were ripe for Laurier to put the stamp of Canadian nationality on the Prairies. The Mintos had left in 1904 and were replaced by Albert Henry George Grey, the 4th Earl Grey, a nice and less pompous man, who, with his wife, Alice, presided over Rideau Hall until 1911. In the election of 3 November 1904 the Canadian people, under Laurier's banner of "Canada first! Always Canada!" gave him his third victory in a row: 139 seats to 75 for the Conservatives. Laurier had also managed to dint the imperial armour by firing the commander-in-chief of the Militia, a martinet by the name of Lord Dundonald. He had opposed Laurier's "disloyal" conviction that, in a free country, the military was subject to political control, and that Canada, independent as it was in internal matters, not the Imperial War Office, had full control over its army. After a bitter debate in which imperialist piety was much displayed — and in which Laurier made one of his few mistakes in the English language, referring to Dundonald as a "foreigner" rather than a "stranger" (both words being *étranger* in French) — Laurier asked that Dundonald be dismissed. The Cabinet agreed; but Minto hesitated when his advisers, conspiring with the Conservatives, were prepared to risk the resignation of Laurier's government and force an election. Minto did as Laurier suggested, though he put his dissent on record. Dundonald, after a short and mischievous campaign, went home, to everybody's relief.

Laurier was ready for his second *projet de pays*: the reorganization of the North-West Territories of Saskatchewan and Alberta into the provinces of Saskatchewan and Alberta. Since his coming to power, the territories had seen a considerable increase in population. In the census of 1891, the aggregate for the North-West Territories was 99,000 inhabitants. By 1901, Saskatchewan alone had 91,000 persons living there, while Alberta had 73,000. The vast majority of these people had come between 1896 and 1901. By 1911, however, Saskatchewan would have a population of 492,000, and Alberta, 374,000. The increase between 1896 and 1905 was largely the result of the dynamism and far-sightedness of Clifford Sifton, Laurier's minister of the interior. He did everything he could to market the area and to people the West: he advertised extensively, made deals with steamship lines, appointed European agents to promote farming on the Prairies, and flattered or enticed financiers and others who could do his bidding. He knew the kind of immigrant he wanted: "I think a stalwart peasant in a sheep-skin coat, born on the soil, whose forefathers have been farmers for ten generations, with a stout wife and a half-dozen children, is good quality." He had no concern about where his farmers came from — whether from Great Britain or from the remotest parts of Europe — or about their language and religion and customs. His critics complained that he was going too fast and that he was indifferent to the problems of integrating and assimilating the thousands of newcomers with whom he constantly made deals. Enthused by Laurier's optimism, he was tireless in pursuing his goal. In the process, he changed the face of Canada — and he made a lot of money.

The two territories had been asking for provincial status for some time when Laurier promised it to them in the election of 1904. He had no illlusion about what that meant. It was bound to bring the school question again to the forefront. However, he hoped that it would not give rise to the "bitter passions on both sides" that had characterized the 1896 turmoil. If it did, it would be his responsibility to find a satisfactory compromise and to "fight the extremists and to place the question where it has been placed by the British North America Act." He would enter "with no misgivings as to the soundness" of his policy and with no apprehension as to the results. Above all, he hoped that Canadians and *Canadiens* would "remember that Confederation was a compromise" that demanded of all "great sacrifices of private opinion." Unfortunately, he had not taken Sifton and Bourassa into account.

There were no great problems with the number of provinces: two were created, Saskatchewan and Alberta. There was little discussion about the control of public lands: the federal government would continue to administer them so no conflict would arise over immigration. And there was agreement over the financial provisions: the annual subsidy of one million dollars per province was said to be generous. However, when it came to the school arrangements, there was much trouble.

Since 1875, and with the unanimous consent of the House of Commons, the North-West Territories Act had permitted the establishment of separate school districts on the request of a religious minority in any given area. In practice that had brought about a dual school system not unlike that in Québec. However, in 1892 and 1901 the council of the Territories reorganized its educational system through new ordinances which strengthened the power of the council over all the schools in the territories and abolished the separate school system that had developed. In practice, however, the ordinance of 1901 maintained the existence of separate schools, which were to be administered by the Department of Education, assisted by an Advisory Educational Council with both Protestant and Catholic representatives. Catholic ratepayers were not obliged to support the public system, and provision was made for optional religious education in all the schools during the last half-hour of the school day. Roman Catholics had their own inspectors, textbooks, and teachers. Such was the system in place in the territories in 1905.

Laurier wanted to continue this system by Article 16 of the autonomy bills (one for Alberta and one for Saskatchewan), which he presented in the House of Commons on 21 February. There would be public and separate schools, and ratepayers would choose between them when they paid their educational taxes, though there would be no separate school system as such. At the same time, he wanted the new provinces to know that their powers in education were limited, so as to avoid any repetition of the crisis in Manitoba that had led to so much confusion and a near religious-racial war. Consequently, he said that section 93, the educational provisions of the British North America Act, "shall apply to the said Province as if, at the date upon which this Act comes into force, the territory comprised therein were already a Province." It was this statement that caused most of the furore with Sifton, Fielding, and others, who argued that since the Laurier formula overlooked the educational ordinance of 1901, a dual administrative system might well develop in time.

Laurier had not consulted Sifton, except to tell him in 1904 what was already in his mind: Article 16 would not guarantee more than was already in place in the North-West, but neither would it provide for less. Sifton agreed with that position, but at the critical time he was out of the country for health reasons and Laurier was not able to show him the final text of Article 16. Fitzpatrick, who was by then minister of justice, a Cabinet post Sifton had coveted, did the drafting after consultations with the permanent apostolic delegate. Later, Bourassa would claim that he had played a large role in it, but he was lying to make himself seem important. Sifton was kept in the dark largely because he hated Fitzpatrick, and Laurier was anxious to avoid an interminable row that might well jeopardize the entire project.

A day before the bills were to be introduced, Laurier wired Sifton, "Bill will be introduced tomorrow." Sifton replied: "I shall be home Friday morning. If any serious difficulty it might be well to postpone final action till then." Laurier telegraphed the following morning: "Important bill should be introduced immediately. Public opinion being worked against us, though not injurious so far. Do not hasten your return. First reading today but cannot come up for discussion for at least a week." Sifton responded by returning home forthwith.

The events that followed fulfilled Laurier's worst fears. He had awakened the sleeping giant of religious and racial division. Where had he gone wrong? Had he been naive? Was there any hope for the dual Canada he was attempting — mostly in vain — to create? Protestant ministers, in their racist and anti-Catholic paranoia, ascended their pulpits again with the message: "The new Provinces shall be bound forever to recognize, maintain, and propagate the Roman Catholic religion." The influential intellectual Goldwin Smith and the Orange lodges also took up the cry. On the other side of the barricades was Henri Bourassa, waiting eager and ready. No doubt some bishops and priests would align with him. The Québec bishops favoured the original Article 16, but the presence of the permanent apostolic delegate prevented the wholesale clerical abuses of 1896 and 1897.

Sifton saw Laurier on the 24th and 26th. In their conversations, the minister rehashed the old arguments: the West should be free to build a society that fit its purposes; one language and one nationality were to be the basis of that society, and a public and non-denominational school system was the best instrument for building a strong Canadianism out of the diverse elements that were pouring into the West; provincial autonomy was sacred, and it was being eroded by Article 16 and by the application of section 93 of the BNA Act, which, in a way, instructed the new provinces on how to proceed with their educational system and which, at the same time, guaranteed a separate school system.

Laurier didn't understand what Sifton was talking about. Provincial autonomy was a Liberal principle, but the Liberal Party had also made itself the guardian of minority rights. Like Mackenzie and Blake before him, he was attempting to reconcile these two postulates. With some irony, he asked Sifton: "Can you really doubt, my dear Sifton, that if the provinces of Alberta and Saskatchewan had been admitted into the Dominion in 1867 instead of now, they would have received the same treatment as was given Ontario and Québec?" Sifton, to his credit, had no answer to that. But Laurier had: "Yes, they would have been treated as Ontario and Québec. I do not think that this can be denied. What I did, which you consider socially and constitutionally and politically unsound, was to give the minority the guarantee of the continuance of its system of schools as it would have had in 1867."

Here Sifton had a counter argument: "You do more than that with your legislation. You potentially remove the separate schools from public regulation. The present Article 16 repeats almost word for word the 1875 federal law, making those administrative compromises that have developed over the years constitutional guarantees. To many of us, this can only mean that Roman Catholics will be empowered to claim that the separate school system has been reinstated and agitate upon it." Even though Laurier held firmly to the opinion that Sifton's statement had no foundation in the act, since Laurier was not creating or imposing a dual educational system, he agreed to amend the law and to remove the ambiguity that Sifton had perceived. In doing so, Laurier hoped to solidify what he intended to have.

With that, Sifton left and Laurier believed he had crossed an important hurdle. On the same day, he was informed that Fielding, who had just returned from Europe, had great reservations about Article 16, as did many from the Maritimes. Obviously, a crisis was brewing. No sooner had Sifton departed than Bourassa arrived, with instructions for Laurier to hold fast and to uphold the national interests of the people he belonged to. Laurier thanked him politely and awaited other developments. Before the end of the day, Sifton resigned. His letter of resignation was dated 27 February.

How was Laurier to hold the government together? Again Bourassa advised him to keep to his course; practically the whole Québec delegation in the House would follow him. Laurier didn't contemplate such ridiculous advice for long. It would split the party irrevocably and force him to pass an important bill through a coalition based on religion. On the other hand, was he to end his career like Mackenzie Bowell, pulled in one direction, then the other, leaving him incapable of action? That was not his way. He was tempted to resign, but, to protect his people, he had to stay at the helm and work towards the day when his dream of a dual Canada would be realized. At whatever cost to him personally, to his reputation, to his leadership of Québec, he would seek a compromise. This would mean accepting the minimum for the minority, but at least it could build on something.

He sought out Sifton and proposed that a new educational clause — a new Article 16 in effect — be drafted along the lines of the Laurier-Greenway Settlement. Sifton agreed, but not in collaboration with Fitzpatrick. After some torment, Laurier accepted that ultimatum. He delayed the second reading of the bills and summoned all the Québec MPs to a meeting. There will be a compromise, he warned, and they should be ready for it; the ride will be rough, but they would pull through. "What sort of compromise?" Bourassa asked angrily. "One based on the Manitoba settlement," came the reply. How could he accept that? Such a solution might have been acceptable in 1897, but not now: "*Canadiens* had the right to claim their country." Laurier did what he generally did in these circumstances; he sat there and waited for the storm to subside. He had anticipated Bourassa's attitude and he sympathized with it. But he was taken aback by Armand Lavergne, Émilie's son, who, to Laurier's delight and not without with his help and influence, had entered Parliament in a by-election in the winter of 1904 and was re-elected in the general election that fall. He, too, lashed out: it was a betrayal and it was totally unacceptable. "Then you will have the Conservatives to deal with," answered Fitzpatrick. "It is as simple as that!" The meeting lasted another hour. Before the end, however, someone asked about the bishops. Again Fitzpatrick answered. Laurier had put him in charge of the government's dealings with the apostolic delegate, Donatus Sbaretti. At the beginning of the crisis, Sbaretti had encouraged Bourassa to hold firm and to press Laurier to do the same. He then came to realize the futility of putting his hope in Bourassa: except for Armand Lavergne, Bourassa was isolated within the ministerial ranks. "His Excellency is prepared to accept a compromise," Fitzpatrick said. Bourassa couldn't believe it. "I have told him," continued Fitzpatrick, "that the great majority of us will not allow Sir Wilfrid to fall and us with him. If he does fall, however, Borden and his friends will take power, and *ce sera pis* — it will be worse. The Catholics will have nothing." Laurier confirmed that Sbaretti was open to an honest compromise. In closing the meeting he said: "Gentlemen, we can think all we want about resigning. Our individual consciences will have to guide us. However, the consequence of resignation would be that the minority, instead of having what it has now, would have nothing at all. For my part, I believe that it is better to remain in office and face this new situation."

On 22 March he moved that the autonomy bills be read a second time. In the face of the "outburst of passion" that had accompanied the first reading, he said, it had become expedient to review the situation. The original Article 16 would lead to confusion and litigation: "We therefore thought it was preferable to have the law made absolutely certain and in order to do that we have incorporated the ordinances under which the law, as it is today, has been established. It may be disappointing to some, but we believe that on the whole it is preferable to have a clear understanding." And so the Roman Catholics and the *Canadiens* in the West had to be satisfied with what their co-religionists and compatriots had in Manitoba.

A considerable agitation, led by Bourassa and seconded by Lavergne, ensued in Québec. For different reasons, the amendment was not well received in Ontario, either. The discontent in Québec laid the foundation of a nationalist movement that was to give Laurier much pain and trouble. As he told David, who was made a senator in 1903, "Bourassa has started a campaign which can become dangerous. There are questions about which it is impossible *de raisonner* with some people." In Ontario, however, the confrontation proved ephemeral. In two by-elections in which the bills were the central issues, the Liberals won. In due time, the bills became law. Though the question of securing the French language in the new provinces came up, motions by Lavergne and a Conservative were defeated.

At the end of August, Laurier and Zoë went west, along with the governor general, his wife, and his daughter, to inaugurate the new provinces. He didn't fret and he didn't second-guess whether he had done the right thing. His party was united. Bourassa and a few hotheads would pursue their dissatisfaction, but he was not the leader of a divided party. He already knew the effects the new Article 16 would have in the West: there would be hardly any agitation at all. The Maritimes were quiet, but he wasn't certain about Ontario. His health was good, the stress was controllable, and, as he had pointed out softly to his cher Armand, he had gained peace. In the back of his mind, though, lingered Bourassa's observation during the debate: "I regret every time I go back to my province to find developing that feeling that Canada is not Canada for all Canadians. We are bound to come to the conclusion that Québec is our only country because we have no liberty elsewhere."

~

Laurier was often troubled in the second half of the first decade of the twentieth century. There were moments of joy and elation, but on the whole he found it difficult to deal with the incessant clamour about him. Important legislation was passed, but it seemed to be mainly housekeeping — with the exception of the naval bill. There were scandals and accusations of more scandals, and it seemed he was forever putting out one fire only to see another lighting up somewhere else. The fanatical puritans of the Lord's Day Alliance badgered the government to pass an act to ensure a stricter observance of Sunday. Laurier, who objected to the government becoming the executive branch of morality, wasn't keen at all. In Québec, Sunday was sacred: you went to Mass, but then you celebrated, went to picnics in the park, and played games; if you lived in the country, you went shopping, for it was the only day you came into the village. The Catholic Church, however, didn't approve of movies on Sunday. Now the *Anglais* were attempting once again to dictate to the *Canadiens*. Still, a bill was introduced to suit the zealots. Laurier admitted later that he hadn't fully understood what it all meant, but that when he did, he had the bill "amended" by the Senate so that the law would not apply to any province that didn't enforce it.

On the bright side, Laurier's salary as prime minister was increased to

$12,000 and his parliamentary indemnity to $2500. He had no objection to a salary to $7000 being awarded to the leader of the opposition, for the first time.

In 1906 two deaths affected him greatly. His brother Henri, married and living in Arthabaska, died on 3 September of a heart attack. It was sudden, unexpected: he was forty-three years old. Laurier had barely recovered when, three days after Christmas, his brother Charlemagne, the merchant of Saint-Lin and the Liberal member for L'Assomption, also died. He was fifty-four. All his life he had suffered from various ailments that were ascribed to the poor condition of his lungs. Of the eight children fathered by Carolus, five were gone with more or less the same symptoms. Beside Laurier, only Carolus (aged forty-six) and Doctorée (aged fifty) remained.

~

On 5 April 1907 Laurier and Zoë went to Europe for yet another Colonial Conference. Even though Chamberlain was gone, the same matters that had been discussed in 1897 were still on the agenda. Laurier's position hadn't changed: he was opposed to an Imperial Council; he said little on the tariff question; and he remained silent on the naval question, as he had plans for a Canadian Navy. When the matter was pressed further, he remarked quietly: "I have said all I have to say on the subject." He established good relations with General Louis Botha of South Africa, and he proposed a fast, all-British steamship line on the Atlantic and the Pacific oceans "under the subsidized control of the governments concerned"; Canada, it was announced later, was prepared to contribute one-half of the $2,500,000 that the promoters insisted they needed for this "All-Red Line Steamship Project." Laurier and Sifton, who were reconciled to each other at the time and were still political allies, worked hard on the idea, but it was not settled satisfactorily.

During his month-long visit to England, Laurier made many speeches. They were eloquent, but not dangerous. He and Zoë were entertained lavishly and extensively. On 21 May they left for Paris, Italy, and Switzerland, and returned home to immense ovations in the middle of July. Laurier was pleased with every aspect of his journey overseas. From London he wrote to his friend, Senator Frédéric-Liguori Béique: "I dreaded very much the voyage to England

and the work that awaited me there. I believe, however, that all has gone well, and even in England the appearance is that the attitude which I have taken meets, not with general, but with a fairly general approval." And to another senator, his friend David, he wrote: "My policy has carried the day." The voyage across the sea had "turned out well."

They went to Arthabaska for a rest under the giant maples he had planted some thirty years before. Refreshed, he returned to Ottawa to face Bourassa.

~

Henri Bourassa was the grandson of Louis-Joseph Papineau. Laurier once remarked rather astutely: "Having known Monsieur Papineau, I can in some measure understand Monsieur Bourassa; having known Monsieur Bourassa, I can in some measure understand Monsieur Papineau." He was an austere, intelligent, and honest man who dedicated his life to the pursuit of the national interests of Québec. Unfortunately, he had no sense of practicality, refused to admit that politics was the art of the possible, and, had Laurier not been in power and leader of the Liberal Party, he would have led the province into the disastrous adventure of separation. He was an Ultramontane Roman Catholic; as such, he was hierarchical, fond of grandiose remarks and attitudes, and dismissive of those who didn't follow his banner. He fixed his actions within the narrow confines of La Ligue Nationaliste founded in 1903, and the Association Catholique de la jeunesse canadienne-française, an organization largely under the control of the church.

Bourassa was very appealing to the clergy, who had been forced to take a secondary role in the politico-national life of Québec since the visit of the papal legate Del Val. Furthermore, the priests who ran the private *collèges classiques*, the only post primary educational system in Québec, were no longer men who spent their time searching out Catholic Liberals. Rather, they hoped to instil in their students respect for "la race, la langue, et la foi." Their graduates were to go out into the world to fight a holy war against the *Anglais*, against the encroachment of others and the dilution of the race, and to keep the fire of faith burning bright. They were, in effect, educating their students to be anti-English, not to associate with English-speaking persons or Protestants, and not to speak English;

otherwise, they would lose their language and eventually their faith. Laurier knew about that: Armand Lavergne refused to learn English and wanted to throw "les Anglais" into the St. Lawrence. In Bourassa, the priests found a natural ally, for "la race, la langue, et la foi" were also at the foundation of his narrow nationalism. An eminent priest once articulated that philosophy in this way:

> We are not only a civilized race, we are the pioneers of civilization; we are not only a religious people, we are the messengers of the religious idea; we are not only submissive sons of the Church, we are, we ought to be, numbered among its zealots, its defenders, and its apostles. Our mission is less to manipulate capital than to change ideas; it consists less in lighting the fire in factories than in maintaining the luminous fire of religion and thought.

Bourassa was particularly fond of this kind of nonsense. It was no wonder, then, that the nationalism he aroused in Québec — and which endured long after him — was tribal, exclusive, messianic, and chauvinistic. But he was very popular, and he did much mischief with that popularity.

Laurier had mixed feelings about Bourassa. He liked him and he wanted him around. He thought he could contain him. Furthermore, Laurier was a political pragmatist, and he shied away from categorical statements and positions. Most things were negotiable, and issues could generally be resolved through compromise and the avoidance of the rigid application of principles and what Armand Lavergne called — generally with his fist up in the air — "l'honneur." Unlike Bourassa, Laurier was also an English Liberal and accepted its emphasis on freedom, liberty, and individuality. He belonged to the Enlightenment, with its accent on the perfectibility of man. Unlike Bourassa, who was a pessimist at heart and thought that perfection was attainable only in the next world, Laurier believed that time would resolve divisive issues. What was important in the imperial struggle was the development of the autonomy of Canada; independence would come in its own good time. What was important in Manitoba in 1897 and in the new western provinces in 1905 was the laying of the foundation on which, in time, the minorities could build. What was important for Laurier in his nation-building was to accept what could be achieved and to wait for the better day that inevitably would come. Bourassa didn't understand any of this approach.

In 1907 Laurier offered to take Bourassa into the Cabinet, but the younger man's demands made that quite impossible. He resigned his federal seat in Labelle in the fall and ran in a provincial by-election, where he was defeated. Laurier offered to have him re-elected in Labelle without opposition, but Bourassa declined. He had other plans, and was successful in the 1908 provincial election.

∼

Joseph-Israël Tarte died in Montréal on Wednesday, 18 December 1907. He had been seriously ill for nine days and in a coma for three. Fifteen hundred people attended his funeral in Montréal at the church of Saint-Louis-de-France, and Laurier was an honorary pallbearer. Laurier had always liked him. "C'est mon ami," he used to say to Pacaud. They had met at the Collège de L'Assomption and they had crossed each other constantly after that, most often as political enemies, then as political associates for a few years, and always as personal friends. Tarte taught Laurier how to fight elections and, above all, how to win them. He showed Laurier the value of organization, the merit in keeping an active press supporting "la cause," and, in many ways, how to face adversity. He and Pacaud were usually at loggerheads, but each, in his own way, had influenced Laurier's political career. Laurier often didn't approve of Tarte's methods, but he was a necessary ally. When they parted in 1902, they did so amicably.

Of his former classmates, there weren't many left.

∼

As far as politics was concerned, 1908 was not much different from the preceding two years. The eight-month session lasted seven days more than in 1903. Laurier was in the House almost constantly, piloting through it two important measures: the extension of the provincial boundaries of Ontario, Québec, and Manitoba, leading to another of those interminable and inimical school-language-religion squabbles; and further pursuit of the Red Line steamship project, to which he was becoming ever more attached. After much hassle and wrangling, Parliament was dissolved on 20 July and an election called for 26 October. Then came the greatest international event ever to take place in Canada up to that time: the Québec tercentenary, from 19 to 31 July.

It was a magnificent affair. The Plaines d'Abraham and some adjoining territory where Wolfe and Montcalm, Lévis and Murray had fought in 1759–60 were made into a national park in the presence of the Marquis de Lévis and le Comte de Montcalm. The Prince of Wales arrived in the *Indomitable,* a vessel of 18,000 tons and the most powerful fighting ship in the world. And the vice-president of the United States was there, as were senior officials from France and from the other dominions. A member of General Botha's government brought a message from Laurier's friend; ships from the navies of France, Great Britain, and the United States sailed up the St. Lawrence, and soldiers from the armies of the same countries paraded in the streets; pageants told noble stories from the past; a pontifical High Mass was celebrated, in the presence of Laurier and the Duke of Norfolk, while the Prince of Wales attended at the Anglican Cathedral; addresses were presented and eminent men were honoured. More than 300,000 people visited the city; journalists from countries around the world wrote of this land so ancient and yet so young; and Laurier made good speeches in which there was one prophetic statement: "We are reaching the day when our Canadian Parliament will claim coequal rights with the British Parliament, and when the only ties binding us together will be a common flag and a common crown." Meanwhile, the *Nationalistes* bitched about everything.

Arthabaska beckoned, and in September the election campaign began. Was he ready? Politically, yes, but in his soul he had some doubts. "I leave tonight," he wrote from Ottawa on 14 September to Pacaud's widow, with whom he was having "an affair of letters" since Ernest's death, "to begin the campaign. Wish me courage and success. I believe in success; I will not lack courage." But "I do not have the same enthusiasm as in the past." Most likely, the fact that "the questions that have to be debated are rather narrow" had sapped his vitality.

Under the slogan inspired by Sifton, "Let Laurier finish his work!" he opened the campaign in Sorel, where ten thousand people came to hear him say: "I have no need to tell you, gentlemen, that the blood which courses in my veins is the blood which flows in yours. I was born here in the Province of Québec of French parents; but, gentlemen, I have never asked my compatriots to support me because I was of their race." In Ontario where he spoke to close to fifty thousand people at seven meetings, the main issues were patronage and conflict-of-interest scandals and charges of extravagance and inefficiency in his administration. He admitted to some, but said he was cleaning everything up. Besides, scandals were not the major issue: "We have great works in hand, we have great works before us." He was proud of his twelve-year record: "In them Canada has been lifted from the humble position of a humble colony to that of a nation. Before 1896, Canada was a mere Colony, hardly known in France, though she was a Mother Country, hardly known in the United States or Europe. In 1908, Canada has become a star to which is directed the gaze of the whole civilized world. That is what we have done." He was in his riding in Québec-Est when he predicted that he would have an overall majority between thirty and forty seats. In Montréal, on 20 October, the city had the largest demonstration it ever had to welcome him. Close to a quarter of a million jubilant people lined the streets and cheered to let him finish his work: "Unity and Harmony among the races of Canada." Thankfully he promised: "If God grants me life, there are many, many things which I would undertake to do; but, unhappily, the years are piling up on my head and this is probably the last time that I shall appeal to my fellow-countrymen of Canada." He looked around, and with tears in his eyes he admitted: "I have grown old."

Laurier was in Ottawa when the results came in on 26 October. The popular vote was 568,476 for the Liberals; 548,494 for the Conservatives. The Liberals had 134 seats, to 87 for the Conservatives. In Québec where the *Nationalistes* had been active, the Liberals had 54 seats, to 11 for the others. He himself was elected in two constituencies: Ottawa and Québec-Est. He rejoiced for a moment, thought about it further, and became ill with a "stupid disease vulgarly known as the 'shingles'," he reported to the governor general at the end of October. Two weeks later, he was still in bed with another malady — "névralgie intercostale," a painful disorder of the muscles that left him weak and limping. He would have to recover, and quickly at that. On 15 November a telegram informed him that Joly de Lotbinière had died in Québec City.

Sick though he might be, Laurier had to think of his Cabinet. Of those who were sworn in on 13 July 1896, only Cartwright in Trade and Commerce, Borden in Militia and Defence, Fisher in Agriculture, Paterson in Customs, and

Fielding in Finance remained. Over the years, the others had resigned or been fired or had died, to be replaced by other men, some of whom were adequate and others severely lacking. After the election of 1908, the Cabinet had, in addition to Laurier and the five from 1896, several new members. Charles Murphy became the secretary of state, and in 1910 was given the additional portfolio of secretary of state for external affairs, another milestone in the development of Canada's independence. Allen Bristol Aylesworth, one of the three Canadian representatives over the Alaska Boundary Tribunal in 1903, was minister of justice and attorney general. Louis Philippe-Brodeur was in Marine and Fisheries, and in 1910 would also become minister of Naval Service. Rodolphe Lemieux was postmaster general, which gave him ample opportunity to carry out missions abroad on behalf of the Canadian government; he was as well minister of labour until June 1909, when William Lyon Mackenzie King replaced him. In Public Works, Laurier named William Pugsley. George Perry Graham, the former leader of the Liberal Party in Ontario, was minister of railways and canals, a portfolio that lent itself easily to excesses of patronage. Frank Oliver, Sifton's successor in the Ministry of the Interior and superintendent general of the Indians, was still in office, though he wasn't as effective as Sifton had been. Finally, William Templeman was minister of both Inland Revenue and Mines, a portfolio created in 1907. Not in the Cabinet but a member of the government was Jacques Bureau as solicitor general.

The same principles that had applied in the making of the 1896 Cabinet applied here, even though Laurier was not able to procure any provincial "stars" this time around. More than adequate Québec representation continued to be a paramount consideration, but Laurier paid close attention to the interests of other regions and provinces as well. He searched for men of proven ability with whom he could plan and realize his agenda. And he rewarded those who had been loyal to him over the years.

The Cabinet would remain mostly unchanged until the next election.

~

Dr. Léandre-Coyteux Prévost had been the Lauriers' family physician since 1906. He was well versed in all aspects of medicine and would refer Zoë or

Wilfrid to specialists as needed. Zoë had been suffering severely from rheumatism for four or five years. She had been to Alabama to ease her pain, and when she went to Europe in 1907 she was often in a sore state. However, the sun of France, Italy, and Switzerland did wonders for her. She was also putting on weight. In recent years, Laurier had noticed that she spoke loudly, at times excessively so, and that he in turn had to speak loudly to her. When they had company, he sat beside her and held her hand, tapping it gently when her voice rose. She also began to drop objects and to bang into doors or miss stairs. Prévost examined her thoroughly, specialists were consulted, and the verdict was clear: Zoë would be totally blind and deaf within the next five years, if not before. It was his responsibility to tell her.

It was the most difficult task of his life. Zoë, however, took it relatively well: "On vieillit! What can I tell you? We are getting old. But life goes on!" Yvonne Coutu, Emma Gauthier's daughter, came to live with them permanently, to be Zoë's companion and help run the house. It was a good addition to their family.

～

The weather is awful, but Zoë has bundled him up well. He takes the streetcar in front of his house. It is crowded. The travellers on their way all over the capital smile at him and a young man gives him his seat. He accepts with gratitude: his muscles ache and the itch in various parts of his body is distracting. By the Parliament Buildings he gets off and walks the short distance to the East Block, where he has his office, Room 221. People greet him and he can see the affection in their eyes. He climbs slowly and awkwardly to his "room," as he calls the place where he conducts the affairs of the country. He needs no assistance beyond some help to remove his coat. He wants to be alone. He sits wearily in his chair and looks out the window at the winter, which he dreads. He sighs and comes back to his task: the time has come to "faire le point."

On 26 October 1908 the Canadian people elected him to a fourth term. In the results, though, there is danger, particularly in Ontario. Robert Borden is catching on. The leader of the opposition is thirteen years younger; he, on the other hand, will be sixty-eight years old in few days. Though his health is generally good, it is taking him a long time to recover from his last illness.

Zoë, his chère amie, needs him more each day. She dismisses his attentions with a wave of her hand, but soon she will be almost an invalid. He feels tired all the time: the job has become less of a challenge, and it is more difficult each day to reconcile so many opposite points of view. And there is the endless succession of scandals.

He has been at the helm twelve years now and, he admits, much has been accomplished. Above all, he has prevented the worst calamity: the break-up of the country through race or religion. He has laid the foundations of the course to take: the West is growing; employment and the economy are relatively healthy; the positioning of Canada in the empire and among the nations of the world is irreversible; the transcontinental will soon provide a new railway link; there is a Ministry of Labour and a method to resolve labour conflicts; a civil service commission will repair the damage done by patronage and scandals; Ottawa is developing as a capital city should; a Canadian Conservation Commission will be established in the next Parliament and he will make Sifton its chairman; and even the perpetual problem of cigarettes and tobacco is getting resolved. The Red Line fleet, the Canadian Navy, and the elusive Americans remain as matters to be settled, but younger men can take those up. Fielding will be good at it.

He picks up his pen and begins to write in his illegible handwriting:

Dear Lord Grey:
After much reflection, I would like to submit my resignation as your First Minister to take effect as soon as Your Excellency has made the necessary arrangements for my successor.
I take the liberty of advising Your Excellency to invite the Hon. William Stevens Fielding to form the government.
With the consent of my successor and at an appropriate moment, I will also resign my position as Leader of the Liberal Party.
Thanking your Excellency —

He doesn't finish the letter. Instead, he rings for his secretary, asks him to find

Fielding, and requests an appointment with the governor general. The letter remains on the desk.

It is still there when Fielding arrives. He had been in conference with a deputation of manufacturers who want to revise the tariff in favour of protection. He jokes about it, but the quip fizzles out as he sees the state his leader is in. Laurier hands him the letter. Fielding reads it and slumps in his chair.

"You can't to do this. Please, spare me the reasons. I know them all. I have thought about them a great deal. We have won the election. Without you, though, we would have been defeated. So you have won them for us. That is clear."

"But . . ."

"My dear Sir Wilfrid, there is no 'but.' You are kind enough to make me your successor. As such, I tell you that I couldn't hold Québec. Without Québec, we shall not be in power."

"There are fine young men in Québec who would assist you."

"No doubt about that. However, you know as well as I that the Conservatives, the Nationalists, would divide it irreparably for us. Furthermore, the agenda of the administration is charged and the Americans are making soft noises. If we are to have a deal with them, only you can sell it to the country."

Fielding stops, leans forward, and replaces the letter on the desk. "Sir Wilfrid, I will give the same advice I gave you some six years ago, at about this time: Think about it. Sleep on it. Don't do it today."

He gets up and prepares to leave: "I have to go back to the manufacturers. Will you be all right?"

Laurier nods his head and again he is alone. "Québec!" he whispers to himself. And the thoughts, the anxiety, pour over him. Can he leave Québec? Is his work done there? What of Bourassa? He is up to mischief; he is a McCarthy in disguise. But he has tamed McCarthy. It will take longer, though, to *apprivoiser* Bourassa. Fielding will not be able to do that. And if it is not done, the province will be turned over to Bourassa. It cannot be allowed.

He sighs, picks up the letter, and tears it into a hundred pieces. The secretary is soon back in the room and the appointment with the governor general is cancelled. Laurier will stay until some time before the next election, presumably four or five years down the road. He dials Zoë:

"How would you like to go to New York for a few days?"

"So, you're not resigning! Yes, I would love to. Yvonne can come with us and some friends."

There is laughter in her voice and a smile on his face as he puts down the receiver and goes back to work.

~

"Home is not the place for all women. If God had intended that, He would have given all women a home." Lady Aberdeen was back in Canada in June 1909, ready to take on the men. It had to do with the right to vote. Women couldn't vote, and they were expected to stay home and fulfil their biological duties as God had intended.

Women's right to vote became an issue in Canada in 1909. Before then, widows and unmarried women who owned property could vote in municipal elections everywhere but in British Columbia; women could graduate from universities, except in Québec; and they could practise law. The Dominion Women's Enfranchisement Association, founded in 1894, made some noises, but it was not until it was reorganized in 1907 as the Canadian Suffrage Association that serious action was taken. In June 1909 two thousand women from all over the world converged on Toronto for the meetings of the International Council of Women. They could hardly go unnoticed, especially with Ishbel in the chair.

The men had hardly recovered from this assault when, in November, Mrs. Emmeline Goulden Pankhurst, the famous English suffragette, arrived in Toronto. To their surprise, even her critics found her "a bright, intelligent, gracious, and feminine personality and a damn good speaker."

For Laurier, the women's issue was a matter for the provincial governments. Still, the seed had been planted, and the women would not go away.

~

Armand Lavergne, Bourassa's cousin, Émilie's and Joseph's son, and Laurier's fond child, had become a thorn in Laurier's flesh. He had watched him grow up, had worried about his inattention at school and his unwillingness to learn, and had guided him as if he were his own son. In his youth and early manhood, Armand had an uncanny resemblance to Laurier largely because of a similar shape of the mouth and arrangement of the teeth. No wonder many concluded that he was his love-son with Émilie. However, on close examination, it was easily revealed that Armand's hair, the shape of his face and eyes, and, above all, his voice were more those of his father, Joseph Lavergne, than of Laurier. In common with Laurier, however, Armand had style, he was romantic, independent, rebellious, and indolent, and he lived on a stage he had erected to play out a drama he was constantly creating. He was, like Laurier, charming and open, and he had a facility with words that was interesting and impressive. He also read an enormous amount of history. He was a nice-looking and bright young man, with a good memory, a sense of humour, a fine orator, and a follower more than a leader. At heart, Armand was a *mousquetaire* and, by temperament, a demagogue. His hatred of the *Anglais* made him a racist. To his credit, though, he was an ardent, if not a wise, *Canadien* nationalist. To the despair of his parents, he espoused Bourassa's cause, became his lieutenant, and devoted much of his energy to embarrassing and defeating Laurier, all the while proclaiming his love.

The four years (1904–08) Lavergne spent in Parliament were not a pleasant time for Laurier. When Armand began his political career, Laurier wrote to him: "Let me give you some advice. It comes from an old friend. Be loyal to your party, to which by tradition, by principle, and by conviction, you belong. Up to now you have been more insubordinate than anything else. Remember that your career will suffer if those who are interested in you are told constantly that your loyalty leaves much to be desired." At the beginning of 1907, he threw Lavergne out of the party for all intents and purposes by removing from him the control of patronage in his constituency. It pained him to do that. He was fond of Armand, but things were out of hand. In the spring of 1908, following Bourassa's example, Lavergne resigned his federal seat to run provincially. He didn't amount to much after that. He was too self-centred to be the team player that politics demanded.

But Armand kept in touch, especially when he needed assistance of some sort. When Laurier appointed Sir Louis-Amable Jetté as chief justice of Québec in 1909, however, Armand was unforgiving. Laurier had humiliated "his dear father," and no explanation could make him change his mind. Furthermore, Armand felt somewhat guilty that his "political attitudes" had endangered "the advancement of my father." Then, on 6 December, came the following letter:

> Only one thing pains me, it is that you may come to think that because I am honest and frank with you, I love you less and the *passé* — the past — doesn't count. Non, believe it does count always, especially when I battle you: the past is quite powerful. Every time duty calls me loudly, the past whispers softly: "Tu quoque Brute." I must appear to you as an ingrate. As God is my witness, I love you; but, and please forgive me, I love my country more!

Armand was, after all, Émilie's son.

~

On Wednesday, 12 January 1910, Laurier introduced a bill to create a Canadian Navy. Service would be voluntary, and the Canadian government could, in an emergency, place all or parts of it "at the disposal of His Majesty for general service in the Royal Navy" — but only with the consent of Parliament. He projected the construction of five cruisers and six destroyers, at a cost of approximately $11 milllion. The annual budget for the running of this Canadian Navy would be $3 million.

The need for Canada to develop this naval instrument was due primarily to the conditions prevailing in Europe. Germany was building a powerful navy. Knowledgeable persons in England estimated that, by 1912, the Germans would have between seventeen and twenty-five large ships threatening Great Britain and causing a general panic. (It turned out to be no more than nine dreadnought battle ships and cruisers.) Canada was under great pressure to help alleviate this threat. There were two ways to do that: one was a contribution in money to a single imperial navy; the other, the Canadian way, was to stand for self-government in naval defence.

The matter was discussed in the House in the session of 1909 and Laurier's resolution for "a Canadian naval force of our own" was adopted without division. In July, an Imperial Conference on Defence was held in London, where Canada was represented by Borden and Brodeur. When the Australians supported the Canadian view, it prevailed.

Then all hell broke loose. The jingoists, who were still quite numerous, rejected Laurier's plan. Rodmond Roblin, premier of Manitoba, branded it a "tin-pot navy." What was needed, they said, was a contribution of money — a sort of tribute to the mother country. In Québec, the *Nationalistes* and the Conservatives came to an understanding: no navy without a referendum. The excitation continued throughout the summer and the fall. And then came Laurier's bill.

Laurier was not interested in the jingoist solution presented by men "who carry abroad upon their foreheads imperial phylacteries, who boldly walk in the temple and there loudly thank the Lord that they are not like other British subjects, that they give tithes of everything they possess, and that in them alone is to be found the true incense of loyalty." As for those like Bourassa who wanted nothing to be done, he found sarcasm to deflate them: "I have dealt with those who blow hot; let me try a word now with those who blow cold." The issue had been talked about since 1902. Had they not read the documents? Were they not forgetting "that Canada was a country with two sea-coasts and exposed coast cities, a country with a large ocean trade and with abounding national revenues? You might as well tell the people of Montréal, with their half-million population, that they do not need any police force." No! "I am a Canadian first, last, and all the time."

The debate went on until 20 April, when Robert Borden's amendment for a contribution of two dreadnoughts to the Royal Navy, and no Canadian Navy without the direct approval of the people, was defeated. The Liberal press everywhere followed Laurier's lead; the Conservative one fought on. In Québec, Bourassa launched a crusade.

As in debates that involved the nationalism of Québec and the jingoism of Ontario, Laurier misread the signs. He was aware that he wasn't as popular as he would like to be, but he sincerely believed that "the sane elements will stay with us, and if so, we have nothing to fear." He was more concerned with the priests than with Bourassa. The clerical journals seized the issue to break the party. That, to Laurier, was "an abuse of religion."

Laurier was attempting once again to reconcile nationhood with empire-hood. Canada's existence as a nation was "the most anomalous that has yet existed." Canadians were British subjects and, at the same time, citizens of "an autonomous nation; we are divided into provinces, we are divided into races, and out of these confused elements, the man at the head of affairs has to sail the ship onwards." It could not be done on "pure idealism." It could only be done by a policy of action that could "appeal on the whole to all sections of the community." This had been his inspiration since he had assumed the leadership of the party, and he was certain it was the right thing to do, for it had brought "peace, harmony, and prosperity" to the country.

On the other hand, it hadn't been done without disappointment and some fancy footwork. He didn't expect this moment to be any different; "it will be of such a character as to give me many troubled hours." The only consolation he could offer to those on whom he was counting for support was that "it will probably be the last one." It was, as before, most necessary not to allow any section of the country to be isolated while nursing its resentment.

Bourassa, Lavergne, and the others were ready too. Bourassa founded *Le Devoir* in January 1910 primarily to beat Laurier. The mighty *nationaliste* leader of Québec had determined that he would replace Laurier in the consciousness and affection of the people. He would be their political and national leader, the prophet and the executor.

The Conservatives weren't any better in Québec or in Ontario. Aided by some Liberal recalcitrants — Sifton was as usual torn and tormented — Laurier was personally pilloried and his policy ridiculed. He read all about it, counteracted some of it, and let the madness go on as the bill passed the House and the Senate. In July, he went west.

〜

He had not been on a similar tour since 1894. He left Ottawa without Zoë on 6 July, travelling in a special car of the Canadian Northern which was attached to the Canadian Pacific Winnipeg Express. His first public meeting was in Port Arthur, and then he would proceed on the transcontinental he had fashioned for the rest of his journey. He would see for himself the "prosperity" he had helped bring to what was once a wilderness. The trip would take him to Winnipeg,

Saskatoon, Regina, Moose Jaw, Edmonton, Calgary, Banff, Vancouver, Victoria, and Prince Rupert, and dozens of places in between.

Everywhere he went, he was enthusiastically received. Thousands of people came to the railway stations to meet him, and thousands more attended his speeches. In many places they lined the road to wave as his train rolled by. Even in the middle of the night, they lit fires or held lanterns to greet him. Many midnights he spent on the platforms of small stations talking to the new citizens of his vast country. He was wined and dined and addressed to death. He took it all with equanimity, basking in his popularity and that of his government and his party. The weather was fine for the most part. Flags and bunting flew in the prairie wind. The press talked of royal welcomes and lauded Laurier as Canada's greatest son. He opened exhibitions, laid corner-stones, participated in parades, received bouquets, spent time with French-speaking Canadians, visited reserves and was created honorary chief, and made speeches — on his way to Edmonton he made seven in one day. Everywhere he went, he was overwhelmed by the growth that he saw. Someone told him that in 1894, Saskatoon had a population of 115 people; when he visited, the population was 14,000.

Children were everywhere — and they were his concern. In Edmonton the rally had to be held outside because there were so many people who wanted to hear him. He spoke from a balcony. All of a sudden, he stopped in his speech. He had noticed a small girl sitting alone on a ledge far above the ground, swinging her feet. He pointed at her and asked the officials: "Is that little one safe?" When they summoned a policeman to see about the child, he resumed his speech. In Manitoba there was another little girl who was not dressed prettily like those who presented him with flowers. She watched him as he stooped down to kiss their cheeks. She wanted to be part of it. Running to a field nearby, she picked an assortment of blooming weeds and came back to where he was. She got close to him, but an official shooed her away. He began to walk in her direction, stopped in front of her, and asked: "Were you good enough to mean those flowers for me?" She blushed and thrust the bouquet in his hands, frightened of what might happen. He bowed, took them, kissed her, and placed a flower in his boutonnière. She was a happy child.

He made speeches about the British Empire and Canada's place in it: "Our experience has no parallel in any part or any age of the world." About free trade:

"I have always been a free trader." About reciprocity with the United States: "Yes — but not at the price of the British preference." About being Canadians: "The newcomer accepts the rights of this land and also the duties of Canadian citizenship, for where there are rights, there are obligations." And about the navy: "The Canadian Navy has not, perhaps, commanded your attention; but it should, for it is your duty to have a share in defending the Empire." In Regina, where he opened the Provincial Fair, a Canadian by the name of Schmitz, who had recently arrived from Germany, told him that in another twenty years he would have a "generation of strong, healthy German boys" to man his navy. He was rather pleased with that. He invited British Columbians to get along with the "Asiatics." He was getting old, he pointed out often, and this was his last trip. But "when my eyes are closing in death, if I can look upon a united people, upon all the races which have been gathered here by our policy; if I can look upon them as true Canadians, all having in their hearts the greater pride of a Canadian nationality; then I will feel that my life has not been lived in vain, and I shall die happy."

However, the trip was not totally without difficulties. Many delegations came to harangue him — or present their views and opinions — on the railway that was his and the new one they wanted to Hudson Bay, on freight rates, on grain elevators, and, above all, on the tariff. The farmers were incensed that no free trade with the United States had followed in the four electoral victories they had given him. With no holds barred, they confronted him, quoting what he had said on his first visit and insisting on his telling them why he had been so reluctant to act. In Saskatoon, he was accused of "treachery" — one newspaper speaking of the "Arraignment of Sir Wilfrid." They were tired of promises; they wanted action. The secretary took copious notes, and Sir Wilfrid promised nothing. He had come to meet and hear the people, to acquaint himself with the new conditions in the West, and to report to his colleagues in Ottawa.

On his way to Edmonton in the first week of August, his train collided with a freight train a few miles from Moose Jaw, Saskatchewan. He was thrown violently to the floor, but was not seriously hurt. His car and those of the journalists were towed to Moose Jaw for a night of repair, and then they went on to Regina. There they switched to the tracks of the Canadian Northern Railway and proceeded directly to Battleford, where he spent a day resting. On 8 August, though, he was in Edmonton for a "western welcome by 7 p.m."

From Edmonton, he went to Banff to spend a day with Zoë, who had arrived by a leisurely route. Then, it was British Columbia, with "royal welcomes" again in Vancouver and Victoria and a boat ride to Prince Rupert, the town his railway had built. The last stop of his tour was on 2 September in Medicine Hat: "I left home a Canadian to the core. I return ten times more a Canadian. I have imbibed the air, spirit and enthusiasm of the West. I am a true Westerner henceforth: nay, I should say a Canadian, for we must in future aim to know the West and the East only in emulation of the best in each other."

By 7 September he was back in Ottawa. He had travelled ten thousand miles "through the boundless resources and regions" of the western part of his beloved country. Two days later, he left on a different voyage.

~

The International Eucharistic Congress of September 1910 was held in Montréal. It was an international event that brought together prelates, priests, nuns, and thousands of lay persons from Québec, from other provinces of Canada, and from all over the world to worship in the streets, to attend pageants, to take part in processions, and to hear sermons and speeches. It wasn't Laurier's kind of public meeting, but he had promised to attend and, as the Roman Catholic prime minister of Canada, it was hard to avoid. No sooner had he seen the program than he wanted to go home: the French-speaking Catholics gathered in one place, Notre Dame, and the English-speaking Catholics in St. Patrick's Church. It was as if God himself couldn't bring unity among His flock to worship Him. However, there were many events in which both groups participated. He was tired and would have preferred to join Zoë in Arthabaska.

It was a spectacular event, both spiritual and profane. The cardinal archbishop of Westminster made a fool of himself; Bishop Fallon of London, Ontario, chose Montréal to begin his crusade against the French or bilingual schools of Ontario, a crusade that almost tore the country apart a few years later; Laurier's speech in Notre Dame was lacklustre: "Our faith is the first duty of our Government, the security of our homes. If those who labour, who struggle, who delve, lose their belief in God, what will rest them?" Bourassa's speech was provocative: "We are only a handful, but we count for what we are, and we have the right to live." The bishops saluted him, the priests exalted him, and the students cheered.

It was at this moment that Laurier realized Bourassa's intention: the formation of a French and Catholic political force. He had worked hard to prevent that challenge, but Bourassa's "wild" speech had undone it all. A Catholic party would destroy the peace and harmony of Canada: "The rest of Canada would be arrayed against it" and "irreparable" harm would be done to the cause of the *Canadiens* and the Roman Catholics. The bishops and their priests didn't care: they were unwilling to realize that "this *furiosus*" was leading them to "the precipice."

Laurier went home rather sad and immediately began to put in effect the plan he had made in August for another appeal to Rome, to his friend Del Val. Lemieux, the postmaster general, was sent to attempt to deflate that new "religious crusade": it was always to be started again, for "these people do not want to learn anything and they do not know how to forget." And Laurier arranged to speak himself at an immense gathering in Montréal in October, a month after the Eucharistic Congress.

He was angry — and terrified of what might happen. He had to stop all this madness swirling around him. A large and enthusiastic crowd looked to his leadership to calm the hotheads in their midst. He succeeded. The navy, he explained, was necessary to defend Canada; it didn't mean conscription, for the service was totally voluntary — those who preached the contrary were liars. However, he wasn't there just for the navy. He was there to give battle for the hundredth time to that abominable sect, *les Castors*. Laurier didn't mince words:

> This violent section — you know it — comprises the Pharisee end of Canadian Catholicism; those who constitute themselves the defenders of a religion which no one attacks; those who handle the holy-water sprinkler as though it were a club; those who arrogate to themselves the monopoly of orthodoxy; those who excommunicate right and left all whose status is a little greater than theirs; those whom the people with their picturesque language designate under the name Castors.

Bourassa was the culprit, and Laurier had no hesitation in identifying him. Bourassa had lied and slandered at will, and was determined to impose his limited vision on the people of Québec.

Three days later, on 13 October 1910, Laurier named Joseph Lavergne's brother, Louis, the member for Drummond-Arthabaska, to the Senate. It was a test. It would become the most important by-election of his prime minister-ship. The campaign lasted until 3 November. Bourassa conducted a racist crusade, frightening the people with lies and distortions, and sending young men in military uniforms to call on the farmers of the county to tell them that their sons would be conscripted to fight wars in far-away continents. The women were asked: "Have you a husband? How many sons? What ages?" and the uniformed men wrote the answers in their large notebooks. "Why do you want to know all that?" the women asked. "We are preparing the lists of available men to serve in the Navy." And on and on it went.

Laurier was stupefied at the antics when he came to Arthabaska the day before the voting. The *Castors,* the clergy — they were at it again, using the same immoral tactics that their predecessors had used to defeat him in 1877. The next day, the Bourassa candidate won by a majority of 207.

"History teaches us that there are defeats which are more honourable than victories," Laurier said in the House during the session that followed. He wasn't discouraged. Pained: yes; doubtful about the future: yes; but discouraged: no. It was "the fate of war."

~

There was another death, that of Edward VII; another coronation, that of George V; and another Imperial Conference. A few hours before Laurier left to attend it, he wrote to Zoë, who was too blind, too deaf, and too incapaci-tated to go.

Château Frontenac, Québec
le 12 mai 1911

Ma chère bonne amie:
I have arrived in Québec and in a few hours, I will board the ship. I

have not left yet and already I want to be back. It would have been more pleasant to stay with you in our home.

Happily, the voyage will not last long and when I return, I will have to go back to work until the next election. When the election is over, whether I win or lose, I will retire. And then, there will be nothing to separate us.

Adieu. Au revoir.
Ton vieux mari qui t'aime toujours.
W.L.

14

"THAT IS ALL!"
6 OCTOBER 1911

A week after leaving Canada, Laurier, accompanied by Borden and Brodeur, arrived in Great Britain as guest of the king and queen. Again he stayed at the Hotel Cecil and was accorded all the courtesies of the previous visits. The Imperial Conference, which opened on 23 May 1911, held twelve sessions before it adjourned on 20 June, three days before the coronation of King George V and Queen Mary. The main topics on the table were the same as in previous conferences, except that New Zealand presented some foggy scheme for an Imperial Parliamentary Federation for the empire which Laurier declared to be "utterly impracticable." He was not about to accept that the government of Canada be responsible to some institution outside the country. While he was in his "negative" mood, he vetoed any attempt to have the British government "consult" with the dominions before undertaking any action that might bind the component parts of the empire: "We may give advice if our advice is sought; but if your advice is sought, or if you tender it, you must be prepared to back that advice with all your strength and take part in the war. We have taken the position in Canada that we do not think we are bound to take part in every war." On the question of trade, he had no more interest in 1911 than he did in 1897 for an imperial *Zollverein*. What he wanted and got was for Great Britain to stop binding Canada and other dominions by "Imperial Trade Treaties." That provision would ease trade negotiations with the United States. As for defence, Canada would build its own navy and it would not contribute money to the Royal Navy.

After the coronation, Laurier left almost immediately for Canada and arrived in Québec City on 10 July, where he was given a rousing welcome. To the 10,000 people massed on the Dufferin Terrace, he said rather proudly: "I am happy to have seen at the Imperial Conference the triumph of the principle which ought to be the basis of the security of the Empire; it is that every community, society, or nation shall govern itself according to the opinion of the people who comprise it." In Montréal 150,000 people greeted him. He had returned to Canada, he told them, "to fight the battle of reciprocity." Accordingly, at the end of July, Parliament was dissolved and an election called for 21 September.

~

By 1911 protectionism was out and free trade was in, at least in so far as the United States and Canada were concerned. Between November 1910 and the following January, the Canadians and the Americans came to a consensus that there ought to be reciprocity of trade between the two countries, and they argued on the form it should take. Then, on 26 January, Fielding presented his project to Parliament. There would be free entry on a wide list of products and manufactured goods; other items would come in at reduced or current rates. Whatever terms were given to the United States would also be granted to the United Kingdom and certain dominions. The reciprocity between Canada and the United States would be enacted through concurrent legislation in Parliament and Congress, instead of by an irrevocable treaty. It was a good deal.

Laurier and Fielding had finally accomplished — almost half a century later — what every government of Canada had attempted to do since the abrogation of the 1854 Reciprocity Treaty in 1864. It was an incredible *projet de pays*. It gave western Canada what it wanted, and it didn't weaken the manufacturing heartland: "All that we ask is to obtain for the man who works in the field the best possible remuneration for his labour." Laurier was convinced the plan could not be opposed.

It was. First came the vested interests of industry, railways, and banks — the same as in 1891. They determined, following Van Horne's advice, "to burst the damned thing." Then came the jingoists and the Imperialists: Canada was on its way to annexation; it was the end of the empire. Others wanted to "let well enough alone." Still others were concerned about risking the prosperity that had been achieved with a tariff that worked well. Some silly Americans didn't help when one of them proclaimed: "I hope to see the day when the American flag will float over every square foot of British North American possession clear to the North Pole."

In the House, every trick was used to delay the passage of the Bill and to agitate outside Parliament until after Laurier had returned from the Imperial Conference. Most of these obstructions were organized by Sifton, who had come to resent not being welcomed back into the Cabinet and who suddenly heard an inner call to defeat his leader. Laurier, who never was able to "fathom the reason" for Sifton's attitude, called him in for a chat:

"Why are you opposed to reciprocity?"

"Because I don't believe in it."

"You did once."

"Yes, but conditions have changed."

"No, it is you who have changed. Your opposition is personal. What is it?"

The conversation ended on that note. Sifton was vengeful towards Laurier, and he didn't care what the issue was. On the other hand, Laurier never believed what he heard about Sifton: that he "carried a knife in his boot for members of the government." He should have. Sifton was secretive, and for him there was only one loyalty: that to himself.

Exasperated by the opposition and the coalition developing against him and his policy in almost every part of the country, Laurier decided to go to the people, some three years into the mandate given to him in 1908. The campaign was all fury. The Conservatives, smelling blood, attacked everywhere, and Sifton led them. He masterminded the attacks against reciprocity both in and out of Parliament. He fought reciprocity in the cities of Ontario and no-popery in the backwoods, and everywhere he argued that Canada's birthright was being sold to the Americans. He agreed with Rudyard Kipling, who wired dramatically: "It is her own soul that Canada risks to-day." Less poetic were the slogans: "Vote against National Suicide," "A vote for Borden is a vote for King and flag," "The flag under which we stand is good enough for us," "A British subject I was born, a British subject I will die." It went on like that for seven weeks.

In Québec, not much attention was paid to reciprocity. Bourassa had no understanding of economics, and tariffs interested him even less. At the beginning, he spoke of it in favourable terms, but since his mission was to defeat

Laurier, he dismissed it as insignificant and concentrated on the navy. He had twenty-eight candidates nominated as *Nationalistes* and he allied them to the Conservative Party headed by an insignificant mouse by the name of Frederick-Debartzch Monk. Throughout the campaign, he branded Laurier as a traitor to his race: he had sold himself to the *Anglais* and had become the chief promoter of conscription and of *Canadien* participation in the wars of the empire; he was the "capitaine de la marine maudite — the captain of the god-damned navy." It was estimated that the capital of Bourassa's paper, *Le Devoir*, was increased by $200,000 during the campaign through Conservative largesse. Those who argued that Bourassa had been "bought" could hardly be accused of defamation.

Throughout the campaign, Laurier was confident and, above all, determined:

> Henry of Navarre at the battle of Ivry said: "Follow my white plume, and you will find it always in the forefront of honour." Like Henry IV, I say to you young men: "Follow my white plume" — the white hairs of sixty-nine years — and you will, I believe I can say it without boasting, find it always in the forefront of honour.

However, some didn't follow his white plume. On the night of 19 September, Laurier was in Montréal on his way towards Québec City. Bourassa, meanwhile, was inflaming a large throng of his followers. When the meeting was over, the mob emptied into the streets. As it happened, Laurier's car was caught in the midst of it: the car was immobilized frequently, powerful fists belonging to ugly faces pounded his windows while their feet kicked the tires, and others threw stones. The jeers and the noise were deafening and terrifying. The chauffeur managed to turn the car around and proceeded quickly to the Gare Viger. But the mob followed the old man right to his train, yelling over and over again and in cadence: "Bourassa! Bourassa!" Laurier was driven out of Montréal.

He went to Ontario and the Maritimes, but stayed much of the time in Québec. For a man of his age, his itinerary was awesome. He didn't spare himself: his policy was right for Canada. He would defend it wherever he could, and convince Canadians and *Canadiens* to accept it. Thousands gathered everywhere to hear him and they cheered for him. The question was, Would they vote for him? He was optimistic that they would:

I am branded in Québec as a traitor to the French, and in Ontario as a traitor to the English. In Québec, I am branded as a Jingo, and in Ontario as a Separatist. In Québec I am attacked as an Imperialist, and in Ontario as an anti-Imperialist.

I am neither. I am a Canadian.

Canada has been the inspiration of my life. I have had before me as a pillar of fire by night and as a pillar of cloud by day a policy of true Canadianism, of moderation, of conciliation. I have followed it consistently since 1896, and I now appeal with confidence to the whole Canadian people to uphold me in this policy of sound Canadianism which makes for the greatness of our country and of the Empire.

By Thursday, 21 September, voting day, he was in Québec City. Zoë stayed close to the telephone.

That day, he lost his gamble with the Canadian people. Though the popular vote was close — a margin of about 47,000 votes — the real determinator, the division of seats, astonished everyone: 134 Conservatives to 87 Liberals. In Ontario, Laurier was able to keep only 14 seats out of 89, and three Cabinet ministers were defeated. In Québec, he lost 27 constituencies to Bourassa (they would vote with the Conservatives), leaving him with 38 Liberals. In the Maritimes he barely hung on, but both Fielding and Borden were defeated. Manitoba voted against him, as did British Columbia, while Alberta and Saskatchewan accepted his reciprocity overwhelmingly. As for himself, he was elected by acclamation in Québec-Est. Later, a Bourassa supporter claimed that he had been drugged and forced to abandon his candidacy, but the wretched "candidate" wasn't able to prove his case.

It was over. The next day he took the train to Montréal, where David and other friends, alerted by the vigilant Zoë, who had talked to him the night before, went to the station to sympathize. He thanked them politely and continued on his journey. In Ottawa, only the chauffeur met him. He drove him home and to Zoë.

~

She is waiting alone in a straight chair in the hall. No one is around. Hardly any lights are turned on. She has had a cold dinner placed in his library. When she faintly hears the engine of the large car and sees dimly the headlights turning the corner of Laurier onto Chapel, she stands, pats her hair, straightens out her dress, and peers into what is now for her an almost total darkness. The door opens and she hardly sees him as he removes his coat and comes near her. She takes his hand and kisses it and tries to hold her tears. He smiles, and his lips find her forehead and linger there for a moment that is important to both of them. Together, they go up the stairs to their bedroom. He entrusts her to her Irish maid, while talking to her softly about going to bed. She nods in agreement and he leaves, turning at the door to smile at her, knowing well that she cannot see that far.

In his study, he hardly eats what has been put before him. His heart is so full of pain. To ease out of it, he walks, talking to himself. Governments are elected to be defeated eventually. He doesn't question the logic of that. So his heart is not breaking because of the loss of power. But he admits that he enjoyed having it and what went with it. Nor does he doubt the soundness of the policies and the record on which the election was fought. So many good men down to defeat, though — Fielding, Borden, Paterson, and Fisher. It wounds him, but it is not for that he grieves.

He sits down in his favourite armchair, now in its winter spot by the fireplace. He realizes then why it is that his heart aches so. "Québec! Mon Québec!" It is not so much that Bourassa robbed him of his victory. Nor is his heart grieving because a great number of his people have chosen Bourassa over him. They were duped! An immoral politician preyed on their fears and anxieties, as the bishops and the clergy had done for a considerable part of his political life. He understands that and he attributes no blame to the farmer and the worker, the father and the brother, or even to the sons who attacked his car a few nights before. His heart is aching because he will not be able to protect them anymore. They have become prisoners of a movement that is inimical to their best interests. They are isolated. He is terrified. And the tears come.

She is not asleep. She feels his tears through the walls that separate them. She gets out of bed, cannot find her slippers, but no matter. She gropes her way to the door, opens it and walks down the hall to where he is, hanging all the way on tables and chairs. Another door. She knows where he is sitting. She kneels beside him and takes him in her arms. She strokes his hair, as she had in Arthabaska in the defeat of 1877. And she whispers: "Le rêve! You still have the dream." And he sobs on her shoulder.

~

In 1911, when Laurier left office, there were 7,204,527 persons living in Canada, an increase of almost two million since the turn of the century. The value of Canada's exports was close to $400 million, while that of the goods imported was in the vicinity of $500 million, bringing slightly under $84 million in duties. The federal revenues were close to $102 million and the expenses chargeable to income were $81 million. It was a fast-growing country, and a prosperous one, that Laurier left to his successor.

His legacy in every aspect of Canadian life was impressive and worth building on — subject only to the capacity of the new government to dream large dreams. Laurier peopled the West. He had not done it by himself, but through his leadership the day was seized, the conditions were exploited, the appropriate men were given free rein to bring in the Canadians-to-be. He succeeded. He stopped emigration to the United States. He harnessed the energy and creativity of the people of Canada to fuel industry, to till vast lands, to build railways that would bring the wheat, lumber, and minerals to market, and to better the condition of the labouring man.

He freed his country from the tentacles that held her bound to an entrenched and arrogant empire. He took Canada as a colony and he made her into a dominion. He was left a dependent country and he fashioned an independent nation, treating with European and Asian countries in the light of her own best interests. He inherited a process that had paralysed Canada in her dealings with the United States, and he made Canada the unquestioned master of that relationship.

Over the years, though, he lost something of his internal power. His first two terms were moments of great creative energy; his third term revealed weaknesses in his leadership and in his management of men which he was not able to overcome; and in the fourth term, he found the spirit again. It was, however, too late. As a party leader, he was too detached, and trusting, and his personal popularity made him feel too secure. His natural indolence took over and he let things go; his instinct to avoid controversy allowed him to tolerate freeloaders and sycophants; and many of his policies, like the railroad one, disintegrated in shambles. He misread the stars too often. He should have seen through Bourassa, Lavergne, and Sifton much earlier than he did, but he hoped for the best too long. And too often he wasn't clear what he wanted to achieve, as he tried to play both sides of the coin at the same time. It injured him.

Did he leave a better Canada, more gentle, more united? On the whole, he thought yes. However, the deep divisions in the land were still acutely present. British Columbia was playing out its phobia against Asians; the West had begun its march to alienation, the victim, it claimed, of the vested interests of central Canada; Ontario was torn by its imperial preoccupation and its Protestant prejudices; Québec was sinking in the morass of a narrow and confining nationalism; and the Maritime provinces often felt excluded — still, after forty-four years of Confederation, uncertain of their future in Canada.

The people of Canada had lived through fifteen years of a dream, a large dream of a Canadianism with compassion, respect, moderation, and conciliation at the centre of it. They might not accept or even live it as fully as Laurier wished, but he had indicated the road to take. Often he marched down it an isolated and lonely figure, but quite visible in the darkness of prejudice and posturing. It was a fine example to bequeath to a country still in its adolescence.

He had the satisfaction, too, of knowing that he went down fighting for a basic Liberal principle — that of free trade. Blake, who had returned to Canada and was near death, understood:

Mr. Blake expressed entire approval of your reciprocity campaign.
This morning the nurse told him of the election and he said slowly:

"I am sorry for Laurier. He is a fine fellow and I always liked him." That is a voice almost from the grave, as I fear we must consider it, the voice of one along with whom you fought many hard battles. Mrs. Blake wishes me to send you her love (that was the word she used) and to say how real are her regrets but, at the same time, how glad she is that you will have a period of comparative rest.

~

Was he to stay? Was he to go? During the campaign, he had said in Saint-Jérome that he would retire if he was defeated. In two months he would be seventy years old. He had served thirty-eight years in the House of Commons, twenty-four as leader of the Liberal Party, and fifteen as prime minister. Was that enough? He was the only one left of the class of 1874. Had he fully satiated the bug of politics? Had not the time come for him to hand over the burden to a younger man? To be with Zoë? To read to his heart's content? To write a history of Canada since Confederation or a life of one of the public men he admired the most, Antoine-Aimé Dorion?

On the Saturday and Sunday following the elections, he talked with Zoë, he telephoned party stalwarts, and David came to dinner. The consensus fitted in with his plans. With Fielding gone, who was there to lead the party, hold it together, keep Québec, and see beyond the immediacy of the moment? He searched as objectively and as dispassionately as he could, but he saw no one. Many could in time, but not at this particular time. Moreover, was he to leave the day after being defeated? What about the policies — reciprocity, the Canadian Navy, the West, the transcontinental railways? Was he to have them discarded by the wayside? What he needed was time to educate and to convince. And what of the dream of Canadianism and of Québec's place within it? If he left, he would abandon his province and his people to Bourassa's folly and mischief. Surely that could not be.

He returned to his office in the East Block and, for two weeks, closed the books on his administration. He was surprised at how much there was to do. Then the day came.

~

When he awoke at his usual hour of 8 a.m., Zoë was already downstairs. More in habit than with a desire to know, he looked at the calendar on his night table. It was Friday, 6 October 1911, the feast of St. Bruno. He didn't remember who that saint was. With the aid of the valet, he dressed and went down to breakfast in the pleasant morning room he and Zoë liked so much.

"Bonjour!" said Zoë, as the maid waited by the kitchen door.

"Bonjour, ma bien aimée! You slept well? I did." He kissed her on the forehead, went to his place, and slowly ate his breakfast. When he had finished and poured himself a cup of tea, she said:

"Aujourd'hui?"

"Oui, today. I have an appointment with his Excellency at three o'clock this afternoon. It is all right, Zoë. Do not fret!"

He went upstairs to his secretary, Lucien Giguère. They handled whatever correspondence there was to do, and Laurier asked that the car be brought around. The butler helped him into his coat and, after seeing Zoë and reassuring her again, he was driven to Parliament Hill.

At 1:30 p.m. the Cabinet assembled in the Privy Council Chamber. The members were all there: Cartwright immediately on his right, a senator, five years his senior, a colleague since 1874 but never a friend; the outgoing Murphy, whom Zoë had plotted often to get married, as she had with the other two bachelors in the Cabinet: Fisher and King; Aylesworth — more deaf every day; the very dependable Lemieux — he was so young when the bug bit him; Sir Frederick William Borden, present at the beginning and now defeated; the newcomer Béland; Fisher, his friend from the Eastern Townships, no longer a member by the will of the people; Pugsley, a former premier of New Brunswick, a colleague since 1907, whom Laurier hardly knew; Fielding to his left, confidant, friend, and successor-to-be — if fate determined it; the ever persistent and faithful Graham, temporarily out of a seat, but to be nurtured for his leadership potential; the fastidious Paterson, there since the beginning; Templeman, the minister from British Columbia; and Mackenzie King, the man to watch. Not at the table, though he had been invited, was Jacques Bureau. All of them, but six, would be around to help him rebuild and refurbish the party. The others, he hoped, would be returned soon.

He remained standing, ever so erect, leaning on the back of his prime ministerial chair. He informed them that he would present his resignation and that of the Cabinet to the governor general, the Duke of Connaught, son of Queen Victoria, at 3 o'clock that afternoon. He asked them to be in their offices should they be needed. The business was done.

Looking at a point above their heads, he said with his voice less audible on the last three words than on the first two: "Well, gentlemen, that is all!" He turned and, with his head held high and a sure gait, he walked quickly to the little door that led into an anteroom.

The dream remained.

15

LEADER OF THE OPPOSITION
1911–1919

Laurier was leader of the opposition. From that position he would reinvigorate the party, educate the population about the meaning and value of his ideas, recapture Québec, confront the Tories, and wait for the seed to germinate and ripen. With the unwilling help of the new prime minister, Robert Borden, he almost did it. His failure was due to a circumstance that changed the history of the world and the nature of Canada: the First World War.

The first task was to mould the caucus into an effective fighting force. He met members regularly; he convened them in small groups to discuss issues of importance; he gave them tools such as an Information Office, which Mackenzie King directed; and he visited as many of their constituencies as time permitted. He worked hard. He followed the same course in his dealings with the party outside the House. He answered his voluminous correspondence on time; he stored away important information that his informants scattered across the country fed him; he revived the political clubs in Québec that Tarte had created so long ago and applauded the creation of the Association de la jeunesse libérale, whose mission it was to wrest the young from Bourassa's embrace; he laid the groundwork for a central party office; and he attended regional and provincial party conventions. He planned well for his inevitable "tussle with the Tories," which would come in 1915 at the latest — and earlier if he could manage it.

The second task was to get Fielding, Graham, Fisher, Borden, and King re-elected. But he was successful only with Graham. Fielding and Borden didn't try, Fisher was defeated in Châteauguay in 1913, and King had to wait for a suitable constituency. One by-election pleased Laurier considerably, even though he didn't allow a Liberal to contest the seat: Hochelaga on the Island of Montréal.

There Bourassa's nationalists battled the *Canadien* Conservative candidate, who, although he had been elected with their support in 1911, didn't want to have anything more to do with them. The Bourassa nominee was soundly beaten. It was, observers said, a "crushing defeat" for Bourassa.

And he did what he did best — he talked. Speech followed upon speech, perhaps sixty in 1912 and 1913. He used them to expose the policies that had been rejected and to educate the electorate in their possibilities. His first public sortie was in Montréal, where the youth association organized a public demonstration for him on 8 January. It was a heartwarming success. They were there by the thousands, not because he could grant them favours, but because they loved him and they wanted him to know it. He thanked them: "The champions of the liberal thought may have been vanquished; but the idea is still there to inspire future victories." He sensed that Bourassa was beginning to pale.

Two months later he was celebrating Graham's victory: "Very deeply do I appreciate the continuance of your wonderful confidence, and I am prepared to remain at the head of the Liberal Party so long as you want me, and so long as God spares me and blesses me with the perfect health that He is giving me today." On another occasion he spoke about reciprocity: "O men of little faith who refused to open the avenues of wider trade: I have more faith in you than you have in yourselves." To him, and he expressed it often, Canada had in its veins "the strength of a young giant." He planned a trip to the West in the fall of 1912, but had to be satisfied with a tour of Québec and Ontario. Between 7 September and 29 October he visited fifteen communities in these two provinces and made thirty-five speeches to 150,000 or 200,000 people. These were remarkable meetings. He was no defeated leader, but the most popular living human being in Canada. He was in close contact again with the affection of the people, the breadth of his popularity, and the magic of his words.

The year 1913 wasn't much different from 1912: he gave as many speeches, in as many cities and towns, and to even more people, particularly young people. He spoke in universities and colleges, where thousands of students flocked to hear him: "If I were your age," he advised, "I would not leave school until I could write and speak French." He courted the business community, which was having serious second thoughts about what it had done to itself in 1911. The seed was germinating and would bear fruit. It was inevitable. Six days after his seventy-third birthday, thousands of telegrams and letters had poured in from the king on down, he addressed the question of the military build-up in Europe: "The condition of Europe is the disgrace and shame of the day. Europe is an armed camp."

It was, though, in Parliament that the weight of the party was to be felt. He took to being the leader of the opposition. It was an honourable legislative post and it paid an additional stipend of $7500. He found, however, that it didn't give him the ample time to himself many had predicted. He was in the House almost every day and he directed the debates. This was particularly so in the tumultuous confrontation over Borden's naval policy in 1913.

In 1909 and 1910 Borden was practically in accord with Laurier on this issue, and in the elections of 1911 he was almost totally silent on it. When he assumed power, he didn't repeal Laurier's Naval Service Act, but he didn't build the navy either. Most of 1912 went by without any policy, even though he kept insisting that "vigorous, earnest action" was necessary. Since Borden was a closet imperialist, he had to wait to unravel his plan until after his visit to Great Britain in the summer of 1912. There, under Winston Churchill's tutorship, Borden embraced the idea of centralizing the empire, against which Laurier had fought so valiantly for fifteen years. When Borden returned to Canada, he introduced his own naval bill on 5 December. Canada was to pay a tribute of $35 million dollars to the British government as her contribution to the naval defence of the empire. With that pledge came an understanding that Canada would have a voice in imperial foreign policy.

In a caucus meeting held the next day, the Liberals agreed unanimously that the battle for the soul of Canada was on and that Laurier's naval policy was the instrument to keep it safe. He led the attack in the House, a hard campaign that lasted until closure was finally imposed on 23 April 1913. Then the Senate — there were sixty-two Liberal senators and nineteen Conservative ones — took over and defeated Borden's naval solution. During the debate, Churchill threatened to cross the ocean to supervise the proceedings in the Canadian Parliament and put some sense in those recalcitrant colonials. He was told to stay home.

Meanwhile, Laurier was reconquering Québec. The alliance between Bourassa and the Conservatives, which had been launched with only one purpose in mind — to dethrone Laurier as leader of the *Canadiens* and to crown Bourassa — had collapsed by the end of 1913. The Conservatives were not as devoted to

Canadien causes as Laurier had been: in the extension of the boundaries of Manitoba, the Laurier-Greenway Settlement didn't even apply, and then came the fatal blow — Borden's naval policy and his view of Canada's place in the empire. Across the province, the people began to feel sorry that they had humiliated Laurier in 1911 by lending an ear to Bourassa's diatribes. They came to recognize Bourassa for what he was: a shallow man, an impotent man, and a man whose ideas were weakening their place in Confederation. He would not even run in any elections. Laurier, in contrast, was still at the centre of the political life of the country; he was the most loved and respected of Canadians; his dignity in defeat, his charm in conciliating diverse points of view, and his tenacity in standing up for his principles turned many of them around. They hoped that soon they would be given an opportunity to repair the damage they had caused in 1911.

~

Séraphin Gauthier passed away in Montréal on 4 January 1912. Laurier and Zoë went to the funeral and remembered their courtship and youth. Edward Blake died in Toronto on 1 March 1912, in the middle of the naval debate. In September, Richard Cartwright followed. There were fewer and fewer left.

Meanwhile, the minister of public charity, Zoë, continued her lobbying for her pet causes, mainly artists. Borden, with his usual courtesy, instructed his ministers to assist her in any way they could.

They took trips together, even though she wasn't as keen as before: her infirmities, limiting as they were, might cause Laurier embarrassment. He would have none of it. And so they went to Virginia for two weeks in January 1912 and to the White Mountains in August, travelling south after that. A year later, they spent some time with the Mulocks in Newmarket, Ontario. And there was always Arthabaska.

On 2 June 1912 the Grand Trunk opened its new $2 million hotel in Ottawa, the Château Laurier. It had been scheduled to open in April, but the sinking of the *Titanic* on 15 April, in which the chairman of the Grand Trunk Railway, Charles Melville Hays, drowned, delayed the opening. Laurier was the first to sign the guest register. However, he wasn't altogether enchanted. The Grand Trunk had commissioned a friend of the Lauriers', the French sculptor

Paul Chèvre, to create a marble bust of Laurier. He came to see it on the day before the opening. He was furious: the nose didn't resemble his in any way, shape, or form. A workman had dropped the sculpture, chipping the elegant nose in the process. A local sculptor had been brought in to repair the damage but Laurier wasn't pleased with the result and left the hotel in a huff.

~

Laurier was in Arthabaska under his maples when the news arrived of the assassination of the Archduke Francis Ferdinand at Sarajevo on 28 June 1914. He didn't grasp fully what it meant either for Europe or for Canada. He stayed where he was and waited for developments. They came with electrifying speed. By the beginning of August, it was apparent that war was imminent and that Great Britain and the empire, including Canada, would be ensnared. On the morning of 4 August he took the train to Ottawa; that night, at 8:00, the governor general was advised that Great Britain had declared war on Germany and her allies. The First World War, with all its tragedies and loss of life, was launched, and Laurier's four-year nightmare began. When the war ended in 1918, all he had struggled for during his entire life seemed to lie in pieces at his feet. But was Canada, really, rent apart on that glorious day when peace returned to the world? Or had he prevented it?

In the first two years of the war, the nightmare was contained. His position was clear and simple: "I have often declared that if the mother country was ever in danger, or if danger ever threatened, Canada would render assistance to the fullest extent of her power." He declared a "truce to party strife" and ordered the members of his caucus, his organizers across the country, his supporters, and the researchers and writers of party publications to abstain from embarrassing Borden's government in that "time of national danger." During the first war session of Parliament in Canada's history, which opened on 18 August, he reiterated his point of view:

> Let the friends and foes of Great Britain know that there is in Canada but one mind and one heart, and that all Canadians stand behind the mother country, conscious and proud that she has

engaged in this war, not from any selfish motive, for any purpose of aggrandizement, but to maintain untarnished the honour of her name, to fulfil her obligations to her allies, to maintain her treaty obligations, and to save civilization from the unbridled lust of conquest and power.

At the same time, he appealed to the young men from among his own people:

If my words can be heard beyond the walls of this House in the province from which I come, among the men whose blood flows in my own veins, I should like them to remember that in taking their place today in the ranks of the Canadian army to fight for the cause of the allied nations, a double honour rests upon them. The very cause for which they are called upon to fight is to them doubly sacred.

That was his policy. That would remain his policy throughout the war. If young men from across Canada volunteered, if older men did no mischief, if everyone was temperate in language, if politicians put aside their political rivalries and concentrated on doing what was right, if conciliation and moderation remained the corner-stones of the edifice of Canada — then the country would pull out of the war united and intact. To achieve all those "ifs," he devoted his time and his energy the next four years.

His recruitment efforts were extraordinary, particularly in Québec. Between the declaration of war in August 1914 and Canada Day in 1916, he made fourteen recruiting speeches to an average audience of 5000; at Sohmer Park in Montréal, 20,000 came to hear him. In addition, he gave more than twenty speeches on various occasions outside the House of Commons, and several in the House. In all those speeches, his message was clear:

Let me tell the young people here tonight that I envy them the youth which enables them to make such sacrifice for Canada, for Great Britain, France and Belgium. It is a sacrifice, for some of those who will go will make a pact with death. Many who will go will never again see their native land. They will sleep in that of their forefathers.

It is a sacrifice that is quite voluntary. Canada is an absolutely free
country. What has been done up to the present, what will be done
in the future, will be absolutely voluntary.

He didn't think of himself or his prestige; nor did he rely on his advanced age
to protect him from his duty. The policy of voluntary recruitment had to work
— and it did. There were approximately 1,270,000 eligible men in Canada.
Borden promised 500,000 of them to the imperial war effort. By 1 June 1916,
334,736 had already enlisted, 210,000 of them in 1915 alone. Laurier was most
optimistic.

He continued to abstain from partisan politics, though doing so was most
difficult. Patronage, corruption, some clever accounting practices, and the need
to take political advantage of the war situation by calling an election were temp-
tations that were hard to overcome. Laurier would have no election — and the
people backed him. The aggressive charlatans of the Conservative Party had to
give way in the face of a strong negative public opinion.

Laurier and Zoë spent some time in Arthabaska, and in July 1915 they
visited Sydney Fisher in the Eastern Townships. By this time, Laurier wasn't well
at all. He was in great pain from an abscess in his mouth, and he felt weak with
the recurrence of the muscle malady that had afflicted him a few years earlier.
He managed, though, to gather his energy and, in early August, he was at Saint-
Lin, where eight thousand people came to honour him. The family — nephews
and nieces, their children and grandchildren — was still there. He enjoyed being
with them and was sorry that Zoë's ailments prevented her from coming out.
"Whatever the vicissitudes and the hazards to which men of politics are
exposed," he said with great emotion, "there is nothing dearer to them than the
corner of the earth where they were born." He challenged the young men of his
audience to enlist and he asserted for the sake of the older members of his audience: "The fear of conscription in Canada is as groundless now as it was in
1911." The war was a "holy cause!"

A month later he was in the hospital in Ottawa. He was at a recruiting rally
in Napanee when, under the intense heat of the day and his dilapidated condition, he fainted. He spent two weeks in hospital, where he was operated on to
remove the abscess. Thousands of telegrams and letters poured in at his home,

at his office, and at party headquarters. When he recovered, he pursued his work: "They who have real patriotism," he said, "are they who are working for reconciliation, who are helping to sweep away the old divisions, who are working to restore harmony among the people on a basis acceptable to all."

The clouds, however, were gathering — and the nightmare became excruciating.

~

For the first two years of the Great War, the Canadian people had sustained an enormous war effort. The sons of Canada were engaged on many fronts on Europe, where their courage, their audacity, and their fortitude became profoundly embedded in the Canadian psyche. In the trenches of France, they discovered each other and liked what they saw. There, "Englishmen" were transformed into Canadians and "French Canadians" into *Canadiens*. On the front at home, the same valour, the same daring, and the same capacity for endurance were also present. Women manned the factories, old men worked the fields, and grandmothers minded the young so their parents could do their part. It was a grand effort.

But the war was taking its dues. There were thousands of casualties, as the strife was to kill 60,661 Canadians and *Canadiens,* wound another 172,950, and leave 20,115 widows, orphans, and dependent parents, and 77,967 with disabilities. The national debt was skyrocketing, as was the cost of living. General dissatisfaction was smouldering under the surface. There was massive corruption in the procuring and manufacturing of munitions. And Borden seemed incapable — or unwilling — to stop it. The country was tense, and mischief almost impossible to avoid.

The life of the twelfth Parliament, elected in 1911, was to expire in the autumn of 1916. Borden wanted its term extended until a year or so after the end of the war. Laurier's caucus was divided on the request and it was left for him to decide. He was of the opinion that an extension was reasonable, but only for a year. That meant that there would have to be an election by 7 October 1917. In the meantime, he and the Liberals agreed that the war situation was of "extreme gravity." Consequently, he pledged, "I will, in the future, as from the first, to the fullest extent of my ability, facilitate all necessary war measures."

Throughout the year, he continued to speak extensively on recruitment and the war effort: "Canada has a direct interest in this war, but I go much further and I say that there is not today a civilized nation in the world which has not an interest in this war." He continued to oppose conscription: "There is to be no conscription in Canada." He was a pacifist, as he had always been and would always be. But all the pacifists of Europe, of Great Britain and the civilized world agreed that Germany must be crushed: "What comes after peace must depend upon the extent of our victory." Still, "love is better than hate; faith better than doubt." In the House of Commons, he battled corruption, fraud, favouritism, extravagance, and injustice.

~

At 9:00 in the evening of Thursday, 3 February 1916, the chief doorkeeper of the House of Commons rushed into the Chamber and called out: "There is a big fire in the reading room; everybody get out quickly." He apologized later to the Speaker for being so bossy. The twenty members who were in the House rushed out of the building without any thought of their belongings. No one picked up the mace.

The fire started in the reading room of the House of Commons situated between the Chamber and the Library of Parliament. Its ceiling, walls, floor, and desks were made of white pine. Two ladies were in the room at the time; one escaped, but her companion remained behind and noticed that the flames were coming from a shelf under one of the desks. A constable attempted to stop the fire with an extinguisher, but the chemicals ignited the newspaper collection in the room. At 8:57 the fire alarm rang at fire station 8 and, within three minutes, the firefighters had arrived. Another alarm was sounded at 9:05, but by then the fire had spread to the roof of the building and the Chamber of the House of Commons was ablaze.

As soon as he saw the fire, the parliamentary librarian closed the heavy iron doors between the Parliament Buildings and the library. A favourable southward wind — favourable at least to the library — pushed the flames away from it towards the Centre Block, and the fire that had started on the roof of the library was quickly extinguished.

However, the destruction continued. The Center Block soon became engulfed in flames and at 11:00 p.m. the fire "began its ascent" of the Victoria Tower, lighting window after window "as it raced from floor to floor." At 9:00, 10:00, and 11:00 p.m. the tower clock struck the hour, as it had done for decades. It was unable to finish its midnight count. "At its last knell, the bell crashed down into the depths of the Tower" and the "clock mechanism faltered at 12:30 a.m. and the hands stopped." An hour later, the crown of the tower collapsed, and at 1:21 a.m. the tower itself "shuddered on its massive foundations and came down with a tragic crash that shook the place for blocks around." By 2:00 a.m. the fire was under control.

Sir Robert Borden was in his office in the new West Wing. As soon as he was told of the fire, he left, crawling on his hands and knees, hatless and coatless, and with a white handkerchief over his face. Someone outside lent him a hat and a fur-lined coat while an aide went to his house to fetch what was needed to keep the prime minister warm. The Speaker rescued his children from his apartment in the Centre Block. The governor general, whose brother, Edward VII, had laid the corner-stone of the building in 1860 when he was Prince of Wales, rushed in from Rideau Hall. Shortly afterwards Laurier drove up in his car. He had been at a concert at the Russell Theatre and, as soon as the news was brought to him, he came to the Hill. The three most important men in the country, along with members of the Senate and the House of Commons and a large number of citizens, stood around powerless to act. Some quick action, though, saved the Senate Chamber from total destruction. Sparks Street was by then filled with people and with cabs of all sorts. The restaurants stayed open practically all night; the Victorian Order of Nurses set up three stations on the site; Sam Hughes, the minister of militia, called in the army; and the mayor of Montréal, who was also an MP, arranged for firefighters and equipment, and for a train to be ready in case of need. The Canadian poet Duncan Campbell Scott described the fire as "terrible and tragic," as the "most terrifying and beautiful sight" he had ever seen.

Laurier's office was in a shambles, like the rest of the building. The reporter for the Montréal *Standard* reported that

Outside Sir Wilfrid Laurier's office, his secretary's room is a mess.

The roll-top desk is smashed in and ice and charcoal abound. The clock upon the wall is burned and broken — and tells twenty-one minutes to nine. In Sir Wilfrid's office, all the furniture is gone. The floor is covered with three-quarters of an inch of yellow ice and knobs of discoloured material — icicles the wrong way up. An ice encrusted cuspidor remains. On the floor by the cupboard, a volume leans against a door embedded in an inch of ice through which the title page is clear, "The Many-Mansioned House and Other Poems" by Edward William Thomson. It is the only poetry of the ice age you have seen, and for a moment you understand the passion which makes a souvenir hunter out of a human being.

On the walls down which the water has streamed, three pictures remain — a photograph of Mr. Asquith behind where Sir Wilfrid used to sit; one of Lloyd George on the western wall, and a water colour scene.

What the reporter didn't write in his article was that many of Laurier's personal and political papers were destroyed.

Seven persons died in the fire: the MP for Yarmouth, Nova Scotia; the assistant clerk of the House of Commons; a constable of the Dominion Police Force; a steamfitter; a post office employee; and two ladies, guests of the Speaker of the House and his wife, who were in the Speaker's apartment. The ladies had run back to fetch their furs. The firefighters found them on the floor at the end of the corridor with "their hands clasped around their heads, hair scorched and garments considerably burned." They had both died of suffocation due to smoke inhalation.

In the middle of the night, Borden held a Cabinet meeting at the Château Laurier and it was decided that the House of Commons would reconvene the next afternoon at 3:00 in the auditorium of the Victoria Memorial Museum on Metcalfe Street. The Senate, which was then in recess, was assigned a large room that "had housed fossils and extinct leviathans." A few nasty souls saw "the hand of political fate" in such an accommodation.

When the House reconvened, the mace and the Speaker's throne came from the Senate Chamber, and there was a table and chairs for the officials of the House, desks for Borden and Laurier, benches for the members of the House of Commons, and a nice rug on the floor. The meeting lasted for forty minutes. Borden read messages from the king and the governor general and spoke sadly of the building that was gone. When his turn came, Laurier was practically in tears. He paid tribute to the building that was now "a mass of ruins" and to those who had died. When he came to the two ladies, he could hardly be heard:

> And what are we to say, Sir, of the loss of those two young ladies, young happy mothers, young happy wives, bright as the lark in the blue sky of the morning, full of life, full of contentment, and appreciating the benefit of their station visiting old friends in their present high station, and now no more.

The fire had been an accident.

~

Three months after the horrible fire, Laurier finally took up the cause of the *Canadiens* in Ontario who were, under Regulation 17, being denied the right to teach their children in the French language. The new assault on language had begun in 1912, when the Keewatin district of the Northwest Territories was annexed to Manitoba. In celebration of that fine moment, *Canadiens* and Roman Catholics living there were deprived of the rights they had always enjoyed. There was no agitation, except for some tempestuous statements by Bourassa and Lavergne. In Ontario, however, it was a different matter, not so much in 1912, but certainly thereafter. Under the influence of Bishop Fallon of London, Ontario, a priest from Ottawa who had always despised *Canadiens* and couldn't understand why they were given the right or the permission to maintain bilingual schools in the capital, the Ontario government in 1912 passed Regulation 17, which forbade teaching in French past grade one and limited it to one hour a day thereafter. *Canadiens* living in Ottawa defied the regulation. Laurier didn't intervene, hoping, as was his wont, that sanity would prevail.

The issue continued to fester, fed by the usual rhetoric on both sides of the great divide. It became more intense in response to the civil disobedience of the mothers and *Canadien* ratepayers of the capital. In 1915, Laurier had tried to effect a compromise through the leader of the provincial Liberals of Ontario, but to no avail. In 1916 it was time to act. At that moment, John Wesley Dafoe came to call. He was by then fifty years old and still the editor-in-chief of the *Manitoba Free Press*. He had heard that the "old man," through "a wonderful stroke of tactics . . . was going to strengthen himself in Québec and at the same time do no harm in Ontario" — and he wished to have his say. On arriving in Ottawa, he found that Laurier wanted a motion about Regulation 17 introduced in the House and voted upon; he would free his party from the usual discipline, but he expected to be supported. Dafoe met him in his office on the third floor of the museum and came quickly to the point: "Sir Wilfrid, you can't go on with this. I appreciate your personal views of the matter, but politically, it is folly. The Ontario and western Liberals are in open revolt. The feeling in Ontario is absolutely in favour of enforcing Regulation 17. The people in that province, as in the West, are utterly opposed to granting greater privileges to the French. Canada is not a bilingual country. One language; one nation. It is the only way Canadians can be made out of the diverse elements of the many races in the West." He paused to estimate the effect of his words. Sir Wilfrid looked out the window and didn't give himself away. Dafoe was left to add, lamely: "The party will be irrevocably split."

Laurier asked quietly: "Is not justice a Liberal principle worth fighting for?" To that, Dafoe replied that since education was a provincial matter, there was no reason to involve the federal Parliament. Laurier agreed but reminded Dafoe that "the dominion Parliament, on both sides, whilst refusing to interfere with provincial legislation, has made representations to legislatures which, in many instances, have produced most salutary effects and a modification of the legislation complained of. That is all I am doing."

The conversation went around in circles. Finally, Laurier zeroed in on what was really bothering Dafoe and his friends: "My dear Dafoe, we have known each other for a long time. I therefore take the liberty of asking you if this attitude of Ontario and of the West which you have just described is not due to . . ."

"Yes, Sir Wilfrid. The French are not doing their part in this war, which is engaging all *our* energies, but not theirs."

Laurier knew that. And he also knew that one of the main reasons for the difficulties in recruitment among *Canadiens* was that Ontario, by Regulation 17, had given Bourassa a splendid opportunity to denounce Canadian participation in the war, since the Ontarians didn't behave much better than the Germans. "Help me remove the irritant, Dafoe, and the situation, I have no doubt, will change."

Dafoe looked sullen. "The party," he said with some viciousness, "will not follow you. Furthermore, Sir Wilfrid, we shall not allow the French to impose their will on the rest of Canada."

"On the other hand, you are allowed to impose your will on us. Isn't that so?"

There was no answer. The old man smiled sadly and said more to himself than to his visitor: "Is this what Liberalism has come to? A party of extremism! I have lived too long." But realizing that he was embarrassing Dafoe, he looked at his guest while leaning on his desk:

"I do not find in the Liberal party of today the same feeling that existed when you and I were younger. You were hardly out of school when I first met you. Now, you too have changed. As for myself, I can honestly say that I have always acted, and the party which I lead has always acted, on the principle that where there was an injustice to undo, I, we, would be there. This, obviously, is no longer the case."

There was no room for reconciliation, so he said simply: "Good afternoon, my dear Dafoe. And thank you for all the help you have given us in the past."

His small office seemed smaller than it was and even more confining than usual, making pacing difficult. It was April, and the weather didn't know how to behave any more than the Liberals. With the help of Ernest Lapointe, who had not spoken a word of English when he first arrived in Ottawa as a young man in 1904 but had managed to teach himself the language, he had prepared a resolution to be presented to the House on 9 May. It invited the Legislative Assembly of Ontario, very respectfully, to see "the wisdom of making it clear that the privilege of the children of French parentage of being taught in their mother tongue be not interfered with," while at the same time recognizing the necessity "of every child being given a thorough English education."

While the caucus was deliberating his resolution, he received letters from Fielding and other political supporters urging him to abandon his plan. To one he advised with annoyance: "Do not commend me for what I have done, or refrained to do, in this matter. It has given me more concern than anybody else in the party, I feel quite sure." To Fielding he wrote: "I believe that my fellow-countrymen of my own race here are unfairly and unjustly treated. Naturally, feeling that way, I am entitled to act accordingly. If I were to remain silent, I would certainly lose my own self-esteem and respect." And to another: "I write with a heavy heart! The party has not advanced; it has sorely retrograded, abandoning position after position before the haughty onslaughts of Toryism."

Lapointe introduced the resolution in English. A western Liberal asked the Speaker not to receive it on the grounds that it was dealing with a purely provincial matter. The Speaker ruled the next day that there was no point of order. A Conservative appealed his ruling, but it failed: only eight members voted against the Speaker, the Conservative and eight western Liberals.

It was with some weariness that Laurier began his speech on 10 May. As he proceeded, though, the members, the public in the galleries, and the reporters saw an unparalleled metamorphosis. He stood straighter and straighter in the narrow space that was to his right, his head held high, the years slipping away from his person. His voice, which had trembled at first, became strong. He was no longer an old man. In an instant, he had rediscovered the passion and emotion of his youth.

With the great intellectual powers that he commanded, he dissected Regulation 17 almost word by word, and he contrasted it with language provisions in the United Kingdom and the empire where freedom of language was paramount and respected, as in Wales, the Highlands of Scotland, India, Egypt, Africa, and Malta: "Today on the battlefield in Flanders there are men who do not speak a word of English but who for England have come forward to fight and die."

But he wasn't there to appeal to the "cold letter of positive law." Nor was he standing in the House of Commons of his land to teach the proponents of "one language and one language only," whether they be in Ontario or in the West, a lesson in British freedom. He was there "to plead before the people of Ontario, on behalf of His Majesty's subjects of French origin in that province," to redress the wrong they complained has been done to them. Granted that the matter lies completely within the purview of provincial jurisdiction, but "Is it forbidden that I respectfully present the petition of a humble servant of French origin?"

He was there speaking to the people of his country for a true Canadianism, one of justice, moderation, and conciliation:

> But, sir, when I ask that we should have the benefit of a French education, will you refuse us the benefit? Is that an unnatural demand? Is that an obnoxious demand? Will the concession do harm to anybody?
>
> I do not believe that any man will refuse us the benefit of a French education.

There was no more to be said. The applause came, but he knew that the minds and hearts of the great majority of those who had listened to him attentively and respectfully were encased in cement. He got up, left the Chamber, and walked slowly and with difficulty to his office, where he was alone with his thoughts. He had, indeed, lived too long. His usefulness was at an end. The party he led no longer stood with him on the central issue of his political life. He should go. There was a knock at the door and Senator Dandurand walked in to give him the caucus report, the members having met province by province to determine how they would vote on the Lapointe motion. He reported that "the Québec members and those from the Maritimes will vote for the resolution; those from the West are all opposed . . ." Laurier interrupted him to ask if the westerners would make any concession. "Non" was Dandurand's answer. Tears came in Laurier's eyes. He brushed them aside and said with anger — an emotion he didn't display often: "And I who have made so many concessions to them."

As for Ontario, Dandurand informed him that all the members were in sympathy, but they would vote for the motion only if he asked them. Laurier's reply to that came swiftly and categorically: "No, I shall not ask them; they should not expect that after all these years." He stood and walked to the window, where he remained for a few minutes absorbed in his thoughts and the pain they gave him. Coming back to his desk, he said to Dandurand: "I have outlived Liberalism. The forces of prejudice in Ontario have been too much for my friends." He sat down and picked up a pen before adding: "It was a mistake for a French Roman Catholic to take the leadership. I told Blake so thirty years ago." He fidgeted with the pen in his hand, then bent his head and scribbled a few lines on a piece of paper. Handing the note to Dandurand, he said: "I am resigning and shall announce my resignation in the House this afternoon. Please give this to George Graham."

And Dandurand left in panic for Graham's office. A meeting of the Ontario Liberals was quickly arranged. They unanimously agreed to support him and urged him not to proceed with his resignation. He accepted their support and granted their wish. Had it all been an exercise in Machiavellianism, or was it the handiwork of Sir Galahad? Who could say? Laurier always did what he had to do.

Lapointe's motion, though, was lost, 107 to 60. Only one Ontario Liberal bolted, and eleven western Liberals. Dafoe responded in his newspaper: "The Ontario Liberals capitulated. The western Liberals were of sterner stuff; they stood to their guns." He didn't mention that they had repudiated whatever was left of Liberalism in their wretched souls. Dafoe made many other stupid comments on this issue. Laurier once described Dafoe as a Liberal with very advanced ideas, even radical ones, but on certain matters "his horizon is the horizon of the sixteenth century," with all its Protestant evangelism and its distrust of anything Catholic and clerical.

A few months later, Laurier was the guest of honour at a concert in Ottawa to raise funds to pay the caretakers in the French schools.

∼

On Monday, 20 November 1916, Wilfrid Laurier celebrated his seventy-fifth birthday. He had no time to *faire le point* — or maybe at his age it was no longer necessary.

Then, almost a year to the day, it began all over again.

∼

The year 1917 was not going well so far as Canada was concerned. Borden's administration was most unpopular. Liberals had won provincial elections, and close to twenty by-elections had not been called because the government feared the results. Corruption, scandals, favouritism, inefficient administration of the war effort, and rising prices all made for confusing times. The real and ever present tragedy, however, was the plight of the men in the trenches of France: 1917 was the year of Vimy Ridge, Passchendaele, Bellevue, and so many more terrible battles. The losses were staggering. Reinforcements were urgently needed if Canadian troops were to be adequately maintained — or so it was said. To achieve that goal, Canada still relied on voluntary recruitment. By the end of 1916, 400,000 men had enlisted, 280,000 had gone overseas, and 150,000 were held in reserve in England. In the first few months of 1917, the monthly enlistment rate was 30,000, then it petered out to about 6000. Conscription was in the air, but Laurier doubted it would happen. He was wrong.

Borden spent most of the winter in England and in France. He returned to Canada on 14 May. Four days later, he informed the House that he would bring down a plan to exchange the voluntary system of recruitment for a compulsory one. Conscription had become a reality. At the end of May he invited Laurier to join him in a coalition government: Borden would be the prime minister; the Liberals and the Conservatives would have an equal number of posts; the policy of the coalition government would be conscription; and the life of Parliament would be extended to a year or so after the end of the war. Negotiations between the two men continued until 6 June. Since Laurier had great reservations about extending the parliamentary term, Borden agreed that once the military service bill was law, the "Coalition Government should seek a mandate from the people."

In the midst of the discussions between Borden and Laurier — apparently the caucuses were not consulted at that time — Clifford Sifton arrived in Ottawa to see Laurier. Deaf, domineering, and determined to have his way in all things, he harangued Laurier over his opposition to conscription and to a coalition with Borden: "That is not good!" he said. "You should agree to an extension of the term of Parliament." He argued that the party was not ready for an election, which it was bound to lose anyhow. Laurier didn't take Sifton's advice and he announced on 6 June that he opposed any extension of the life of Parliament. Five days later, Borden introduced the Military Service Act, which would bring in conscription. Laurier said no to that too.

In the midst of an acrimonious debate in the Canadian Parliament and among the Canadian people, the fiftieth anniversary of Confederation passed on

1 July 1917 almost unnoticed. Twenty-three days later, the Commons agreed to conscription by a majority of fifty-eight, and a few days later it became the law of the land.

Why did Laurier oppose both conscription and a coalition? If Borden had offered a coalition in 1914, Laurier would have taken it. However, it would not have worked. There was a difference in attitude between the two men which in many ways affected their decisions and actions. Borden saw the war as Canada's war. Laurier saw it as arising out of Canada's duty and responsibility as part of the empire. Consequently, the war didn't mean the same thing to them. Borden, and most Canadians, would have gone to war in 1914 regardless of whether they were part of the empire or not. Laurier, and most *Canadiens*, would have participated, but to a limited degree. It wouldn't have been what it came to demand from Borden and the others: a total effort. All Laurier's interventions during the war had that same caveat: We are in it because Great Britain is in it.

When, three years into the war, Borden, to achieve his policy of compulsory military service and to save his own neck, offered a coalition to Laurier, it was too late. And the basis for the coalition — conscription — was not acceptable. In addition, there were many other differences between the two parties and the leaders — the relationship between Canada and the empire, the economic question, and the railway question, to cite but a few — which would have made it difficult, if not impossible, for Laurier to form a government with Borden.

Furthermore, a coalition would not have lasted long. Laurier could never have accepted Borden's Wartime Elections Act that Arthur Meighen, the secretary of state, introduced in September 1917 with one of the most racist speeches ever pronounced in the Canadian House of Commons. The act disenfranchised all immigrants "of alien enemy birth or of other European birth and of alien enemy mother tongue or native language, who have been naturalized since the 31st March, 1902," in order that in the coming election "the real view of the Canadian people" would be expressed. To Laurier this was an "infamous act" that caused a grave injustice to "men who are by the laws of the land our fellow-citizens." It would have been most unnatural for Laurier to sanction that affront to human dignity and tolerance.

The fundamental difference between Laurier and Borden, however, was conscription. Laurier couldn't accept it. He was a pacifist and, as such, he naturally distrusted military solutions to the problems of human conflict; he was a liberal and, consequently, he rejected compulsion as a motive for social behaviour; he was a *Canadien,* and embedded in his being was the century-old conviction that *corvées* and compulsory military service — which the French authorities had imposed all through the era of New France — were inimical to the interests of the new land of Canada; and he was a man whose life was dedicated to a Canadianism of moderation and conciliation. He was not about to "create a line of cleavage in the population, the consequences of which I know too well and for which I will not be responsible."

Laurier recognized that conscription might help the war effort, though he doubted it. Even if it did, it would, in the end, injure the country. It was not only the people of Québec "who are opposed to conscription," but elsewhere in Canada "there is amongst the masses an undercurrent indicating that they will be sore and bitter if at the moment, a conscription law is forced upon them." If conscription had to be, then the people should have been prepared for it and the consent of both the Canadians and the *Canadiens* should have been obtained. There was a "singular want of foresight on the part of the government."

He knew that if he accepted conscription, he would simply hand over the province of Québec to the extremists. "I would lose the respect of the people whom I thus addressed," he said, "and I would deserve it. I would lose not only their respect, but my own self-respect also." He had no delusions: there were extremists in Québec who, roused by Bourassa's rhetoric, by Lavergne's demagoguery, and by the not too tacit clerical collaboration, particularly that of the Jesuits, could enflame passions that would be most destructive. He saw no danger of civil war: "To talk of civil war in Québec is simply sheer nonsense." But he was concerned about acts of violent agitation: "To arouse passion and prejudice may be the work of a moment; to quell a storm may be the work of years." Laurier, more than anyone else of his time, saw clearly that Bourassa (a man "of great ability, but his ability is negative and destructive") wished to bring about a cleavage between the "races" in Canada so as to isolate the people of Québec from the rest of the country and to make them a separate body. Laurier's duty, as he understood it, was to limit the damage and to prevent the calamity he feared so much. "The result may be my own end," he wrote to his friend and colleague Sir Allen Aylesworth, but "I will go down with colours flying high at the topmast."

Conscription had not only to do with winning the war but with winning elections. Of that Laurier was convinced. "How many men will conscription bring in?" he asked. "Just a few slackers, exactly the same as in England." He projected a similar result in Canada: "The number of men who can be spared from agriculture and industry is infinitesimally small. Conscription will take a few farmers and schoolboys; this will be the supreme triumph of Toryism, but Toryism will once more have asserted its undying spirit of domination." Laurier proved to be right. Exemptions were quite numerous. In Ontario, for instance, there were 125,750 draft-age men; 118,128 of them asked to be excused, only 4 percent less than in Québec. This high percentage of claimants was the same all across Canada, except in the Yukon.

The sentiment, though, for a greater participatory effort to be achieved through conscription was a popular idea in many sections of the country. Borden seized upon it to prop up his sagging fortunes. And he followed it with the Military Voters Act, which gave the vote to all enlisted men and women regardless of their date of arrival in Canada, and the Wartime Elections Act, which removed many from the voters' lists but added considerably more by allowing "the wives, the widows, the mothers, the sisters, and the daughters" of all those serving — or who had served — overseas to vote. These two acts were ample proof to Laurier that the government intended "to win elections" more than "to win the war." He was as aware as Borden that most of Meighen's undesirables generally voted Liberal.

At bottom, conscription had much to do with the determination of men like Dafoe, Sifton, members of the Orange Order, ministers of various Protestant churches, Willison, and knee-jerk Liberals and Tories to put Québec in its place. Laurier had no doubt about that either: "Is it not true that the main reason advocated for conscription — not so much publicly as privately, not shouted but whispered — is that Québec must be made to do her part, and French Canadians forced to enlist compulsorily since they did not enlist voluntarily? Is this not the main reason?"

In the Canada of the Canadians, there was a great deal of dissatisfaction and anger about Québec's poor enlistment record. Laurier admitted as much in speeches and in letters to his partisans: "No one regrets it more than I do." He attributed the low numbers to several factors — tradition, the low urban population, the small number of British-born residents, the general in charge in Québec who didn't speak a word of French, the Methodist minister in Montréal who was the chief recruiting officer, the oft-repeated pledge by the government that conscription would not be imposed — but the most important reason was the unholy alliance between Bourassa's *nationalistes* and the Tories in 1911. It had falsified the normal democratic process and had encouraged a negative nationalist fervour. All through the war, even though Bourassa became more of a spent force as the years rolled by, it was most difficult to undo the immense damage he had done. Therefore, recruitment was low and the next electoral campaign would be fought on the back of "French Québec." He would not allow it. There was no one of his prestige and popularity who could minimize the danger that such tactics would certainly cause: "If a general election is held shortly, a racial cry will be inevitable and English will be pitted against French and French against English, and there will follow years of bitterness."

What of the party he led? From the very beginning of the war, he realized that the party might end up divided — but not, he hoped, beyond repair. He consulted as broadly as he could, he kept informed of every development, and he intervened often. He made his position quite clear and asked for support, but he understood if it was withheld. In Ontario and in Manitoba, the party, in conventions and in meetings, reaffirmed confidence in his leadership. But it was not very deep. Some favoured a coalition government, which they called a "National Government," and many more supported conscription. There were defections every day. And then came October.

~

It is early in the afternoon of Sunday, 7 October. He is in his study reading, and the ever-in-attendance Giguère informs him that Fielding and three others wish to see him. He hasn't seen Fielding in a few months, and his companions are all friends. They come in and are made welcome. He soon finds out the purpose of their unannounced visit: they wish him to resign. They have a better chance, they argue, to win the forthcoming election with a new leader, one who is in favour of conscription, one who is not a *Canadien* but Canadian.

He looks intently at each one of them, for the request takes him by surprise. He asks their spokesman to be so kind as to repeat his statement. As he does so, Laurier watches the eyes of the members of the delegation. Only Fielding has the decency not to look directly at him.

So that is it: because he is a *Canadien*, he cannot be the leader of the Liberal Party. It annoys him, but he will not dwell on it so as not to arouse anger. Often in the past he has wanted to resign; many times he has been of the opinion that it was difficult for the "English" and the Protestants to accept a *Canadien* and a Catholic as leader. But never has he been told before that because of his "race," or origin, he cannot lead a Canadian political party. He controls himself and responds: "If such is the wish of the party, I will undoubtedly resign. However, the matter cannot be decided this Sunday. I will have to refer it to the party itself. Is there anything else? Well, thank you, gentlemen."

And he rings for the secretary to show his friends out. As they leave, he shakes their hands and wishes them well.

~

Laurier considered the talk confidential, but "a distorted announcement was made in the press that he had resigned." The result, he said, was "a shower of representations showing me conclusively that the feeling was far from unanimous, and if I may judge, the feeling is preponderant that I should continue at my post."

It was around this time that Bourassa came to see him in Ottawa. Laurier greeted him with some warmth and they talked of conscription, Québec, and the railway. Laurier was charming; Bourassa, non-committal. He did, though, praise Laurier for his anti-conscriptionist position, though he believed that Laurier would flinch. As for Laurier, he still had great reservations about Bourassa: he had, after all, created the storm; it would be difficult for him to calm the wind.

Laurier might not favour a coalition, but many Liberals accepted Borden's invitation to support him in his war efforts and to form a government made up of Conservatives and Liberals to be known as Unionists and to fight the forth-coming general election under his leadership. On 12 October Borden announced what he called his "Union Cabinet." Only three Liberals from Laurier's caucus agreed to serve, and the other seven came from the second string of the party leadership. No Liberals came from Québec. By the middle of November Laurier was facing "a murderous winter election." He accepted it fully "even if I have to die for it." It certainly was not "the time to abandon the ship."

However, it was not going to be easy. The party was split; outside Québec he had only a couple of friendly newspapers; there was hardly any money; the vast majority of the men of power and wealth were Unionists and conscription-ists; and the defections were mounting every day. Moreover, he was an old man. All through November his health was so bad that he held only three meetings: in Montréal, Ottawa, and Arnprior. That didn't mean that he rested. From his study he directed the campaign, seeing visitors, writing letters, and preparing speeches. Zoë feared the worst. A chill could bring disastrous results, but it was impossible to stop him. So she sent him out in the cold with furs and knitted mittens and scarves and sturdy galoshes. She admonished his handlers that she would hold them personally responsible if anything happened to him. They were to guard him with their lives. And she let him go.

At the beginning of the campaign, he assessed his chances. In Québec he was on sure ground. He had little hope for Ontario, but he didn't despair of the Maritimes, even though Fielding was a Unionist candidate there. Many of his best organizers and the bulk of his organizations in Saskatchewan and, to a certain degree, in Manitoba had passed into Conservative hands. In Alberta, there were good possibilities: "The new local government will be with us, and we can look to a good account there." As for British Columbia, he wasn't certain: the conscrip-tionist sentiment was very strong in that province. Such was the way of politics.

On 7 December he went west in a private car, the "Matapedia," put at his disposal by the CPR. On the 10th he spoke to eight thousand people in Winnipeg, in temperatures that were 20 degrees Fahrenheit below zero. The next day he was in Regina, where "great throngs sought to hear him." The day after that he had four large meetings in Calgary — it was almost 30 degrees below zero, the train was late, and a blizzard raged. Two days later there were five immense gatherings in Vancouver — and it rained. Everywhere the message was the same. The cost of living was far too high owing to the incompetence of the government. The Franchise Act was "iniquitous." He was in the war "to the end"; but "if we are to win this war, if we are to get men to go to the fighting-line, the proper way is by appealing to the soul, not to coercion of the conscience." As for Québec, he had done his best to appeal to the soul of the young men of his province, but he had not been successful. However, he intoned, "If I had been in office, I would not have been stupid enough to take the methods taken by this Government."

Meanwhile, he suffered the abuse of those who hated Québec, who abrogated to themselves the virtue of patriotism, who misquoted him deliberately, who were racist and prejudiced, who called him "Kaiser," a demagogue, a charlatan, and a mountebank. He bore with those who ascended their Protestant pulpits to declare that a vote against Laurier was a sacred duty, or who prepared a new map of Canada with Québec painted over in black because it was "the foul blot on Canada." He turned a blind eye to Bishop Fallon, who slandered him and his province in the name of the new god, the Unionist government, and to those who had worked with him for many years and now reviled him. It hurt — but he didn't complain.

Everywhere, people cheered for him, but they did not vote for him. On the day of the election, 17 December, he was on the train coming back to Ottawa. On that day, the Canadian people elected 153 candidates who supported the government, and 82 for the Liberals. Of those, 62 were in Québec, 10 in the Maritimes, 8 in Ontario, 1 in Manitoba, 1 in Alberta, and none in Saskatchewan, British Columbia, and the Yukon. Laurier was re-elected in Québec-Est, but defeated in Ottawa.

Laurier's post mortem of the election was short: "It has been my lot to run the whole gamut of prejudices in Canada. In 1896 I was excommunicated by the Roman priests and in 1917 by Protestant parsons. Let us take it cheerfully, however, and be prepared to continue the fight for the good cause."

~

The New Year brought increasing rumours about his possible resignation. He didn't even bother to deal with them. The party did, though, and expressed its full confidence in the leader. In the House he tended to be quiet, and he avoided controversies of any kind that might push the Liberal Unionists into the arms of Borden's Conservatives. He did not judge those who had abandoned him, nor did he want the party to eviscerate them: "Do not think hard of them," he pleaded, "for I do not." He understood their dilemma and "the difficulties which faced them." One day they would return. In the meantime, he would wait patiently for them as he rebuilt his party.

During Holy Week, between 28 March 1918 and 1 April, there were violent riots in Québec City over conscription, the high cost of living, and the arrests by the military police of those suspected of avoiding the draft. Four civilians were killed by the police, ten soldiers were wounded, as were many residents of the city, and fifty-two were arrested. In the House, Laurier said: "If the law is applied in such a way as to respect the rights of the people, my honourable friend can be certain that it will not be resisted." In other words, had he been in power, the whole bloody mess would have been avoided. He searched for conciliation, but many others opted for confrontation.

On Monday, 13 May 1918, Laurier and Zoë celebrated their golden wedding anniversary. Fifty years! There were no public festivities — it wouldn't have been proper in wartime — just a family dinner with the closest of friends and the nephews and nieces and their children. Flowers were everywhere in the house, and letters and congratulatory messages poured in, including one from the king and queen. The members of the caucus sent splendid gifts: a golden salver for both of them and gold knitting needles for Zoë. The day before, they had gone to Mass together at Sacré-Coeur, as they always did on Sunday. The church was full, and those who had not been able to find seats waited on the street. They arrived in their large car. She looked frail as she walked up the aisle on his arm while with his right hand he held hers. He did that now all the time when they were together. She was more than legally blind, but her mind was in no way impaired. She knew the Mass by heart. He looked splendid in his morning coat, his white hair long and full, his eyes shining with pride, and his mouth quivering with emotion. Fifty years!

A month later he was quite ill, and in July he took the train to David's house in Val Morin. He spent a month there recuperating, talking endlessly with David and with friends who dropped by, including Bourassa, who spent two hours with him. On the day of his departure by car, he had the chauffeur drive to L'Assomption. No one had been told of his visit. The students were on holiday, but the priests were still there. They fussed over him and he bowed ceremoniously, asking the superior to give him his blessing. The priests, most of them with tears streaming down their faces, blessed him all together. He walked around the buildings he knew, touching the stones and remembering. After an hour or so he left — his memory intact.

The following month passed easily enough, working on party matters. He also attended the Liberal Conference in Ottawa on 17 September, and gave a speech in Montréal on the 29th: "These are my last words to you, my fellow-countrymen. We are a nation divided in many ways; we must all unite to work together to bring a just and fair peace amongst ourselves and with all the nations of the earth." Then, on 11 November 1918, the Great War ended.

Ten days later Laurier spent his seventy-seventh birthday in London, Ontario. To the Young Liberals of that city, to his countrymen — then and future — and to the citizens of the world he said:

> Banish doubt and hate from your life. Let your souls be ever open to the prompting of faith and the gentle influence of brotherly love. Be adamant against the haughty, be gentle and kind to the weak. Let your aim and purpose, in good report or ill, in victory or defeat, be so to live, so to strive, so to serve as to do your part to raise ever higher the standard of life and of living.

These were his last words and his enduring testament.

On Saturday, 15 February 1919, Laurier attended a Canadian Club luncheon at the Château Laurier. Afterwards, he was driven to his office at the Victoria Memorial Museum. He had been working for a couple of hours when he suddenly felt dizzy. He stood up and, the next thing he knew, he was on the floor with a bump on his forehead. With difficulty he raised himself up, struggled into his coat, and, instead of summoning his driver, took the streetcar home. It was around 5:30.

16

"C'est Fini"
17 February 1919

I
t is Sunday morning. He has slept a troubled sleep, tossing and turning, but ever conscious of not awakening Zoë next to him. As usual, she gets up earlier than he does and, more than a little tired, he falls into a deep sleep. His valet wakes him at 9:00 so he will be ready for the High Mass at Sacré Coeur at 10:00. He has difficulty getting out of bed, and the bump on his forehead is now a nasty blue colour. He brushes his teeth; the valet shaves his face and helps him dress. That done, Wilfrid sits down on the side of the bed to put on his shoes. He faints. Dr. Rodolphe Chevrier is called.

The doctor orders him to remain in bed all day and rest. There is nothing to worry about. Zoë goes back to the morning room. He sleeps until the sound of the lunch gong awakens him. He gets out of bed, puts on his dressing gown, walks to the door, and the noise of his body hitting the rug is not heard except by Giguère, who is working in the library. Dr. Chevrier is summoned again, while the valet, the butler, and the secretary put Wilfrid gently back to bed. He has not regained consciousness.

At 6:30 p.m. he is more alert and takes comfort in Zoë being at his side. No one has yet told her that he has had a stroke. He takes a few sips of rye and aqua and continues to fall in and out of consciousness. The night passes.

The early morning of Monday does not find him well, even though his hands are warmer and his heart is still regular and strong. Suddenly his pulse weakens and cold sweat appears on his forehead. His breathing becomes shorter and more difficult, as spasms rock his body at regular intervals. It goes on like this for hours. The priest comes to administer the last rites of the church. Wilfrid is hardly aware of it. But Zoë is there and wants to stay. Around 11:40 a.m. she does not hear him say softly: "C'est fini!"

At noon she has to leave him for a moment to welcome the governor general, who is downstairs in the drawing room. He pays his respects and leaves her with his best wishes and the assurance of his prayers. Sir Thomas White, the acting prime minister in the absence of Robert Borden, who is in Paris at the Peace Conference, follows shortly thereafter. With her usual dignity and simplicity she receives him. Mercifully, he does not stay long and she returns to their room.

At 2:50 in the afternoon of Monday, 17 February 1919, Henry-Charles-Wilfrid Laurier dies. She brings his hand to her lips and whispers: "Wilfrid! Mon Wilfrid."

~

Since Laurier's will, dated 27 July 1912, did not specify where he was to be buried, it was decided to delay the decision to another day. He couldn't be buried in the ground anyhow, since the earth was frozen solid. After the state funeral, he would be taken to Ottawa's Catholic cemetery, Notre Dame, and his coffin would be placed in a lead casket and stored in the crypt until the following spring. In April 1919 the family bought a plot in which Laurier was buried. After Zoë's death, a larger and more prominent space was found and he was moved by her side.

Zoë agreed to a state funeral provided that Wilfrid would remain in their house for the prescribed three days. In those days, Roman Catholics followed the tradition that the body remained at home for three days, signifying Christ's time spent in the tomb. She also expressed the wish that the Funeral Mass be conducted at their parish church, Sacré Coeur, though she was persuaded to accept the Basilica on Sussex Street.

From approximately 2:00 a.m. on Tuesday, 18 February, until 5 p.m. on Thursday, 20 February, Wilfrid lay in his own house, dressed in the uniform he had worn at official and court functions — the Windsor uniform with its scarlet jacket and gold braid, its satin breeches, white silk stockings, and low black shoes. Floral arrangements and telegrams arrived from the mighty and the powerful, and from his colleagues and the ordinary citizens of his country. The nuns prayed, as did a succession of prelates and priests. Zoë prayed with them.

Then it was 4:00 p.m. on Thursday. Everyone had left, except the immediate family and some very close friends. The curé said the prescribed prayers and blessed Wilfrid. Zoë approached the casket and silently said her farewell to the man who had been her husband and "Mon Wilfrid" since 1868. Refusing to leave the room, she stayed while the casket was closed and the policemen carried him to the hearse waiting in the front of the house. She followed him to the porch and, when the horses had disappeared from view Yvonne took her upstairs. Wilfrid was now in the hands of Canada.

The country did well by him. All the seats in the temporary House of Commons in the Victoria Memorial Museum were removed, except his, and the room was adorned in the purple and black colours of mourning. He lay in the centre of the room in his open casket, candles surrounding him, flowers banked in profusion, and police officers guarding him. After the officials had passed by, the doors were opened to the general public. From about 7:00 p.m. on Thursday until the early hours of Saturday morning, fifty thousand of his countrymen and -women, many with their children, came to bid him farewell.

Meanwhile, Ottawa, Hull, and neighbouring municipalities were inundated with a mass of humanity. Every hotel, *pension*, and empty room was occupied as, by every means of transport available, thirty-five thousand people came to take part in the national moment.

Saturday, 22 February 1919, was a calm day with a fluttering of spring in the air. By 9:00 a.m. thousands of people were already on the streets through which the funeral procession would pass. Soon thereafter, close to a hundred thousand were lined, six rows deep in many places, to await Wilfrid's passage. The battery of "moving picture machines" was installed at the Château Laurier and on Connaught Place. People filled windows and ledges and roofs, and the agile among them climbed trees and telephone poles.

At 10:00 a.m. the mile-long procession of sleighs began its slow journey from the museum to the Basilica along Metcalfe, Wellington, St. Patrick, and Sussex streets. At the head came a squad of Dominion Police, six abreast. They were followed by the priests and clergy who would officiate at the solemn High Mass; the undertaker and the policemen who would serve as pallbearers; the sleighs containing floral tributes; the hearse pulled by four black horses; the honorary pallbearers, among whom was David; the chief mourners, including Carolus and numerous nephews and cousins, the governor general, and other dignitaries; and the Ottawa branch of the Great War Veterans' Association.

At 10:30, as the procession proceeded down Metcalfe Street, every train in the country, from the Atlantic to the Pacific, stopped, wherever it was, for one minute.

Silence accompanied the passage of the hearse. Many bowed their heads, removed their hats, or signed themselves with the Sign of the Cross. At the Basilica, which was all draped in black and gold, his curé received him and led him to rest on an immense catafalque of gold and black in the middle of the main aisle and in front of the altar. Archbishops, bishops, canons, priests, seminarians, and representatives of all the religious communities of Ottawa filled the sanctuary as the apostolic delegate celebrated the Funeral Mass. The archbishop of Regina delivered the eulogy in French, and a Paulist Father, John Burke, whom Wilfrid had known personally, followed in English. A booklet in both languages was published so that all those in the Basilica could follow the service.

After the final blessing of Wilfrid's body, he was taken to Notre Dame Cemetery in Ottawa. He lies just inside the front gates, in a plot of Canadian soil overlooking the peaceful countryside.

~

Zoë's turn came two years later, at 11:46 a.m. on Tuesday, 1 November 1921. She had been no worse than usual when she fell into a coma a couple of days before. She was eighty years old.

The family assembled again for the Funeral Mass at Sacré Coeur on Friday, 4 November. Thousands lined the streets from her house to her parish church. After the Mass, she was laid in Notre Dame Cemetery with her Wilfrid.

And so ends the story of Wilfrid and Zoë.

Wilfrid Laurier loved Canada. He began his life in a little corner of it, but by the time he died he knew all of it and the people who inhabited it. Early on he acquired the prejudices of the day about the place his people held in the scheme of Canada, but he came to discard every one of them in favour of a broad Canadianism that became the compelling passion of his life.

He did not have an easy time living with that passion. The demands it made on his mind and on his heart often left him in momentary despair. There was so much to reconcile, so much to forgo, so much to do that was objectionable. But the passion compelled.

Laurier sacrificed much to it. He began his political career in Ottawa in 1874 with the explicit purpose of bringing "amity" between "the races," as he called the Canadians and the *Canadiens*. He ended his political life with them at each other's throat. Did he fail in his mission? No. He was able to buy time; he was able to prevent the more "extremist" elements from gaining momentum; he was able to be the conscience for a better day. That Canada did not fragment into irreconcilable parts was due to him.

Nor did he fail in his leadership of the Liberal Party. True, men abandoned him and he ended up with a caucus drawn mainly from Québec — but that was not because of something he did. Had he been prime minister in 1914, the clashes and the divisions and the animosity would have been there, but he would have contained them and turned them around. Furthermore, he gave the Liberal Party its mission and its raison d'être. He dedicated it to the tasks of enlarging the freedom available to the Canadian people; of fostering a feeling for the land

and those who live on it; of raising "ever higher the standard of life and of living"; and of supporting a policy of true "Canadianism" — a policy of moderation and of conciliation.

"I am a Canadian. Canada has been the inspiration of my life." These were not the empty words of a politician on the make. They were the constant that made the pain bearable and the joy exquisite. He was not an easy man to live with, to be a colleague of, or to try to understand. He was complex, at times unscrupulous, at other times imponderable; and he appeared too often inconsistent. But he stayed the course — and that is to his credit.

Today, Canadians and *Canadiens* are living a drama of their own — a malaise that is partly constitutional and political, partly social and economic, and mostly attitudinal. Extremists on both sides of the barricades are vying for the souls of their countrymen and women. The country over which Laurier presided had a malaise of its own, too, but since history never quite repeats itself, those problems differ from the ones that afflict us in our own time. However, the negative attitudes are the same as in his day: the madness of alienation, of doubt, of retribution, and of imposing the will of the many on the few. The mischief, caused by illusions, ignorance, prejudice, and a political agenda that goes against the betterment of the commonwealth, is not much different from in Laurier's time.

What to do, then? From the depth of Laurier's life come the words that ennoble, the spirit that inspires. Canada was not an insignificant little colony to Wilfrid Laurier. It was the prototype for the dominions in the British Empire. "Mighty nations, indeed," he said, "may well come to us to seek a lesson in justice and humanity." The value of Canada for him resided in its diversity — and he was convinced that it was because of that diversity that Canada became a federal state and not a legislative union. Québec spearheaded that movement, realizing full well that there would be no Québec without Canadian federalism. Laurier led a party that was the champion of provincial autonomy. But that autonomy was not limitless: it had to live within the context of a federal state. Too often, in his opinion, that simple and basic truism was forgotten.

At the end of the twentieth century, Canada continues to be the prototype for the political ensembles of the century that is coming. Federalism is still vital as the sinew that binds our regions, our provinces, and our peoples together. Without it, we degenerate into insignificant little principalities. Furthermore, only federalism makes possible the unity in diversity that we have given to ourselves. Without a conscious recognition of the diversity that exists among their people, states sink into ethnic cleansing, unilingualism, and conflicting levels of citizenship. The pursuit of "One Country, One Language, One Nationality" by D'Alton McCarthy, John Dafoe, John Willison, and so many others was an affront to the nature of Canada and to decency. In our time, there are many who, in their own way, preach uniformity. It is as indecent in this day as it was in the yesterday of Wilfrid Laurier.

To Laurier, Québec had a distinct personality because of the nature of most of its residents — the *Canadiens*. "We, French Canadians, belong to one country, Canada. Canada is for us the whole world." That distinction gave Québec a particular responsibility both in Canada and in the North American continent. Laurier strove to have Canadians recognize that fact — not through special status of any kind for Québec but through the recognition of consent.

Did Laurier believe that *Canadiens* had the same rights outside Québec as they had inside the province? He did, but those rights were not guaranteed as they were in Québec. Consequently, "the French tongue has nothing to look for aside from whatever sentiments the justice of the cause may arouse and whatever influence may be brought to bear on the majority." On the other hand, he was conscious that "we have reached a critical period in the development of Confederation, with regard to the rights of the French language." In three school crises, he pushed the majority to live by certain "sentiments of justice." He was not as successful as he hoped to be, but he was the first to advocate that Canada belonged to his people as well as to those others who lived with them.

What of Québec itself? Where did it fit into the scheme of Canada? To Laurier, it had always been a part of Canada. At one point, it was Canada. Laurier saw clearly the consequences of an extreme nationalism that becomes, by the force of words and deeds, an exclusive one, regardless of the rhetoric that tries to camouflage that sentiment. That was the essence of his battle with Henri Bourassa. He did not want Québec to become a prison for *Canadiens*. And Laurier certainly saw to it that Canada did not become the prison for Québec.

"Canada is a difficult country to govern," Laurier once said. So it was, and so it is. But he left his words to make men and women of good will keep the faith:

As for you who stand today on the threshold of life, with a long horizon open before you for a long career of usefulness to your native land, if you will permit me, after a long life, I shall remind you that already many problems rise before you: problems of race division, problems of creed differences; problems of economic conflict, problems of national duty and national aspiration. Let me tell you that for the solution of these problems you have a safe guide, an unfailing light, if you remember that faith is better than doubt and love is better than hate.

Vive le Canada!

I n reasearching this book, I read various collections in the National Archives of Canada, Laurier House in Arthabaska, Laurier House in Ottawa, the McCord Museum in Montréal, and the Collège de L'Assomption. Of great importance, of course, were the Laurier Papers in the National Archives and those of his immediate colleagues. Unfortunately, much of Laurier's correspondence was destroyed in the 1916 fire in the Parliament Buildings, while some was also lost through other causes.

I consulted a large number of newspapers of Laurier's times, and I found the biographies, memoirs, journals, reminiscences, and printed collections of letters of those who knew Laurier most useful.

In addition, I have used many of the fine books, articles, and theses written by scholars who have described and assessed Laurier's life and accomplishments. Among those, I should mention in particular O.D. Skelton's *Life and Letters of Sir Wilfrid Laurier*, 2 vols. (Toronto: Oxford University Press 1921), Joseph Schull's *Laurier: The First Canadian* (Toronto: Macmillan 1965), and Réal Bélanger's *Wilfrid Laurier: Quand la politique devient passion* (Montréal: Entreprises Radio Canada 1986).

The reader interested in Wilfrid Laurier and his times would also do well to consult Robert Craig Brown and Ramsay Cook, *Canada 1896–1921: A Nation Transformed* (Toronto: McClelland and Stewart 1974), Laurent-Olivier David, *Laurier, sa vie, ses oeuvres* (Beauceville: L'Eclaireur 1919), Charles Fisher, *Dearest Émilie Lavergne* (Toronto: NC Press 1989), Sandra Gwyn, *The Private Capital: Ambition and Love in the Age of Macdonald and Laurier* (Toronto: McClelland & Stewart 1984), H. Blair Neatby, *Laurier and a Liberal Québec* (Toronto:

McClelland and Stewart 1973), Lucien Pacaud, *Sir Wilfrid Laurier: Letters to My Father and Mother, 1867–1919* (Toronto: Ryerson Press 1935; the French version was published in 1934), Heather Robertson, *More Than a Rose: Prime Ministers' Wives and Other Women* (Toronto: Seal Books 1991), Robert Rumilly, *Histoire de la Province de Québec*, 40 vols. (Montréal: Montréal Editions 1940–69), John T. Saywell, ed., *The Canadian Journal of Lady Aberdeen* (Toronto: Champlain Society 1960), Maggie Siggins, *Riel: A Life of Revolution* (Toronto: Harper Collins 1994), Mason Wade, *The French-Canadians, 1760–1945* (Toronto: Macmillian 1956), Peter B. Waite, *Arduous Destiny* (Toronto: McClelland and Stewart 1971), and John S. Willison, *Sir Wilfrid Laurier and the Liberal Party* (London: John Murray 1903).

For Laurier's speeches, see Ulric Barthe, *Wilfrid Laurier on the Platform* (Québec City: Turcotte and Ménard's Steam Printing Office 1890), Alfred D. Decelles, *Discours de Sir Wilfrid Laurier de 1889 à 1911* (Montréal: Librairie Beauchemin 1920), Skelton, above, various newspapers, and the pertinent *Official Report of the Debates of the House of Commons of the Dominion of Canada*.

From those and many other sources has come my reconstruction of Laurier's life and times.

INDEX

Navy
  Canadian. *See* Canadian Navy
  Royal. *See* Royal Navy
North-West Rebellion, 81
North-West Territories, Council of the, 184
North-West Territories Act, 299

O'Brien, William Edward, 158
O'Connell, Daniel, 91
Oliver, Frank, 311
Ontario, early. *See* Canada West; Upper Canada
Ontario Government Regulation 17, 348–353
Orange Order, 158
Ottawa, fires in, 272
Ottawa Improvement Commission, 264

Pacaud, Édouard-Louis, 111
Pacaud, Ernest, 88, 123, 126, 292
  and Baie des Chaleurs Scandal, 172–174
  as editor of *Le Journal d'Arthabaska*, 111
  as editor of *L'Electeur*, 119
  as political and campaign organizer, 96, 100, 101–102, 112, 146, 215
Pacaud, Louis-Édouard, 111
Pacaud, Philippe-Napoléon, 111
Pacific Scandal of 1873, 77
Papineau, Louis-Joseph, 37, 40, 41, 306
Papin, Joseph, 29
Parliament, extension on life of, 354
Parliament Hill, fire on, 345–348
parties, political. *See* Castors; Conservative Party; Liberal Party; National Party; Parti national; Programmistes
Parti national, 65, 78, 138, 146
Paterson, William, 225, 310, 464
La Patrie (newspaper), 121
Le Pays (newspaper), 45
Philippe-Brodeur, Louis, 311
Poisson, Médéric and Madame, 58
Poisson, Roméo, 107
Pope, Joseph, 261
Postmaster General, 225, 276, 311
La Presse (newspaper), 52
Prévost, Dr. Léandre-Coyteux, 311–312
Privileges and Elections, Select Standing Committee on, 171, 172
Programme catholique (political manifesto), 63–64, 65, 227–232
Programmistes, 66, 67, 74, 76, 99–100, 120. *See also* Ultramontanes

prohibition, 262–263
Proulx, Jean-Baptiste, 213, 232–234, 296
provincial autonomy, 301
"Public Charity," "Ministry of," 287, 340
Public Works, ministry of, 225, 311
Pugsley, William, 311, 335

Québec, 309. *See also* Canada East; Lower Canada
Québécois. *See Canadiens*
Queen Victoria's Diamond Jubilee, 239–245

Railway Commissioners, Board of, 290
railway expansion, 288–292
Railways. *See* Canadian Northern Railway; Canadian Pacific Railway; Drummond County Railway; Grand Trunk Pacific Railway; Grand Trunk Railway/ Intercolonial Railway
Railways and Canals, ministry of, 225, 290, 311
reciprocity, 157, 169–170, 321, 327–328, 338
Reciprocity Treaty (1864), 155
Red River Colony, 129–130
Reform Club of Ottawa, 190
Reformers of Canada West, 40
Regulation 17 (Ontario Government), 348–353
Report on the Affairs of British North America (Durham), 38–39
representation by population, 40, 51
responsible government, 38–39, 40, 41, 51
Revenue, ministry of, 95, 225, 311
Richard, Édouard, 112
Riel, Louis, 79–83, 127–145
Riel rebellions, 130, 134, 139, 140
rights, women's, 315
Riopel, Louis-Joseph, 26, 35
Roblin, Rodmond, 318
Roosevelt, Theodore, 284, 293–294, 295
Rouge (newspaper), 56–57
Rouges/Rougeisme, 29, 33, 40, 41, 44–45, 47, 53, 55, 65, 226
Routhier, Justice, 228
Royal Navy, 317, 318, 326
Russell, Charles, 234
Russell, John, 91

Saskatchewan, provincial status for, 298–304
Sbaretti, Donatus, 302–303
Schultz, John Christian, 128–129

PICTURE CREDITS

Laurier, as portrayed by Marc-Aurèle de Foy Suzor-Côté. Crown Collection, National Capital Commission, gift of Mrs. Marie Giguère, Montréal, through the Canadiana Fund, photo NCC/CCN

Laurier the member of parliament for Drummond-Arthabaska in 1874. Photographed by William Topley. National Archives of Canada (NA), PA 26430

Zoë Laurier in 1878. Photographer William Topley. NA, PA 26528

Le Collège de L'Assomption. NA, C 3564

The Laurier home among the maples in Arthabaska. NA, C 51786

Laurier House in Ottawa. NA, PA 28196

The Honourable Wilfrid Laurier, leader of the opposition, 1891. NA, C 1977

An elegant Zoë in 1900. Photographer William Topley. NA, PA 27936

The Lauriers in their chauffeur-driven automobile with unidentified friends. NA, C 63517

Wilfrid and Zoë on their golden wedding day, 13 May 1918. NA, C 1964

Sir Wilfrid Laurier. Photographer William Topley. NA, PA 12279

Lady Zoë Laurier in 1911. Photographer William Topley. NA, PA 28100

Laurier entering the Parliament Buildings in Ottawa. NA, C 21313

Laurier's office in the Parliament Buildings around 1902. Photographer William Topley. NA, PA 8980

Laurier relaxing at the races. NA, C 5626

Laurier lying in state in the Victoria Memorial Museum in Ottawa, 21 February 1919. NA, C 22355

Laurier's funeral procession passing the Château Laurier, with the Parliament Buildings in the background. NA, PA 24973

The Laurier memorial in Notre Dame Cemetery in Ottawa. NA, PA 34430